✤ Preface ✤

The future belongs to those who believe in the beauty of their dreams.

미래는 자신의 꿈의 아름다움을 믿는 사람들의 것이다.

-Eleanor Roosevelt-

이 책의 **구성과 특징**

Words

교과서 어휘

교과서 어휘 익히기

교과서에 제시된 주요 단어와 숙어를 정리하고, 어휘 익히기를 통해 학습한 어휘를 연습할 수 있습니다.

Structures

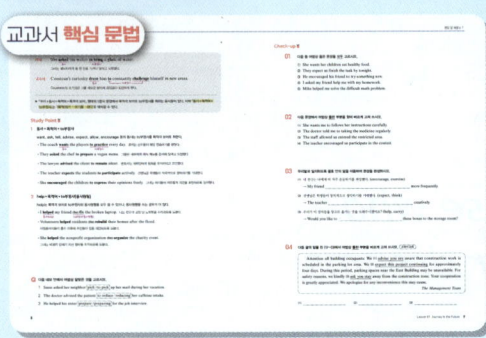
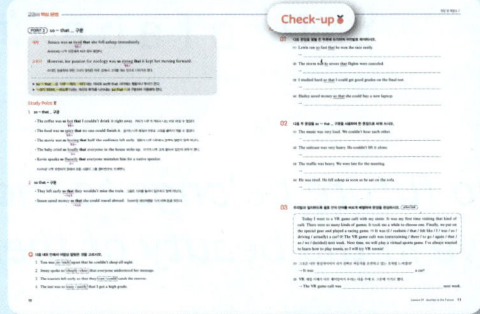

교과서 핵심 문법 / Check-up

교과서 단원별 핵심 문법 POINT를 정리하였으며, Check-up을 통해 학습한 내용을 연습할 수 있습니다.

Reading

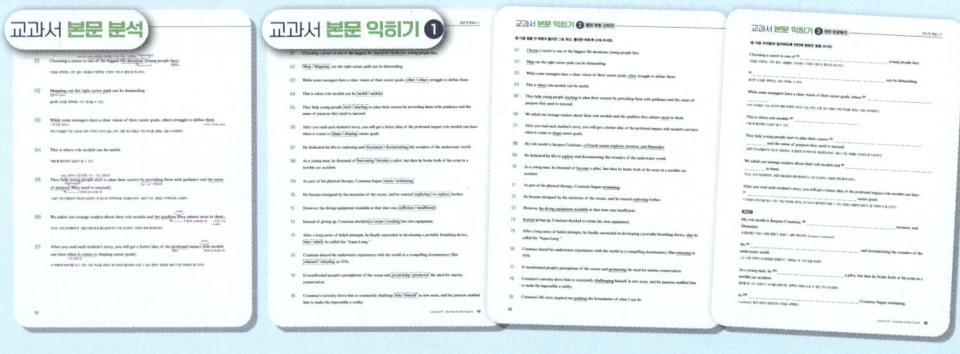

교과서 본문 분석

교과서 본문 익히기 ❶ ❷ ❸

교과서 본문의 모든 문장에 대한 첨삭식 해설과 해석을 제시하였으며, 옳은 어법·어휘 고르기, 틀린 부분 고치기, 빈칸 완성하기 활동을 통해 각 문장을 정확하게 이해하고 있는지 확인할 수 있습니다.

내신 백신

고등 기출문제집

English I

오선영

내신 1등급 공략

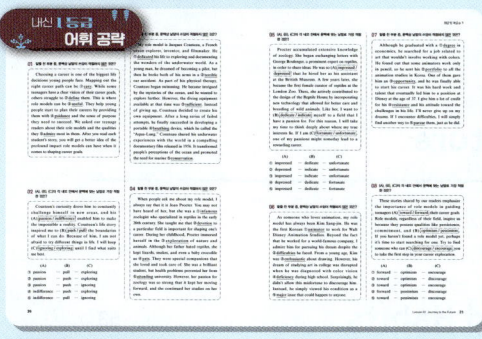

내신 1등급 어휘 공략
내신 1등급 어법 공략

교과서 지문을 이용하여 수능 어휘와 어법 문제 유형을 집중 연습할 수 있도록 구성하였습니다.

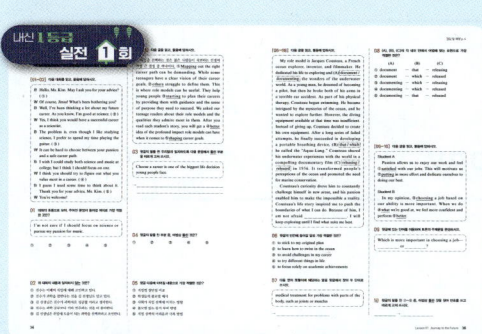

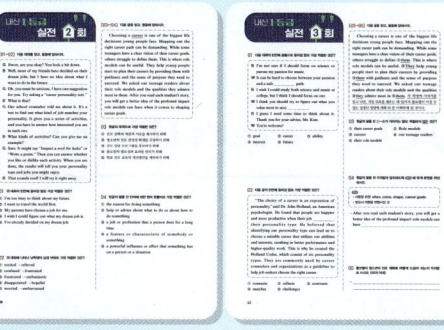

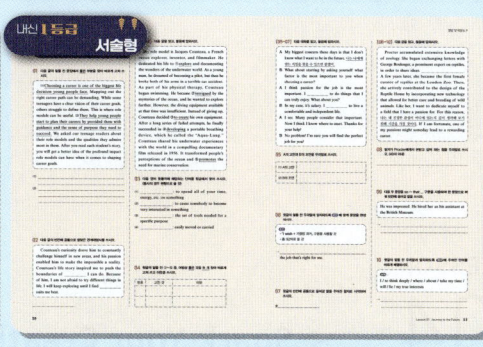

내신 1등급 실전 1회~3회

실제 학교 내신 기출 문제에서 엄선한 내신 기출 문제와 내신 시험에 나올 확률이 높은 문제들로 구성된 내신 1등급 실전 문제를 통해 풍부한 실전 경험을 쌓을 수 있습니다.

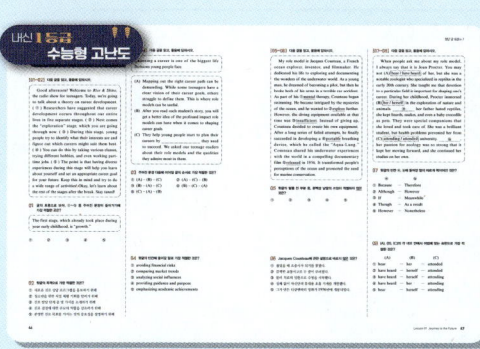

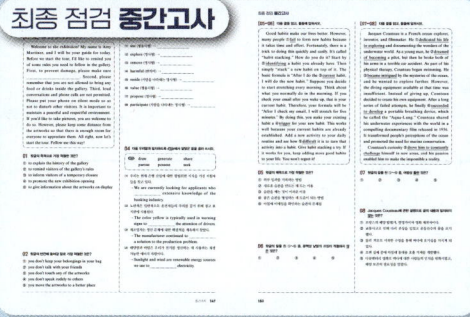

내신 1등급 수능형 고난도
내신 1등급 서술형

수능에서 3점으로 자주 출제되는 10개 유형(빈칸, 제목, 주제, 요약문, 어휘, 어법, 글의 순서, 주어진 문장, 무관한 문장, 함축 의미)으로 구성하여 고난도 문제에 효과적으로 대비할 수 있습니다. 또한 까다로운 서술형 문항을 집중 학습할 수 있도록 구성하였습니다.

중간고사, 기말고사

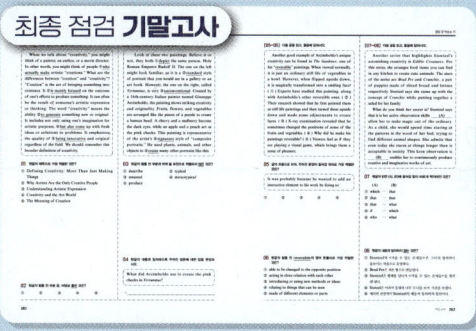

중간고사
기말고사

최종 점검 중간고사와 기말고사를 통해 학교 내신 1등급에 완벽하게 대비할 수 있습니다.

이 책의 **차례**

LESSON
01
✤ **Journey to the Future**   5

LESSON
02
✤ **The Power of Good Habits**   53

LESSON
03
✤ **Let's Live in Harmony**   101

중간고사   149

LESSON
04
✤ **Spark Your Creativity**   155

LESSON
05
✤ **Rise Above Challenges**   203

SPECIAL LESSON
✤ **The Open Window**   251

기말고사   282

01

Journey to the Future

Functions

▶ 선호 표현하기
I prefer to spend my time playing the guitar.

▶ 바람 표현하기
I wish I could study both science and music at college.

Structures

▶ Cousteau's curiosity **drove** him **to** constantly **challenge** himself in new areas.

▶ However, her passion for zoology was **so** strong **that** it kept her moving forward.

교과서 어휘

☐ career	명 직업
☐ demanding	형 힘든
☐ struggle	동 분투하다, 어려움을 겪다
☐ define	동 정하다
☐ guidance	명 지도
☐ quality	명 (사람의) 자질
☐ admire	동 존경하다 (admiration 명 존경)
☐ profound	형 엄청난
☐ impact	명 영향
☐ explorer	명 탐험가 (explore 동 탐험하다)
☐ dedicate	동 전념하다, 바치다
☐ terrible	형 끔찍한
☐ intrigue	동 호기심을 불러일으키다
☐ equipment	명 장비
☐ available	형 이용할 수 있는
☐ insufficient	형 불충분한 (↔ sufficient 충분한)
☐ attempt	명 시도
☐ portable	형 휴대용의
☐ compelling	형 매우 흥미로운, 강렬한
☐ transform	동 바꾸다, 변형시키다
☐ perception	명 인식 (perceive 동 인식하다)
☐ promote	동 홍보하다 (promotion 명 홍보)
☐ conservation	명 보존, 보호
☐ constantly	부 끊임없이 (constant 형 끊임없는)
☐ inspire	동 고무[격려]하다, 영감을 주다
☐ boundary	명 한계, 경계
☐ suit	동 맞다, 어울리다
☐ notable	형 저명한, 유명한
☐ zoologist	명 동물학자
☐ specialize	동 전문적으로 하다

☐ reptile	명 파충류
☐ devotion	명 전념, 몰두 (devote 동 전념하다)
☐ companion	명 친구, 동반자
☐ accumulate	동 모으다
☐ extensive	형 광범위한
☐ prominent	형 유명한, 중요한
☐ impressed	형 인상 깊게 생각하는
☐ assistant	명 조수
☐ curator	명 큐레이터
☐ contribute	동 기여하다 (contribution 명 기여)
☐ incorporate	동 포함하다
☐ breeding	명 번식
☐ rewarding	형 보람 있는
☐ pursue	동 추구하다 (pursuit 명 추구)
☐ enthusiastic	형 열렬한, 열정적인
☐ disrupt	동 지장을 주다 (disruption 명 방해)
☐ diagnose	동 진단하다 (diagnosis 명 진단)
☐ misfortune	명 불운, 불행 (↔ fortune 운, 행운)
☐ discourage	동 좌절시키다
☐ economics	명 경제학
☐ involve	동 수반하다, 포함하다
☐ opportunity	명 기회 (= chance)
☐ credit	명 칭찬, 인정
☐ persistence	명 끈기
☐ encounter	동 맞닥뜨리다
☐ emphasize	동 강조하다 (emphasis 명 강조)
☐ possess	동 (자질·특징을) 지니다
☐ commitment	명 헌신 (commit 동 헌신하다)
☐ optimism	명 낙관주의 (↔ pessimism 비관주의)
☐ encourage	동 격려하다 (encouragement 명 격려)

☐ map out	계획하다
☐ when it comes to	~에 관한 한
☐ physical therapy	물리 치료
☐ immerse oneself in	~에 몰두하다

☐ allow for	가능하게 하다
☐ lead to	~으로 이어지다
☐ related to	~과 관련 있는
☐ regardless of	~에 상관없이

교과서 어휘 익히기

✤ 다음 영어는 우리말로, 우리말은 영어로 쓰시오.

01	guidance	명	_____	26	명 탐험가	_____
02	devotion	명	_____	27	명 번식	_____
03	equipment	명	_____	28	형 불충분한	_____
04	available	형	_____	29	명 시도	_____
05	map out		_____	30	동 바꾸다, 변형시키다	_____
06	emphasize	동	_____	31	명 경제학	_____
07	career	명	_____	32	동 정하다	_____
08	profound	형	_____	33	명 파충류	_____
09	boundary	명	_____	34	동 추구하다	_____
10	commitment	명	_____	35	형 보람 있는	_____
11	encourage	동	_____	36	명 인식	_____
12	misfortune	명	_____	37	동 진단하다	_____
13	conservation	명	_____	38	형 휴대용의	_____
14	prominent	형	_____	39	형 광범위한	_____
15	intrigue	동	_____	40	명 친구, 동반자	_____
16	opportunity	명	_____	41	동 맞닥뜨리다	_____
17	demanding	형	_____	42	~에 관한 한	_____
18	accumulate	동	_____	43	동 좌절시키다	_____
19	enthusiastic	형	_____	44	명 끈기	_____
20	disrupt	동	_____	45	동 전념하다, 바치다	_____
21	notable	형	_____	46	물리 치료	_____
22	involve	동	_____	47	형 매우 흥미로운, 강렬한	_____
23	zoologist	명	_____	48	동 고무[격려]하다	_____
24	optimism	명	_____	49	동 전문적으로 하다	_____
25	immerse oneself in		_____	50	~에 상관없이	_____

교과서 핵심 문법

POINT 1 to부정사를 목적격 보어로 취하는 동사

예제 She **asked** the waiter **to bring** a glass of water.
　　　　　　　 동사　　　　　　　　　 to부정사
그녀는 웨이터에게 물 한 잔을 가져다 달라고 요청했다.

교과서 Cousteau's curiosity **drove** him **to** constantly **challenge** himself in new areas.
　　　　　　　　　　　　　　　 동사　　　　└──── to부정사 ────┘
Cousteau의 호기심은 그를 새로운 분야에 끊임없이 도전하게 했다.

▶ 「주어＋동사＋목적어＋목적격 보어」 형태의 5형식 문장에서 목적격 보어로 to부정사를 취하는 동사들이 있다. 이때 「동사＋목적어＋to부정사」는 '(목적어)가 ~하기를 …하다'로 해석할 수 있다.

Study Point 🍑

1 동사＋목적어＋to부정사

want, ask, tell, advise, expect, allow, encourage 등의 동사는 to부정사를 목적격 보어로 취한다.

- The coach **wants** the players **to practice** every day. 코치는 선수들이 매일 연습하기를 원한다.
　　　　　　 동사　　　　　　　　 to부정사
- They **asked** the chef **to prepare** a vegan menu. 그들은 셰프에게 채식 메뉴를 준비해 달라고 요청했다.
- The lawyer **advised** the client **to remain** silent. 변호사는 의뢰인에게 침묵을 유지하라고 조언했다.
- The teacher **expects** the students **to participate** actively. 선생님은 학생들이 적극적으로 참여하기를 기대한다.
- She **encouraged** the chlidren **to express** their opinions freely. 그녀는 아이들이 자유롭게 의견을 표현하도록 장려했다.

2 help＋목적어＋to부정사[동사원형]

help는 목적격 보어로 to부정사와 동사원형을 모두 쓸 수 있으나, 동사원형을 쓰는 경우가 더 많다.

- I **helped** my friend **(to) fix** the broken laptop. 나는 친구가 고장 난 노트북을 수리하도록 도왔다.
　 동사(help)　　　　　　 to부정사[동사원형]
- Volunteers **helped** residents **(to) rebuild** their homes after the flood.
  자원봉사자들이 홍수 이후에 주민들이 집을 재건하도록 도왔다.
- She **helped** the nonprofit organization **(to) organize** the charity event.
  그녀는 비영리 단체가 자선 행사를 조직하도록 도왔다.

Q 다음 네모 안에서 어법상 알맞은 것을 고르시오.

1 Susie asked her neighbor | pick / to pick | up her mail during her vacation.

2 The doctor advised the patient | to reduce / reducing | her caffeine intake.

3 He helped his sister | prepare / preparing | for the job interview.

Check-up 🍎

01 다음 중 어법상 옳은 문장을 <u>모두</u> 고르시오.

① She wants her children eat healthy food.
② They expect us finish the task by tonight.
③ He encouraged his friend to try something new.
④ I asked my friend help me with my homework.
⑤ Mike helped me solve the difficult math problem.

02 다음 문장에서 어법상 <u>틀린</u> 부분을 찾아 바르게 고쳐 쓰시오.

(1) She wants me to follows her instructions carefully.
(2) The doctor told me to taking the medicine regularly.
(3) The staff allowed us entered the restricted area.
(4) The teacher encouraged us participate in the contest.

03 우리말과 일치하도록 괄호 안의 말을 이용하여 문장을 완성하시오.

(1) 내 친구는 나에게 더 자주 운동하기를 권장했다. (encourage, exercise)

→ My friend _____ more frequently.

(2) 선생님은 학생들이 창의적으로 생각하기를 기대했다. (expect, think)

→ The teacher _____ creatively.

(3) 우리가 이 상자들을 창고로 옮기는 것을 도와주시겠어요? (help, carry)

→ Would you like to _____ these boxes to the storage room?

04 다음 글의 밑줄 친 (1)~(3)에서 어법상 <u>틀린</u> 부분을 바르게 고쳐 쓰시오. (교과서 25쪽)

Attention all building occupants: We (1) <u>advise you are</u> aware that construction work is scheduled in the parking lot area. We (2) <u>expect this project continuing</u> for approximately four days. During this period, parking spaces near the East Building may be unavailable. For safety reasons, we kindly (3) <u>ask you stay</u> away from the construction zone. Your cooperation is greatly appreciated. We apologize for any inconvenience this may cause.

The Management Team

(1) _____   (2) _____   (3) _____

POINT 2 so ~ that ... 구문

예제	Jessica was **so** tired **that** she fell asleep immediately. 　　　　　　　형용사 Jessica는 너무 피곤해서 바로 잠이 들었다.
교과서	However, her passion for zoology was **so** strong **that** it kept her moving forward. 　　　　　　　　　　　　　　　　　　　　　형용사 하지만, 동물학에 대한 그녀의 열정은 아주 강해서 그녀를 계속 앞으로 나아가게 했다.

▶ so ~ that ...은 '너무 ~해서 …하다'라는 의미로 so와 that 사이에는 형용사나 부사가 온다.
▶ '~하기 위하여, ~하도록'이라는 의미의 목적을 나타내는 so that ~과 구분하여 사용해야 한다.

Study Point 🍊

1 so ~ that ... 구문

- The coffee was **so** hot **that** I couldn't drink it right away. 커피가 너무 뜨거워서 나는 바로 마실 수 없었다.
  　　　　　　　　형용사
- The food was **so** spicy **that** no one could finish it. 음식이 너무 매워서 아무도 그것을 끝까지 먹을 수 없었다.
  　　　　　　　형용사
- The movie was **so** boring **that** half the audience left early. 영화가 너무 지루해서 관객의 절반이 일찍 떠났다.
  　　　　　　　　형용사
- The baby cried **so** loudly **that** everyone in the house woke up. 아기가 너무 크게 울어서 집안의 모두가 깼다.
  　　　　　　　　부사
- Kevin speaks **so** fluently **that** everyone mistakes him for a native speaker.
  　　　　　　　　　부사
  Kevin은 너무 유창하게 말해서 모든 사람이 그를 원어민으로 오해한다.

2 so that ~ 구문

- They left early **so that** they wouldn't miss the train. 그들은 기차를 놓치지 않으려고 일찍 떠났다.
  　　　　　　　~하도록
- Susan saved money **so that** she could travel abroad. Susan은 해외여행을 가기 위해 돈을 모았다.
  　　　　　　　　~하도록

Q 다음 네모 안에서 어법상 알맞은 것을 고르시오.

1 Tom was so / such upset that he couldn't sleep all night.

2 Jenny spoke so clearly / clear that everyone understood her message.

3 The tourists left early so that they can / could catch the sunrise.

4 The test was so easy / easily that I got a high grade.

Check-up 🍊

01 다음 문장을 밑줄 친 부분에 유의하여 우리말로 해석하시오.

(1) Lewis ran <u>so</u> fast <u>that</u> he won the race easily.

→ _____

(2) The storm was <u>so</u> severe <u>that</u> flights were canceled.

→ _____

(3) I studied hard <u>so that</u> I could get good grades on the final test.

→ _____

(4) Hailey saved money <u>so that</u> she could buy a new laptop.

→ _____

02 다음 두 문장을 so ~ that ... 구문을 사용하여 한 문장으로 바꿔 쓰시오.

(1) The music was very loud. We couldn't hear each other.

→ _____

(2) The suitcase was very heavy. He couldn't lift it alone.

→ _____

(3) The traffic was heavy. We were late for the meeting.

→ _____

(4) He was tired. He fell asleep as soon as he sat on the sofa.

→ _____

03 우리말과 일치하도록 괄호 안의 단어를 바르게 배열하여 문장을 완성하시오. (교과서 25쪽)

> Today I went to a VR game café with my sister. It was my first time visiting that kind of café. There were so many kinds of games. It took me a while to choose one. Finally, we put on the special gear and played a racing game. (1) It was (I / realistic / that / felt like / I / was / so / driving / actually) a car! (2) The VR game café was (entertaining / there / to go / again / that / so / we / decided) next week. Next time, we will play a virtual sports game. I've always wanted to learn how to play tennis, so I will try VR tennis!

(1) 그것은 너무 현실적이어서 내가 진짜로 자동차를 운전하고 있는 것처럼 느껴졌다!

→ It was _____ a car!

(2) VR 게임 카페가 너무 재미있어서 우리는 다음 주에 또 그곳에 가기로 했다.

→ The VR game café was _____ next week.

교과서 본문 분석

Who Is Your Role Model?
당신의 롤모델은 누구인가?

01
one of + the + 최상급 + 복수명사: 가장 ~한 … 중 하나 (that[which])
Choosing a career is one of the biggest life decisions [young people face].
직면하다

직업을 선택하는 것은 젊은 사람들이 직면하는 인생의 가장 큰 결정 중 하나이다.

02
Mapping out the right career path can be demanding.
동명사구 (주어)

올바른 진로를 계획하는 것은 어려울 수 있다.

03
While some teenagers have a clear vision of their career goals, others struggle to define them.
~인 반면 (접속사)   = their career goals

어떤 10대들은 직업 목표에 대해 뚜렷한 비전이 있는 반면, 다른 청소년들은 직업 목표를 정하는 것을 어려워한다.

04
This is where role models can be useful.

이럴 때 롤모델이 도움이 될 수 있다.

05
help + 목적어 + 동사원형: ~이 …하는 것을 돕다
They help young people start to plan their careers by providing them with guidance and the sense
            (that[which])   by v-ing: ~함으로써
of purpose [they need to succeed].
                    목적격 관계대명사절

그들은 청소년들에게 지도와 성공하는 데 필요한 목적의식을 제공함으로써 그들이 진로 계획을 시작하도록 도와준다.

06
                                                              (that)
We asked our teenage readers about their role models and the qualities [they admire most in them].
                                                              목적격 관계대명사절   = their role
                                                                                      models

우리는 10대 독자들에게 그들의 롤모델과 롤모델에서 가장 존경하는 자질에 대해 물어보았다.

07
                                                                            (that)
After you read each student's story, you will get a better idea of the profound impact [role models
                                                              엄청난   목적격 관계대명사절
can have when it comes to shaping career goals].
        ~에 관한 한

각 학생의 이야기를 읽고 나면, 직업 목표를 세우는 데 있어서 롤모델이 미칠 수 있는 엄청난 영향에 대해 더 잘 이해하게 될 것이다.

Minji

08 My role model is Jacques Cousteau, a French ocean explorer, inventor, and filmmaker.

내 롤모델은 프랑스 해양 탐험가, 발명가, 영화 제작자인 Jacques Cousteau다.

09 He dedicated his life to exploring and documenting the wonders of the underwater world.
병렬 구조 (전치사 to의 목적어)   경이(로운 것)

그는 수중 세계의 경이로움을 탐험하고 기록하는 데 그의 삶을 바쳤다.

10 As a young man, he dreamed of [becoming a pilot], but then he broke both of his arms in a
동명사구 (전치사 of의 목적어)
terrible car accident.

젊었을 때 그는 조종사가 되기를 꿈꿨지만, 끔찍한 교통사고로 두 팔이 모두 부러졌다.

11 As part of his physical therapy, Cousteau began swimming.
물리 치료   동명사, to부정사 둘 다 목적어로 취하는 동사

Cousteau는 물리 치료의 일환으로 수영을 시작했다.

12 He became intrigued by the mysteries of the ocean, and he wanted to explore further.
아주 흥미로워 하는

그는 해양의 신비로움에 호기심을 가지게 되었고, 더 깊이 탐험하고 싶어 했다.

13 However, the diving equipment [available at that time] was insufficient.
(that[which] was)   그때(에)   불충분한, 부족한

하지만 그 당시에 사용할 수 있었던 잠수 장비는 부적합했다.

14 Instead of giving up, Cousteau decided [to create his own equipment].
~ 대신에 (전치사)   명사적 용법 (decided의 목적어)

Cousteau는 포기하는 대신 자신만의 장비를 만들기로 결심했다.

15 After a long series of failed attempts, he finally succeeded in developing a portable breathing
과거분사   succeed in v-ing: ~하는 데 성공하다
device, [which he called the "Aqua-Lung."]
계속적 용법의 목적격 관계대명사절

오랜 실패 끝에 그는 마침내 휴대용 호흡 기계를 개발하는 데 성공했고, 이 장비를 'Aqua-Lung'이라고 불렀다.

16 Cousteau shared his underwater experiences with the world in a compelling documentary film
매우 흥미로운

[released in 1956].
과거분사구

Cousteau는 1956년 개봉한 흥미로운 다큐멘터리 영화로 그의 수중 세계 경험을 세상과 공유했다.

17 It transformed people's perceptions of the ocean and promoted the need for marine conservation.
동사 1   동사 2   보존, 보호

이 영화는 바다에 대한 사람들의 인식을 바꾸었고, 해양 보존에 대한 필요성을 널리 알렸다.

18 Cousteau's curiosity drove him to constantly challenge himself in new areas, and his passion
drive + 목적어 + to-v: ~이 …하게 만들다   재귀대명사 (재귀용법)

enabled him to make the impossible a reality.
enable + 목적어 + to-v: ~이 …할 수 있게 하다

Cousteau의 호기심은 그를 새로운 분야에 끊임없이 도전하게 했고, 그의 열정은 불가능한 것을 현실로 만들게 했다.

19 Cousteau's life story inspired me to push the boundaries of what I can do.
선행사를 포함하는 관계대명사

Cousteau의 인생 이야기는 내가 할 수 있는 것의 한계를 뛰어넘도록 격려했다.

20 Because of him, I am not afraid to try different things in life.
~ 때문에 (전치사)

Cousteau 덕분에 나는 인생에서 다양한 것들에 도전하는 것이 두렵지 않다.

21 I will keep exploring until I find [what suits me best].
keep v-ing: 계속 ~하다   ~까지 (접속사)   명사절 (find의 목적어)

나에게 가장 잘 맞는 것을 찾을 때까지 나는 계속 탐구할 것이다.

Sunho

22 When people ask me about my role model, I always say that it is Joan Procter.
접속사   = my role model

사람들이 내 롤모델에 대해 물어보면 나는 항상 Joan Procter라고 말한다.

23 You may not have heard of her, but she was a notable zoologist [who specialized in reptiles] in the
may have p.p.: ~했을지도 모른다   주격 관계대명사절

early 20th century.

그녀에 대해 들어보지 못했을지도 모르지만, 그녀는 20세기 초반에 파충류를 전문으로 다룬 저명한 동물학자였다.

24 She taught me [that devotion to a particular field is important for shaping one's career].

간접목적어 (~에게)
직접목적어(~을)
동명사구 (전치사 for의 목적어)

그녀는 내게 특정 분야에 전념하는 것은 한 사람의 경력을 형성하는 데 중요하다는 것을 가르쳐 주었다.

25 During her childhood, Procter immersed herself in the exploration of nature and animals.

~ 동안 (전치사)
immerse oneself in: ~에 몰두하다

Procter는 어린 시절에 자연과 동물을 탐험하는 것에 몰두했다.

26 Although her father hated reptiles, she kept lizards, snakes, and even a baby crocodile as pets.

비록 ~이지만 (접속사)
~로서 (전치사)

비록 그녀의 아버지가 파충류를 싫어했지만, 그녀는 도마뱀, 뱀, 심지어 새끼 악어도 반려동물로 키웠다.

27 They were special companions [that she loved and took care of].

목적격 관계대명사절
take care of: ~을 돌보다

그들은 그녀가 사랑하고 돌봐주었던 특별한 친구들이었다.

28 She was a brilliant student, but health problems prevented her from attending university.

prevent A from v-ing: A가 ~하는 것을 막다

그녀는 뛰어난 학생이었지만, 건강 문제로 대학에 진학하지 못했다.

29 However, her passion for zoology was so strong that it kept her moving forward, and she continued her studies on her own.

so ~ that ...: 너무 ~해서 …하다
on one's own: 혼자서, 자력으로

하지만, 동물학에 대한 그녀의 열정은 아주 강해서 그녀를 계속 앞으로 나아가게 했고, 그녀는 혼자 힘으로 공부를 계속했다.

30 Procter accumulated extensive knowledge of zoology.

accumulate: 모으다

Procter는 동물학에 대한 광범위한 지식을 쌓았다.

31 She began exchanging letters with George Boulenger, a prominent expert on reptiles, in order to share ideas.

in order to-v: ~하기 위해서

그녀는 유명한 파충류 전문가였던 George Boulenger와 의견을 나누기 위해 편지를 주고받기 시작했다.

32 He was so impressed that he hired her as his assistant at the British Museum.

so ~ that ...: 너무 ~해서 ···하다   조수

그는 그녀에게 아주 깊은 인상을 받아서 그녀를 British Museum에서 자신의 조수로 채용했다.

33 A few years later, she became the first female curator of reptiles at the London Zoo.

a few + 셀 수 있는 명사의 복수형

몇 년 후, 그녀는 London Zoo의 첫 번째 여성 파충류 큐레이터가 되었다.

34 There, she actively contributed to the design of the Reptile House by incorporating new technology [that allowed for better care and breeding of wild animals].

contribute to: ~에 기여하다   by v-ing: ~함으로써   주격 관계대명사절

그곳에서 그녀는 야생 동물을 더 잘 돌보고 번식시킬 수 있게 하는 새로운 기술을 포함시킴으로써 Reptile House의 설계에 적극적으로 기여했다.

35 Like her, I want to dedicate myself to a field [that I have a passion for].

~처럼 (전치사)   재귀대명사 (재귀용법)   목적격 관계대명사절

나도 그녀처럼 내가 열정을 가지고 있는 분야에 전념하고 싶다.

36 For this reason, I will take my time to think deeply about [where my true interests lie].

부사적 용법 〈목적〉   간접의문문

이러한 이유로, 나는 내 진정한 관심이 어디에 있는지 깊이 생각해 보기 위해 시간을 가질 것이다.

37 If I am fortunate, one of my passions might someday lead to a rewarding career.

one of + 복수 명사: ~ 중의 하나   보람 있는

운이 좋다면 언젠가 내 열정 중 하나가 보람 있는 직업으로 이어질 것이다.

Yubin

38 As someone [who loves animation], my role model has always been Kim Sang-jin.

주격 관계대명사절   현재완료

애니메이션을 좋아하는 사람으로서, 내 롤모델은 항상 김상진이었다.

39 He was the first Korean animator [to work for Walt Disney Animation Studios].

형용사적 용법

그는 Walt Disney 애니메이션 스튜디오에서 일한 최초의 한국인 애니메이터였다.

40 Beyond the fact that he worked for a world-famous company, I admire him for pursuing his
동격의 that   세계적으로 유명한
dream despite the difficulties [he faced].
~에도 불구하고 (전치사)   (that[which])

나는 그가 세계적으로 유명한 회사에서 일했다는 사실을 넘어, 그가 마주했던 어려움에도 불구하고 자신의 꿈을 추구했다는 점에서 그를 존경한다.

41 From a young age, Kim was enthusiastic about drawing.

그는 어렸을 때부터 그림 그리는 것에 열정적이었다.

42 However, his dream of studying art in college was disrupted when he was diagnosed with color
                    =   수동태   be diagnosed with: ~으로 진단받다
vision deficiency during high school.

하지만 고등학교 때 색약 진단을 받으면서 대학에서 미술을 공부하고자 했던 그의 꿈에 지장이 갔다.

43 Surprisingly, he didn't allow this misfortune to discourage him.
놀랍게도   allow + 목적어 + to-v: ~이 …하게 하다

놀랍게도 그는 이 불행으로 좌절하지 않았다.

44 Instead, he simply viewed his condition as a minor issue [that could happen to anyone].
              view A as B: A를 B로 여기다   주격 관계대명사절   누구든지

대신에, 그는 자신의 상태를 단지 누구에게나 일어날 수 있는 사소한 문제로 여겼다.

45 [Although he graduated with a degree in economics], he searched for a job [related to art] [that
부사절 <양보>   과거분사구
wouldn't involve working with colors].
주격 관계대명사절

그는 경제학 학위를 받고 졸업했지만, 색을 다루지 않으면서 미술과 관련된 직업을 찾았다.

46 He found out that some animators work only in pencil, so he sent his portfolio to all the animation
              접속사
studios in Korea.

그는 몇몇 애니메이터들이 오직 연필만으로 작업한다는 것을 알아냈고, 한국에 있는 모든 애니메이션 스튜디오에 자신의 포트폴리오를 보냈다.

47 One of them gave him an opportunity, and he was finally able to start his career.
        = the animation studios in Korea   be able to-v: ~할 수 있다

그중 한 곳에서 그에게 기회를 주었고, 그는 마침내 그의 커리어를 시작할 수 있었다.

48 It was his hard work and talent that eventually led him to a position at Disney at the age of 37.
It is[was] ~ that 강조 구문

그가 37세에 결국 Disney에서 일할 수 있게 했던 것은 그의 노력과 재능이었다.

49 I give him a lot of credit for his persistence and his attitude toward the challenges in his life.
칭찬, 인정   끈기

나는 그의 끈기와 인생에서의 어려움을 대하는 태도를 높이 평가한다.

50 I'll never give up on my dreams.

나도 절대 내 꿈을 포기하지 않을 것이다.

51 If I encounter difficulties, I will simply find another way [to pursue them], just as he did.
단순 조건문: if + 주어 + 동사의 현재형, 주어 + will + 동사원형   형용사적 용법   = my dreams

만약 어려움을 맞닥뜨리게 된다면, 그가 그랬던 것처럼 그저 꿈을 추구하는 다른 방법을 찾을 것이다.

52 These stories [shared by our readers] emphasize the importance of role models in [guiding
주어   과거분사구   동사   동명사구 (전치사 in의 목적어)
teenagers toward their career goals].

독자들이 공유한 이야기들은 청소년들을 직업 목표로 인도하는 데 있어서 롤모델의 중요성을 강조한다.

53 Role models, regardless of their field, inspire us because they possess qualities like persistence,
주어   <삽입구>   동사   전치사 (~같은)
commitment, and optimism.
          낙관주의

분야에 상관없이 롤모델은 끈기, 헌신, 낙관주의와 같은 자질을 가지고 있어서 우리에게 영감을 준다.

54 If you haven't found a role model yet, perhaps it's time to start searching for one.
현재완료 부정형   it's time to-v: ~할 시간이다   = a role model

아직 롤모델을 찾지 못했다면 어쩌면 이제 롤모델을 찾기 시작할 때일지도 모른다.

55 Try to find someone [who can encourage you to take the first step in your career exploration].
                          주격 관계대명사절

진로 탐색에서의 첫걸음을 내딛도록 당신을 격려할 수 있는 누군가를 찾아보아라.

교과서 본문 익히기 ① 옳은 어법·어휘 고르기

♣ 다음 네모 안에서 옳은 것을 고르시오.

01 Choosing a career is one of the biggest life decision / decisions young people face.

02 Map / Mapping out the right career path can be demanding.

03 While some teenagers have a clear vision of their career goals, other / others struggle to define them.

04 This is where role models can be useful / useless .

05 They help young people start / starting to plan their careers by providing them with guidance and the sense of purpose they need to succeed.

06 After you read each student's story, you will get a better idea of the profound impact role models can have when it comes to shape / shaping career goals.

07 He dedicated his life to exploring and document / documenting the wonders of the underwater world.

08 As a young man, he dreamed of becoming / became a pilot, but then he broke both of his arms in a terrible car accident.

09 As part of his physical therapy, Cousteau began swam / swimming .

10 He became intrigued by the mysteries of the ocean, and he wanted exploring / to explore further.

11 However, the diving equipment available at that time was sufficient / insufficient .

12 Instead of giving up, Cousteau decided to create / creating his own equipment.

13 After a long series of failed attempts, he finally succeeded in developing a portable breathing device, that / which he called the "Aqua-Lung."

14 Cousteau shared his underwater experiences with the world in a compelling documentary film released / releasing in 1956.

15 It transformed people's perceptions of the ocean and promoting / promoted the need for marine conservation.

16 Cousteau's curiosity drove him to constantly challenge him / himself in new areas, and his passion enabled him to make the impossible a reality.

17　Cousteau's life story inspired me pushing / to push the boundaries of what I can do.

18　 Because / Because of him, I am not afraid to try different things in life.

19　I will keep exploring until I find what / that suits me best.

20　When people ask me about my role model, I always say that / what it is Joan Procter.

21　You may not have heard of her, but she was a notable zoologist who / whom specialized in reptiles in the early 20th century.

22　During her childhood, Procter immersed her / herself in the exploration of nature and animals.

23　 Although / Despite her father hated reptiles, she kept lizards, snakes, and even a baby crocodile as pets.

24　They were special companions that she loved and took care / took care of .

25　She was a brilliant student, but health problems prevented her from / of attending university.

26　However, her passion for zoology was so / such strong that it kept her moving forward, and she continued her studies on her own.

27　He was so impressed what / that he hired her as his assistant at the British Museum.

28　A few years later, she became the first male / female curator of reptiles at the London Zoo.

29　There, she actively contributed to the design of the Reptile House by incorporating / incorporated new technology that allowed for better care and breeding of wild animals.

30　Like her, I want to dedicate me / myself to a field that I have a passion for.

31　For this reason, I will take my time to think deeply about what / where my true interests lie.

32　If I am fortunate, one of my passion / passions might someday lead to a rewarding career.

33　As someone who / which loves animation, my role model has always been Kim Sang-jin.

34　He was the first Korean animator worked / to work for Walt Disney Animation Studios.

35 Beyond the fact that he worked for a world-famous company, I admire him for pursuing his dream despite / although the difficulties he faced.

36 From a young age, Kim was enthusiastic / exhausted about drawing.

37 However, his dream of studying art in college was disrupted when he was diagnosed with color vision deficiency / sufficiency during high school.

38 Surprisingly, he didn't allow this misfortune discouraging / to discourage him.

39 Instead, he simply viewed his condition as / like a minor issue that could happen to anyone.

40 Although he graduated from / with a degree in economics, he searched for a job related to art that wouldn't involve working with colors.

41 He found out that some animators work only in pencil, so / because he sent his portfolio to all the animation studios in Korea.

42 One of them gave him an opportunity, and he was finally able to start / finish his career.

43 It was his hard work and talent which / that eventually led him to a position at Disney at the age of 37.

44 I give him a lot of credit for his persistence and his attitude toward the challenges / opportunities in his life.

45 If / Unless I encounter difficulties, I will simply find another way to pursue them, just as he did.

46 These stories sharing / shared by our readers emphasize the importance of role models in guiding teenagers toward their career goals.

47 Role models, regardless of their field, inspire us because they possess qualities like persistence, commitment, and optimism / pessimism.

48 If you haven't found a role model yet, perhaps it's time to start waiting / searching for one.

49 Try to find someone who can encourage you taking / to take the first step in your career exploration.

✤ 다음 밑줄 친 부분이 옳으면 ○표 하고, 틀리면 바르게 고쳐 쓰시오.

01 <u>Choose</u> a career is one of the biggest life decisions young people face.

02 <u>Map</u> out the right career path can be demanding.

03 While some teenagers have a clear vision of their career goals, <u>other</u> struggle to define them.

04 This is <u>where</u> role models can be useful.

05 They help young people <u>starting</u> to plan their careers by providing them with guidance and the sense of purpose they need to succeed.

06 We asked our teenage readers about their role models and the qualities they admire <u>most</u> in them.

07 After you read each student's story, you will get a better idea of the profound impact role models can have when it comes to <u>shape</u> career goals.

08 My role model is Jacques Cousteau, <u>a French ocean explorer, inventor, and filmmaker</u>.

09 He dedicated his life to <u>explore</u> and documenting the wonders of the underwater world.

10 As a young man, he dreamed of <u>become</u> a pilot, but then he broke both of his arms in a terrible car accident.

11 As part of his physical therapy, Cousteau began <u>swimming</u>.

12 He became intrigued by the mysteries of the ocean, and he wanted <u>exploring</u> further.

13 However, <u>the diving equipment available</u> at that time was insufficient.

14 <u>Instead</u> giving up, Cousteau decided to create his own equipment.

15 After a long series of failed attempts, he finally succeeded in developing a portable breathing device, <u>that</u> he called the "Aqua-Lung."

16 Cousteau shared his underwater experiences with the world in a compelling documentary film <u>releasing</u> in 1956.

17 It transformed people's perceptions of the ocean and <u>promoting</u> the need for marine conservation.

18 Cousteau's curiosity drove him to constantly <u>challenging</u> himself in new areas, and his passion enabled him to make the impossible a reality.

19 Cousteau's life story inspired me <u>pushing</u> the boundaries of what I can do.

20 <u>Because</u> him, I am not afraid to try different things in life.

21 I will keep exploring until I find <u>that</u> suits me best.

22 When people ask me about my role model, I always say <u>that</u> it is Joan Procter.

23 You may not <u>hear</u> of her, but she was a notable zoologist who specialized in reptiles in the early 20th century.

24 She taught me <u>it</u> devotion to a particular field is important for shaping one's career.

25 <u>For</u> her childhood, Procter immersed herself in the exploration of nature and animals.

26 <u>Despite</u> her father hated reptiles, she kept lizards, snakes, and even a baby crocodile as pets.

27 They were special companions that she loved and <u>took care of</u>.

28 She was a brilliant student, but health problems prevented her <u>from attending</u> university.

29 However, her passion for zoology was <u>such</u> strong that it kept her moving forward, and she continued her studies on her own.

30 Procter accumulated extensive <u>know</u> of zoology.

31 She began <u>exchanging</u> letters with George Boulenger, a prominent expert on reptiles, in order to share ideas.

32 He was so <u>impressing</u> that he hired her as his assistant at the British Museum.

33 A few years later, she became the first <u>male</u> curator of reptiles at the London Zoo.

34 There, she actively contributed to the design of the Reptile House by incorporating new technology that <u>allowed to</u> better care and breeding of wild animals.

35 Like her, I want to dedicate <u>me</u> to a field that I have a passion for.

36 For this reason, I will take my time to think <u>deep</u> about where my true interests lie.

37 If I am fortunate, one of my passions might someday <u>lead to</u> a rewarding career.

38 As someone <u>which</u> loves animation, my role model has always been Kim Sang-jin.

39 He was the first Korean animator <u>to work</u> for Walt Disney Animation Studios.

40 Beyond the fact that he worked for a world-famous company, I admire him for pursuing his dream <u>although</u> the difficulties he faced.

41 From a young age, Kim was enthusiastic about <u>drawing</u>.

42 However, his dream of studying art in college was <u>disrupting</u> when he was diagnosed with color vision deficiency during high school.

43 Surprisingly, he didn't allow this misfortune <u>discouraging</u> him.

44 Instead, he simply viewed his condition <u>as</u> a minor issue that could happen to anyone.

45 Although he graduated with a degree in <u>economic</u>, he searched for a job related to art that wouldn't involve working with colors.

46 He found out that some animators work only in pencil, <u>so</u> he sent his portfolio to all the animation studios in Korea.

47 One of them gave him an opportunity, and he was finally able to <u>starting</u> his career.

48 It was his hard work and talent <u>which</u> eventually led him to a position at Disney at the age of 37.

49 I give him <u>a lot</u> credit for his persistence and his attitude toward the challenges in his life.

50 I'll never <u>give up</u> on my dreams.

51 If I <u>will encounter</u> difficulties, I will simply find another way to pursue them, just as he did.

52 These stories <u>sharing</u> by our readers emphasize the importance of role models in guiding teenagers toward their career goals.

53 Role models, regardless of their field, inspire us <u>because</u> they possess qualities like persistence, commitment, and optimism.

54 If you haven't found a role model yet, perhaps it's time to start <u>search for</u> one.

55 Try to find someone who can encourage you <u>taking</u> the first step in your career exploration.

교과서 본문 익히기 ③ 빈칸 완성하기

❖ 다음 우리말과 일치하도록 빈칸에 알맞은 말을 쓰시오.

Choosing a career is one of (1) _____ _____ _____ _____ young people face.

직업을 선택하는 것은 젊은 사람들이 직면하는 인생의 가장 큰 결정 중 하나이다.

(2) _____ _____ _____ _____ _____ _____ can be demanding.

올바른 진로를 계획하는 것은 어려울 수 있다.

While some teenagers have a clear vision of their career goals, others (3) _____ _____ _____ _____.

어떤 10대들은 직업 목표에 대해 뚜렷한 비전이 있는 반면, 다른 청소년들은 직업 목표를 정하는 것을 어려워한다.

This is where role models (4) _____ _____ _____.

이럴 때 롤모델이 도움이 될 수 있다.

They help young people start to plan their careers (5) _____ _____ _____ _____ _____ and the sense of purpose they need to succeed.

그들은 청소년들에게 지도와 성공하는 데 필요한 목적의식을 제공함으로써 그들이 진로 계획을 시작하도록 도와준다.

We asked our teenage readers about their role models and (6) _____ _____ _____ _____ _____ in them.

우리는 10대 독자들에게 그들의 롤모델과 롤모델에게서 가장 존경하는 자질에 대해 물어보았다.

After you read each student's story, you will get a better idea of the profound impact role models can have (7) _____ _____ _____ _____ _____ career goals.

각 학생의 이야기를 읽고 나면, 직업 목표를 세우는 데 있어서 롤모델이 미칠 수 있는 엄청난 영향에 대해 더 잘 이해하게 될 것이다.

`Minji`

My role model is Jacques Cousteau, (8) _____ _____ _____ _____, inventor, and filmmaker.

내 롤모델은 프랑스 해양 탐험가, 발명가, 영화 제작자인 Jacques Cousteau다.

He (9) _____ _____ _____ _____ _____ and documenting the wonders of the underwater world.

그는 수중 세계의 경이로움을 탐험하고 기록하는 데 그의 삶을 바쳤다.

As a young man, he (10) _____ _____ _____ a pilot, but then he broke both of his arms in a terrible car accident.

젊었을 때 그는 조종사가 되기를 꿈꿨지만, 끔찍한 교통사고로 두 팔이 모두 부러졌다.

As (11) _____ _____ _____, Cousteau began swimming.

Cousteau는 물리 치료의 일환으로 수영을 시작했다.

He (12) _____ _____ _____ the mysteries of the ocean, and he wanted to explore further.

그는 해양의 신비로움에 호기심을 가지게 되었고, 더 깊이 탐험하고 싶어 했다.

However, (13) _____ _____ _____ _____ at that time was insufficient.

하지만 그 당시에 사용할 수 있었던 잠수 장비는 부적합했다.

Instead of giving up, Cousteau decided to (14) _____ _____ _____ _____ .

Cousteau는 포기하는 대신 자신만의 장비를 만들기로 결심했다.

After a long series of failed attempts, he finally (15) _____ _____ _____ a portable breathing device, which he called the "Aqua-Lung."

오랜 실패 끝에 그는 마침내 휴대용 호흡 기계를 개발하는 데 성공했고, 이 장비를 'Aqua-Lung'이라고 불렀다.

Cousteau (16) _____ _____ _____ _____ with the world in a compelling documentary film released in 1956.

Cousteau는 1956년 개봉한 흥미로운 다큐멘터리 영화로 그의 수중 세계 경험을 세상과 공유했다.

It transformed people's perceptions of the ocean and promoted (17) _____ _____ _____ _____ _____ .

이 영화는 바다에 대한 사람들의 인식을 바꾸었고, 해양 보존에 대한 필요성을 널리 알렸다.

Cousteau's curiosity (18) _____ _____ _____ _____ _____ in new areas, and his passion enabled him to make the impossible a reality.

Cousteau의 호기심은 그를 새로운 분야에 끊임없이 도전하게 했고, 그의 열정은 불가능한 것을 현실로 만들게 했다.

Cousteau's life story (19) _____ _____ _____ _____ the boundaries of what I can do.

Cousteau의 인생 이야기는 내가 할 수 있는 것의 한계를 뛰어넘도록 격려했다.

Because of him, I am not afraid to (20) _____ _____ _____ in life.

Cousteau 덕분에 나는 인생에서 다양한 것들에 도전하는 것이 두렵지 않다.

I will keep exploring until I find (21) _____ _____ _____ _____ .

나에게 가장 잘 맞는 것을 찾을 때까지 나는 계속 탐구할 것이다.

Sunho

When people (22) _____ _____ _____ _____ _____ , I always say that it is Joan Procter.

사람들이 내 롤모델에 대해 물어보면 나는 항상 Joan Procter라고 말한다.

You (23) _____ _____ _____ _____ _____ her, but she was a notable zoologist (24) _____ _____ _____ _____ in the early 20th century.

그녀에 대해 들어보지 못했을지도 모르지만, 그녀는 20세기 초반에 파충류를 전문으로 다룬 저명한 동물학자였다.

She taught me that (25) _____ _____ _____ _____ _____ is important for shaping one's career.

그녀는 내게 특정 분야에 전념하는 것은 한 사람의 경력을 형성하는 데 중요하다는 것을 가르쳐 주었다.

During her childhood, Procter (26) _____ _____ _____ the exploration of nature and animals.

Procter는 어린 시절에 자연과 동물을 탐험하는 것에 몰두했다.

Although (27) _____ _____ _____ _____, she kept lizards, snakes, and even a baby crocodile as pets.

비록 그녀의 아버지가 파충류를 싫어했지만, 그녀는 도마뱀, 뱀, 심지어 새끼 악어도 반려동물로 키웠다.

They were special companions that she loved and (28) _____ _____ _____.

그들은 그녀가 사랑하고 돌봐주었던 특별한 친구들이었다.

She was a brilliant student, but health problems (29) _____ _____ _____ _____ university.

그녀는 뛰어난 학생이었지만, 건강 문제로 대학에 진학하지 못했다.

However, her passion for zoology was (30) _____ _____ _____ it kept her moving forward, and she continued her studies on her own.

하지만, 동물학에 대한 그녀의 열정은 아주 강해서 그녀를 계속 앞으로 나아가게 했고, 그녀는 혼자 힘으로 공부를 계속했다.

Procter (31) _____ _____ _____ of zoology.

Procter는 동물학에 대한 광범위한 지식을 쌓았다.

She began exchanging letters with George Boulenger, a prominent expert on reptiles, (32) _____ _____ _____ _____ ideas.

그녀는 유명한 파충류 전문가였던 George Boulenger와 의견을 나누기 위해 편지를 주고받기 시작했다.

He was (33) _____ _____ _____ _____ _____ her as his assistant at the British Museum.

그는 그녀에게 아주 깊은 인상을 받아서 그녀를 British Museum에서 자신의 조수로 채용했다.

A few years later, she became (34) _____ _____ _____ _____ of reptiles at the London Zoo.

몇 년 후, 그녀는 London Zoo의 첫 번째 여성 파충류 큐레이터가 되었다.

There, she actively (35) _____ _____ the design of the Reptile House by incorporating new technology that (36) _____ _____ _____ _____ and breeding of wild animals.

그곳에서 그녀는 야생 동물을 더 잘 돌보고 번식시킬 수 있게 하는 새로운 기술을 포함시킴으로써 Reptile House의 설계에 적극적으로 기여했다.

Like her, I (37) _____ _____ _____ _____ _____ a field that I have a passion for.

나도 그녀처럼 내가 열정을 가지고 있는 분야에 전념하고 싶다.

For this reason, I will take my time to think deeply about (38) _____ _____ _____
_____.

이러한 이유로, 나는 내 진정한 관심이 어디에 있는지 깊이 생각해 보기 위해 시간을 가질 것이다.

If I am fortunate, one of my passions might someday (39) _____ _____ _____ _____
_____.

운이 좋다면 언젠가 내 열정 중 하나가 보람 있는 직업으로 이어질 것이다.

Yubin

As someone (40) _____ _____ _____, my role model has always been Kim Sang-jin.
애니메이션을 좋아하는 사람으로서, 내 롤모델은 항상 김상진이었다.

He was (41) _____ _____ _____ _____ to work for Walt Disney Animation Studios.
그는 Walt Disney 애니메이션 스튜디오에서 일한 최초의 한국인 애니메이터였다.

(42) _____ _____ _____ _____ he worked for a world-famous company, I admire him for
pursuing his dream (43) _____ _____ _____ _____ _____.
나는 그가 세계적으로 유명한 회사에서 일했다는 사실을 넘어, 그가 마주했던 어려움에도 불구하고 자신의 꿈을 추구했다는 점에서 그를 존경한다.

From a young age, Kim was (44) _____ _____ _____.
그는 어렸을 때부터 그림 그리는 것에 열정적이었다.

However, his dream of studying art in college was disrupted when he (45) _____ _____ _____
color vision deficiency during high school.
하지만 고등학교 때 색약 진단을 받으면서 대학에서 미술을 공부하고자 했던 그의 꿈에 지장이 갔다.

Surprisingly, he didn't (46) _____ _____ _____ _____ _____ him.
놀랍게도 그는 이 불행으로 좌절하지 않았다.

Instead, he simply (47) _____ _____ _____ _____ a minor issue that could happen to
anyone.
대신에, 그는 자신의 상태를 단지 누구에게나 일어날 수 있는 사소한 문제로 여겼다.

Although he (48) _____ _____ _____ _____ _____ _____, he searched for a
job (49) _____ _____ _____ that wouldn't involve working with colors.
그는 경제학 학위를 받고 졸업했지만, 색을 다루지 않으면서 미술과 관련된 직업을 찾았다.

He found out that some animators work only in pencil, so he (50) _____ _____ _____
_____ all the animation studios in Korea.
그는 몇몇 애니메이터들이 오직 연필만으로 작업한다는 것을 알아냈고, 한국에 있는 모든 애니메이션 스튜디오에 자신의 포트폴리오를 보냈다.

One of them (51) _____ _____ _____ _____, and he was finally able to start his career.

그중 한 곳에서 그에게 기회를 주었고, 그는 마침내 그의 커리어를 시작할 수 있었다.

(52) _____ _____ _____ _____ _____ _____ that eventually led him to a position at Disney at the age of 37.

그가 37세에 결국 Disney에서 일할 수 있게 했던 것은 그의 노력과 재능이었다.

I give him a lot of (53) _____ _____ _____ _____ and his attitude toward the challenges in his life.

나는 그의 끈기와 인생에서의 어려움을 대하는 태도를 높이 평가한다.

I'll (54) _____ _____ _____ _____ on my dreams.

나도 절대 내 꿈을 포기하지 않을 것이다.

If I (55) _____ _____, I will simply find another way to pursue them, just as he did.

만약 어려움을 맞닥뜨리게 된다면, 그가 그랬던 것처럼 그저 꿈을 추구하는 다른 방법을 찾을 것이다.

These stories shared by our readers (56) _____ _____ _____ _____ role models in guiding teenagers toward their career goals.

독자들이 공유한 이야기들은 청소년들을 직업 목표로 인도하는 데 있어서 롤모델의 중요성을 강조한다.

Role models, (57) _____ _____ _____ _____, inspire us because they possess qualities like persistence, commitment, and optimism.

분야에 상관없이 롤모델은 끈기, 헌신, 낙관주의와 같은 자질을 가지고 있어서 우리에게 영감을 준다.

(58) _____ _____ _____ _____ a role model yet, perhaps it's time to start searching for one.

아직 롤모델을 찾지 못했다면 어쩌면 이제 롤모델을 찾기 시작할 때일지도 모른다.

(59) _____ _____ _____ someone who can (60) _____ _____ _____ _____ the first step in your career exploration.

진로 탐색에서의 첫걸음을 내딛도록 당신을 격려할 수 있는 누군가를 찾아보아라.

01 밑줄 친 부분 중, 문맥상 낱말의 쓰임이 적절하지 않은 것은?

Choosing a career is one of the biggest life decisions young people face. Mapping out the right career path can be ①easy. While some teenagers have a clear vision of their career goals, others struggle to ②define them. This is where role models can be ③useful. They help young people start to plan their careers by providing them with ④guidance and the sense of purpose they need to succeed. We asked our teenage readers about their role models and the qualities they ⑤admire most in them. After you read each student's story, you will get a better idea of the profound impact role models can have when it comes to shaping career goals.

02 (A), (B), (C)의 각 네모 안에서 문맥에 맞는 낱말로 가장 적절한 것은?

Cousteau's curiosity drove him to constantly challenge himself in new areas, and his (A) passion / indifference enabled him to make the impossible a reality. Cousteau's life story inspired me to (B) push / pull the boundaries of what I can do. Because of him, I am not afraid to try different things in life. I will keep (C) ignoring / exploring until I find what suits me best.

	(A)	(B)	(C)
①	passion	… pull	… exploring
②	passion	… push	… exploring
③	passion	… push	… ignoring
④	indifference	… push	… exploring
⑤	indifference	… pull	… ignoring

03 밑줄 친 부분 중, 문맥상 낱말의 쓰임이 적절하지 않은 것은?

My role model is Jacques Cousteau, a French ocean explorer, inventor, and filmmaker. He ①dedicated his life to exploring and documenting the wonders of the underwater world. As a young man, he dreamed of becoming a pilot, but then he broke both of his arms in a ②terrible car accident. As part of his physical therapy, Cousteau began swimming. He became intrigued by the mysteries of the ocean, and he wanted to explore further. However, the diving equipment available at that time was ③sufficient. Instead of giving up, Cousteau decided to create his own equipment. After a long series of failed attempts, he finally succeeded in developing a portable ④breathing device, which he called the "Aqua-Lung." Cousteau shared his underwater experiences with the world in a compelling documentary film released in 1956. It transformed people's perceptions of the ocean and promoted the need for marine ⑤conservation.

04 밑줄 친 부분 중, 문맥상 낱말의 쓰임이 적절하지 않은 것은?

When people ask me about my role model, I always say that it is Joan Procter. You may not have heard of her, but she was a ①infamous zoologist who specialized in reptiles in the early 20th century. She taught me that ②devotion to a particular field is important for shaping one's career. During her childhood, Procter immersed herself in the ③exploration of nature and animals. Although her father hated reptiles, she kept lizards, snakes, and even a baby crocodile as ④pets. They were special companions that she loved and took care of. She was a brilliant student, but health problems prevented her from ⑤attending university. However, her passion for zoology was so strong that it kept her moving forward, and she continued her studies on her own.

05 (A), (B), (C)의 각 네모 안에서 문맥에 맞는 낱말로 가장 적절한 것은?

Procter accumulated extensive knowledge of zoology. She began exchanging letters with George Boulenger, a prominent expert on reptiles, in order to share ideas. He was so (A) impressed / depressed that he hired her as his assistant at the British Museum. A few years later, she became the first female curator of reptiles at the London Zoo. There, she actively contributed to the design of the Reptile House by incorporating new technology that allowed for better care and breeding of wild animals. Like her, I want to (B) dedicate / indicate myself to a field that I have a passion for. For this reason, I will take my time to think deeply about where my true interests lie. If I am (C) fortunate / unfortunate, one of my passions might someday lead to a rewarding career.

	(A)		(B)		(C)
①	impressed	⋯	dedicate	⋯	unfortunate
②	depressed	⋯	indicate	⋯	unfortunate
③	impressed	⋯	indicate	⋯	unfortunate
④	depressed	⋯	dedicate	⋯	fortunate
⑤	impressed	⋯	dedicate	⋯	fortunate

06 밑줄 친 부분 중, 문맥상 낱말의 쓰임이 적절하지 않은 것은?

As someone who loves animation, my role model has always been Kim Sang-jin. He was the first Korean ①animator to work for Walt Disney Animation Studios. Beyond the fact that he worked for a world-famous company, I admire him for pursuing his dream despite the ②difficulties he faced. From a young age, Kim was ③enthusiastic about drawing. However, his dream of studying art in college was disrupted when he was diagnosed with color vision ④deficiency during high school. Surprisingly, he didn't allow this misfortune to discourage him. Instead, he simply viewed his condition as a ⑤major issue that could happen to anyone.

07 밑줄 친 부분 중, 문맥상 낱말의 쓰임이 적절하지 않은 것은?

Although he graduated with a ①degree in economics, he searched for a job related to art that wouldn't involve working with colors. He found out that some animators work only in pencil, so he sent his ②portfolio to all the animation studios in Korea. One of them gave him an ③opportunity, and he was finally able to start his career. It was his hard work and talent that eventually led him to a position at Disney at the age of 37. I give him a lot of credit for his ④resistance and his attitude toward the challenges in his life. I'll never give up on my dreams. If I encounter difficulties, I will simply find another way to ⑤pursue them, just as he did.

08 (A), (B), (C)의 각 네모 안에서 문맥에 맞는 낱말로 가장 적절한 것은?

These stories shared by our readers emphasize the importance of role models in guiding teenagers (A) toward / forward their career goals. Role models, regardless of their field, inspire us because they possess qualities like persistence, commitment, and (B) optimism / pessimism. If you haven't found a role model yet, perhaps it's time to start searching for one. Try to find someone who can (C) discourage / encourage you to take the first step in your career exploration.

	(A)		(B)		(C)
①	forward	⋯	optimism	⋯	encourage
②	toward	⋯	optimism	⋯	discourage
③	toward	⋯	optimism	⋯	encourage
④	forward	⋯	pessimism	⋯	discourage
⑤	toward	⋯	pessimism	⋯	encourage

01 다음 글의 밑줄 친 부분 중, 어법상 틀린 것은?

Choosing a career is one of the biggest life ① decisions young people face. Mapping out the right career path can be demanding. While some teenagers have a clear vision of their career goals, ② others struggle to define them. This is where role models can be useful. They help young people ③ starting to plan their careers by providing them with guidance and the sense of purpose they need to succeed. We asked our teenage readers about their role models and the qualities they admire ④ most in them. After you read each student's story, you will get a better idea of the profound impact role models can have when it comes to ⑤ shaping career goals.

02 (A), (B), (C)의 각 네모 안에서 어법에 맞는 표현으로 가장 적절한 것은?

Cousteau's curiosity drove him to constantly challenge himself in new areas, and his passion enabled him (A) making / to make the impossible a reality. Cousteau's life story inspired me to push the boundaries of (B) what / that I can do. Because of him, I am not afraid to try different things in life. I will keep (C) exploring / to explore until I find what suits me best.

	(A)	(B)	(C)
①	making	that	exploring
②	to make	what	exploring
③	making	what	to explore
④	to make	what	to explore
⑤	to make	that	exploring

03 다음 글의 밑줄 친 부분 중, 어법상 틀린 것은?

My role model is Jacques Cousteau, a French ocean explorer, inventor, and filmmaker. He dedicated his life to ① exploring and documenting the wonders of the underwater world. As a young man, he dreamed of ② becoming a pilot, but then he broke both of his arms in a terrible car accident. As part of his physical therapy, Cousteau began swimming. He became ③ intrigued by the mysteries of the ocean, and he wanted to explore further. However, the diving equipment available at that time was insufficient. Instead of giving up, Cousteau decided to create his own equipment. After a long series of failed attempts, he finally succeeded in developing a portable ④ breathing device, which he called the "Aqua-Lung." Cousteau shared his underwater experiences with the world in a compelling documentary film ⑤ releasing in 1956. It transformed people's perceptions of the ocean and promoted the need for marine conservation.

04 다음 글의 밑줄 친 부분 중, 어법상 틀린 것은?

When people ask me about my role model, I always say that it is Joan Procter. You may not have heard of her, but she was a notable zoologist ① who specialized in reptiles in the early 20th century. She taught me that devotion to a particular field is important for shaping one's career. ② During her childhood, Procter immersed herself in the exploration of nature and animals. ③ Although her father hated reptiles, she kept lizards, snakes, and even a baby crocodile as pets. They were special companions that she loved and took care of. She was a brilliant student, but health problems prevented her from ④ attending university. However, her passion for zoology was ⑤ such strong that it kept her moving forward, and she continued her studies on her own.

05 (A), (B), (C)의 각 네모 안에서 어법에 맞는 표현으로 가장 적절한 것은?

Procter accumulated extensive knowledge of zoology. She began exchanging letters with George Boulenger, a prominent expert on reptiles, in order to share ideas. He was so (A) impressing / impressed that he hired her as his assistant at the British Museum. A few years later, she became the first female curator of reptiles at the London Zoo. There, she actively contributed to the design of the Reptile House by incorporating new technology that allowed for better care and breeding of wild animals. Like her, I want to dedicate (B) me / myself to a field that I have a passion for. For this reason, I will take my time to think deeply about where my true interests lie. If I am fortunate, one of my (C) passion / passions might someday lead to a rewarding career.

	(A)		(B)		(C)
①	impressing	⋯	me	⋯	passions
②	impressing	⋯	myself	⋯	passions
③	impressed	⋯	me	⋯	passion
④	impressed	⋯	myself	⋯	passions
⑤	impressed	⋯	myself	⋯	passion

06 다음 글의 밑줄 친 부분 중, 어법상 틀린 것은?

As someone ①who loves animation, my role model has always been Kim Sang-jin. He was the first Korean animator to work for Walt Disney Animation Studios. Beyond the fact that he worked for a world-famous company, I admire him for pursuing his dream ②despite the difficulties he faced. From a young age, Kim was enthusiastic about drawing. However, his dream ③that studying art in college was disrupted when he was diagnosed with color vision deficiency ④during high school. Surprisingly, he didn't allow this misfortune ⑤to discourage him. Instead, he simply viewed his condition as a minor issue that could happen to anyone.

07 (A), (B), (C)의 각 네모 안에서 어법에 맞는 표현으로 가장 적절한 것은?

Although he graduated with a degree in economics, he searched for a job (A) relating / related to art that wouldn't involve working with colors. He found out that some animators work only in pencil, so he sent his portfolio to all the animation studios in Korea. One of them gave him an opportunity, and he was finally able to start his career. It was his hard work and talent (B) that / which eventually led him to a position at Disney at the age of 37. I give him a lot of credit for his persistence and his attitude toward the challenges in his life. I'll never give up on my dreams. If I (C) encounter / will encounter difficulties, I will simply find another way to pursue them, just as he did.

	(A)		(B)		(C)
①	relating	⋯	that	⋯	encounter
②	relating	⋯	which	⋯	will encounter
③	related	⋯	that	⋯	encounter
④	related	⋯	that	⋯	will encounter
⑤	related	⋯	which	⋯	encounter

08 다음 글의 밑줄 친 부분 중, 어법상 틀린 것은?

These stories ①sharing by our readers emphasize the importance of role models in guiding teenagers toward their career goals. Role models, regardless of their field, ②inspire us because they possess qualities like persistence, commitment, and optimism. If you ③haven't found a role model yet, perhaps it's time to start searching for one. Try to find someone ④who can encourage you ⑤to take the first step in your career exploration.

[01~02] 다음 대화를 읽고, 물음에 답하시오.

B Hello, Ms. Kim. May I ask you for your advice? (①)

W Of course, Jinsu! What's been bothering you?

B Well, I've been thinking a lot about my future career. As you know, I'm good at science. (②)

W Yes, I think you would have a successful career as a scientist.

B The problem is, even though I like studying science, I prefer to spend my time playing the guitar. (③)

W It can be hard to choose between your passion and a safe career path.

B I wish I could study both science and music at college, but I think I should focus on one.

W I think you should try to figure out what you value most in a career. (④)

B I guess I need some time to think about it. Thank you for your advice, Ms. Kim. (⑤)

W You're welcome!

01 대화의 흐름으로 보아, 주어진 문장이 들어갈 위치로 가장 적절한 곳은?

I'm not sure if I should focus on science or pursue my passion for music.

①   ②   ③   ④   ⑤

02 위 대화의 내용과 일치하지 <u>않는</u> 것은?

① 진수는 미래의 직업에 대해 고민하고 있다.
② 진수가 과학을 잘한다는 것을 김 선생님도 알고 있다.
③ 김 선생님은 진수가 과학자로 성공할 거라고 생각한다.
④ 진수는 과학 공부보다 기타 연주하는 것을 더 좋아한다.
⑤ 김 선생님은 취업에 도움이 되는 과학을 선택하라고 조언한다.

[03~05] 다음 글을 읽고, 물음에 답하시오.

직업을 선택하는 것은 젊은 사람들이 직면하는 인생의 가장 큰 결정 중 하나이다. ①Mapping out the right career path can be demanding. While some teenagers have a clear vision of their career goals, ②others struggle to define them. This is where role models can be useful. They help young people ③starting to plan their careers by providing them with guidance and the sense of purpose they need to succeed. We asked our teenage readers about their role models and the qualities they admire most in them. After you read each student's story, you will get a ④better idea of the profound impact role models can have when it comes to ⑤shaping career goals.

03 윗글의 밑줄 친 우리말과 일치하도록 다음 문장에서 <u>틀린</u> 부분을 바르게 고쳐 쓰시오.

Choose a career is one of the biggest life decision young people face.

→ _____

04 윗글의 밑줄 친 부분 중, 어법상 틀린 것은?

①   ②   ③   ④   ⑤

05 윗글 다음에 이어질 내용으로 가장 적절한 것은?

① 직업별 장단점 비교
② 학생들의 롤모델 예시
③ 사회가 직업 선택에 미치는 영향
④ 롤모델 없는 동기 부여 방법
⑤ 직업 선택의 어려움과 극복 방법

[06~08] 다음 글을 읽고, 물음에 답하시오.

My role model is Jacques Cousteau, a French ocean explorer, inventor, and filmmaker. He dedicated his life to exploring and (A) document / documenting the wonders of the underwater world. As a young man, he dreamed of becoming a pilot, but then he broke both of his arms in a terrible car accident. As part of his physical therapy, Cousteau began swimming. He became intrigued by the mysteries of the ocean, and he wanted to explore further. However, the diving equipment available at that time was insufficient. Instead of giving up, Cousteau decided to create his own equipment. After a long series of failed attempts, he finally succeeded in developing a portable breathing device, (B) that / which he called the "Aqua-Lung." Cousteau shared his underwater experiences with the world in a compelling documentary film (C) releasing / released in 1956. It transformed people's perceptions of the ocean and promoted the need for marine conservation.

Cousteau's curiosity drove him to constantly challenge himself in new areas, and his passion enabled him to make the impossible a reality. Cousteau's life story inspired me to push the boundaries of what I can do. Because of him, I am not afraid _____. I will keep exploring until I find what suits me best.

06 윗글의 빈칸에 들어갈 말로 가장 적절한 것은?

① to stick to my original plan
② to learn how to swim in the ocean
③ to avoid challenges in my career
④ to try different things in life
⑤ to focus solely on academic achievements

07 다음 영어 뜻풀이에 해당하는 말을 윗글에서 찾아 두 단어로 쓰시오.

medical treatment for problems with parts of the body, such as joints or muscles

→ _____

08 (A), (B), (C)의 각 네모 안에서 어법에 맞는 표현으로 가장 적절한 것은?

	(A)	(B)	(C)
①	document	… that	… releasing
②	document	… which	… released
③	documenting	… which	… releasing
④	documenting	… which	… released
⑤	documenting	… that	… released

[09~10] 다음 글을 읽고, 물음에 답하시오.

Student A

Passion allows us to enjoy our work and feel ①satisfied with our jobs. This will motivate us ②putting in more effort and dedicate ourselves to doing our best.

Student B

In my opinion, ③choosing a job based on our ability is more important. When we do ④what we're good at, we feel more confident and perform ⑤better.

09 윗글에 있는 단어를 이용하여 토론의 주제문을 완성하시오.

Which is more important in choosing a job— _____ or _____?

10 윗글의 밑줄 친 ①~⑤ 중, 어법상 틀린 것을 찾아 번호를 쓰고 바르게 고쳐 쓰시오.

_____ → _____

[11~12] 다음 글을 읽고, 물음에 답하시오.

When people ask me about my role model, I always say ①that it is Joan Procter. You may not have heard of her, but she was a notable zoologist ②who specialized in reptiles in the early 20th century. She taught me that devotion to a particular field is important for ③shaping one's career. During her childhood, Procter immersed ④herself in the exploration of nature and animals. Although her father hated reptiles, she kept lizards, snakes, and even a baby crocodile ⑤as pets. They were special companions that she loved and took care of. She was a brilliant student, but health problems prevented her from attending university. 하지만, 동물학에 대한 그녀의 열정은 아주 강해서 그녀를 계속 앞으로 나아가게 했고, 그녀는 혼자 힘으로 계속 공부했다.

11 윗글의 밑줄 친 ①~⑤ 중, 설명이 바르지 <u>않은</u> 것은?

① 목적어 역할을 하는 명사절을 이끄는 접속사이다.
② 선행사가 zoologist인 주격 관계대명사이다.
③ 전치사의 목적어 역할을 하는 동명사이다.
④ 강조 용법으로 쓰인 재귀대명사로 생략할 수 있다.
⑤ '~로서'라는 뜻의 전치사이다.

12 윗글의 밑줄 친 우리말과 일치하도록 [보기]에 주어진 단어를 바르게 배열하시오.

[보기]

so / that / it / her / was / moving forward / strong / kept

→ However, her passion for zoology _____

_____ ,

and she continued her studies on her own.

[13~14] 다음 글을 읽고, 물음에 답하시오.

Procter accumulated extensive knowledge of zoology. She began exchanging letters with George Boulenger, a prominent expert on reptiles, in order to share ideas. He was so impressed that he hired her as his assistant at the British Museum. A few years later, she became the first female curator of reptiles at the London Zoo. There, she actively contributed to the design of the Reptile House by incorporating new technology that allowed for better care and breeding of wild animals. Like her, I want to dedicate myself to a field that I have a passion for. For this reason, I will take my time to think deeply about where my true interests lie. If I am fortunate, one of my passions might someday lead to a rewarding career.

13 윗글에 나타난 필자의 태도로 가장 적절한 것은?

① envious ② pleased ③ determined
④ satisfied ⑤ depressed

14 윗글의 밑줄 친 부분과 쓰임이 <u>다른</u> 것을 <u>모두</u> 고르면?

① They decided to volunteer at the animal shelter every weekend.
② Scientists developed a vaccine to prevent the spread of the virus.
③ Lisa joined a debate club to enhance her public speaking abilities.
④ Tony tried his best to become a professional athlete.
⑤ It was surprising to discover the ancient artifact in the urban area.

As someone who loves animation, my role model has always been Kim Sang-jin. He was the first Korean animator to work for Walt Disney Animation Studios. Beyond the fact that he worked for a world-famous company, I admire him for (A) pursuing / abandoning his dream despite the difficulties he faced. From a young age, Kim was enthusiastic about drawing. However, his dream of studying art in college was (B) maintained / disrupted when he was diagnosed with color vision deficiency during high school. Surprisingly, he didn't allow this misfortune to (C) encourage / discourage him. Instead, he simply viewed his condition as a minor issue that could happen to anyone.

15 윗글의 주제로 가장 적절한 것은?

① 색약을 극복하는 다양한 방법
② 디즈니 애니메이션의 기술적 발전
③ 미술 교육 시스템의 한계
④ 장애 극복을 통한 꿈의 추구
⑤ 애니메이션의 해외 진출의 중요성

16 (A), (B), (C)의 각 네모 안에서 문맥에 맞는 낱말로 가장 적절한 것은?

	(A)	(B)	(C)
①	pursuing	⋯ disrupted	⋯ encourage
②	abandoning	⋯ disrupted	⋯ discourage
③	abandoning	⋯ maintained	⋯ encourage
④	pursuing	⋯ maintained	⋯ discourage
⑤	pursuing	⋯ disrupted	⋯ discourage

Although Kim Sang-jin graduated with a degree in economics, he searched for a job related to art that wouldn't involve working with colors. He found out that some animators work only in pencil, so he sent his portfolio to all the animation studios in Korea. One of them gave him an opportunity, and he was finally able to start his career. It was his hard work and talent that eventually led him to a position at Disney at the age of 37. I give him a lot of credit for his persistence and his attitude toward the challenges in his life. I'll never give up on my dreams. 만약 어려움을 맞닥뜨리게 된다면, 그가 그랬던 것처럼 그저 꿈을 추구하는 다른 방법을 찾을 것이다.

17 윗글의 밑줄 친 우리말과 일치하도록 보기 에 주어진 단어를 배열하여 문장을 완성하시오.

> 보기
>
> encounter / I / them / find / I / to pursue / will / difficulties / simply / another way

→ If _____,

_____,

just as he did.

18 다음 영어 뜻풀이에 해당하는 단어를 윗글에서 찾아 쓰시오.

> the quality that allows somebody to keep doing something even if it is difficult

→ _____

[01~02] 다음 대화를 읽고, 물음에 답하시오.

G Jiwon, are you okay? You look a bit down.

B Well, most of my friends have decided on their dream jobs, but I have no idea about what I want to do in the future. _____

G Oh, you must be anxious. I have one suggestion for you. Try taking a "career personality test."

B What is that?

G Our school counselor told me about it. It's a test to find out what kind of job matches your personality. It gives you a series of activities, and you have to answer how interested you are in each one.

B What kinds of activities? Can you give me an example?

G Sure. It might say "Inspect a roof for leaks" or "Write a poem." Then you can answer whether you like or dislike each activity. When you are done, the results will tell you your personality type and jobs you might enjoy.

B That sounds cool! I will try it right away.

01 위 대화의 빈칸에 들어갈 말로 가장 적절한 것은?

① I'm too busy to think about my future.

② I want to travel the world first.

③ My parents have chosen a job for me.

④ I wish I could figure out what my dream job is.

⑤ I've already decided on my dream job.

02 위 대화에 나타난 남학생의 심경 변화로 가장 적절한 것은?

① excited → relieved

② confused → frustrated

③ frustrated → enthusiastic

④ disappointed → hopeful

⑤ worried → embarrassed

[03~04] 다음 글을 읽고, 물음에 답하시오.

Choosing a career is one of the biggest life decisions young people face. Mapping out the right career path can be demanding. While some teenagers have a clear vision of their career goals, others struggle to define them. This is where role models can be useful. They help young people start to plan their careers by providing them with guidance and the sense of purpose they need to succeed. We asked our teenage readers about their role models and the qualities they admire most in them. After you read each student's story, you will get a better idea of the profound impact role models can have when it comes to shaping career goals.

03 윗글의 목적으로 가장 적절한 것은?

① 진로 선택의 객관적 기준을 제시하기 위해

② 청소년의 진로 결정권 확대를 주장하기 위해

③ 진로 상담 프로그램을 홍보하기 위해

④ 롤모델의 필요성과 효과를 알리기 위해

⑤ 학교 진로 교육의 개선방안을 제안하기 위해

04 윗글의 밑줄 친 단어에 대한 영어 뜻풀이로 가장 적절한 것은?

① the reason for doing something

② help or advice about what to do or about how to do something

③ a job or profession that a person does for a long time

④ a feature or characteristic of somebody or something

⑤ a powerful influence or effect that something has on a person or a situation

[05~07] 다음 글을 읽고, 물음에 답하시오.

My role model is Jacques Cousteau, a French ocean explorer, inventor, and filmmaker. He ① dedicated his life to exploring and documenting the wonders of the underwater world. As a young man, he ② dreamed of becoming a pilot, but then he broke both of his arms in a terrible car accident. As part of his physical therapy, Cousteau began swimming. He ③ became intrigued by the mysteries of the ocean, and he wanted to explore further. However, the diving equipment available at that time was insufficient. Instead of giving up, Cousteau decided to create his own equipment. After a long series of failed attempts, he finally ④ succeeded in developing a portable breathing device, which he called the "Aqua-Lung." Cousteau shared his underwater experiences with the world in a compelling documentary film released in 1956. It transformed people's perceptions of the ocean and promoted the need for marine conservation. Cousteau의 호기심은 그를 새로운 분야에 끊임없이 도전하게 했고, and his passion enabled him to make the impossible a reality. Cousteau's life story ⑤ inspired me to push the boundaries of what I can do. Because of him, I am not afraid to try different things in life. I will keep exploring until I find what suits me best.

05 윗글의 주제로 가장 적절한 것은?

① 사고 후 재활의 중요성
② 해양 생태계의 복잡성
③ 해양 탐사 장비의 변천사
④ 다큐멘터리 제작 기술의 발전
⑤ 어려움 극복을 통한 성취와 영향력

06 윗글의 밑줄 친 ①~⑤ 중, 우리말 해석이 바르지 않은 것은?

① 탐험하는 데 그의 삶을 바쳤다
② 조종사가 되기를 꿈꿨다
③ 해양의 신비로움에 두려움을 느꼈다
④ 휴대용 호흡 기계를 개발하는 데 성공했다
⑤ 한계를 뛰어넘도록 영감을 주었다

07 윗글의 밑줄 친 우리말과 일치하도록 보기 에 주어진 단어를 바르게 배열하시오.

보기
Cousteau's curiosity / in / him / to / himself / constantly / new / drove / areas / challenge

→ _____

08 다음 글의 밑줄 친 ①~⑤ 중, 어법상 틀린 것은?

As someone ① who loves animation, my role model has always been Kim Sang-jin. He was the first Korean animator ② to work for Walt Disney Animation Studios. Beyond the fact ③ of he worked for a world-famous company, I admire him for pursuing his dream despite the difficulties he faced. From a young age, Kim was enthusiastic about ④ drawing. However, his dream of studying art in college was disrupted when he was diagnosed with color vision deficiency during high school. Surprisingly, he didn't allow this misfortune ⑤ to discourage him. Instead, he simply viewed his condition as a minor issue that could happen to anyone.

①   ②   ③   ④   ⑤

[09~10] 다음 글을 읽고, 물음에 답하시오.

When people ask me about my role model, I always say that it is Joan Procter. You may not have heard of her, but she was a notable zoologist who specialized in reptiles in the early 20th century. She taught me that devotion to a particular field is important for shaping one's career. During her childhood, Procter immersed herself in the exploration of nature and animals. Although her father hated reptiles, she kept lizards, snakes, and even a baby crocodile as pets. They were special companions that she loved and took care of. She was a brilliant student, but (health problems / her / university / from / prevented / attending). However, her passion for zoology was so strong that it kept her moving forward, and she continued her studies on her own.

09 Joan Procter에 관한 설명으로 글의 내용과 일치하지 <u>않는</u> 것은?

① 20세기 초반의 저명한 동물학자였다.

② 어린 시절부터 자연과 동물 탐험에 몰두했다.

③ 아버지를 따라 파충류에 관심을 가지게 되었다.

④ 새끼 악어를 반려동물로 키운 적도 있다.

⑤ 혼자 힘으로 동물학에 대한 공부를 꾸준히 했다.

10 윗글의 괄호 안에 주어진 단어를 알맞게 배열하여 문장을 완성하시오.

She was a brilliant student, but _____

_____ .

[11~12] 다음 글을 읽고, 물음에 답하시오.

Procter accumulated extensive knowledge of zoology. ① She began exchanging letters with George Boulenger, a prominent expert on reptiles, in order to share ideas. He was so ____(A)____ that he hired her as his assistant at the British Museum. ② A few years later, she became the first female curator of reptiles at the London Zoo. There, she actively contributed to the design of the Reptile House by ____(B)____ new technology that allowed for better care and breeding of wild animals. ③ Interestingly, the London Zoo is also home to one of the oldest surviving reptile houses in the world, attracting thousands of visitors each year. ④ Like her, I want to dedicate myself to a field that I have a passion for. ⑤ For this reason, I will take my time to think deeply about where my true interests lie. If I ____(C)____ fortunate, one of my passions might someday lead to a rewarding career.

11 윗글의 전체 흐름상, 관계 <u>없는</u> 문장은?

①   ②   ③   ④   ⑤

12 윗글의 빈칸 (A)~(C)에 들어갈 말을 어법에 맞는 형태로 바꿔 쓰시오.

(A) impress → _____

(B) incorporate → _____

(C) be → _____

Although Kim Sang-jin graduated with a degree in economics, he searched for a job ①related to art that wouldn't involve working with colors. He found out ②that some animators work only in pencil, so he sent his portfolio to all the animation studios in Korea. One of ③them gave him an opportunity, and he was finally able to start his career. It was his hard work and talent ④that eventually led him to a position at Disney at the age of 37. I give him a lot of credit for his persistence and his attitude toward the challenges in his life. I'll never give up on my dreams. ⑤If I encounter difficulties, I will simply find another way to pursue them, just as he did.

13 윗글의 밑줄 친 ①~⑤ 중, 설명이 바르지 않은 것은?

① 앞의 명사 a job을 수식하는 과거분사구이다.
② 목적어 역할을 하는 명사절을 이끄는 접속사이다.
③ 앞 문장에 나온 animation studios를 가리킨다.
④ his hard work and talent를 수식하는 관계대명사이다.
⑤ '만약 ~라면'이라는 의미의 조건을 나타내는 접속사이다.

14 윗글을 통해 답을 찾을 수 없는 질문을 모두 고르면?

① 김상진의 대학 전공은 무엇인가?
② 김상진은 어떤 종류의 직업을 찾으려고 했는가?
③ 김상진이 일했던 한국의 애니메이션 스튜디오는 어디인가?
④ 김상진은 몇 살에 디즈니에서 일하게 되었는가?
⑤ 김상진은 디즈니에서 어떤 애니메이션 작품에 참여했는가?

My future goal is to become a veterinarian. In my first year of high school, I regularly volunteered at an animal shelter. Through this experience, I discovered my passion for animals and their welfare. After graduation, I would like to enroll in a veterinary school. I will study relevant subjects like medicine and surgery to gain valuable knowledge in this field. When I finally become a veterinarian, I will help animals that are brought to my clinic. I plan to keep studying and expanding my expertise. Later, when I have enough experience, I will travel to rural areas and do volunteer work using my expertise. I hope I can have a fulfilling life as a successful veterinarian!

15 윗글의 제목으로 가장 적절한 것은?

① My Dream to Become a Veterinarian
② The Importance of Volunteering at Animal Shelters
③ How to Take Care of Pets at Home
④ The Challenges of Studying Medicine
⑤ My Experience Traveling in Rural Areas

16 윗글의 밑줄 친 this experience가 의미하는 바를 우리말로 쓰시오. (20자 이내)

01 다음 대화의 빈칸에 공통으로 들어갈 말로 가장 적절한 것은?

> B I'm not sure if I should focus on science or pursue my passion for music.
>
> W It can be hard to choose between your passion and a safe _____ path.
>
> B I wish I could study both science and music at college, but I think I should focus on one.
>
> W I think you should try to figure out what you value most in a(n) _____.
>
> B I guess I need some time to think about it. Thank you for your advice, Ms. Kim.
>
> W You're welcome!

① goal   ② career   ③ ability
④ interest   ⑤ future

02 다음 글의 빈칸에 들어갈 말로 가장 적절한 것은?

> "The choice of a career is an expression of personality," said Dr. John Holland, an American psychologist. He found that people are happier and more productive when their job _____ their personality type. He believed that identifying our personality type can lead us to choose a suitable career that utilizes our abilities and interests, resulting in better performance and higher-quality work. This is why he created the Holland Codes, which consist of six personality types. They are commonly used by career counselors and organizations as a guideline to help job seekers choose the right career.

① connects   ② reflects   ③ contrasts
④ matches   ⑤ challenges

[03~05] 다음 글을 읽고, 물음에 답하시오.

> Choosing a career is one of the biggest life decisions young people face. Mapping out the right career path can be demanding. While some teenagers have a clear vision of their career goals, others struggle to define ①them. This is where role models can be useful. ②They help young people start to plan their careers by providing ③them with guidance and the sense of purpose they need to succeed. We asked our teenage readers about their role models and the qualities ④they admire most in ⑤them. 각 학생의 이야기를 읽고 나면, 직업 목표를 세우는 데 있어서 롤모델이 미칠 수 있는 엄청난 영향에 대해 더 잘 이해하게 될 것이다.

03 윗글의 밑줄 친 ①~⑤가 가리키는 말로 적절하지 않은 것은?

① their career goals   ② Role models
③ careers   ④ our teenage readers
⑤ their role models

04 윗글의 밑줄 친 우리말과 일치하도록 조건에 맞게 문장을 완성하시오.

> 조건
> • 사용할 표현: when, come, shape, career goals
> • 필요시 어형을 변형시킬 것

→ After you read each student's story, you will get a better idea of the profound impact role models can have _____

_____ .

05 롤모델이 청소년의 진로 계획에 어떻게 도움이 되는지 우리말로 쓰시오. (50자 이내)

→ _____

_____

[06~07] 다음 글을 읽고, 물음에 답하시오.

My role model is Jacques Cousteau, a French ocean explorer, inventor, and filmmaker. He dedicated his life to ①exploring and documenting the wonders of the underwater world. As a young man, he dreamed of becoming a pilot, but then he broke both of his arms in a terrible car accident. As part of his physical therapy, Cousteau began swimming. He became ②intrigued by the mysteries of the ocean, and he wanted to explore further. However, the diving equipment available at that time was insufficient. Instead of giving up, Cousteau decided ③to create his own equipment. After a long series of failed attempts, he finally succeeded in ④developing a portable breathing device, which he called the "Aqua-Lung." Cousteau shared his underwater experiences with the world in a compelling documentary film ⑤releasing in 1956. It transformed people's perceptions of the ocean and promoted the need for marine conservation.

06 윗글의 밑줄 친 ①~⑤ 중, 어법상 **틀린** 것은?

① ② ③ ④ ⑤

07 윗글의 밑줄 친 which와 쓰임이 같은 것끼리 묶은 것은?

ⓐ He bought the painting, which was created in 1920.
ⓑ I don't know which route I should take to avoid traffic.
ⓒ My friend gave me a book, which was very interesting.
ⓓ I visited the old museum, which was founded in the 19th century.
ⓔ Which do you think is more important, health or success?

① ⓐ, ⓑ
② ⓐ, ⓒ, ⓓ
③ ⓑ, ⓒ
④ ⓒ, ⓓ
⑤ ⓒ, ⓓ, ⓔ

[08~09] 다음 글을 읽고, 물음에 답하시오.

When people ask me about my role model, I always say that it is Joan Procter. You may not have heard of her, but she was a notable zoologist who specialized in reptiles in the early 20th century. She taught me (A) that / what devotion to a particular field is important for shaping one's career. During her childhood, Procter immersed herself in the exploration of nature and animals. (B) Despite / Although her father hated reptiles, she kept lizards, snakes, and even a baby crocodile as pets. They were special companions that she loved and took care of. She was a brilliant student, but health problems prevented her from attending university. However, her passion for zoology was (C) so / such strong that it kept her moving forward, and she continued her studies on her own.

08 다음 영어 뜻풀이에 해당하는 단어를 윗글에서 찾아 쓰시오.

very important and famous

→ _____

09 (A), (B), (C)의 각 네모 안에서 어법에 맞는 표현으로 가장 적절한 것은?

	(A)	(B)	(C)
①	what	Despite	so
②	that	Although	such
③	what	Although	so
④	that	Although	so
⑤	that	Despite	such

[10~11] 다음 글을 읽고, 물음에 답하시오.

Procter accumulated extensive knowledge of zoology. She began exchanging letters with George Boulenger, a prominent expert on reptiles, in order to share ideas. ① He was so impressed that he hired her as his assistant at the British Museum. A few years later, ② she became the first female curator of reptiles at the London Zoo. There, she actively contributed to the design of the Reptile House by incorporating new technology that allowed for better care and breeding of wild animals. Like her, ③ I want to dedicate me to a field that I have a passion for. For this reason, ④ I will take my time to think deeply about where my true interests lie. ⑤ If I am fortunate, one of my passions might someday lead to a rewarding career.

10 윗글의 밑줄 친 ①~⑤ 중, 어법상 틀린 문장을 찾아 번호를 쓰고 바르게 고쳐 쓰시오.

_____ → _____

_____

11 윗글의 내용과 일치하지 <u>않는</u> 것은?

① Procter는 동물학에 대한 광범위한 지식을 쌓았다.
② George Boulenger는 유명한 파충류 전문가였다.
③ Procter는 정기적으로 George Boulenger를 만나 대화했다.
④ George Boulenger는 대영 박물관에서 Procter를 조수로 고용했다.
⑤ Procter는 새로운 기술을 도입해 파충류관 설계에 기여했다.

[12~13] 다음 글을 읽고, 물음에 답하시오.

As someone who loves animation, my role model has always been Kim Sang-jin. He was the first Korean animator to work for Walt Disney Animation Studios. Beyond the fact that he worked ①for a world-famous company, I admire him for pursuing his dream despite the difficulties he faced. From a young age, Kim was enthusiastic ②about drawing. However, his dream ③from studying art in college was disrupted when he was diagnosed with color vision deficiency ④during high school. Surprisingly, he didn't allow this misfortune to (A)discourage him. Instead, he simply viewed his condition ⑤as a minor issue that could happen to anyone.

12 윗글의 밑줄 친 ①~⑤ 중, 전치사의 쓰임이 바르지 <u>않은</u> 것은?

①   ②   ③   ④   ⑤

13 윗글의 밑줄 친 (A)discourage의 영어 뜻풀이로 가장 적절한 것은?

① to try to do or achieve something, often over a long period of time
② to make somebody less hopeful, confident, or positive about something
③ to prevent something from continuing as usual or as expected
④ to identify an illness or the cause of a problem
⑤ to gather or acquire something over a long period of time

Although Kim Sang-jin graduated with a degree in economics, he searched for a job related to art that wouldn't involve working with colors. He found out that some animators work only in pencil, so he sent his portfolio to all the animation studios in Korea. One of them gave him an opportunity, and he was finally able to start his career. His hard work and talent eventually led him to a position at Disney at the age of 37. I give him a lot of credit for his persistence and his attitude toward the challenges in his life. I'll never give up on my dreams. If I encounter difficulties, I will simply find another way to pursue them, just as he did.

14 윗글의 밑줄 친 문장을 조건 에 맞게 바꿔 쓰시오.

조건
• 「It is[was] ~ that」 강조 구문을 사용할 것
• 주어를 강조할 것

→ _____

_____

15 윗글의 내용과 일치하지 않는 것은?

① Kim Sang-jin majored in economics at university.
② Kim Sang-jin wanted to work in an art-related job that did not require using colors.
③ Kim Sang-jin was immediately hired by Disney after sending his portfolio.
④ Some animators work only in pencil, without using colors.
⑤ The writer admires Kim Sang-jin's persistence.

Today I will introduce the six "work personality types" in the Holland Codes. The first group is doers. Doers are realistic and practical people who are good at making or fixing things with their hands. They often become mechanics or engineers. The next group is thinkers. These logical people like to solve problems related to math or science. Computer programmer or scientist can be the best career choice for them. Creators, the third personality type, are artistic and enjoy creative activities like drawing and writing. Many creators become book editors, graphic designers, or actors. People who like doing things for others are helpers. They prefer to work with other people. Nurses and social workers usually have this personality type. We also have persuaders. These energetic and confident people like to persuade or lead others in a group. They are a good fit for jobs like sales manager, school principal, or lawyer. The final group is organizers. They enjoy repeating specific tasks and following fixed routines or procedures. Because of their strong sense of responsibility for their work, they often become bank clerks or secretaries.

16 Holland Codes의 'Organizers' 유형에 관한 설명으로 옳은 것은?

① 창의적 활동을 선호하며 예술 분야에 적합하다.
② 논리적 사고로 과학이나 수학 문제 해결에 강점이 있다.
③ 체계적 업무와 규칙 준수를 중시하여 은행원이 적합하다.
④ 타인을 돕는 일을 추구하며 사회 복지사로 진출한다.
⑤ 리더십을 발휘하며 변호사나 영업 관리자로 활약한다.

17 직업 성격 유형과 그에 해당하는 직업이 바르게 연결되지 않은 것은?

① Doers – mechanic, engineer
② Thinkers – computer programmer, scientist
③ Creators – book editor, graphic designer, actor
④ Helpers – nurse, social worker
⑤ Persuaders – accountant, bank clerk

[01~02] 다음 글을 읽고, 물음에 답하시오.

Good afternoon! Welcome to *Rise & Shine,* the radio show for teenagers. Today, we're going to talk about a theory on career development. (①) Researchers have suggested that career development occurs throughout our entire lives in five separate stages. (②) Next comes the "exploration" stage, which you are going through now. (③) During this stage, young people try to identify what their interests are and figure out which careers might suit them best. (④) You can do this by taking various classes, trying different hobbies, and even working part-time jobs. (⑤) The point is that having diverse experiences during this stage will help you learn about yourself and set an appropriate career goal for your future. Keep this in mind and try to do a wide range of activities! Okay, let's learn about the rest of the stages after the break. Stay tuned!

01 글의 흐름으로 보아, ①~⑤ 중 주어진 문장이 들어가기에 가장 적절한 곳은?

The first stage, which already took place during your early childhood, is "growth."

①   ②   ③   ④   ⑤

02 윗글의 목적으로 가장 적절한 것은?
① 새로운 진로 상담 프로그램을 홍보하기 위해
② 청소년을 위한 직업 체험 기회를 알리기 위해
③ 진로 발달 단계 중 몇 가지를 소개하기 위해
④ 진로 결정에 대한 부모의 역할을 강조하기 위해
⑤ 분명한 진로 목표를 가지는 것의 중요성을 설명하기 위해

[03~04] 다음 글을 읽고, 물음에 답하시오.

Choosing a career is one of the biggest life decisions young people face.

(A) Mapping out the right career path can be demanding. While some teenagers have a clear vision of their career goals, others struggle to define them. This is where role models can be useful.

(B) After you read each student's story, you will get a better idea of the profound impact role models can have when it comes to shaping career goals.

(C) They help young people start to plan their careers by _____ they need to succeed. We asked our teenage readers about their role models and the qualities they admire most in them.

03 주어진 문장 다음에 이어질 글의 순서로 가장 적절한 것은?
① (A) – (B) – (C)   ② (A) – (C) – (B)
③ (B) – (A) – (C)   ④ (B) – (C) – (A)
⑤ (C) – (A) – (B)

04 윗글의 빈칸에 들어갈 말로 가장 적절한 것은?
① avoiding financial risks
② comparing market trends
③ analyzing social influences
④ providing guidance and purpose
⑤ emphasizing academic achievements

[05~06] 다음 글을 읽고, 물음에 답하시오.

My role model is Jacques Cousteau, a French ocean explorer, inventor, and filmmaker. He dedicated his life to exploring and documenting the wonders of the underwater world. As a young man, he dreamed of becoming a pilot, but then he broke both of his arms in a terrible car accident. As part of his ① mental therapy, Cousteau began swimming. He became intrigued by the mysteries of the ocean, and he wanted to ② explore further. However, the diving equipment available at that time was ③ insufficient. Instead of giving up, Cousteau decided to create his own equipment. After a long series of failed attempts, he finally succeeded in developing a ④ portable breathing device, which he called the "Aqua-Lung." Cousteau shared his underwater experiences with the world in a compelling documentary film ⑤ released in 1956. It transformed people's perceptions of the ocean and promoted the need for marine conservation.

05 윗글의 밑줄 친 부분 중, 문맥상 낱말의 쓰임이 적절하지 <u>않은</u> 것은?

①   ②   ③   ④   ⑤

06 Jacques Cousteau에 관한 설명으로 바르지 <u>않은</u> 것은?

① 젊었을 때 조종사가 되기를 꿈꿨다.
② 끔찍한 교통사고로 두 팔이 부러졌다.
③ 물리 치료의 일환으로 수영을 시작했다.
④ 실패 없이 자신만의 휴대용 호흡 기계를 개발했다.
⑤ 그가 만든 다큐멘터리 영화가 1956년에 개봉되었다.

[07~08] 다음 글을 읽고, 물음에 답하시오.

When people ask me about my role model, I always say that it is Joan Procter. You may not (A) hear / have heard of her, but she was a notable zoologist who specialized in reptiles in the early 20th century. She taught me that devotion to a particular field is important for shaping one's career. During her childhood, Procter immersed (B) her / herself in the exploration of nature and animals. ____ⓐ____ her father hated reptiles, she kept lizards, snakes, and even a baby crocodile as pets. They were special companions that she loved and took care of. She was a brilliant student, but health problems prevented her from (C) attending / attended university. ____ⓑ____, her passion for zoology was so strong that it kept her moving forward, and she continued her studies on her own.

07 윗글의 빈칸 ⓐ, ⓑ에 들어갈 말이 바르게 짝지어진 것은?

	ⓐ		ⓑ
①	Because	…	Therefore
②	Although	…	However
③	If	…	Meanwhile
④	Though	…	As a result
⑤	However	…	Nonetheless

08 (A), (B), (C)의 각 네모 안에서 어법에 맞는 표현으로 가장 적절한 것은?

	(A)		(B)		(C)
①	hear	…	her	…	attended
②	have heard	…	herself	…	attended
③	have heard	…	herself	…	attending
④	have heard	…	her	…	attending
⑤	hear	…	herself	…	attending

09 글의 흐름으로 보아, 주어진 문장이 들어갈 위치로 가장 적절한 곳은?

A few years later, she became the first female curator of reptiles at the London Zoo.

Procter accumulated extensive knowledge of zoology. (①) She began exchanging letters with George Boulenger, a prominent expert on reptiles, in order to share ideas. (②) He was so impressed that he hired her as his assistant at the British Museum. (③) There, she actively contributed to the design of the Reptile House by incorporating new technology that allowed for better care and breeding of wild animals. (④) Like her, I want to dedicate myself to a field that I have a passion for. (⑤) For this reason, I will take my time to think deeply about where my true interests lie. If I am fortunate, one of my passions might someday lead to a rewarding career.

①   ②   ③   ④   ⑤

10 다음 글의 밑줄 친 부분 중, 문맥상 낱말의 쓰임이 적절하지 않은 것은?

Today I went to a VR game café with my sister. It was my first time visiting that ①kind of café. There were so many kinds of games. It took me a while to choose one. Finally, we ②took off the special gear and played a racing game. It was so ③realistic that I felt like I was actually driving a car! The VR game café was so entertaining that we decided to go there again next week. Next time, we will play a ④virtual sports game. I've always wanted to learn how to play tennis, so I will ⑤try VR tennis!

①   ②   ③   ④   ⑤

[11~12] 다음 글을 읽고, 물음에 답하시오.

"The choice of a career is an expression of personality," said Dr. John Holland, an American psychologist. He found that people are happier and ①more productive when their job matches their personality type. He believed that ②identifying our personality type can lead us to choose a suitable career that utilizes our abilities and interests, ③resulting in better performance and higher-quality work. This is ④why he created the Holland Codes, which consist of six personality types. They are commonly ⑤using by career counselors and organizations as a guideline to help job seekers choose the right career.

11 윗글의 밑줄 친 ①~⑤ 중, 어법상 틀린 것은?

①   ②   ③   ④   ⑤

12 윗글의 내용과 일치하도록 할 때, 빈칸 ⓐ, ⓑ에 들어갈 말이 바르게 짝지어진 것은?

According to Dr. Holland, it is important to identify what your _____ⓐ_____ type is because finding a career that matches it will make you happier and more _____ⓑ_____ at work.

	ⓐ	ⓑ
①	ability	successful
②	interest	efficient
③	skill	organized
④	personality	productive
⑤	future	satisfied

[13~16] 다음 글을 읽고, 물음에 답하시오.

As someone who loves animation, my role model has always been Kim Sang-jin. He was the first Korean animator to work for Walt Disney Animation Studios. Beyond the fact ①that he worked for a world-famous company, I admire him for pursuing his dream despite the difficulties he faced. From a young age, Kim was enthusiastic about drawing. However, his dream ②of studying art in college was disrupted when he was diagnosed with color vision deficiency during high school. Surprisingly, he didn't allow this misfortune ③to discourage him. Instead, he simply viewed his condition as a minor issue that could happen to anyone.

Although he graduated with a degree in economics, he searched for a job ④relating to art that wouldn't involve working with colors. He found out that some animators work only in pencil, so he sent his portfolio to all the animation studios in Korea. One of them gave him an opportunity, and he was finally able to start his career. It was ＿＿＿＿＿＿＿＿ that eventually led him to a position at Disney at the age of 37. I give him a lot of credit for his persistence and his attitude toward the challenges in his life. I'll never give up on my dreams. If I ⑤encounter difficulties, I will simply find another way to pursue them, just as he did.

13 김상진에 관한 설명으로 글의 내용과 일치하지 <u>않는</u> 것은?

① 어렸을 때부터 그림 그리는 것에 열정적이었다.
② 고등학교 시절 색약 진단을 받았다.
③ 대학에서 미술 대신 경제학을 전공했다.
④ 애니메이터로서의 일을 월트 디즈니에서 처음 시작했다.
⑤ 월트 디즈니에서 일한 최초의 한국인 애니메이터였다.

14 윗글의 밑줄 친 ①~⑤ 중, 어법상 틀린 것은?

①   ②   ③   ④   ⑤

15 윗글의 빈칸에 들어갈 말로 가장 적절한 것은?

① his luck and timing
② his hard work and talent
③ his connections in the industry
④ his family's financial support
⑤ his degree in economics

16 윗글의 내용을 다음과 같이 요약할 때 빈칸에 들어갈 말로 가장 적절한 것은?

Kim Sang-jin ＿＿(A)＿＿ color vision deficiency and kept ＿＿(B)＿＿ his passion for animation. As a result, he became the first Korean animator at Walt Disney Animation Studios, inspiring others with his ＿＿(C)＿＿.

	(A)	(B)	(C)
①	overcame	pursuing	persistence
②	overcame	abandoning	persistence
③	diagnosed	abandoning	persuasion
④	overcame	pursuing	persuasion
⑤	diagnosed	pursuing	persistence

내신 1등급 서술형

01 다음 글의 밑줄 친 문장에서 틀린 부분을 찾아 바르게 고쳐 쓰시오.

(1)Choosing a career is one of the biggest life decision young people face. Mapping out the right career path can be demanding. While some teenagers have a clear vision of their career goals, others struggle to define them. This is where role models can be useful. (2)They help young people start to plan their careers by provided them with guidance and the sense of purpose they need to succeed. We asked our teenage readers about their role models and the qualities they admire most in them. After you read each student's story, you will get a better idea of the profound impact role models can have when it comes to shaping career goals.

(1) _____

_____

(2) _____

_____

02 다음 글의 빈칸에 공통으로 알맞은 관계대명사를 쓰시오.

Cousteau's curiosity drove him to constantly challenge himself in new areas, and his passion enabled him to make the impossible a reality. Cousteau's life story inspired me to push the boundaries of _____ I can do. Because of him, I am not afraid to try different things in life. I will keep exploring until I find _____ suits me best.

[03~04] 다음 글을 읽고, 물음에 답하시오.

My role model is Jacques Cousteau, a French ocean explorer, inventor, and filmmaker. He dedicated his life to ①explore and documenting the wonders of the underwater world. As a young man, he dreamed of becoming a pilot, but then he broke both of his arms in a terrible car accident. As part of his physical therapy, Cousteau began swimming. He became ②intrigued by the mysteries of the ocean, and he wanted to explore further. However, the diving equipment available at that time was insufficient. Instead of giving up, Cousteau decided ③to create his own equipment. After a long series of failed attempts, he finally succeeded in ④developing a portable breathing device, which he called the "Aqua-Lung." Cousteau shared his underwater experiences with the world in a compelling documentary film released in 1956. It transformed people's perceptions of the ocean and ⑤promotes the need for marine conservation.

03 다음 영어 뜻풀이에 해당하는 단어를 윗글에서 찾아 쓰시오. (동사의 경우 원형으로 쓸 것)

(1) _____ : to spend all of your time, energy, etc. on something

(2) _____ : to cause somebody to become very interested in something

(3) _____ : the set of tools needed for a specific purpose

(4) _____ : easily moved or carried

04 윗글의 밑줄 친 ①~⑤ 중, 어법상 틀린 것을 두 개 찾아 바르게 고쳐 쓰고 이유를 쓰시오.

번호	고친 것	이유

50

[05~07] 다음 대화를 읽고, 물음에 답하시오.

A My biggest concern these days is that I don't know what I want to be in the future. <u>나는 나에게 맞는 직업을 찾을 수 있으면 좋겠어.</u>

B What about starting by asking yourself what factor is the most important to you when choosing a career?

A I think passion for the job is the most important. I _____ to do things that I can truly enjoy. What about you?

B In my case, it's salary. I _____ to live a comfortable and independent life.

A I see. Many people consider that important. Now I think I know where to start. Thanks for your help!

B No problem! I'm sure you will find the perfect job for you!

05 A의 고민과 B의 조언을 우리말로 쓰시오.

(1) A의 고민	
(2) B의 조언	

06 윗글의 밑줄 친 우리말과 일치하도록 조건 에 맞게 문장을 완성하시오.

> **조건**
> • 「I wish + 가정법 과거」 구문을 사용할 것
> • 총 5단어로 쓸 것

→ _____

the job that's right for me.

07 윗글의 빈칸에 공통으로 들어갈 말을 주어진 철자로 시작하여 쓰시오.

p_____

[08~10] 다음 글을 읽고, 물음에 답하시오.

Procter accumulated extensive knowledge of zoology. She began exchanging letters with George Boulenger, a prominent expert on reptiles, in order to share ideas. _____
A few years later, she became the first female curator of reptiles at the London Zoo. There, she actively contributed to the design of the Reptile House by incorporating new technology that allowed for better care and breeding of wild animals. Like her, I want to dedicate myself to a field that I have a passion for. For this reason, <u>나는 내 진정한 관심이 어디에 있는지 깊이 생각해 보기 위해 시간을 가질 것이다.</u> If I am fortunate, one of my passions might someday lead to a rewarding career.

08 필자가 Procter에게서 본받고 싶어 하는 점을 우리말로 쓰시오. (40자 이내)

_____

09 다음 두 문장을 so ~ that ... 구문을 사용하여 한 문장으로 바꿔 빈칸에 들어갈 말을 쓰시오.

He was impressed. He hired her as his assistant at the British Museum.

→ _____

_____

10 윗글의 밑줄 친 우리말과 일치하도록 보기 에 주어진 단어를 바르게 배열하시오.

> **보기**
> I / to think deeply / where / about / take my time / will / lie / my true interests

→ _____

_____

[11~13] 다음 글을 읽고, 물음에 답하시오.

As someone who loves animation, my role model has always been Kim Sang-jin. He was the first Korean animator to work for Walt Disney Animation Studios. Beyond the fact that he worked _____ⓐ_____ a world-famous company, I admire him for pursuing his dream despite the difficulties he faced. From a young age, Kim was enthusiastic about drawing. However, his dream _____ⓑ_____ studying art in college was disrupted when he was diagnosed _____ⓒ_____ color vision deficiency during high school. Surprisingly, he didn't allow this misfortune to discourage him. Instead, he simply viewed his condition _____ⓓ_____ a minor issue that could happen to anyone.

11 윗글의 밑줄 친 this misfortune이 의미하는 바를 우리말로 쓰시오. (50자 이내)

_____

_____

12 윗글의 빈칸에 들어갈 전치사로 알맞은 것을 보기 에서 찾아 쓰시오.

> 보기 of   with   from   as   for   about

ⓐ _____   ⓑ _____

ⓒ _____   ⓓ _____

13 다음 영어 뜻풀이에 해당하는 단어를 윗글에서 찾아 쓰시오.

> feeling or showing interest or excitement about somebody or something

→ _____

[14~15] 다음 글을 읽고, 물음에 답하시오.

When people ask me about my role model, I always say that it is Joan Procter. You may not have heard of her, but (1)she was a notable zoologist whom specialized in reptiles in the early 20th century. She taught me that ⓐdevote to a particular field is important for shaping one's career. During her childhood, Procter immersed herself in the ⓑexplore of nature and animals. Although her father hated reptiles, she kept lizards, snakes, and even a baby crocodile as pets. They were special companions that she loved and took care of. She was a brilliant student, but health problems prevented her from attending university. However, (2)her passion for zoology was such strong that it kept her moving forward, and she continued her studies on her own.

14 윗글의 밑줄 친 동사 ⓐ, ⓑ를 어법상 알맞은 형태로 고쳐 쓰시오.

ⓐ _____   ⓑ _____

15 윗글의 밑줄 친 (1), (2)에서 틀린 부분을 찾아 바르게 고쳐 쓰시오.

번호	틀린 것	고친 것
(1)		
(2)		

02

The Power of Good Habits

Functions

▶ 의도 표현하기
  I'm actually **planning to** make a habit of running after school.

▶ 기대 표현하기
  I hope this habit keeps me fit and strong!

Structures

▶ **If** you **pause**, **take** your time, and carefully **think** about it, you will realize your mistake.

▶ They can also develop a habit **of** accepting things to be true even though they have never been proven.

교과서 어휘

□ neuroscience	몡 신경 과학	□ dependable	혱 믿을 수 있는
□ audience	몡 청중, 관중	□ reasonable	혱 합리적인, 타당한
□ purchase	됭 사다, 구입하다	□ critical	혱 대단히 중요한
□ calculation	몡 계산 (calculate 됭 계산하다)	□ reliant	혱 의존하는 (rely 됭 의존하다)
□ reveal	됭 드러내 보이다, 밝히다	□ confront	됭 직면하다
□ fundamental	혱 근본적인	□ intense	혱 굉장한, 강렬한
□ utilize	됭 활용[이용]하다	□ concentration	몡 집중 (concentrate 됭 집중하다)
□ instinct	몡 본능	□ essential	혱 필수적인
□ conscious	혱 의식적인 (consciousness 몡 의식)	□ intelligence	몡 지성, 지능
□ apply	됭 적용하다 (application 몡 적용)	□ frequently	붕 자주 (frequent 혱 잦은)
□ countless	혱 셀 수 없이 많은	□ resist	됭 이겨내다, 저항하다
□ advertisement	몡 광고 (advertise 됭 광고하다)	□ deliberate	혱 의도적인
□ continuously	붕 계속해서 (continuous 혱 끊임없는)	□ generate	됭 만들어 내다
□ process	됭 처리하다 몡 과정, 진행	□ option	몡 선택(지)
□ enormous	혱 엄청난, 거대한	□ conclusion	몡 결론
□ initially	붕 처음에 (initial 혱 처음의)	□ investigate	됭 조사하다
□ automatic	혱 자동적인	□ unfamiliar	혱 잘 모르는, 낯선 (↔ familiar 친숙한)
□ response	몡 반응, 응답 (respond 됭 대답하다)	□ multiple	혱 많은
□ fascinating	혱 대단히 흥미로운	□ angle	몡 관점, 시각
□ rapid	혱 빠른	□ foundation	몡 토대, 기초
□ regularly	붕 자주	□ stimulate	됭 자극하다
□ reasoning	몡 추리, 추론	□ efficiently	붕 효율적으로 (efficient 혱 효율적인)
□ feature	몡 특징, 특성	□ creature	몡 생물, 동물
□ validity	몡 타당성 (valid 혱 타당한)	□ careless	혱 부주의한 (↔ careful 주의 깊은)
□ argument	몡 주장 (argue 됭 주장하다)	□ balanced	혱 균형 잡힌
□ mental	혱 정신의, 마음의 (↔ physical 신체의, 육체의)	□ invest	됭 투자하다 (investment 몡 투자)
□ reliable	혱 믿을 만한	□ alert	혱 경계하는
□ reflect	됭 곰곰이 생각하다	□ harmoniously	붕 조화롭게 (harmonious 혱 조화로운)
□ shortcut	몡 지름길, 손쉬운 방법	□ reinforce	됭 강화하다
□ incorrectly	붕 부정확하게 (incorrect 혱 부정확한)	□ capability	몡 능력, 역량 (capable 혱 ~을 할 수 있는)

□ work out	운동하다	□ rely on	~에 의존하다
□ pop into one's head	갑자기 생각나다	□ dive into	~에 대해 파고들다
□ come up with	생각해 내다	□ serve as	~의 역할을 하다
□ be responsible for	~을 책임지다	□ fall into	~에 빠지다

교과서 어휘 익히기

❖ 다음 영어는 우리말로, 우리말은 영어로 쓰시오.

01	response	명	26	명 관점, 시각	
02	validity	명	27	명 주장	
03	advertisement	명	28	명 본능	
04	continuously	부	29	동 조사하다	
05	utilize	동	30	형 합리적인, 타당한	
06	feature	명	31	동 사다, 구입하다	
07	reliable	형	32	명 청중, 관중	
08	come up with		33	형 경계하는	
09	neuroscience	명	34	명 선택(지)	
10	enormous	형	35	동 직면하다	
11	initially	부	36	동 강화하다	
12	efficiently	부	37	형 의존하는	
13	generate	동	38	명 지성, 지능	
14	dependable	형	39	형 자동적인	
15	calculation	명	40	명 결론	
16	reasoning	명	41	부 자주	
17	stimulate	동	42	동 드러내 보이다, 밝히다	
18	incorrectly	부	43	~에 의존하다	
19	essential	형	44	형 잘 모르는, 낯선	
20	critical	형	45	형 능력, 역량	
21	shortcut	명	46	형 근본적인	
22	intense	형	47	동 이겨내다, 저항하다	
23	fascinating	형	48	형 셀 수 없이 많은	
24	deliberate	형	49	동 곰곰이 생각하다	
25	pop into one's head		50	~을 책임지다	

교과서 핵심 문법

POINT 1 단순 조건문 (if 조건문)

예제
If it **rains** tomorrow, we **will cancel** the picnic.
동사의 현재형   will + 동사원형
내일 비가 오면 우리는 소풍을 취소할 것이다.

교과서
If you **pause**, **take** your time, and carefully **think** about it, you **will realize** your mistake.
└─────── 동사의 현재형 ───────┘   will + 동사원형
잠시 멈추고 시간을 가지면서 그것에 대해 신중하게 생각해 보면 여러분의 실수를 알아챌 수 있을 것이다.

▶ 미래의 불확실한 상황에 대해 말할 때 if를 활용한 단순 조건문을 쓸 수 있다.
▶ 현재의 사실에 반대되는 사실을 가정·상상하는 가정법 과거와 구분해서 사용해야 한다.

Study Point 🍒

1 단순 조건문

단순 조건문은 「if + 주어 + 동사의 현재형, 주어 + will + 동사원형」의 형태로 쓸 수 있다. 조건을 나타내는 if절에는 미래시제 대신 현재시제를 쓴다는 점에 주의한다.

- If I **have** time tomorrow, I **will cook** dinner for my family.   내일 시간이 있으면 나는 가족을 위해 저녁을 요리할 것이다.
  동사의 현재형   will + 동사원형
- If you **help** me with my homework, I **will finish** it sooner.   네가 내 숙제를 도와준다면, 나는 그것을 더 빨리 끝낼 수 있을 것이다.
  동사의 현재형   will + 동사원형
- If she **gets** a new job, she **will buy** a new car.   그녀가 새 직장을 구하면 새 차를 살 것이다.
  동사의 현재형   will + 동사원형
- If you **lose** your phone, you **won't be** able to contact anyone easily.
  동사의 현재형   won't + 동사원형
  만약 네가 휴대폰을 잃어버리면, 쉽게 아무에게도 연락할 수 없을 것이다.

2 가정법 과거

현재의 사실에 반대되는 사실을 가정·상상하는 가정법 과거는 「if + 주어 + 동사의 과거형, 주어 + 조동사의 과거형(would/could/might) + 동사원형」의 형태로 쓴다.

- If it **were** sunny today, we **would go** to the beach.   만약 오늘 날씨가 맑다면, 우리는 해변에 갈 텐데.
  동사의 과거형   과거형 조동사 + 동사원형
- If you **practiced** daily, you **could become** a great pianist.   만약 네가 매일 연습한다면, 훌륭한 피아니스트가 될 수 있을 텐데.
  동사의 과거형   과거형 조동사 + 동사원형

Q 다음 네모 안에서 어법상 알맞은 것을 고르시오.

1 If it [rains / will rain] tomorrow, we will watch movies at home.

2 If she [study / studies] hard, she will get the highest score in class.

3 If the tourists don't hurry, they [miss / will miss] the train.

4 If I [am / were] a bird, I would fly over mountains and seas.

5 If I knew the truth, I [will / would] tell you immediately.

Check-up

01 다음 중 어법상 **틀린** 문장을 고르시오.

① If the weather is cold, we will play board games inside.
② If you wake up early, you will enjoy a quiet morning.
③ If you practice harder, you will improve your skills.
④ If I were you, I will take a different approach.
⑤ If he doesn't call me back, I will message him again.

02 다음 문장의 밑줄 친 부분을 어법에 맞게 고쳐 쓰시오.

(1) If the weather will get hotter, I will turn on the air conditioner.
(2) If you take this medicine, you feel much better.
(3) If John had more time, he can start a new hobby.

03 우리말과 일치하도록 괄호 안의 말을 이용하여 문장을 완성하시오.

(1) 내가 할인 쿠폰을 가지고 있으면, 그 영화를 볼 것이다. (have, watch)

→ If I _____ a discount coupon, I _____ that movie.

(2) 도서관이 열려 있다면, 나는 재미있는 소설을 대출할 것이다. (be, borrow)

→ If the library _____ open, I _____ an interesting novel.

(3) 구매 전에 리뷰를 읽으면, 너는 더 나은 결정을 할 것이다. (read, make)

→ If you _____ reviews before buying, you _____ a better decision.

(4) 그녀가 영어를 유창하게 한다면, 해외에서 일할 수 있을 텐데. (speak, work)

→ If she _____ English fluently, she _____ _____ abroad.

04 다음 글의 밑줄 친 ①~⑤ 중, 어법상 **틀린** 것을 찾아 번호를 쓰고 바르게 고쳐 쓰시오. (교과서 51쪽)

Good morning, everyone! Welcome to today's weather forecast. If you ①have plans to do any activities outside, you will have to cancel them. It ②is expected to rain heavily all day long. If you drive, you ③need to be extra careful since the roads will be wet. Also, traffic is expected to be slower around 9:00 a.m. because of the heavy rain. If you ④leave earlier, you ⑤will be able to avoid the traffic.

_____ → _____

(**POINT 2**) **동격을 나타내는 전치사 of**

| 예제 | The idea **of** moving to a new city excites her.
생각 = 새로운 도시로 이사하는 것
새 도시로 이사한다는 생각이 그녀를 들뜨게 한다. |
|---|---|
| 교과서 | They can also develop a habit **of** accepting things to be true even though they have never been proven.
습관 = 그것들을 사실로 받아들이는 것

그들은 또한 어떠한 사실이 한 번도 증명되지 않았음에도 불구하고 그것을 사실로 받아들이는 습관을 키울 수도 있다. |

▶ 전치사 of를 사용하여 명사에 대한 구체적인 설명을 덧붙여 줄 수 있다.
▶ 이때 「명사+of+동명사(구)」의 형태로 주로 쓰이며, of는 '~이라고 하는, ~인, ~의' 등으로 해석한다.

Study Point 🏅

1 동격을 나타내는 전치사 of

동격을 나타내는 전치사 of는 명사 dream, idea, fact, goal, habit, possibility 등을 설명하기 위해 자주 쓰이며 전치사 of의 앞뒤에 있는 명사(구)가 서로 동격임을 나타낸다.

• The dream **of** becoming a pilot motivated him to study hard.
꿈 = 조종사가 되는 것
조종사가 되고자 하는 꿈이 그가 열심히 공부하도록 동기를 부여했다.

• The news **of** winning the competition shocked everyone. 대회에서 우승했다는 소식이 모두를 놀라게 했다.
소식 = 대회에서 우승하는 것
• The possibility **of** traveling abroad makes me nervous. 해외여행을 할 가능성이 나를 긴장하게 만든다.
가능성 = 해외여행 하는 것
• The fear **of** failing the exam kept him awake all night. 시험에 떨어질까 하는 두려움이 그를 밤새 잠 못 들게 했다.
두려움 = 시험에 떨어지는 것

2 동격을 나타내는 that절

동격을 나타내는 that절은 주로 특정 명사 뒤에 위치하여 그 명사를 구체적으로 설명하거나 정의하는 역할을 하며, that 뒤에는 「주어+동사」의 절이 온다.

• The news **that** the vaccine is effective spread quickly. 백신이 효과적이라는 소식이 빠르게 퍼졌다.
소식 = 백신이 효과적이라는 것
• The idea **that** we should reduce plastic use is changing our behavior.
생각 = 우리가 플라스틱 사용을 줄여야 한다는 것
플라스틱 사용을 줄여야 한다는 생각이 우리의 행동을 바꾸고 있다.

Q 다음 밑줄 친 부분과 동격에 해당하는 것에 밑줄을 치시오.

1 They set a goal of reducing plastic waste by 50 percent this year.

2 The possibility of finding a cure for the disease gives patients hope.

3 The fact that global warming is accelerating worries many scientists.

Check-up 🍎

01 다음 문장을 밑줄 친 부분에 유의하여 우리말로 해석하시오.

(1) His dream of exploring space began in his childhood.

→ _____

(2) The habit of reading books daily helps expand knowledge.

→ _____

(3) Danny has a dream of becoming a famous musician.

→ _____

(4) Susie was excited by the idea of traveling around the world.

→ _____

02 우리말과 일치하도록 괄호 안의 말을 이용하여 문장을 완성하시오.

(1) 가수가 되고자 하는 그녀의 꿈이 그녀로 하여금 보컬 레슨을 받게 만들었다. (her dream, become a singer)

→ _____ made her take vocal lessons.

(2) 그는 좋아하는 아티스트를 만난다는 생각에 매우 흥분했다. (the idea, meet his favorite artist)

→ He was thrilled by _____.

(3) 새로운 사업을 시작하는 과정은 신중한 준비를 필요로 한다. (the process, start a new business)

→ _____ requires careful preparation.

(4) 우승하리라는 희망은 팀이 더 열심히 훈련하도록 동기를 부여한다. (the hope, win the championship)

→ _____ motivates the team to train harder.

03 다음 (1)~(3)의 괄호 안에 주어진 단어를 바르게 배열하시오. (교과서 51쪽)

Due to environmental pollution, many plant and animal species are in (1) (of / becoming / danger / extinct). As an environmental group, we have developed numerous plans for restoring natural diversity. To put these plans into action, we need your help. Please make a donation and protect our beautiful planet! Your support is essential for us to accomplish (2) (conserving / of / our goal / endangered species). Join us to fulfill (3) (protecting / the dream / all living things / of / on earth)!

(1) _____

(2) _____

(3) _____

교과서 본문 분석

Wake Up Your Lazy Brain!
당신의 게으른 뇌를 깨워라!

Host

01 Hello, everyone! Welcome to *Science Report*. I'm your host, Alvin Stuart.

안녕하세요, 여러분! Science Report에 오신 걸 환영합니다. 저는 진행자 Alvin Stuart입니다.

02 We all know [how important it is for us {to exercise our bodies}]. But what about our brains?

간접의문문 (「의문사 + 주어 + 동사」의 어순) ┌ to부정사의 의미상의 주어
가주어 <it>   진주어 <to부정사구>

우리 모두 몸을 운동시키는 것이 얼마나 중요한지 알고 있습니다. 하지만 우리의 뇌는 어떨까요?

03 Did you know that it's important [to work out your mind], too?

진주어 <to부정사구>
접속사 가주어 <it>   운동하다

우리의 정신도 운동시키는 것이 중요하단 걸 아셨나요?

04 Dr. Caitlin Yoon, a professor of neuroscience at Central University, is here with us today
to talk about [how we can become better thinkers]. Thank you for joining us, Dr. Yoon!

부사적 용법 <목적>   간접의문문

Central 대학의 신경 과학 교수 Caitlin Yoon 박사님께서 더 잘 생각하는 사람이 될 수 있는 방법에 대해 이야기하고자 오늘 이 자리에 오셨습니다.
Yoon 박사님, 저희와 함께 해주셔서 감사합니다!

Doctor

05 Thank you for having me.

저를 초대해 주셔서 감사합니다.

Host

06 Doctor, what is the secret to [becoming a better thinker]?

동명사구 (전치사 to의 목적어)

박사님, 더 잘 생각하는 사람이 되는 비결이 뭔가요?

Doctor

07 Well, I want to begin by asking the audience a question.

by v-ing: ~함으로써

자, 청중에게 질문하면서 시작해 보고 싶습니다.

08 Suppose you go into a store to purchase a notebook and a pen.

(that)
부사적 용법 <목적>

여러분이 공책과 펜을 사기 위해 가게에 들어갔다고 가정해 봅시다.

09 The total price is $1.10, and the notebook costs $1 more than the pen. What is the price of the pen?

총가격은 1.10달러이고, 공책이 펜보다 1달러 더 비쌉니다. 그렇다면 펜의 가격은 얼마일까요?

10 Raise your hand if "$0.10" was the first thing [that came to mind].

주격 관계대명사절

come to mind: 생각이 떠오르다

'0.10달러'가 가장 먼저 떠올랐다면 손을 들어주세요.

Host

11 That's what popped into my head.

pop into one's head: 갑자기 생각나다

저도 그게 머릿속에서 떠올랐습니다.

Doctor

12 The correct answer is "$0.05." Now, think again. Do you see the error in your calculation?

정답은 '0.05달러'입니다. 자, 다시 생각해 보세요. 여러분의 계산에서 오류를 발견했나요?

13 If the price of the pen was $0.10, then the notebook would cost $1.10. That would make the total price $1.20.

가정법 과거 「if + 주어 + 동사의 과거형, 주어 + 조동사의 과거형 + 동사원형」

펜의 가격이 0.10달러였다면 공책은 1.10달러일 겁니다. 그러면 총가격이 1.20달러가 됩니다.

Host

14 It seems like an easy question now.

seem like: ~처럼 보이다

이제 쉬운 문제 같아 보이네요.

Doctor

15 If you pause, take your time, and carefully think about it, you will realize your mistake.

단순 조건문 「if + 주어 + 동사의 현재형, 주어 + will + 동사원형」

잠시 멈추고 시간을 가지면서 그것에 대해 신중하게 생각해 보면 여러분의 실수를 알아챌 수 있을 겁니다.

16 This simple question reveals the fundamental way that our brains work.

reveal: 드러내 보이다

이 간단한 문제는 우리의 뇌가 작동하는 근본적인 방법을 보여줍니다.

17 They actually have two different systems [that they can utilize]: System 1 and System 2.
= Our brains   목적격 관계대명사절

실제로 뇌가 이용할 수 있는 두 가지 다른 시스템이 있는데, 그것은 System 1과 System 2입니다.

18 System 1 is based on instinct, and it works without our conscious control.
~에 기초하다, ~에 근거하다   의식적인

System 1은 본능을 기반으로 하고, 의식적인 통제 없이 작동합니다.

19 Our brains naturally apply this system in countless everyday situations, such as when we hear
셀 수 없이 많은   ~과 같은   동사 1
simple sentences, see large words on advertisements, or encounter easy questions like "2+2=?".
동사 2   동사 3

우리의 뇌는 간단한 문장을 듣거나, 광고에 크게 쓰인 단어를 보거나, '2+2=?'처럼 쉬운 문제를 접할 때와 같이 무수히 많은 일상적인 상황들에 자연스럽게 이 시스템을 적용합니다.

20 This system works very quickly, because it needs to continuously process enormous amounts of
= System 1   처리하다
information [coming in through our senses].
현재분사구

이 시스템은 매우 빠르게 작동하는데, 우리의 감각 기관을 통해 들어오는 엄청난 양의 정보를 계속해서 처리해야 하기 때문입니다.

21 If you initially came up with the answer "$0.10" to the question [(that) I asked earlier], that was the
come up with: 생각해 내다   목적격 관계대명사절
automatic response of System 1.

제가 앞서 질문했던 문제에 '0.10달러'라는 답을 먼저 생각해 냈다면, 그것은 System 1의 자동적인 반응이었습니다.

Host

22 That is fascinating! So if System 1 produces these rapid, automatic responses to situations [(that[which])
we regularly encounter in daily life], what is the role of System 2?
목적격 관계대명사절

대단히 흥미롭네요! System 1이 우리가 일상생활에서 자주 마주치는 상황에 대한 빠르고 자동적인 반응을 만들어낸다면, System 2의 역할은 무엇인가요?

Doctor

23 System 2 is responsible for our reasoning and deeper decision-making processes.
be responsible for: ~을 책임지다   과정, 절차

System 2는 추론과 더 깊은 의사 결정 과정을 책임집니다.

24 Our brains use this system [when we compare the prices and features of products, check the validity of an argument, or encounter difficult questions like "238×79×451=?"].

우리가 제품의 가격과 특징을 비교하고, 어떠한 주장의 타당성을 확인하거나, '238x79x451=?'처럼 어려운 문제를 마주할 때 우리의 뇌는 이 시스템을 사용합니다.

25 It controls conscious mental activities when we need to focus or make careful choices.

그것은 우리가 집중하거나 신중한 선택을 해야 할 때 의식적인 정신 활동을 통제합니다.

26 However, while System 2 is more reliable, its application requires time and effort.

그러나 System 2가 더 믿을 만하긴 하지만, 그것을 적용하는 데는 시간과 노력이 필요합니다.

27 If you got the right answer to the notebook and pen question after taking a few seconds to reflect, then your brain used System 2 [to check System 1's initial response].

여러분이 곰곰이 생각할 시간을 가진 후에 공책과 펜 문제의 정답을 알아냈다면, 여러분의 뇌는 System 1의 첫 응답을 검토하기 위해 System 2를 사용한 것입니다.

28 However, our brains tend to rely heavily on [taking mental shortcuts with System 1].

하지만 우리의 뇌는 System 1을 통해 정신적 지름길을 이용하는 것에 매우 의존하는 경향이 있습니다.

29 That is why it's common for people [to answer the question incorrectly at first].

그것이 사람들이 흔히 처음에 그 문제에 틀리게 답하는 이유입니다.

Host

30 So, Doctor, why do we rely on these mental shortcuts when System 1 is not as dependable as System 2?

박사님, 그럼 System 1을 System 2만큼 믿을 수 없는데도 불구하고 왜 우리는 이러한 정신적 지름길에 의존하나요?

Doctor

31 Well, we make about 35,000 decisions every day without realizing it, and it is impossible [to make every one of these consciously].

자, 우리는 알아차리지 못한 채 매일 약 35,000번의 결정을 내리는데, 그 모든 결정 하나하나를 의식적으로 내리는 것은 불가능합니다.

32

to부정사의 의미상의 주어

So it's quite reasonable and effective for the brain [to be a bit lazy sometimes].

가주어 〈it〉   병렬 구조   진주어 〈to부정사구〉

그래서 뇌가 때때로 약간 게을러지는 것은 꽤 합리적이고 효과적입니다.

33

Having a lazy brain allows us to save energy for critical tasks [that require our focus and attention].

주어 (동명사구)   allow + 목적어 + to-v: ~이 …하게 하다   주격 관계대명사절

게으른 뇌를 가지고 있는 것은 우리가 집중력과 주의력을 필요로 하는 중요한 일을 하기 위한 에너지를 아끼게 해줍니다.

34

However, it is dangerous when this becomes a habit.

= having a lazy brain

하지만 이것이 습관이 되면 위험합니다.

35

If your brain becomes too reliant on System 1, it will not be able to apply System 2 when you confront a problem [that requires intense concentration].

단순 조건문 「if + 주어 + 동사의 현재형, 주어 + will + 동사원형」

주격 관계대명사절

여러분의 뇌가 System 1에 너무 의존하게 되면, 고도의 집중력을 필요로 하는 문제를 직면했을 때 System 2를 적용할 수 없을 것입니다.

36

System 2 is essential for [exercising human intelligence], so the less you use it, the more likely you are to become a lazy thinker.

동명사구 (전치사 for의 목적어)   the + 비교급, the + 비교급: ~할수록 …하다

System 2는 인간의 지성을 발휘하는 데 필수적이므로, 그것을 덜 사용할수록 게으르게 생각하는 사람이 될 가능성이 더 커집니다.

37

Those [who have an overly lazy brain] frequently make errors and bad decisions.

주격 관계대명사절   동사

지나치게 게으른 뇌를 가진 사람들은 자주 실수를 하고 잘못된 결정을 내립니다.

38

They can also develop a habit of [accepting things to be true even though they have never been proven].

=   ~에도 불구하고 (접속사)   현재완료 수동태 부정형

그들은 또한 어떠한 사실이 한 번도 증명되지 않았음에도 불구하고 그것을 사실로 받아들이는 습관을 키울 수도 있습니다.

39

Therefore, it can be harmful [to develop lazy brain habits].

가주어 〈it〉   진주어 〈to부정사구〉

그러므로 게으른 두뇌 습관을 기르는 것은 해로울 수 있습니다.

40　So how can we resist these lazy brain habits?

그러면 우리는 어떻게 이 게으른 두뇌 습관을 이겨낼 수 있을까요?

Doctor

41　We can make a deliberate effort [to practice thinking deeply with System 2 more often].
　　　　　　　　　　　　　　　　　　　　형용사적 용법

우리는 System 2를 사용해서 깊이 생각하는 연습을 더 자주 하도록 의도적인 노력을 할 수 있습니다.

42　Here are some tips: First, reconsider your initial thoughts instead of [accepting them right away].
　　　　　　　　　　　　　　　　　　　　　　　　　　　　~ 대신에　　　　　　　= your initial thoughts
　　　　　　　　　　　　　　　　　　　　　　　동명사구 (전치사 instead of의 목적어)

팁을 알려드릴게요. 첫 번째로, 여러분의 처음 생각을 곧바로 받아들이는 대신, 다시 생각해 보세요.

43　Keep generating more ideas and carefully compare the available options before making a decision.
　　　　동사 1　　　　　　　　　　　　　　　　　동사 2

계속해서 더 많은 아이디어를 생각해 내고, 결정을 내리기 전 가능한 선택지들을 신중하게 비교하세요.

44　Ask yourself if the information [you have gathered] supports your original conclusion. If not, then
　　　재귀대명사 (재귀용법)　　　　　　(that[which])　　현재완료
think again.

여러분이 모은 정보가 처음에 생각한 결론을 뒷받침하는지 스스로에게 물어보세요. 그렇지 않다면, 다시 생각해 보세요.

45　Next, make use of your natural curiosity. Curiosity can motivate us [to investigate unfamiliar
　　　　　~을 이용하다　　　　　　　　　　　　　　　　　　　　　명사적 용법 (목적격 보어)
topics and ideas].

다음으로, 타고난 호기심을 이용하세요. 호기심은 우리가 잘 모르는 주제나 개념을 조사하도록 동기를 부여해줄 수 있습니다.

46　It encourages us to dive deeper into a subject and explore it from multiple angles.
　　= Curiosity　　　　　목적격 보어 1　　　　　　　　　(to)　　= a subject
　　　　　　　　　　　　　　　　　　　　　　　　　목적격 보어 2

그것은 우리가 주제에 대해 더 깊이 파고들고, 그것을 다양한 관점에서 탐구하도록 권장합니다.

47　Therefore, it can serve as a foundation for [building deeper thinking habits].
　　　　　　　　　　　~의 역할을 하다　토대, 기초　동명사구 (전치사 for의 목적어)

그러므로 그것은 더 깊이 생각하는 습관을 만들기 위한 토대의 역할을 할 수 있습니다.

48　Finally, learn something new in order to stimulate your brain and become more intelligent.
　　　　　　　　　　　　　　　　in order to-v: ~하기 위해서　　(to)

마지막으로, 여러분의 뇌를 자극하고 더 똑똑해지기 위해서 새로운 무언가를 배워 보세요.

49 [Learning a language or a musical instrument] might not be easy, but these new activities will
동명사구 (주어)   allow + 목적어 + to-v: ~이 …하게 하다
create new paths [that allow information to flow through your brain more efficiently].
주격 관계대명사절

언어나 악기를 배우는 것은 쉽지 않을 수 있지만, 이 새로운 활동들은 여러분의 뇌에서 정보가 더 효율적으로 흐르게 해주는 새로운 길을 만들 겁니다.

Host

50 That sounds like excellent advice, Doctor. Do you have any final words for our audience?

좋은 조언 같네요, 박사님. 청중들에게 마지막으로 하고 싶은 말이 있으신가요?

Doctor

51 Yes. We are creatures of habit, so it is vitally important [that we develop well-balanced thinking
극도로, 지극히
가주어 <it>   진주어 <that절>   균형이 잘 잡힌
habits].

네. 우리는 습관의 동물이므로, 균형이 잘 잡힌 사고 습관을 기르는 것은 지극히 중요합니다.

52 We should remain alert so that we do not fall into the trap of making careless decisions.
~하도록   동격의 of

우리는 부주의한 결정을 내리는 함정에 빠지지 않도록 경계심을 유지해야 합니다.

53 We should invest time into learning how to think deeply in order to use both System 1 and System
how to-v: ~하는 방법   both A and B: A와 B 둘 다
2 harmoniously.

우리는 System 1과 System 2를 모두 조화롭게 사용하기 위해서 깊이 사고하는 방법을 배우는 데 시간을 투자해야 합니다.

54 That way, instead of developing a habit of relying too much on a lazy brain, you can exercise your
(can)   동격의 of   동사 1
intelligence and reinforce your mental capabilities.
동사 2

그렇게 하면 게으른 뇌에 과도하게 의존하는 습관을 기르는 대신, 여러분은 지성을 발휘하고 지적 능력을 강화할 수 있습니다.

Host

55 Okay, Dr. Yoon. Thanks for the great advice! Please give her a big hand!
give A a big hand: A에게 큰 박수를 보내다

그렇군요, Yoon 박사님. 좋은 조언을 해주셔서 감사합니다! 박사님께 큰 박수 부탁드립니다!

교과서 본문 익히기 ❶ 옳은 어법·어휘 고르기

✦ 다음 네모 안에서 옳은 것을 고르시오.

01 We all know how important | it is / is it | for us to exercise our bodies.

02 Did you know that it's important | working / to work | out your mind, too?

03 Doctor, what is the secret to | become / becoming | a better thinker?

04 Well, I want to begin by | asking / asked | the audience a question.

05 Suppose you go into a store | purchasing / to purchase | a notebook and a pen.

06 Raise your hand if "$0.10" was the first thing | that / what | came to mind.

07 That's | which / what | popped into my head.

08 If the price of the pen was $0.10, then the notebook | will / would | cost $1.10.

09 If you pause, take your time, and carefully think about it, you | realize / will realize | your mistake.

10 This simple question reveals the fundamental way | how / that | our brains work.

11 System 1 is based on instinct, and it works | with / without | our conscious control.

12 Our brains naturally apply this system in countless everyday situations, such as when we hear simple sentences, see large words on advertisements, or encounter easy questions | like / as | "2+2=?".

13 This system works very quickly, because it needs to continuously process enormous amounts of information | come / coming | in through our senses.

14 If you initially came up | with / of | the answer "$0.10" to the question I asked earlier, that was the automatic response of System 1.

15 So if System 1 produces these rapid, automatic responses to situations we | regular / regularly | encounter in daily life, what is the role of System 2?

16 System 2 is responsible | for / of | our reasoning and deeper decision-making processes.

17 Our brains use this system when we compare the prices and features of products, check the validity of an argument, or encourage / encounter difficult questions like "238×79×451=?".

18 It controls conscious mental activities when we need to focus or make / take careful choices.

19 However, while System 2 is more reliable, its / it's application requires time and effort.

20 If you got the right answer to the notebook and pen question after taking a few / a little seconds to reflect, then your brain used System 2 to check System 1's initial response.

21 However, our brains tend to rely heavily on / in taking mental shortcuts with System 1.

22 That is why it's common of / for people to answer the question incorrectly at first.

23 So, Doctor, why do we rely on these mental shortcuts when System 1 is not as dependable as / than System 2?

24 Well, we make about 35,000 decisions every day without realizing it, and it / that is impossible to make every one of these consciously.

25 So it's quite reasonable and effective for the brain being / to be a bit lazy sometimes.

26 Having a lazy brain allows us saving / to save energy for critical tasks that require our focus and attention.

27 If your brain becomes too reliant on System 1, it will not be able to apply System 2 when you confront a problem that / what requires intense concentration.

28 System 2 is essential for exercising human intelligence, so the little / less you use it, the more likely you are to become a lazy thinker.

29 Those who have an overly lazy brain frequently make / take errors and bad decisions.

30 They can also develop a habit of accept / accepting things to be true even though they have never been proven.

31 Therefore, it can be useful / harmful to develop lazy brain habits.

32 We can make a deliberate effort to practice thinking deep / deeply with System 2 more often.

33 First, reconsider your initial thoughts instead / instead of accepting them right away.

34 Keep generating / to generate more ideas and carefully compare the available options before making a decision.

35 Ask yourself if / that the information you have gathered supports your original conclusion.

36 Curiosity can motivate us to investigate familiar / unfamiliar topics and ideas.

37 It encourages us diving / to dive deeper into a subject and explore it from multiple angles.

38 Therefore, it can serve as / like a foundation for building deeper thinking habits.

39 Finally, learn new something / something new in order to stimulate your brain and become more intelligent.

40 Learn / Learning a language or a musical instrument might not be easy, but these new activities will create new paths that allow information to flow through your brain more efficiently.

41 Do you have some / any final words for our audience?

42 We are creatures of habit, so it is vital / vitally important that we develop well-balanced thinking habits.

43 We should remain alert so / such that we do not fall into the trap of making careless decisions.

44 We should invest time into learning how to think deeply in order to use both System 1 or / and System 2 harmoniously.

45 That way, instead of developing a habit of / for relying too much on a lazy brain, you can exercise your intelligence and reinforce your mental capabilities.

46 Please give her / to her a big hand!

♣ 다음 밑줄 친 부분이 옳으면 ○표 하고, 틀리면 바르게 고쳐 쓰시오.

01 We all know <u>how important is it</u> for us to exercise our bodies.

02 Did you know that it's important <u>to work out</u> your mind, too?

03 Doctor, what is the secret <u>to become</u> a better thinker?

04 Well, I want <u>to begin</u> by asking the audience a question.

05 Suppose you go into a store <u>to purchasing</u> a notebook and a pen.

06 Raise your hand <u>if</u> "$0.10" was the first thing that came to mind.

07 That's <u>which</u> popped into my head.

08 If the price of the pen was $0.10, then the notebook <u>would cost</u> $1.10.

09 If you <u>will pause</u>, take your time, and carefully think about it, you will realize your mistake.

10 This simple question reveals the fundamental way <u>how</u> our brains work.

11 They actually have two different systems that they <u>can utilize</u>: System 1 and System 2.

12 System 1 <u>bases on</u> instinct, and it works <u>without</u> our conscious control.

13 Our brains naturally apply this system in countless everyday situations, <u>such as</u> when we hear simple sentences, see large words on advertisements, or encounter easy questions like "2+2=?".

14 This system works very quickly, <u>because of</u> it needs to continuously process enormous amounts of information <u>coming in through</u> our senses.

15 <u>If</u> you initially came up with the answer "$0.10" to the question I asked <u>earlier</u>, that was the automatic response of System 1.

16 So if System 1 produces these rapid, automatic responses to situations we <u>regular encounter</u> in daily life, what is the role of System 2?

17 System 2 <u>is responsible for</u> our reasoning and deeper decision-making processes.

18 Our brains use this system when we compare the prices and features of products, check the validity of an argument, or <u>encounters</u> difficult questions like "238×79×451=?".

19 It controls conscious mental activities when we <u>need focusing</u> or make careful choices.

20 However, <u>while</u> System 2 is more reliable, <u>it's</u> application requires time and effort.

21 If you got the right answer to the notebook and pen question after taking <u>a few</u> seconds to reflect, then your brain used System 2 <u>checking</u> System 1's initial response.

22 However, our brains <u>tend to rely heavily on</u> taking mental shortcuts with System 1.

23 <u>That is how</u> it's common for people to answer the question incorrectly at first.

24 So, Doctor, why do we rely on these mental shortcuts when System 1 is not <u>as dependable than</u> System 2?

25 Well, we make about 35,000 decisions every day <u>without realizing</u> it, and it is impossible <u>to make</u> every one of these consciously.

26 So it's quite reasonable and effective <u>for the brain</u> to be a bit lazy sometimes.

27 <u>Have</u> a lazy brain allows us to save energy for critical tasks <u>that requires</u> our focus and attention.

28 <u>However,</u> it is dangerous when this becomes a habit.

29 If your brain <u>will become</u> too reliant on System 1, it will not be able to apply System 2 when you confront a problem that requires intense concentration.

30 System 2 is essential for exercising human intelligence, so the less you use it, <u>the better likely</u> you are to become a lazy thinker.

31 <u>Those which</u> have an overly lazy brain frequently make errors and bad decisions.

32 They can also develop a habit of <u>accepting</u> things to be true even though they <u>have never proven</u>.

33 Therefore, it can be harmful <u>to develop</u> lazy brain habits.

34 So how can we resist <u>this</u> lazy brain habits?

35 We can make a deliberate effort to practice <u>to think</u> deeply with System 2 more often.

36 Here are some tips: First, reconsider your initial thoughts <u>instead</u> accepting them right away.

37 Keep <u>to generate</u> more ideas and carefully compare the available options before making a decision.

38 <u>Ask yourself</u> if the information you have gathered supports your original conclusion.

39 Curiosity can motivate us <u>to investigate</u> unfamiliar topics and ideas.

40 It encourages us <u>diving</u> deeper into a subject and explore it from multiple angles.

41   Therefore, it can serve <u>like</u> a foundation for building deeper thinking habits.

42   Finally, learn <u>new something</u> in order to stimulate your brain and become more intelligent.

43   <u>Learning</u> a language or a musical instrument might not be easy, but these new activities will create new paths that allow information to flow through your brain <u>more efficient</u>.

44   Do you have <u>some</u> final words for our audience?

45   We are creatures of habit, so it is vitally important <u>what</u> we develop well-balanced thinking habits.

46   We should remain alert <u>such that</u> we do not fall into the trap of making careless decisions.

47   We should invest time into learning how to think deeply <u>in order to using</u> both System 1 and System 2 harmoniously.

48   That way, instead of developing <u>a habit of relying</u> too much on a lazy brain, you can exercise your intelligence and reinforce your mental capabilities.

49   Please give <u>to her</u> a big hand!

교과서 본문 익히기 ③ 빈칸 완성하기

✦ 다음 우리말과 일치하도록 빈칸에 알맞은 말을 쓰시오.

Host

Hello, everyone! (1) _____ _____ Science Report. I'm your host, Alvin Stuart.

안녕하세요, 여러분! Science Report에 오신 걸 환영합니다. 저는 진행자 Alvin Stuart입니다.

We all know (2) _____ _____ _____ _____ for us to exercise our bodies.
But what about our brains?

우리 모두 몸을 운동시키는 것이 얼마나 중요한지 알고 있습니다. 하지만 우리의 뇌는 어떨까요?

Did you know that it's important (3) _____ _____ _____ _____ _____, too?

우리의 정신도 운동시키는 것이 중요하단 걸 아셨나요?

Dr. Caitlin Yoon, a professor of neuroscience at Central University, is here with us today to talk about how
(4) _____ _____ _____ _____ _____. Thank you for joining us, Dr. Yoon!

Central 대학의 신경 과학 교수 Caitlin Yoon 박사님께서 더 잘 생각하는 사람이 될 수 있는 방법에 대해 이야기하고자 오늘 이 자리에 오셨습니다.
Yoon 박사님, 저희와 함께 해주셔서 감사합니다!

Doctor

(5) _____ _____ _____ _____ me.

저를 초대해 주셔서 감사합니다.

Host

Doctor, (6) _____ _____ _____ _____ _____ becoming a better thinker?

박사님, 더 잘 생각하는 사람이 되는 비결이 뭔가요?

Doctor

Well, I want to begin (7) _____ _____ _____ _____ a question.

자, 청중에게 질문하면서 시작해 보고 싶습니다.

(8) _____ you go into a store (9) _____ _____ a notebook and a pen.

여러분이 공책과 펜을 사기 위해 가게에 들어갔다고 가정해 봅시다.

(10) _____ _____ _____ _____ $1.10, and the notebook costs $1 more than the pen.
What is the price of the pen?

총가격은 1.10달러이고, 공책이 펜보다 1달러 더 비쌉니다. 그렇다면 펜의 가격은 얼마일까요?

(11) _____ your hand if "$0.10" was the first thing (12) _____ _____ _____ _____.

'0.10달러'가 가장 먼저 떠올랐다면 손을 들어주세요.

Host

That's what (13) _____ _____ _____ _____.

저도 그게 머릿속에서 떠올랐습니다.

Doctor

The correct answer is "$0.05." Now, think again. Do you see **(14)** _____ _____ _____ _____ _____ ?

정답은 '0.05달러'입니다. 자, 다시 생각해 보세요. 여러분의 계산에서 오류를 발견했나요?

If the price of the pen was $0.10, then the notebook would cost $1.10. That would **(15)** _____ _____ _____ _____ $1.20.

펜의 가격이 0.10달러였다면 공책은 1.10달러일 겁니다. 그러면 총가격이 1.20달러가 됩니다.

Host

(16) _____ _____ _____ an easy question now.

이제 쉬운 문제 같아 보이네요.

Doctor

If you pause, take your time, and carefully think about it, you will **(17)** _____ _____ _____ .

잠시 멈추고 시간을 가지면서 그것에 대해 신중하게 생각해 보면 여러분의 실수를 알아챌 수 있을 겁니다.

This simple question **(18)** _____ _____ _____ _____ that our brains work.

이 간단한 문제는 우리의 뇌가 작동하는 근본적인 방법을 보여줍니다.

They actually **(19)** _____ _____ _____ _____ that they can utilize: System 1 and System 2.

실제로 뇌가 이용할 수 있는 두 가지 다른 시스템이 있는데, 그것은 System 1과 System 2입니다.

System 1 **(20)** _____ _____ _____ _____ , and it works **(21)** _____ _____ _____ _____ .

System 1은 본능을 기반으로 하고, 의식적인 통제 없이 작동합니다.

Our brains naturally apply this system in countless everyday situations, such as when we hear simple sentences, see **(22)** _____ _____ _____ _____ , or encounter easy questions like "2+2=?".

우리의 뇌는 간단한 문장을 듣거나, 광고에 크게 쓰인 단어를 보거나, '2+2=?'처럼 쉬운 문제를 접할 때와 같이 무수히 많은 일상적인 상황들에 자연스럽게 이 시스템을 적용합니다.

This system works very quickly, because it needs to continuously **(23)** _____ _____ _____ _____ _____ coming in through our senses.

이 시스템은 매우 빠르게 작동하는데, 우리의 감각 기관을 통해 들어오는 엄청난 양의 정보를 계속해서 처리해야 하기 때문입니다.

If you initially **(24)** _____ _____ _____ the answer "$0.10" to the question I asked earlier, that was the automatic response of System 1.

제가 앞서 질문했던 문제에 '0.10달러'라는 답을 먼저 생각해 냈다면, 그것은 System 1의 자동적인 반응이었습니다.

Host

That is fascinating! So if System 1 produces these rapid, automatic responses to situations **(25)** _____ _____ _____ in daily life, what is the role of System 2?

대단히 흥미롭네요! System 1이 우리가 일상생활에서 자주 마주치는 상황에 대한 빠르고 자동적인 반응을 만들어낸다면, System 2의 역할은 무엇인가요?

System 2 (26) _____ _____ _____ our reasoning and deeper decision-making processes.

System 2는 추론과 더 깊은 의사 결정 과정을 책임집니다.

Our brains use this system when we compare the prices and features of products, check (27) _____ _____ _____ _____ _____, or encounter difficult questions like "238×79×451=?".

우리가 제품의 가격과 특징을 비교하고, 어떠한 주장의 타당성을 확인하거나, '238x79x451=?'처럼 어려운 문제를 마주할 때 우리의 뇌는 이 시스템을 사용합니다.

It controls (28) _____ _____ _____ when we need to focus or make careful choices.

그것은 우리가 집중하거나 신중한 선택을 해야 할 때 의식적인 정신 활동을 통제합니다.

However, while System 2 is more reliable, its application (29) _____ _____ _____ _____.

그러나 System 2가 더 믿을 만하긴 하지만, 그것을 적용하는 데는 시간과 노력이 필요합니다.

If you got the right answer to the notebook and pen question after (30) _____ _____ _____ _____ _____ _____, then your brain used System 2 to check System 1's initial response.

여러분이 곰곰이 생각할 시간을 가진 후에 공책과 펜 문제의 정답을 알아냈다면, 여러분의 뇌는 System 1의 첫 응답을 검토하기 위해 System 2를 사용한 것입니다.

However, our brains (31) _____ _____ _____ _____ _____ taking mental shortcuts with System 1.

하지만 우리의 뇌는 System 1을 통해 정신적 지름길을 이용하는 것에 매우 의존하는 경향이 있습니다.

(32) _____ _____ _____ _____ _____ for people to answer the question incorrectly at first.

그것이 사람들이 흔히 처음에 그 문제에 틀리게 답하는 이유입니다.

So, Doctor, why do we rely on these mental shortcuts when System 1 is (33) _____ _____ _____ _____ System 2?

박사님, 그럼 System 1을 System 2만큼 믿을 수 없는데도 불구하고 왜 우리는 이러한 정신적 지름길에 의존하나요?

Well, we make about 35,000 decisions every day without realizing it, and (34) _____ _____ _____ _____ _____ every one of these consciously.

자, 우리는 알아차리지 못한 채 매일 약 35,000번의 결정을 내리는데, 그 모든 결정 하나하나를 의식적으로 내리는 것은 불가능합니다.

So it's (35) _____ _____ _____ _____ for the brain to be a bit lazy sometimes.

그래서 뇌가 때때로 약간 게을러지는 것은 꽤 합리적이고 효과적입니다.

Having a lazy brain (36) _____ _____ _____ _____ _____ for critical tasks that require our focus and attention.

게으른 뇌를 가지고 있는 것은 우리가 집중력과 주의력을 필요로 하는 중요한 일을 하기 위한 에너지를 아끼게 해줍니다.

However, it is dangerous when this (37) _____ _____ _____.

하지만 이것이 습관이 되면 위험합니다.

If your brain becomes too reliant on System 1, it will not be able to apply System 2 when you confront a problem that (38) _____.

여러분의 뇌가 System 1에 너무 의존하게 되면, 고도의 집중력을 필요로 하는 문제를 직면했을 때 System 2를 적용할 수 없을 것입니다.

System 2 is essential for exercising human intelligence, so (39) _____ _____ you use it, (40) _____ _____ _____ you are to become a lazy thinker.

System 2는 인간의 지성을 발휘하는 데 필수적이므로, 그것을 덜 사용할수록 게으르게 생각하는 사람이 될 가능성이 더 커집니다.

Those who have an overly lazy brain frequently (41) _____ _____ _____ _____

_____.

지나치게 게으른 뇌를 가진 사람들은 자주 실수를 하고 잘못된 결정을 내립니다.

They can also (42) _____ _____ _____ _____ _____ things to be true even though they have never been proven.

그들은 또한 어떠한 사실이 한 번도 증명되지 않았음에도 불구하고 그것을 사실로 받아들이는 습관을 키울 수도 있습니다.

Therefore, it (43) _____ _____ _____ to develop lazy brain habits.

그러므로 게으른 두뇌 습관을 기르는 것은 해로울 수 있습니다.

Host

So how can we resist (44) _____ _____ _____ _____?

그러면 우리는 어떻게 이 게으른 두뇌 습관을 이겨낼 수 있을까요?

Doctor

We can make a deliberate effort to (45) _____ _____ _____ with System 2 more often.

우리는 System 2를 사용해서 깊이 생각하는 연습을 더 자주 하도록 의도적인 노력을 할 수 있습니다.

Here are some tips: First, (46) _____ _____ _____ _____ instead of accepting them right away.

팁을 알려드릴게요. 첫 번째로, 여러분의 처음 생각을 곧바로 받아들이는 대신, 다시 생각해 보세요.

(47) _____ _____ _____ _____ and carefully compare the available options before making a decision.

계속해서 더 많은 아이디어를 생각해 내고, 결정을 내리기 전 가능한 선택지들을 신중하게 비교하세요.

Ask yourself if the information you have gathered (48) _____ _____ _____.

(49) _____ _____, then think again.

여러분이 모은 정보가 처음에 생각한 결론을 뒷받침하는지 스스로에게 물어보세요. 그렇지 않다면, 다시 생각해 보세요.

Next, (50) _____ _____ _____ your natural curiosity. Curiosity can (51) _____

_____ _____ _____ unfamiliar topics and ideas.

다음으로, 타고난 호기심을 이용하세요. 호기심은 우리가 잘 모르는 주제나 개념을 조사하도록 동기를 부여해줄 수 있습니다.

It encourages us to dive deeper into a subject and explore it (52) _____ _____ _____.

그것은 우리가 주제에 대해 더 깊이 파고들고, 그것을 다양한 관점에서 탐구하도록 권장합니다.

Therefore, it can (53) _____ _____ _____ _____ _____ building deeper thinking habits.

그러므로 그것은 더 깊이 생각하는 습관을 만들기 위한 토대의 역할을 할 수 있습니다.

Finally, learn something new (54) _____ _____ _____ _____ _____ _____ and become more intelligent.

마지막으로, 여러분의 뇌를 자극하고 더 똑똑해지기 위해서 새로운 무언가를 배워 보세요.

Learning a language or a musical instrument might not be easy, but these new activities will create new paths that (55) _____ _____ _____ _____ _____ your brain more efficiently.

언어나 악기를 배우는 것은 쉽지 않을 수 있지만, 이 새로운 활동들은 여러분의 뇌에서 정보가 더 효율적으로 흐르게 해주는 새로운 길을 만들 겁니다.

Host

That sounds like excellent advice, Doctor. Do you have any (56) _____ _____ _____ _____ _____ ?

좋은 조언 같네요, 박사님. 청중들에게 마지막으로 하고 싶은 말이 있으신가요?

Doctor

Yes. We are (57) _____ _____ _____ , so it is (58) _____ _____ that we develop well-balanced thinking habits.

네. 우리는 습관의 동물이므로, 균형이 잘 잡힌 사고 습관을 기르는 것은 지극히 중요합니다.

We should (59) _____ _____ _____ _____ we do not fall into the trap of making careless decisions.

우리는 부주의한 결정을 내리는 함정에 빠지지 않도록 경계심을 유지해야 합니다.

We should invest time into learning (60) _____ _____ _____ _____ in order to use both System 1 and System 2 harmoniously.

우리는 System 1과 System 2를 모두 조화롭게 사용하기 위해서 깊이 사고하는 방법을 배우는 데 시간을 투자해야 합니다.

That way, instead of developing a habit of (61) _____ _____ _____ _____ a lazy brain, you can exercise your intelligence and (62) _____ _____ _____ _____ .

그렇게 하면 게으른 뇌에 과도하게 의존하는 습관을 기르는 대신, 여러분은 지성을 발휘하고 지적 능력을 강화할 수 있습니다.

Host

Okay, Dr. Yoon. Thanks for the great advice! Please (63) _____ _____ _____ _____ _____ !

그렇군요, Yoon 박사님. 좋은 조언을 해주셔서 감사합니다! 박사님께 큰 박수 부탁드립니다!

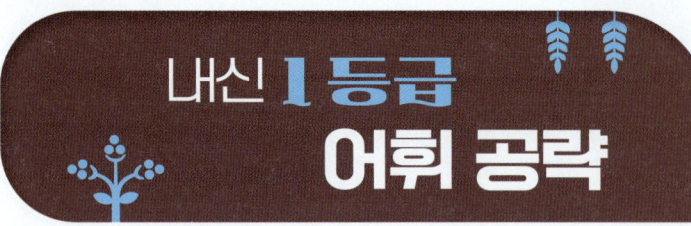

01 밑줄 친 부분 중, 문맥상 낱말의 쓰임이 적절하지 <u>않은</u> 것은?

If you pause, take your time, and carefully think about it, you will realize your ①mistake. This simple question reveals the fundamental way that our brains work. They actually have two different systems that they can utilize: System 1 and System 2. System 1 is based on ②instinct, and it works without our conscious control. Our brains naturally apply this system in countless everyday situations, such as when we hear simple sentences, see large words on advertisements, or ③encounter easy questions like "2+2=?". This system works very ④slowly, because it needs to continuously process enormous amounts of information coming in through our senses.

If you initially came up with the answer "$0.10" to the question I asked earlier, that was the automatic ⑤response of System 1.

02 (A), (B), (C)의 각 네모 안에서 문맥에 맞는 낱말로 가장 적절한 것은?

Hello, everyone! Welcome to *Science Report*. I'm your host, Alvin Stuart. We all know how important it is for us to (A) exercise / rest our bodies. But what about our brains? Did you know that it's important to work out your (B) body / mind , too? Dr. Caitlin Yoon, a professor of neuroscience at Central University, is here with us today to talk about how we can become better thinkers. Thank you for (C) joining / inviting us, Dr. Yoon!

	(A)	(B)	(C)
①	rest	… body	… inviting
②	rest	… mind	… joining
③	exercise	… mind	… joining
④	exercise	… mind	… inviting
⑤	exercise	… body	… joining

03 (A), (B), (C)의 각 네모 안에서 문맥에 맞는 낱말로 가장 적절한 것은?

System 2 is responsible for our reasoning and deeper decision-making processes. Our brains use this system when we compare the prices and features of products, check the validity of an argument, or encounter difficult questions like "238×79×451=?". It controls conscious mental activities when we need to focus or make careful choices. However, while System 2 is more reliable, its application (A) requires / acquires time and effort.

If you got the right answer to the notebook and pen question after taking a few seconds to reflect, then your brain used System 2 to check System 1's (B) final / initial response. However, our brains tend to rely heavily on taking mental shortcuts with System 1. That is why it's (C) common / uncommon for people to answer the question incorrectly at first.

	(A)	(B)	(C)
①	requires	… final	… uncommon
②	acquires	… final	… common
③	requires	… initial	… uncommon
④	acquires	… initial	… common
⑤	requires	… initial	… common

04 (A), (B), (C)의 각 네모 안에서 문맥에 맞는 낱말로 가장 적절한 것은?

We make about 35,000 decisions every day without realizing it, and it is (A) possible / impossible to make every one of these consciously. So it's quite reasonable and effective for the brain to be a bit lazy sometimes. Having a lazy brain (B) allows / prevents us to save energy for critical tasks that require our focus and attention. However, it is dangerous when this becomes a habit. If your brain becomes too reliant on System 1, it will not be able to apply System 2 when you confront a problem that requires (C) intense / extensive concentration. System 2 is essential for exercising human intelligence, so the less you use it, the more likely you are to become a lazy thinker. Those who have an overly lazy brain frequently make errors and bad decisions. They can also develop a habit of accepting things to be true even though they have never been proven. Therefore, it can be harmful to develop lazy brain habits.

	(A)		(B)		(C)
①	possible	…	prevents	…	intense
②	possible	…	allows	…	intense
③	impossible	…	allows	…	extensive
④	impossible	…	allows	…	intense
⑤	impossible	…	prevents	…	extensive

05 밑줄 친 부분 중, 문맥상 낱말의 쓰임이 적절하지 않은 것은?

We are ①creatures of habit, so it is vitally important that we develop well-balanced thinking habits. We should remain ②alert so that we do not fall into the trap of making careless decisions. We should ③save time into learning how to think deeply in order to use both System 1 and System 2 harmoniously. That way, instead of developing a habit of relying too much on a ④lazy brain, you can exercise your intelligence and ⑤reinforce your mental capabilities.

06 밑줄 친 부분 중, 문맥상 낱말의 쓰임이 적절하지 않은 것은?

We can make a deliberate effort to practice thinking deeply with System 2 more often. Here are some tips:

First, reconsider your initial thoughts instead of ①rejecting them right away. Keep generating more ideas and carefully compare the available ②options before making a decision. Ask yourself if the information you have gathered supports your original conclusion. If not, then think again.

Next, make use of your natural curiosity. Curiosity can motivate us to investigate ③unfamiliar topics and ideas. It encourages us to dive deeper into a subject and explore it from ④multiple angles. Therefore, it can serve as a foundation for building deeper thinking habits.

Finally, learn something new in order to ⑤stimulate your brain and become more intelligent. Learning a language or a musical instrument might not be easy, but these new activities will create new paths that allow information to flow through your brain more efficiently.

07 밑줄 친 부분 중, 문맥상 낱말의 쓰임이 적절하지 않은 것은?

If you have failed to make a new habit ①stick, understanding the structure of habits can be helpful. A habit has three phases: the trigger, the action, and the reward. The trigger is a ②signal that prompts you to take a certain action. It can be a sound, a place, or an event. It is like an alarm clock telling you to do something. Next, the action is the activity of the habit. Now comes the reward. This is the part where you ③give something good for doing the desired activity. For example, you might allow yourself to eat a ④piece of chocolate after you work out. If your brain successfully associates a certain behavior with the reward, your habit will naturally become part of your ⑤routine.

01 (A), (B), (C)의 각 네모 안에서 어법에 맞는 표현으로 가장 적절한 것은?

> **Host** Doctor, what is the secret to (A) become / becoming a better thinker?
>
> **Doctor** Well, I want to begin by asking the audience a question. Suppose you go into a store (B) purchasing / to purchase a notebook and a pen. The total price is $1.10, and the notebook costs $1 more than the pen. What is the price of the pen? (C) Raise / Raising your hand if "$0.10" was the first thing that came to mind.

	(A)	(B)	(C)
①	becoming	···	to purchase	···	Raising
②	become	···	purchasing	···	Raising
③	becoming	···	to purchase	···	Raise
④	becoming	···	purchasing	···	Raise
⑤	become	···	to purchase	···	Raise

02 다음 글의 밑줄 친 부분 중, 어법상 틀린 것은?

> **Host** That's ①what popped into my head.
>
> **Doctor** The correct answer is "$0.05." Now, think again. Do you see the error in your calculation? If the price of the pen was $0.10, then the notebook ②will cost $1.10. That would make the total price $1.20.
>
> **Host** It seems like an easy question now.
>
> **Doctor** If you ③pause, take your time, and carefully think about it, you will realize your mistake. This simple question reveals the fundamental way ④that our brains work. They actually have two different systems that they can utilize: System 1 and System 2. System 1 is based on instinct, and it works without our conscious control. Our brains naturally apply this system in countless everyday situations, such as when we hear simple sentences, see large words on advertisements, or encounter easy questions like "2+2=?". This system works very quickly, because it needs to continuously process enormous amounts of information ⑤coming in through our senses.
>
> If you initially came up with the answer "$0.10" to the question I asked earlier, that was the automatic response of System 1.

03 (A), (B), (C)의 각 네모 안에서 어법에 맞는 표현으로 가장 적절한 것은?

> System 2 is responsible for our reasoning and deeper decision-making processes. Our brains use this system when we compare the prices and features of products, check the validity of an argument, or (A) encounter / encountering difficult questions like "238×79×451=?". It controls conscious mental activities when we need to focus or make careful choices. However, while System 2 is more reliable, its application requires time and effort.
>
> If you got the right answer to the notebook and pen question after taking (B) a few / a little seconds to reflect, then your brain used System 2 to check System 1's initial response. However, our brains tend to rely heavily on taking mental shortcuts with System 1. That is (C) how / why it's common for people to answer the question incorrectly at first.

	(A)	(B)	(C)
①	encountering	···	a little	···	how
②	encountering	···	a few	···	why
③	encounter	···	a few	···	how
④	encounter	···	a few	···	why
⑤	encounter	···	a little	···	why

04 다음 글의 밑줄 친 부분 중, 어법상 틀린 것은?

We make about 35,000 decisions every day ① without realizing it, and it is impossible to make every one of these consciously. So it's quite reasonable and effective for the brain to be a bit lazy sometimes. Having a lazy brain ② allows us to save energy for critical tasks that require our focus and attention. However, it is dangerous when this becomes a habit. If your brain ③ becomes too reliant on System 1, it will not be able to apply System 2 when you confront a problem that requires intense concentration. System 2 is essential for exercising human intelligence, so ④ the little you use it, the more likely you are to become a lazy thinker. Those who have an overly lazy brain frequently make errors and bad decisions. They can also develop a habit of accepting things to be true even though they ⑤ have never been proven. Therefore, it can be harmful to develop lazy brain habits.

05 다음 글의 밑줄 친 부분 중, 어법상 틀린 것은?

We can make a deliberate effort to practice thinking deeply with System 2 more often. Here are some tips:

First, reconsider your initial thoughts instead of accepting them right away. Keep ① generating more ideas and carefully compare the available options before making a decision. Ask yourself ② if the information you have gathered supports your original conclusion. If not, then think again.

Next, make use of your natural curiosity. Curiosity can motivate us to investigate unfamiliar topics and ideas. It encourages us to dive deeper into a subject and explore it from multiple angles. Therefore, it can serve as a foundation for building deeper thinking habits.

Finally, learn ③ new something in order to stimulate your brain and become more intelligent. ④ Learning a language or a musical instrument might not be easy, but these new activities will create new paths that allow information ⑤ to flow through your brain more efficiently.

06 (A), (B), (C)의 각 네모 안에서 어법에 맞는 표현으로 가장 적절한 것은?

Host Do you have (A) some / any final words for our audience?

Doctor Yes. We are creatures of habit, so it is vitally important that we develop well-balanced thinking habits. We should remain alert (B) so / such that we do not fall into the trap of making careless decisions. We should invest time into learning (C) what / how to think deeply in order to use both System 1 and System 2 harmoniously. That way, instead of developing a habit of relying too much on a lazy brain, you can exercise your intelligence and reinforce your mental capabilities.

	(A)	(B)	(C)
①	some	such	what
②	any	so	how
③	any	so	what
④	any	such	how
⑤	some	such	how

07 다음 글의 밑줄 친 부분 중, 어법상 틀린 것은?

If you have failed to make a new habit stick, ① understanding the structure of habits can be helpful. A habit has three phases: the trigger, the action, and the reward. The trigger is a signal ② that prompts you to take a certain action. It can be a sound, a place, or an event. It is like an alarm clock ③ telling you to do something. Next, the action is the activity of the habit. Now comes the reward. This is the part ④ where you receive something good for doing the desired activity. For example, you might allow yourself ⑤ eating a piece of chocolate after you work out. If your brain successfully associates a certain behavior with the reward, your habit will naturally become part of your routine.

[01~02] 다음 대화를 읽고, 물음에 답하시오.

G Hey, Minho. Where are you heading now?

B I'm going to the park. I run for 30 minutes every day.

G That's amazing! I'm actually planning to make a habit of running after school, but it's not easy for me. Do you have any tips?

B Starting small is key to making it a habit. I suggest creating a running playlist with energetic songs. Initially, run for just three songs. That's how I began.

G That would only take around 10 minutes, right? That sounds doable!

B Exactly. After you get used to it, try running for four songs. Then go for five songs!

G That way, I can increase my running time bit by bit!

B That's the spirit. Over time, you'll find yourself able to run for 30 minutes.

G All right. I'll start with making that playlist. I hope this habit keeps me fit and strong!

01 위 대화에 어울리는 속담으로 가장 적절한 것은?

① Seeing is believing.
② Practice makes perfect.
③ Strike while the iron is hot.
④ Actions speak louder than words.
⑤ A journey of a thousand miles begins with a single step.

02 위 대화 후 여학생이 할 일로 가장 적절한 것은?

① 휴대폰에 달리기 앱 설치하기
② 30분 동안 달리기하기
③ 신나는 노래로 플레이리스트 만들기
④ 달리기 동아리 가입하기
⑤ 달리기 대회 참가하기

[03~05] 다음 대화를 읽고, 물음에 답하시오.

M Welcome to *Morning Talk*. Today, we will dive deep into the world of habits and see how we can make use of them for a better life. Habits are the things we do again and again, often without thinking. Right, Zahara?

W Right, Tom. Unfortunately, we all have bad habits. For example, you might habitually waste time looking at your phone. And getting rid of such habits can be difficult. However, a great way to do this is to _____ them with good habits. Start by recognizing your bad habits. Ask yourself when and how often they typically occur each day.

M Then find positive replacements. If you want to stop looking at your phone too often, put it away and do something better! You could listen to music, read a book, take a walk, or chat with your family. As time passes, these good habits will take the place of your bad habits.

03 위 대화의 주제로 가장 적절한 것은?

① 좋은 습관을 만드는 다양한 방법
② 스마트폰 사용의 장점
③ 나쁜 습관을 좋은 습관으로 바꾸는 방법
④ 가족과 함께하는 시간의 중요성
⑤ 운동이 건강에 미치는 영향

04 위 대화의 빈칸에 들어갈 말로 가장 적절한 것은?

① support   ② combine   ③ compare
④ replace   ⑤ recognize

05 위 대화에서 너무 자주 휴대폰을 보는 것의 대안으로 언급되지 **않은** 것은?

① 책 읽기   ② 일기 쓰기
③ 산책하기   ④ 음악 듣기
⑤ 가족과 가벼운 대화하기

06 다음 글을 읽고, 각 물건의 가격을 빈칸에 쓰시오.

Suppose you go into a store to purchase a notebook and a pen. The total price is $1.10, and the notebook costs $1 more than the pen. What is the price of the pen?

(1) 공책: $ _____ (2) 펜: $ _____

[07~08] 다음 글을 읽고, 물음에 답하시오.

Our brains ① actually have two different systems that they can utilize: System 1 and System 2. System 1 is based on instinct, and it works without our conscious control. Our brains ② naturally apply this system in countless everyday situations, such as when we hear ③ simply sentences, see large words on advertisements, or encounter easy questions like "2+2=?". This system works very ④ quickly, because it needs to ⑤ continuously process enormous amounts of information coming in through our senses.

07 윗글의 밑줄 친 ①~⑤ 중, 어법상 틀린 것은?

①   ②   ③   ④   ⑤

08 System 1에 관해 글의 내용과 일치하지 않는 것은?

① 본능을 기반으로 한다.
② 의식적인 통제에 따라 작동한다.
③ 무수히 많은 일상적인 상황들에 적용된다.
④ 매우 빠르게 작동한다.
⑤ 엄청난 양의 정보를 계속해서 처리한다.

[09~10] 다음 글을 읽고, 물음에 답하시오.

System 2 is responsible for our reasoning and deeper decision-making processes. Our brains use this system when we compare the prices and features of products, check the validity of an argument, or encounter difficult questions like "238×79×451=?". It controls conscious mental activities when we need to focus or make careful choices. However, while System 2 is more reliable, its application requires time and effort.

If you got the right answer to the notebook and pen question after taking a few seconds to reflect, then your brain used System 2 to check System 1's initial response. However, our brains tend to rely heavily on taking mental shortcuts with System 1. That is why it's common for people to answer the question incorrectly at first.

09 윗글의 밑줄 친 mental shortcuts의 의미로 가장 적절한 것은?

① correct calculations   ② careful analysis
③ detailed planning   ④ logical reasoning
⑤ unconscious processes

10 윗글의 내용과 일치하지 않는 것은?

① System 2는 복잡한 문제를 해결할 때 사용된다.
② System 2는 시간과 노력이 더 많이 필요하다.
③ System 1은 신중한 결정에 주로 사용된다.
④ 많은 사람들이 공책과 펜 문제에 처음에는 틀린 답을 내놓는다.
⑤ System 2는 논리적 사고를 담당한다.

[11~12] 다음 글을 읽고, 물음에 답하시오.

We make about 35,000 (A) mistakes / decisions every day without realizing it, and it is impossible to make every one of these consciously. So it's quite reasonable and effective for the brain to be a bit lazy sometimes. Having a lazy brain allows us to save energy for critical tasks that require our focus and (B) intention / attention . However, it is dangerous when this becomes a habit. If your brain becomes too reliant on System 1, it will not be able to apply System 2 when you confront a problem that requires intense concentration. System 2 is essential for exercising human intelligence, so 여러분이 그것을 덜 사용할수록 게으르게 생각하는 사람이 될 가능성이 더 커집니다. Those who have an overly lazy brain frequently make errors and bad decisions. They can also develop a (C) habit / fact of accepting things to be true even though they have never been proven. Therefore, it can be harmful to develop lazy brain habits.

11 (A), (B), (C)의 각 네모 안에서 문맥에 맞는 낱말로 가장 적절한 것은?

	(A)		(B)		(C)
①	mistakes	…	intention	…	fact
②	decisions	…	attention	…	habit
③	decisions	…	attention	…	fact
④	mistakes	…	attention	…	habit
⑤	decisions	…	intention	…	habit

12 윗글의 밑줄 친 우리말과 일치하도록 빈칸에 알맞은 말을 넣어 문장을 완성하시오. (반드시 비교급을 사용할 것)

→ System 2 is essential for exercising human intelligence, so _____ _____ you use it, _____ _____ _____ you are to become a lazy thinker.

[13~14] 다음 글을 읽고, 물음에 답하시오.

We can make a deliberate effort to practice thinking deeply with System 2 more often. Here are some tips:

First, reconsider your initial thoughts instead of accepting them right away. Keep generating more ideas and carefully compare the available options before making a decision. Ask yourself if the information you have gathered supports your original conclusion. If not, then think again.

Next, make use of your natural curiosity. Curiosity can motivate us to investigate unfamiliar topics and ideas. It encourages us to dive deeper into a subject and explore it from multiple angles. Therefore, it can serve as a foundation for building deeper thinking habits.

Finally, learn something new in order to stimulate your brain and become more intelligent. Learning a language or a musical instrument might not be easy, but these new activities will create new paths that allow information to flow through your brain more efficiently.

13 윗글의 필자가 주장하는 바로 가장 적절한 것은?

① The brain should always rely on System 1 for efficiency.
② Deep thinking, curiosity, and learning new things help overcome lazy brain habits.
③ Accepting initial thoughts is the best way to make decisions.
④ Learning new things is not easy, but necessary.
⑤ Thinking with System 2 requires more energy.

14 다음 영어 뜻풀이에 해당하는 단어를 윗글에서 찾아 주어진 철자로 시작하여 쓰시오.

to create more activity, especially in the mind or body

→ s_____

Good habits make our lives better. However, many people fail to form new habits because it takes time and effort. Fortunately, there is a trick to doing this quickly and easily. It's (A) calling / called "habit stacking." How do you do it? Start by identifying a habit you already have. Then simply "stack" a new habit on top of it. The basic formula is "After I do the current habit, I will do the new habit." Suppose you decide to start stretching every morning. Think about (B) what / which you normally do in the morning. If you check your email after you wake up, that is your current habit. Therefore, your formula will be "After I check my email, I will stretch for five minutes." By doing this, you make your existing habit a trigger for your new habit. This works well because your current habits are already established. Add a new activity to your daily routine and see how easy it is (C) turning / to turn that activity into a habit. Give habit stacking a try. If it works for you, keep adding more good habits to your life. You won't regret it!

15 윗글의 밑줄 친 habit stacking의 목적으로 가장 적절한 것은?

① to break bad habits
② to avoid starting new habits
③ to stick to your current routine
④ to form new habits effectively
⑤ to make your daily routine more complicated

16 (A), (B), (C)의 각 네모 안에서 어법에 맞는 표현으로 가장 적절한 것은?

	(A)		(B)		(C)
①	called	…	what	…	to turn
②	called	…	what	…	turning
③	called	…	which	…	to turn
④	calling	…	what	…	to turn
⑤	calling	…	which	…	turning

17 다음 글의 내용을 한 문장으로 요약할 때, 빈칸에 알맞은 말을 쓰시오.

Hello! My name is Jiwoo. We can get rid of bad habits by replacing them with good ones. Let me tell you about one of my bad habits and my plan to replace it. The habit I plan to replace is constantly eating sugary snacks. I want to get rid of this habit because it is harmful to my health. To replace this habit, I plan to eat healthier snacks like nuts instead. I believe this change will be helpful for me.

↓

Jiwoo plans to _____ _____ snacks like nuts instead of _____ snacks.

18 다음 글의 밑줄 친 우리말과 일치하도록 보기 의 단어를 바르게 배열하시오.

Host Do you have any final words for our audience?

Doctor Yes. We are creatures of habit, so it is vitally important that we develop well-balanced thinking habits. 우리는 부주의한 결정을 내리는 함정에 빠지지 않도록 경계심을 유지해야 합니다. We should invest time into learning how to think deeply in order to use both System 1 and System 2 harmoniously. That way, instead of developing a habit of relying too much on a lazy brain, you can exercise your intelligence and reinforce your mental capabilities.

Host Okay, Dr. Yoon. Thanks for the great advice! Please give her a big hand!

보기 of / careless / the trap / making / decisions

We should remain alert so that we do not fall into _____.

[01~02] 다음 대화를 읽고, 물음에 답하시오.

> A I'm planning to make a habit of reading books. (①)
>
> B Oh, that sounds like a good idea! Do you have a specific plan to develop this new habit?
>
> A Of course! (②)
>
> B That's great! Forming a new habit isn't easy, so we need to set small and achievable goals. (③)
>
> A You're right. I hope I can improve my language skills and learn new information with this habit. (④)
>
> B I'm sure you can do it. Good luck! (⑤)

01 위 대화의 주제로 가장 적절한 것은?

① 책 읽는 습관의 장점
② 독서 동아리 활동 방법
③ 독서 습관을 만들기 위한 계획
④ 책에서 얻은 정보를 정리하는 방법
⑤ 언어 능력을 향상시키는 여러 가지 방법

02 위 대화의 흐름으로 보아, 주어진 말이 들어갈 위치로 가장 적절한 곳은?

> I'll start by reading for ten minutes a day and gradually increase the amount of time.

①   ②   ③   ④   ⑤

[03~04] 다음 글을 읽고, 물음에 답하시오.

> Hello! My name is Jiwoo. We can get rid of bad habits by replacing them with good ones. Let me tell you about one of my bad habits and my plan to replace it. The habit I plan to replace is constantly eating sugary snacks. I want to get rid of (A)this habit because it is harmful to my health. To replace this habit, I plan to eat healthier snacks like nuts instead. I believe (B)this change will be helpful for me.

03 윗글의 밑줄 친 (A), (B)가 가리키는 바를 영어로 쓰시오.

(A) this habit: _____

(B) this change: _____

04 윗글의 내용과 일치하는 것은?

① Jiwoo plans to eat more sugary snacks.
② Jiwoo thinks his current habit is good for his health.
③ Jiwoo wants to replace his bad habit with a healthier one.
④ Jiwoo doesn't know how to change his habits.
⑤ Jiwoo will stop eating snacks altogether.

05 다음 우리말과 일치하도록 괄호 안의 단어를 알맞은 형태로 바꿔 쓰시오.

(1) 운전자는 그의 부주의한 운전이 사고의 원인이었다는 것을 인정했다. (care)
→ The driver admitted that his _____ driving was the cause of the accident.

(2) 그들은 어려움에도 불구하고 주목할 만한 업적을 만들었다. (remark)
→ They made a _____ achievement despite their hardships.

[06~08] 다음 글을 읽고, 물음에 답하시오.

Host Hello, everyone! Welcome to *Science Report*. I'm your host, Alvin Stuart. We all know how important it is ①for us to exercise our bodies. But what about our brains? Did you know that it's important ②to work out your mind, too? Dr. Caitlin Yoon, a professor of neuroscience at Central University, is here with us today to talk about (how / become / can / better / we / thinkers). Thank you for joining us, Dr. Yoon!

Doctor Thank you for having me.

Host Doctor, what is the secret to ③become a better thinker?

Doctor Well, I want to begin by ④asking the audience a question. Suppose you go into a store to purchase a notebook and a pen. The total price is $1.10, and the notebook costs $1 more than the pen. What is the price of the pen? Raise your hand if "$0.10" was the first thing ⑤that came to mind.

06 윗글의 밑줄 친 ①~⑤ 중, 어법상 틀린 것은?

①   ②   ③   ④   ⑤

07 윗글의 밑줄 친 to purchase와 쓰임이 다른 것은?

① She studies hard to achieve her dream of becoming a doctor.
② He left early to avoid the heavy traffic on the highway.
③ To succeed in business, you must understand your customers well.
④ The company hired experts to improve the quality of their products.
⑤ It's exciting to explore new cultures when traveling abroad alone.

08 윗글의 괄호 안에 주어진 단어를 바르게 배열하시오.

→ _____

[09~10] 다음 글을 읽고, 물음에 답하시오.

Due to environmental pollution, many plant and animal species are in danger _____ becoming extinct. As an environmental group, we have developed numerous plans for restoring natural diversity. To put these plans into action, we need your help. Please make a donation and protect our beautiful planet! Your support is essential for us to accomplish our goal _____ conserving endangered species. Join us to fulfill the dream _____ protecting all living things on earth!

09 윗글의 목적으로 가장 적절한 것은?

① 환경 오염을 일으키는 기업을 비판하기 위해
② 멸종 위기에 처한 동식물의 종류를 알리기 위해
③ 종 다양성 보존을 위한 활동에 후원을 요청하기 위해
④ 다양한 영역에서 자원봉사 활동을 독려하기 위해
⑤ 꿈을 이루기 위한 노력의 중요성을 강조하기 위해

10 윗글의 빈칸에 공통으로 들어갈 말로 가장 적절한 것은?

① of   ② for   ③ about
④ to   ⑤ from

[11~12] 다음 글을 읽고, 물음에 답하시오.

We make about 35,000 decisions every day without realizing it, and it is impossible to make every one of these consciously. So it's quite reasonable and effective for the brain to be a bit lazy sometimes. Having a lazy brain allows us to save energy for critical tasks that require our focus and attention. However, it is dangerous when this becomes a habit. If your brain (A) becomes / will become too reliant on System 1, it will not be able to apply System 2 when you confront a problem that requires intense concentration. System 2 is essential for exercising human intelligence, so the (B) little / less you use it, the more likely you are to become a lazy thinker. Those who have an overly lazy brain frequently make errors and bad decisions. They can also develop a habit of accepting things to be true even though they have never (C) proven / been proven. Therefore, it can be harmful to develop lazy brain habits.

11 (A), (B), (C)의 각 네모 안에서 어법에 맞는 표현으로 가장 적절한 것은?

	(A)		(B)		(C)
①	becomes	…	less	…	proven
②	becomes	…	little	…	been proven
③	will become	…	less	…	proven
④	becomes	…	less	…	been proven
⑤	will become	…	little	…	been proven

12 윗글의 밑줄 친 a lazy brain이 의미하는 바와 가장 가까운 것은?

① a brain that is always active
② a brain that avoids effortful thinking
③ a brain that never makes mistakes
④ a brain that only uses System 2
⑤ a brain that questions everything

[13~14] 다음 글을 읽고, 물음에 답하시오.

We can make a deliberate effort to practice thinking deeply with System 2 more often. Here are some tips:

First, _____ instead of accepting them right away. Keep ①proving more ideas and carefully compare the available options before making a decision. Ask yourself if the information you have gathered supports your original ②conclusion. If not, then think again.

Next, make use of your natural curiosity. Curiosity can motivate us to investigate unfamiliar topics and ideas. It encourages us to dive deeper into a subject and explore it from ③multiple angles. Therefore, it can serve as a foundation for building deeper thinking habits.

Finally, learn something new in order to stimulate your brain and become more ④intelligent. Learning a language or a musical instrument might not be easy, but these new activities will create new paths that allow information to flow through your brain more ⑤efficiently.

13 윗글의 빈칸에 들어갈 말로 가장 적절한 것은?

① make immediate decisions
② complain about others' ideas
③ reconsider your initial thoughts
④ understand other people's points of view
⑤ come up with as many creative ideas as possible

14 윗글의 밑줄 친 부분 중, 문맥상 낱말의 쓰임이 적절하지 <u>않은</u> 것은?

① ② ③ ④ ⑤

Host Do you have any final words for our audience?

Doctor Yes. We are creatures of habit, so it is vitally important that we develop well-balanced thinking habits. We should remain alert _____ we do not fall into the trap of making careless decisions. We should invest time into learning how to think deeply in order to use both System 1 and System 2 harmoniously. That way, instead of developing a habit of relying too much on a lazy brain, you can exercise your intelligence and reinforce your mental capabilities.

Host Okay, Dr. Yoon. Thanks for the great advice! Please give her a big hand!

15 Dr. Yoon이 주장하는 바로 가장 적절한 것은?

① System 1의 한계를 비판하려고
② 부주의한 결정을 내리는 사례를 설명하려고
③ 균형 잡힌 사고 습관을 기르는 것을 권장하려고
④ System 1보다 System 2를 더 많이 사용하게 하려고
⑤ 유연한 사고를 위한 뇌 운동에 대해 소개하려고

16 윗글의 빈칸에 들어갈 말로 가장 적절한 것은?

① since   ② unless
③ such as   ④ so that
⑤ even though

17 다음 글의 밑줄 친 ①~⑤ 중, 어법상 틀린 것은?

Good morning, everyone! Welcome to today's weather forecast. If you have plans to do any activities outside, you ①will have to cancel them. It ②is expected to rain heavily all day long. If you ③will drive, you will need to be extra careful since the roads will be wet. Also, traffic is expected to be slower around 9:00 a.m. ④because of the heavy rain. If you leave ⑤earlier, you will be able to avoid the traffic.

①   ②   ③   ④   ⑤

18 다음 중 어법상 틀린 문장끼리 묶은 것은?

ⓐ If the weather is nice, we will be able to go camping.
ⓑ You will feel much better if you will take this medicine.
ⓒ Katie is concerned about her habit of staying up too late every night.
ⓓ Tourists should be aware of the danger from getting lost in the forest.
ⓔ If the restaurant is open, we will have dinner there.

① ⓐ, ⓑ   ② ⓑ, ⓒ   ③ ⓑ, ⓓ
④ ⓒ, ⓓ   ⑤ ⓓ, ⓔ

01 대화의 흐름으로 보아, 주어진 문장이 들어갈 위치로 가장 적절한 곳은?

> I find self-rewarding quite effective when trying to form a new habit.

> B   What are you doing, Sera?
> G   I am creating a habit tracking chart because I'm planning to develop a new habit. (①)
> B   A habit tracking chart? What's that?
> G   It's essentially a calendar that tracks a specific habit that you want to develop. (②) My goal is to take a walk after dinner every day. (③) I will mark whether I do it from Monday to Sunday. (④)
> B   So if you walk after dinner on Monday, do you put a circle in the Monday box?
> G   Exactly. And if I mark more than five days in a week, I'll reward myself. (⑤)
> B   That will definitely keep you motivated!

①   ②   ③   ④   ⑤

02 다음 글의 빈칸에 알맞은 말을 보기 에 주어진 단어를 배열하여 쓰시오.

> Hello, everyone! Welcome to *Science Report*. I'm your host, Alvin Stuart. We all know _____. But what about our brains? Did you know that it's important to work out your mind, too? Dr. Caitlin Yoon, a professor of neuroscience at Central University, is here with us today to talk about how we can become better thinkers. Thank you for joining us, Dr. Yoon!

> 보기   it / how / is / to exercise / for us / important / our bodies

[03~05] 다음 대화를 읽고, 물음에 답하시오.

> W   Unfortunately, we all have bad habits. ___(A)___, you might habitually waste time looking at your phone. And getting rid of such habits can be difficult. ___(B)___, a great way to do this is to replace them with good habits. Start by recognizing your bad habits. Ask yourself when and how often they typically occur each day.
> M   Then find positive replace. ___(C)___ you want to stop looking at your phone too often, put it away and do something better! You could listen to music, read a book, take a walk, or chat with your family. As time passes, these good habits will take the place of your bad habits.

03 위 대화의 목적으로 가장 적절한 것은?

① To explain the benefits of using smartphones
② To introduce ways to listen to music
③ To describe how to spend more time with family
④ To emphasize the importance of exercise
⑤ To suggest ways to replace bad habits with good ones

04 위 대화의 빈칸 (A)~(C)에 들어갈 말로 가장 적절한 것은?

	(A)		(B)		(C)
①	In addition	…	Therefore	…	Unless
②	For example	…	However	…	If
③	As a result	…	Also	…	When
④	Otherwise	…	For instance	…	Because
⑤	Moreover	…	Meanwhile	…	Although

05 위 대화의 밑줄 친 replace를 알맞은 형태로 바꿔 쓰시오. (필요시 복수형으로 쓸 것)

[06~08] 다음 글을 읽고, 물음에 답하시오.

If you have failed to make a new habit ①stick, understanding the structure of habits can be helpful. A habit has three phases: the trigger, the action, and the reward. The trigger is a signal ②that prompts you to take a certain action. It can be a sound, a place, or an event. It is like an alarm clock telling you ③to do something. Next, the action is the activity of the habit. Now comes the reward. This is the part ④where you receive something good for doing the desired activity. _____, you might allow yourself to eat a piece of chocolate after you work out. If your brain successfully ⑤will associate a certain behavior with the reward, your habit will naturally become part of your routine.

06 윗글의 밑줄 친 부분 중, 어법상 틀린 것은?

①   ②   ③   ④   ⑤

07 윗글의 빈칸에 들어갈 말로 가장 적절한 것은?

① For example   ② In conclusion
③ However   ④ In addition
⑤ On the other hand

08 윗글의 내용과 일치하도록 다음 질문에 대한 답을 완전한 문장으로 쓰시오.

Q What are the three phases of a habit?
A _____

[09~10] 다음 글을 읽고, 물음에 답하시오.

Doctor The correct answer is "$0.05." Now, think again. Do you see the error in your calculation? If the price of the pen was $0.10, then the notebook would cost $1.10. That would make the total price $1.20.
Host It seems like an easy question.
Doctor If you pause, take your time, and carefully think about it, you will realize your mistake. (①) This simple question reveals the fundamental way that our brains work. (②) System 1 is based on instinct, and it works without our conscious control. (③) Our brains naturally apply this system in _____ everyday situations, such as when we hear simple sentences, see large words on advertisements, or encounter easy questions like "2+2=?". (④) This system works very quickly, because it needs to continuously process enormous amounts of information coming in through our senses. (⑤)

09 글의 흐름으로 보아, 주어진 문장이 들어가기에 가장 적절한 곳은?

They actually have two different systems that they can utilize: System 1 and System 2.

①   ②   ③   ④   ⑤

10 윗글의 빈칸에 들어갈 말로 가장 적절한 것은?

① careless   ② harmless   ③ countless
④ useless   ⑤ meaningless

[11~12] 다음 글을 읽고, 물음에 답하시오.

System 2 is responsible for our reasoning and deeper decision-making processes. Our brains use this system when we compare the prices and features of products, check the validity of an argument, or encounter difficult questions like "238×79×451=?". It controls conscious mental activities when we need to focus or make careful choices. However, while System 2 is more reliable, its application requires time and effort.

If you got the right answer to the notebook and pen question after taking a few seconds to reflect, then your brain used System 2 to check System 1's initial response. However, our brains tend to rely heavily on taking mental shortcuts with System 1. That is why it's common for people to answer the question incorrectly at first.

11 윗글의 밑줄 친 compare에 해당하는 영어 뜻풀이로 가장 적절한 것은?

① to think deeply about
② to think about a situation as if it were real
③ to show something that was unknown
④ to use an idea or method in a certain situation
⑤ to look at the similarities and differences between two or more things

12 윗글에서 언급된 System 2에 관한 설명이 아닌 것은?

① 우리가 신중한 결정을 내릴 때 작동한다.
② System 2를 사용하는 데는 시간과 노력이 필요하다.
③ 논리적 추론과 깊은 사고를 담당한다.
④ 어려운 문제를 풀 때 활성화된다.
⑤ 우리가 정신적 지름길로서 의존한다.

[13~15] 다음 글을 읽고, 물음에 답하시오.

We make about 35,000 decisions every day without realizing it, and it is impossible to make every one of these consciously. So it's quite reasonable and effective for the brain to be a bit lazy sometimes. Having a lazy brain allows us to save energy for critical tasks that require our focus and attention. However, it is dangerous when this becomes a habit. If your brain becomes too reliant on System 1, it will not be able to apply System 2 when you confront a problem that requires intense concentration. System 2 is essential for exercising human intelligence, so the less you use it, the more likely you are to become a lazy thinker. Those who have an overly lazy brain frequently make errors and bad decisions. They can also develop a habit of accepting things to be true even though they have never been proven. Therefore, it can be harmful to develop lazy brain habits.

13 윗글의 주제로 가장 적절한 것은?

① 인간의 뇌가 결정을 내리는 방식
② System 1과 System 2의 정의
③ 게으른 뇌가 가져오는 위험성
④ 집중력 향상 방법
⑤ 무의식적 사고의 장점

14 윗글의 밑줄 친 부분을 우리말로 해석하시오.

_____

15 윗글을 한 문장으로 요약할 때, 빈칸에 들어갈 말로 가장 적절한 것은?

> According to the passage above, relying too much on System 1 can be dangerous because _____.

① it always saves energy
② it helps us make better decisions
③ it never makes mistakes
④ it makes us more intelligent
⑤ it prevents us from using System 2 when necessary

16 다음 글의 ①~⑤ 중, 어법상 틀린 것을 두 개 찾아 번호를 쓰고 바르게 고쳐 쓰시오.

> **Host** ① Do you have any final words for our audience?
>
> **Doctor** Yes. ② We are creatures of habit, so it is vitally important that we develop well-balanced thinking habits. ③ We should remain alert such that we do not fall into the trap of making careless decisions. ④ We should invest time into learning how to think deeply in order to use both System 1 and System 2 harmoniously. ⑤ That way, instead of developing a habit from relying too much on a lazy brain, you can exercise your intelligence and reinforce your mental capabilities.
>
> **Host** Okay, Dr. Yoon. Thanks for the great advice! Please give her a big hand!

번호	틀린 것	고친 것

[17~18] 다음 글을 읽고, 물음에 답하시오.

> We can make a deliberate effort to practice thinking deeply with System 2 more often. Here are some tips:
>
> First, reconsider your initial thoughts instead of accepting them right away. Keep generating more ideas and carefully compare the available options before making a decision. Ask yourself if the information you have gathered supports your original conclusion. If not, then think again.
>
> Next, make use of your natural curiosity. Curiosity can motivate us to investigate unfamiliar topics and ideas. It encourages us to dive deeper into a subject and explore it from multiple angles. Therefore, it can serve as a foundation for building deeper thinking habits.
>
> Finally, learn something new in order to stimulate your brain and become more intelligent. Learning a language or a musical instrument might not be easy, but these new activities will create new paths that allow information to flow through your brain more efficiently.

17 윗글의 밑줄 친 learn something new가 어떻게 깊이 생각하는 데 도움이 되는지 우리말로 쓰시오. (30자 이내)

_____

_____

18 윗글에서 게으른 두뇌 습관을 이겨내는 방법으로 언급되지 <u>않은</u> 것은?

① Reconsidering your initial thoughts
② Comparing multiple options before making decisions
③ Relying solely on intuition
④ Using curiosity to explore new topics
⑤ Learning a new language or instrument

01 다음 대화의 주제로 가장 적절한 것은?

A I'm planning to make a habit of reading books.

B Oh, that sounds like a good idea! Do you have a specific plan to develop this new habit?

A Of course! I'll start by reading for ten minutes a day and gradually increase the amount of time.

B That's great! Forming a new habit isn't easy, so we need to set small and achievable goals.

A You're right. I hope I can improve my language skills and learn new information with this habit.

B I'm sure you can do it. Good luck!

① ways to improve language skills
② the benefits of reading books
③ the secret to developing a new habit
④ how to set achievable goals
⑤ tips for spending free time wisely

02 다음 글의 밑줄 친 ①~⑤ 중, 어법상 틀린 것은?

Student News interviewed Jeon Heeju to find out about one of her good habits and how she developed it. She has ① a habit of waking up early. She wakes up at 6:00 a.m. every morning. She said, "To develop this habit, I began by ② waking up ten minutes early than usual every day for two weeks. After I ③ got used to this pattern, I repeated the process with an even earlier wake-up time." She explained that she didn't ④ have enough time to exercise in the morning before. However, since she developed this habit, she has had more time in the morning and has become more productive. Heeju's habit ⑤ seems to be worth adopting for our own personal growth.

①   ②   ③   ④   ⑤

[03~04] 다음 대화를 읽고, 물음에 답하시오.

M Welcome to *Morning Talk*. Today, we will dive deep into the world of habits and see how we can make use of them for a better life. Habits are the things we do again and again, often without thinking. Right, Zahara?

W Right, Tom. Unfortunately, we all have bad habits. For example, you might habitually waste time looking at your phone. And getting rid of such habits can be difficult. However, a great way to do this is to replace them with good habits. Start by recognizing your bad habits. Ask yourself when and how often they typically occur each day.

M Then find positive replacements. If you want to stop looking at your phone too often, put it away and _____! You could listen to music, read a book, take a walk, or chat with your family. As time passes, these good habits will take the place of your bad habits.

03 위 대화의 제목으로 가장 적절한 것은?

① Ways to Exercise Regularly
② How to Replace Bad Habits
③ Tips for Reading More Books
④ The Importance of Family Conversations
⑤ How to Spend Less Time on Your Phone

04 위 대화의 빈칸에 들어갈 말로 가장 적절한 것은?

① go to the library
② get rid of bad habits
③ do something better
④ find another way to communicate
⑤ make a list of what you should do

[05~07] 다음 글을 읽고, 물음에 답하시오.

System 2 is responsible for our reasoning and deeper decision-making processes. Our brains use this system when we _____(A)_____ the prices and features of products, check the validity of an argument, or encounter difficult questions like "238×79×451=?". It controls conscious mental activities when we need to focus or make careful choices. _____(B)_____, while System 2 is more reliable, its application requires time and effort.

If you got the right answer to the notebook and pen question after taking a few seconds to reflect, then your brain used System 2 to check System 1's initial response. _____(C)_____, our brains tend to rely heavily on taking mental shortcuts with System 1. That is why it's common for people to answer the question incorrectly at first.

05 윗글의 주제로 가장 적절한 것은?

① similarities between System 1 and System 2
② the impact of System 2 on everyday tasks
③ the role and characteristics of System 2
④ the influence of System 1 on decision- making
⑤ the necessity of System 2 in cognitive processing

06 윗글의 빈칸 (A)에 들어갈 말로 가장 적절한 것은?

① ignore   ② forget   ③ purchase
④ compare   ⑤ generate

07 윗글의 빈칸 (B)와 (C)에 공통으로 들어갈 말로 가장 적절한 것은?

① However   ② Therefore   ③ Finally
④ Moreover   ⑤ As a result

[08~09] 다음 글을 읽고, 물음에 답하시오.

We make about 35,000 decisions every day without realizing it, and it is impossible to make every one of these consciously. (①) So it's quite reasonable and effective for the brain to be a bit lazy sometimes. (②) Having a lazy brain allows us to save energy for critical tasks that require our focus and attention. (③) If your brain becomes too reliant on System 1, it will not be able to apply System 2 when you confront a problem that requires intense concentration. (④) System 2 is essential for exercising human intelligence, so the less you use it, the more likely you are to become a lazy thinker. (⑤) Those who have an overly lazy brain frequently make errors and bad decisions. They can also develop a habit of accepting things to be true even though they have never been proven. Therefore, it can be harmful to develop lazy brain habits.

08 글의 흐름으로 보아, 주어진 문장이 들어가기에 가장 적절한 곳은?

However, it is dangerous when this becomes a habit.

①   ②   ③   ④   ⑤

09 윗글의 내용과 일치하지 <u>않는</u> 것은?

① 우리는 하루에 수만 번의 결정을 내린다.
② System 1에 지나치게 의존하면 오류가 잦아질 수 있다.
③ System 2는 집중이 필요한 문제 해결에 필수적이다.
④ System 1을 많이 사용하면 인간의 지능이 높아진다.
⑤ 게으른 뇌 습관은 잘못된 판단을 유발할 수 있다.

[10~11] 다음 글을 읽고, 물음에 답하시오.

If you have failed to make a new habit (A) stick / to stick , understanding the structure of habits can be helpful. A habit has three phases: the trigger, the action, and the reward. The trigger is a signal that prompts you to take a certain action. It can be a sound, a place, or an event. It is like an alarm clock (B) telling / told you to do something. Next, the action is the activity of the habit. Now comes the reward. This is the part where you receive something good for doing the desired activity. For example, you might allow yourself to eat a piece of chocolate after you work out. If your brain successfully (C) associates / will associate a certain behavior with the reward, your habit will naturally become part of your routine.

10 윗글의 제목으로 가장 적절한 것은?

① How to Reward Yourself After Working Out
② The Importance of Alarm Clocks in Daily Life
③ Understanding the Three Phases of Habits
④ Why Bad Habits Are Hard to Break
⑤ Tips for Saving Time During the Day

11 (A), (B), (C)의 각 네모 안에서 어법에 맞는 표현으로 가장 적절한 것은?

	(A)	(B)	(C)
①	stick	… telling	… associates
②	stick	… told	… will associate
③	to stick	… telling	… associates
④	stick	… telling	… will associate
⑤	to stick	… told	… will associate

[12~14] 다음 글을 읽고, 물음에 답하시오.

Host How can we resist these lazy brain habits?
Doctor We can make a deliberate effort to practice thinking deeply with System 2 more often. Here are some tips:

First, reconsider your initial thoughts instead of ①accepting them right away. Keep generating more ideas and carefully compare the available options before making a decision. Ask ②yourself if the information you have gathered supports your original conclusion. If not, then think again.

Next, make use of your natural curiosity. Curiosity can motivate us ③investigating unfamiliar topics and ideas. It encourages us to dive deeper into a subject and explore it from multiple angles. Therefore, it can serve as a foundation for building deeper thinking habits.

Finally, learn ④something new in order to stimulate your brain and become more intelligent. ⑤Learning a language or a musical instrument might not be easy, but these new activities will create new paths that allow information to flow through your brain more efficiently.

12 윗글의 밑줄 친 lazy brain habits가 가리키는 것으로 가장 적절한 것은?

① learning new skills regularly
② using curiosity to explore
③ habits that encourage deep thinking
④ always questioning your own conclusions
⑤ relying too much on automatic, effortless thinking

13 윗글의 밑줄 친 ①~⑤ 중 어법상 틀린 것은?

①   ②   ③   ④   ⑤

14 윗글의 내용을 참고할 때, 다음 문장의 빈칸에 들어갈 말로 가장 적절한 것은?

> According to the doctor, curiosity is important because it _____.

① leads us to rely more on System 1
② keeps us from making decisions
③ encourages us to avoid new experiences
④ motivates us to investigate and think deeply
⑤ makes us accept things as true without evidence

[15~16] 다음 대화를 읽고, 물음에 답하시오.

> **G** Hey, Minho. Where are you heading now?
> **B** I'm going to the park. I run for 30 minutes every day.
> **G** That's amazing! I'm actually planning to make a (A) habit / fact of running after school, but it's not easy for me. Do you have any tips?
> **B** Starting (B) big / small is key to making it a habit. I suggest creating a running playlist with energetic songs. Initially, run for just three songs. That's how I began.
> **G** That would only take around 10 minutes, right? That sounds doable!
> **B** Exactly. After you get used to it, try running for four songs. Then go for five songs!
> **G** That way, I can (C) increase / decrease my running time bit by bit!
> **B** That's the spirit. Over time, you'll find yourself able to run for 30 minutes.
> **G** All right. I'll start with making that playlist. I hope this habit keeps me fit and strong!

15 (A), (B), (C)의 각 네모 안에서 문맥에 맞는 낱말로 가장 적절한 것은?

	(A)	(B)	(C)
①	fact	… big	… decrease
②	habit	… small	… increase
③	habit	… small	… decrease
④	habit	… big	… increase
⑤	fact	… small	… increase

16 위 대화의 내용과 일치하지 <u>않는</u> 것은?

① Minho runs for 30 minutes every day.
② The girl plans to make a running playlist.
③ Minho suggests starting with running for three songs.
④ The girl finds it easy to make running a habit.
⑤ The girl hopes the habit will keep her fit and strong.

17 다음 글의 ①~⑤ 중, 전체 흐름과 관계 <u>없는</u> 문장은?

> **Host** Do you have any final words for our audience?
> **Doctor** Yes. We are creatures of habit, so it is vitally important that we develop well-balanced thinking habits. ① We should remain alert so that we do not fall into the trap of making careless decisions. ② Many people enjoy reading books or listening to music in their free time. ③ We should invest time into learning how to think deeply in order to use both System 1 and System 2 harmoniously. ④ That way, instead of developing a habit of relying too much on a lazy brain, you can exercise your intelligence and reinforce your mental capabilities.
> **Host** Okay, Dr. Yoon. Thanks for the great advice! ⑤ Please give her a big hand!

①   ②   ③   ④   ⑤

[01~03] 다음 글을 읽고, 물음에 답하시오.

Hello! My name is Jiwoo. We can get rid of bad habits by replacing them with good ⓐ ones. Let me tell you about one of my bad habits and my plan to replace it. The habit I plan to replace is constantly eating sugary snacks. I want to get rid of this habit because it is ⓑ harmless to my health. To replace this habit, I plan to eat healthier snacks like nuts instead. I believe this change will be helpful for me.

01 윗글을 읽고 지우의 나쁜 습관과 습관을 바꾸기 위한 계획을 우리말로 쓰시오.

(1) 나쁜 습관: _____

(2) 습관을 바꾸기 위한 계획: _____

02 윗글의 밑줄 친 ⓐ가 가리키는 것을 찾아 쓰시오.

_____

03 윗글의 밑줄 친 ⓑ를 문맥상 알맞은 형태로 고쳐 쓰시오.

_____

[04~06] 다음 대화를 읽고, 물음에 답하시오.

M Welcome to *Morning Talk*. Today, we will dive deep into the world of habits and see how we can make use of them for a better life. Habits are the things we do again and again, often without thinking. Right, Zahara?

W Right, Tom. Unfortunately, we all have bad habits. For example, you might habitually waste time looking at your phone. And getting rid of such habits can be difficult. However, a great way to do ⓐ this is to replace them with good habits. Start by recognizing your bad habits. Ask yourself when and how often they typically occur each day.

M Then find positive replacements. If you want to stop looking at your phone too often, put it away and do ⓑ something better! You could listen to music, read a book, take a walk, or chat with your family. As time passes, these good habits will take the place of your bad habits.

04 위 대화의 밑줄 친 ⓐ this가 가리키는 바를 우리말로 쓰시오.

_____

05 위 대화의 밑줄 친 ⓑ something better의 예시로 언급된 것을 모두 쓰시오.

_____

06 위 대화의 요약문을 다음과 같이 완성할 때, 빈칸에 알맞은 말을 글에서 찾아 쓰시오.

The best way to break bad _____ is to first recognize them and understand when and how often they occur. Then, _____ those bad habits with _____ ones.

[07~08] 다음 글을 읽고, 물음에 답하시오.

We make about 35,000 decisions every day without realizing it, and it is impossible to make every one of these consciously. So it's quite ⓐreason and effective for the brain to be a bit lazy sometimes. Having a lazy brain allows us to save energy for critical tasks that require our focus and attention. However, it is dangerous when this becomes a habit. If your brain becomes too ⓑrely on System 1, it will not be able to apply System 2 when you confront a problem that requires intense ⓒconcentrate. System 2 is essential for exercising human intelligence, so the less you use it, the more likely you are to become a lazy thinker. ⓓThose who have an overly lazy brain frequently make errors and bad decisions. They can also develop a habit of accepting things to be true even though they have never been proven.

07 윗글의 밑줄 친 ⓐ, ⓑ, ⓒ를 알맞은 형태로 바꿔 쓰시오.

ⓐ reason → _____

ⓑ rely → _____

ⓒ concentrate → _____

08 윗글의 밑줄 친 ⓓThose who have an overly lazy brain 이 겪는 문제 두 가지를 윗글에서 찾아 우리말로 쓰시오. (각 30자 이내)

(1) _____

(2) _____

09 다음 대화의 밑줄 친 this habit이 의미하는 바를 우리말로 쓰시오.

A I'm planning to make a habit of reading books.

B Oh, that sounds like a good idea! Do you have a specific plan to develop this new habit?

A Of course! I'll start by reading for ten minutes a day and gradually increase the amount of time.

B That's great! Forming a new habit isn't easy, so we need to set small and achievable goals.

A You're right. I hope I can improve my language skills and learn new information with this habit.

B I'm sure you can do it. Good luck!

10 다음 빈칸에 들어갈 말을 보기 에서 골라 쓰시오.

보기 | rely on   pay attention   dive into
        serve as   come up with

(1) 선생님은 중요한 발표를 하기 전에 우리에게 집중하라고 말했다.
→ The teacher told us to _____ before she made an important announcement.

(2) 동굴 안에 빛이 없었기 때문에 그들은 작은 손전등에 의존해야 했다.
→ They had to _____ their small flashlight, as there was no light in the cave.

(3) 그 회사는 더 많은 고객을 끌어 모으기 위한 새로운 아이디어를 생각해 내려고 애썼다.
→ The company struggled to _____ a new idea to attract more customers.

[11~12] 다음 글을 읽고, 물음에 답하시오.

> **Host** How can we resist these lazy brain habits?
> **Doctor** We can make a deliberate effort to practice thinking deeply with System 2 more often. Here are some tips:
>
> First, reconsider your initial thoughts instead of accepting them right away. Keep ___(A)___ more ideas and carefully compare the available options before making a decision. Ask yourself if the information you have gathered supports your original conclusion. If not, then think again.
>
> Next, make use of your natural curiosity. Curiosity can motivate us to investigate unfamiliar topics and ideas. It encourages us ___(B)___ deeper into a subject and explore it from multiple angles. Therefore, it can serve as a foundation for building deeper thinking habits.
>
> Finally, learn something new in order to stimulate your brain and become more intelligent. ___(C)___ a language or a musical instrument might not be easy, but these new activities will create new paths that allow information to flow through your brain more efficiently.

11 윗글에서 게으른 두뇌 습관을 이겨내는 방법으로 언급한 세 가지를 우리말로 쓰시오.

(1)	
(2)	
(3)	

12 윗글의 빈칸 (A)~(C)에 들어갈 말을 **보기**에서 골라 알맞은 형태로 바꿔 쓰시오. (필요시 단어를 추가할 것)

> **보기**   dive   learn   generate

(A) _____

(B) _____

(C) _____

[13~14] 다음 글을 읽고, 물음에 답하시오.

> We are creatures of habit, so it is vitally important that we develop well-balanced thinking habits. We should remain alert so that we do not fall into the trap _____ making careless decisions. We should (think / invest / into / how / time / learning / to / deeply) in order to use both System 1 and System 2 harmoniously. That way, instead of developing a habit _____ relying too much on a lazy brain, you can exercise your intelligence and reinforce your mental capabilities.

13 윗글의 빈칸에 공통으로 알맞은 전치사를 쓰시오.

_____

14 윗글의 괄호 안에 주어진 단어를 바르게 배열하여 쓰시오.

_____

15 다음 문장에서 어법상 **틀린** 부분을 찾아 바르게 고쳐 쓰시오.

(1) If she will take the early train, she will arrive at her destination before noon.

_____ → _____

(2) If you won't hurry, you will be late for class.

_____ → _____

03

—

Let's Live in Harmony

Functions

▶ 경고하기
Make sure you don't touch any of the artworks.

▶ 강조하기
It is important to maintain a peaceful and respectful environment.

Structures

▶ Humanitas is a yellow brick house **located** in the city of Deventer, the Netherlands.

▶ Sometimes I teach them things, such as **how to use** social media.

교과서 어휘

Words

□ brick	명 벽돌		□ proposal	명 제안, 제의 (propose 동 제안하다)
□ locate	동 위치하다, 있다		□ intriguing	형 아주 흥미로운
□ house	동 수용하다		□ live-in	형 입주해서 사는
□ elderly	형 연세가 드신		□ knowledge	명 지식
□ resident	명 거주자, 주민		□ acquire	동 습득하다, 얻다
□ require	동 필요로 하다		□ obviously	부 확실히, 분명히 (obvious 형 분명한)
□ assistance	명 도움, 지원		□ meaningful	형 의미 있는
□ supportive	형 지원하는		□ intend	동 ~할 작정이다, 의도하다
□ unusual	형 특이한 (↔ usual 보통의)		□ grateful	형 감사하는, 고마워하는
□ neighbor	명 이웃(사람)		□ transformative	형 변화시키는
□ unique	형 독특한, 특별한		□ experience	명 경험 동 경험하다
□ intergenerational	형 세대 간의		□ inform	동 알리다, 알아내다
□ budget	명 예산, 비용		□ energetic	형 활기찬
□ funding	명 자금		□ decent	형 괜찮은, 제대로 된
□ reduction	명 삭감, 축소 (reduce 동 줄이다)		□ recently	부 최근에 (recent 형 최근의)
□ loss	명 손실 (lose 동 잃다)		□ grief	명 큰 슬픔, 비통
□ essential	형 필수적인		□ comfort	명 위로, 위안 동 위로하다
□ social	형 사회의		□ remind	동 상기시키다, 생각나게 하다
□ educational	형 교육의, 교육적인		□ nearly	부 거의
□ counseling	명 상담, 조언		□ vibrant	형 활기찬
□ affordable	형 적당한, 감당할 수 있는		□ currently	부 현재 (current 형 현재의)
□ removal	명 제거 (remove 동 제거하다)		□ spot	명 장소, 자리
□ numerous	형 많은		□ youthful	형 젊은
□ accommodation	명 거처, 숙소		□ perspective	명 관점, 시각
□ struggle	동 ~하려고 애쓰다 명 투쟁		□ valuable	형 소중한, 귀중한 (value 명 가치)
□ afford	동 ~할 여유가 되다		□ harmony	명 조화

Phrases

□ along with	~과 함께		□ rush around	분주히 돌아다니다
□ in return for	~의 대가로		□ move in	이사 오다
□ in exchange for	~의 대가로, ~대신에		□ compared to	~과 비교하여
□ hang out with	~와 시간을 보내다		□ go through	~을 겪다

102

교과서 어휘 익히기

♣ 다음 영어는 우리말로, 우리말은 영어로 쓰시오.

01 budget ⑲	26 ⑲ 거주자, 주민	
02 locate ⑧	27 ⑲ 제거	
03 loss ⑲	28 ⑲ 경험	
04 youthful ⑲	29 ⑲ 도움, 지원	
05 numerous ⑲	30 ⑲ 최근에	
06 live-in ⑲	31 ⑲ 특이한	
07 require ⑧	32 ⑲ 이웃(사람)	
08 vibrant ⑲	33 ⑲ 사회의	
09 intriguing ⑲	34 ⑲ 관점, 시각	
10 in exchange for	35 ⑲ 연세가 드신	
11 inform ⑧	36 ⑲ 삭감, 축소	
12 along with	37 ~을 겪다	
13 grateful ⑲	38 ⑲ 지식	
14 comfort ⑲	39 ⑲ 장소, 자리	
15 remind ⑧	40 ⑧ 습득하다, 얻다	
16 grief ⑲	41 분주히 돌아다니다	
17 valuable ⑲	42 ⑲ 거처, 숙소	
18 affordable ⑲	43 ⑲ 독특한, 특별한	
19 currently ⑲	44 ⑲ 상담, 조언	
20 nearly ⑲	45 ~의 대가로	
21 intend ⑧	46 ⑲ 의미 있는	
22 obviously ⑲	47 ⑲ 변화시키는	
23 decent ⑲	48 ⑲ 지원하는	
24 intergenerational ⑲	49 ⑲ 교육의, 교육적인	
25 hang out with	50 ⑲ 제안, 제의	

교과서 핵심 문법 ─────────

POINT 1 분사의 후치수식

예제	The house [**surrounded by trees**] looks peaceful.
	나무들로 둘러싸인 그 집은 평화로워 보인다.
교과서	Humanitas is a yellow brick house [**located in the city of Deventer, the Netherlands**].
	Humanitas는 네덜란드의 데벤터르시에 위치한 노란 벽돌집이다.

▶ 분사는 명사의 앞이나 뒤에서 명사를 수식할 수 있다.
▶ 분사와 수식을 받는 명사 사이의 관계가 <mark>능동·진행(~한, ~하고 있는)일 때는 현재분사를 쓰고, 수동·완료(~된)일 때는 과거분사를</mark> 쓴다.

Study Point 🍑

1 분사의 후치수식

분사에 목적어나 수식어(구) 등이 있을 때는 명사의 뒤에서 명사를 수식한다.

- The book [**written by the famous author**] was sold out. 유명 작가가 쓴 그 책은 매진되었다.
  과거분사구
- The car [**parked in front of the building**] had a flat tire. 건물 앞에 주차된 차는 타이어가 펑크가 났다.
  과거분사구
- Do you know the man [**standing near the door**]? 문 근처에 서 있는 남자를 아시나요?
  현재분사구
- The chef [**preparing the meal**] has won several cooking awards.
  현재분사구

  식사를 준비하고 있는 그 셰프는 여러 번의 요리상을 수상한 적이 있다.

2 분사의 전치수식

분사가 단독으로 명사를 수식할 때는 명사의 앞에서 명사를 수식한다.

- The policeman found the **stolen** necklace. 경찰관은 도난당한 목걸이를 찾았다.
  과거분사
- The **frozen** lake became a popular skating spot. 얼어붙은 호수는 인기 있는 스케이트장이 되었다.
  과거분사
- A **burning** candle filled the room with a sweet scent. 타고 있는 양초가 방을 달콤한 향기로 가득 채웠다.
  현재분사

Q 다음 네모 안에서 어법상 알맞은 것을 고르시오.

1 The falling / fallen leaves covered the entire path.

2 A crying / cried baby kept the whole family awake.

3 The trees covering / covered with snow in the park look great.

4 The woman wearing / worn a yellow dress is our new math teacher.

Check-up 🍑

01 다음 괄호 안의 단어를 알맞은 형태로 바꿔 문장을 완성하시오.

(1) Look at the stars _____ brightly in the night sky. (shine)

(2) This bakery is famous for its cakes _____ with fresh fruit. (decorate)

(3) The treasure _____ in the cave was discovered by adventurers. (hide)

02 다음 문장에서 어법상 **틀린** 부분을 찾아 바르게 고쳐 쓰시오.

(1) The musician lived in a house building by a famous architect.

(2) The players worn the red uniform won the championship.

(3) The broken window by a stranger was repaired quickly.

03 우리말과 일치하도록 괄호 안의 말을 바르게 배열하여 문장을 완성하시오.

(1) 우리는 셰프가 추천한 특별 요리를 주문했다. (the chef / the special dishes / by / recommended)
→ We ordered _____.

(2) 교통사고로 부상당한 사람들은 병원으로 이송되었다. (injured / the traffic accident / in / the people)
→ _____ were taken to the hospital.

(3) 그는 우리에게 신체적 장애를 극복한 한 남자를 소개하는 영상을 보여주었다. (a man / introducing / a video)
→ He showed us _____ who overcame a physical disability.

04 다음 글의 밑줄 친 (1), (2)를 어법상 알맞은 형태로 고쳐 쓰시오. ⟨교과서 77쪽⟩

> *Dumplin'* is an inspiring story (1) <u>write</u> by Julie Murphy. It tells the story of a teenage girl (2) <u>name</u> Willowdean Dickson. Willowdean is overweight, but she is proud of who she is. She decides to enter a beauty contest, and, along the way, she learns to stand up for what she believes in. This book will keep you inspired and teach you an important lesson about self-acceptance. I recommend this book to anyone who enjoys reading humorous and moving stories.

(1) _____   (2) _____

POINT 2 의문사 + to부정사

예제	They talked about **where to go** for the next holiday.

의문사 + to부정사

그들은 다음 휴가를 어디로 갈지에 대해 이야기했다.

교과서	Sometimes I teach them things, such as **how to use** social media.

의문사 + to부정사

나는 때로는 그분들에게 소셜 미디어를 사용하는 법과 같은 것들을 가르쳐 드린다.

▶ 「의문사+to부정사」는 명사구 역할을 하며, 문장에서 주어, 목적어, 보어로 쓰일 수 있다.
▶ 단, why는 to부정사와 함께 「why+to부정사」의 형태로 쓰이지 않는다는 것에 주의한다.

Study Point 🍎

1 의문사 + to부정사

「의문사 + to부정사」는 '(의문사) ~할지'와 같이 해석한다.

- Can you tell me **what to do** in this situation? 이 상황에서 내가 무엇을 해야 할지 말해 줄 수 있나요?
  what to-v: 무엇을 ~할지
- She explained **where to find** the best coffee in town. 그녀는 동네에서 최고의 커피를 어디서 찾을 수 있는지 설명해 주었다.
  where to-v: 어디서 ~할지
- He taught me **when to use** formal language in Korean. 그는 나에게 한국어에서 언제 존댓말을 써야 하는지 가르쳐 주었다.
  when to-v: 언제 ~할지
- Tell me **whom to contact** for technical support. 기술 지원을 위해 누구에게 연락해야 하는지 말해 주세요.
  who(m) to-v: 누구를[누구와] ~할지
- They learned **how to solve** complex math problems. 그들은 복잡한 수학 문제를 푸는 방법을 배웠다.
  how to-v: 어떻게 ~할지

2 명사구를 명사절로 전환하기

「의문사+to부정사」 형태의 명사구는 「의문사+주어+조동사+동사원형」 형태의 명사절로 전환할 수 있다.

- Do you know **when to submit** the application? 신청서를 언제 제출해야 하는지 알고 있나요?
  명사구
  → Do you know **when I should submit** the application?
  명사절
- Can you show me **how to use** this machine? 이 기계를 어떻게 사용하는지 보여줄 수 있나요?
  명사구
  → Can you show me **how I can use** this machine?
  명사절

Q 다음 문장의 밑줄 친 명사절을 명사구로 바꿔 쓰시오.

1 We'll determine when we should launch the product.

2 Jessica is learning how she can write song lyrics.

3 Can you tell me what I should say in the interview?

Check-up 🍊

01 우리말과 일치하도록 괄호 안의 단어를 이용하여 문장을 완성하시오.

(1) 우리는 여름 휴가를 어디로 갈지 결정해야 한다. (go)

→ We need to decide _____ _____ _____ for our summer vacation.

(2) 그 건물에 있는 누구도 이 상황에서 무엇을 해야 할지 모른다. (do)

→ No one in the building knows _____ _____ _____ in this situation.

(3) 내 친구들 중 몇몇은 소셜 미디어에서 누구를 팔로우할지 선택하지 못한다. (follow)

→ Some of my friends can't choose _____ _____ _____ on social media.

(4) 크림 파스타를 어떻게 요리할지 가르쳐 줄 수 있나요? (make)

→ Can you teach me _____ _____ _____ creamy pasta?

02 우리말과 일치하도록 괄호 안의 말을 바르게 배열하여 문장을 완성하시오.

(1) 그녀는 도서관 책을 언제 반납해야 하는지 물었다. (to / return / when / the library books)

→ She asked _____.

(2) 그는 새 기계를 어떻게 작동시키는지 설명했다. (operate / to / the new machine / how)

→ He explained _____.

(3) 그녀는 나에게 신뢰할 수 있는 정보를 어디서 찾는지 가르쳐 주었다. (reliable / find / where / to / information)

→ She taught me _____.

(4) 나는 전시회 티켓을 어디서 살지 모르겠다. (buy / where / to / tickets)

→ I don't know _____ for the exhibition.

03 다음 밑줄 친 우리말과 일치하도록 의문사와 동사를 각각 하나씩 골라 문장을 완성하시오. (교과서 77쪽)

> where   what   how   get   do   recover

> To whom it may concern,
> I recently purchased a computer from your store, and I am disappointed with its quality. (1) <u>나는 무엇을 해야 할지 모르겠습니다</u>, as it makes too much noise and the screen keeps turning off. Also, some of my data was lost, and (2) <u>그것을 어떻게 복구해야 할지 모르겠습니다</u>. (3) <u>어디에서 그것을 고칠 수 있는지 알려주세요.</u>

(1) I don't know _____

(2) I have no idea _____ it

(3) Please let me know _____ it fixed.

교과서 본문 분석

Under a Shared Roof
같은 지붕 아래

01 Humanitas is a yellow brick house [located in the city of Deventer, the Netherlands].
└─ 과거분사구

Humanitas는 네덜란드의 데벤터르시에 위치한 노란 벽돌집이다.

02 It is a care center [that houses more than 160 elderly residents {who require assistance}].
요양 시설 · house: 수용하다 · 주격 관계대명사절 · 주격 관계대명사절

그것은 도움이 필요한 160명 이상의 노인 거주자들을 수용하고 있는 요양 시설이다.

03 Along with its supportive environment, Humanitas offers something unusual: young neighbors.
= Humanitas's

Humanitas는 그곳의 지원적인 환경과 함께, 젊은 이웃이라는 특이한 요소를 제공한다.

04 At Humanitas, elderly residents share their living space with university students.
└─ share A with B: A를 B와 공유하다 ─┘

Humanitas에서 노인 거주자들은 그들의 생활공간을 대학생들과 공유한다.

05 This unique "intergenerational living" project began in 2012, after budget cuts reduced the amount
세대 간의 · 예산 삭감 · ~의 양
of money [(that) care homes in the Netherlands received].
└─ 목적격 관계대명사절

이 독특한 '세대 간 생활' 프로젝트는 네덜란드의 요양원이 받았던 돈이 예산 삭감으로 줄어든 후였던 2012년에 시작되었다.

06 This funding reduction led to the loss of many essential elderly care programs, including social,
lead to: ~으로 이어지다 · ~을 포함하여 (전치사)
educational, and counseling services.

이 자금 삭감은 사회, 교육, 그리고 상담 서비스를 포함한 여러 가지 필수적인 노인 돌봄 프로그램의 손실로 이어졌다.

07 Humanitas needed to seek an affordable solution to fill the gap [left by the removal of these
└─ 과거분사구
services].

Humanitas는 이 서비스들이 사라지면서 남은 공백을 메우기 위해 적당한 해결책을 찾아야 했다.

08 Since the building had numerous empty rooms available, the director decided to offer local
~ 때문에 (접속사) 후치수식 형용사
university students free accommodations in return for [spending time with the elderly residents].
offer B A: B에게 A를 제공하다 (= offer A to B) 동명사구 (전치사 for의 목적어)

그 건물에는 사용 가능한 빈 방이 많았기 때문에, 시설장은 지역 대학생들에게 노인 거주자들과 함께 시간을 보내는 것의 대가로 무료 거처를 제공하기로 결정했다.

09 Many students were struggling to afford the area's high rents, so the proposal was a true win-win
과거진행형 모두에게 유리한
situation.

많은 학생들이 그 지역의 높은 임대료를 감당하기 어려워하고 있었고, 그래서 그 제안은 진정으로 모두에게 유리한 상황이었다.

10 Now, let's hear more about this intriguing place from two of the residents.

이제 두 명의 주민으로부터 이 흥미진진한 공간에 대해 더 들어보자.

More Than a Free Place to Stay
형용사적 용법
무료로 머무를 수 있는 곳, 그 이상

11 Hi! My name is Jacob Jansen, and I've been living at Humanitas for over two years.
현재완료 진행형 ~이상
I've really enjoyed my time here.
현재완료

안녕하세요! 제 이름은 Jacob Jansen이고, 2년 넘게 Humanitas에서 살고 있어요. 저는 이곳에서 정말 즐겁게 지내고 있어요.

12 As a live-in student, I'm required to spend at least 30 hours per month with my elderly neighbors
~로서 (전치사) 수동태 적어도, 최소한 ~당
in exchange for free accommodations.

입주 학생으로서, 저는 무료 거처에 대한 대가로 한 달에 최소 30시간을 노인 이웃들과 함께 보내야 하죠.

13 In reality, however, we spend a lot more time together than that.
사실은, 실제로는 훨씬 (비교급 강조) = 30 hours

하지만 실제로 우린 그것보다 훨씬 더 많은 시간을 함께 보내요.

14 Sometimes I teach them things, such as how to use social media, and other times I just hang out
= elderly neighbors　　　　how to-v: ～하는 방법
with them.

전 때로는 그분들에게 소셜 미디어를 사용하는 법과 같은 것들을 가르쳐 주고, 다른 때에는 그저 함께 시간을 보내요.

15 We have meals together, play games, and go shopping.
동사 1　　　　　　　동사 2　　　　　동사 3

우리는 밥을 같이 먹고, 게임도 하고, 쇼핑을 가기도 하죠.

16 Humanitas doesn't feel like a care home to me.

Humanitas는 제게 요양원처럼 느껴지지 않아요.

17 Instead, I consider it a community [that I am a part of].
목적격 관계대명사절

대신, 저는 그곳을 제가 속한 공동체라고 생각해요.

18 Every time I come home, I tell my neighbors about my day.
～할 때마다

집에 올 때마다, 저는 이웃들에게 저의 하루에 대해 이야기하죠.

19 When I have a problem, they always have useful advice to share.
형용사적 용법

제가 고민이 있을 때, 그분들은 항상 공유해 줄 수 있는 유용한 조언이 있어요.

20 With so much experience [gathered over a lifetime], they possess knowledge [that I
과거분사구　　　　　　　　　　　　　　　　　　　목적격 관계대명사절
have yet to acquire].
have yet to-v: 아직 ～하지 않았다

평생 동안 쌓은 많은 경험과 함께, 그분들은 제가 아직 얻지 못한 지식을 가지고 있어요.

21 They also teach me lots of little but important things, often without realizing it.
전치사 + 동명사

또한 그분들은 모르는 사이에 사소하지만 중요한 것들을 제게 많이 가르쳐 줘요.

22 For example, I've learned the value of [having a casual chat over a cup of coffee] from them.
현재완료　　　　　　　　동명사구 (전치사 of의 목적어)　　　～하는 동안에 (전치사)

예를 들어, 저는 그분들에게서 커피 한 잔과 함께 가볍게 이야기를 나누는 것의 가치를 배웠어요.

23

= having a casual chat over a cup of coffee

It's a really great way [to take a break from rushing around all the time].

그건 항상 분주하게 돌아다니던 것에서 벗어나 잠시 휴식을 취할 수 있는 정말 좋은 방법이에요.

24

the + 형용사: ~한 사람들

(that)

I used to feel sorry for the elderly because I focused only on the things [they *can't* do].

used to + 동사원형: (과거에) ~하곤 했다

focus on: ~에 초점을 맞추다

저는 어르신들이 할 수 없는 일들에만 초점을 맞추었기 때문에, 그분들에 대해 안타까움을 느끼곤 했어요.

25

(that)

When I look at them now, however, I see all the things [they *can* do].

= the elderly

하지만 이제 그분들을 볼 때, 그분들이 할 수 있는 모든 것들이 보여요.

26

Obviously, Humanitas provides me with much more than a free place to stay.

확실히 Humanitas는 제게 무료로 머물 수 있는 공간 이상의 많은 것을 제공해 줘요.

27

I've made deep, meaningful friendships [that I'll never forget] here.

목적격 관계대명사절

여기서 절대로 잊지 못할 깊고 의미 있는 우정을 쌓았죠.

28

I intend to stay at Humanitas for at least one more year.

intend to-v: ~할 작정이다

저는 Humanitas에서 적어도 1년은 더 지내려고 해요.

29

(that)

Living here has changed my life in ways [I never thought possible], and I'm really grateful for this

주어 (동명사구)   동사 (현재완료)

be grateful for: ~에 감사하다

transformative experience.

여기서 사는 것은 제가 가능하다고 생각하지 못했던 방식으로 제 삶을 변화시켰고, 이러한 변화의 경험에 정말 감사함을 느껴요.

30

(접속사 that)

I have learned so much from my neighbors already, but I'm sure there is still a lot more [that they

현재완료

비교급 강조

can teach me].

제 이웃들에게 이미 많은 것을 배웠지만, 그분들이 제게 가르쳐 줄 수 있는 것이 아직 훨씬 더 많다고 확신해요.

A Breath of Fresh Air
신선한 공기의 숨결

31 My name is Helena Smit, and I am 93 years old. I have been living at Humanitas for the past 15
현재완료 진행형
years, so I remember [when we were first informed that we would have young people as neighbors].
접속사   ~로서 (전치사)

제 이름은 Helena Smit이고, 93살이에요. 저는 지난 15년간 Humanitas에서 살아왔기에, 젊은이들이 이웃으로 온다는 것을 처음 알게 되었을 때를 기억해요.

32 Believe me, not everyone was happy about it! But that quickly changed once they moved in.
모두 ~인 것은 아니다 (부분부정)   = having young people as neighbors   접속사 (~하자마자)

정말로, 모든 사람들이 다 그것을 반기지는 않았어요! 하지만 그들이 입주하자마자, 그것은 빠르게 바뀌었죠.

33 The students here are energetic, friendly, and caring. They make us laugh and create a joyful
                                                                                                동사 1   동사 2
mood.
make + 목적어 + 동사원형: ~이 … 하게 하다

이곳의 학생들은 활기차고, 친절하고, 배려심이 많아요. 그들은 우리를 웃게 하고 즐거운 분위기를 만들죠.

34 Humanitas was already a decent place to live [before the students arrived], but it has become a lot
                                                형용사적 용법   부사절 <시간>   현재완료
more fun since they moved in.
~한 이후로 (접속사)

Humanitas는 학생들이 오기 전에도 이미 살기 괜찮은 곳이었지만, 그들이 입주하고 나서 훨씬 더 즐거워졌어요.

35 Recently, the students held a pajama party and invited us to join them.
                                        동사 1   동사 2

최근에 학생들은 잠옷 파티를 열었고, 그들과 함께 하자고 우리를 초대했어요.

36 They taught us how to play some new games, and we all had a great time. It was like we were
                        how to-v: ~하는 방법   마치 ~인 것 같았다
in our 20s again.
in one's 20s: 20대인

그들은 우리에게 새로운 게임을 하는 방법도 가르쳐 주었고, 우린 모두 즐거운 시간을 보냈죠. 마치 우리가 다시 20대로 돌아간 기분이었어요.

37 I sometimes hear loud music from my young next-door neighbor's apartment, but that is okay.

가끔은 옆집 젊은 이웃의 아파트에서 큰 음악 소리가 들리긴 하지만, 괜찮아요.

38 It's a small matter compared to [what they've brought to our lives].
~과 비교하여   선행사를 포함하는 관계대명사
명사절 (전치사 to의 목적어)

그것은 그들이 우리 인생에 가져다준 것에 비해서는 사소한 문제거든요.

39 I'm grateful every day that they have become part of our community.
접속사   현재완료

그들이 우리 공동체의 일원이 된 것에 저는 매일 감사해요.

40 Speaking of my young neighbor, she has been here for more than two years now.
~에 대해 말하자면   현재완료

제 젊은 이웃에 대해 이야기하자면, 그녀는 이제 여기서 2년 넘게 지내왔어요.

41 Last year, she went through a difficult time of grief [after she lost her father], so I did what came
go through: ~을 겪다   부사절 <시간>   선행사를 포함하는 관계대명사
naturally.

그녀는 작년에 아버지를 여의고 나서 힘든 슬픔의 시간을 겪었고, 저는 자연스럽게 하게 되는 일을 했어요.

42 I stayed with her, held her hands [when she cried], and listened to [what she said].
동사 1   동사 2   부사절 <시간>   동사 3   명사절 (전치사 to의 목적어)

저는 그녀와 함께 있어 주었고, 그녀가 울 때 손을 잡아주었고, 그녀가 말하는 것을 들어주었죠.

43 She later told me that I was a great comfort during that difficult time, which made me feel very
접속사   ~ 동안 (전치사)   계속적 용법의 주격 관계대명사
good.

나중에 그녀는 그 힘든 시기에 제가 큰 위로가 되었다고 말해주었는데, 그 사실이 저를 매우 기분 좋게 해주었어요.

44 It always feels nice [to be reminded that I'm still capable of doing things for others].
가주어 <it>   진주어 <to부정사>   접속사 be capable of: ~할 수 있다   동명사구 (전치사 of의 목적어)

제가 아직 다른 사람을 위해 무언가 할 수 있다는 것이 생각날 땐 항상 기분이 좋아요.

45 I am nearly 100 years old, and I have bad knees. I understand that my knees aren't going to
거의   접속사
get any better.
좋아지다

저는 거의 100살이고, 무릎이 좋지 않아요. 저의 무릎이 더는 좋아지지 않을 거라는 것을 잘 알죠.

46 There is nothing much [the doctors can do about the pain].
(that)
목적격 관계대명사절

이 통증에 관해서 의사가 해줄 수 있는 것이 별로 없어요.

47 But [having young, vibrant people around] helps me forget about the pain and enjoy my life!
주어 (동명사구)   동사   목적격 보어 1   목적격 보어 2

하지만 젊고 활기찬 사람들을 곁에 두는 것은 이 통증을 잊고 제 삶을 즐길 수 있게 도와준답니다!

48 There are currently six students [living at Humanitas], with a long waiting list of others [hoping to
현재분사구   현재분사구
be offered a spot].

현재 Humanitas에 살고 있는 여섯 명의 학생들이 있고, 한 자리를 얻길 원하는 다른 학생들의 긴 대기 목록도 있다.

49 Humanitas is a great example of [how people of different ages can help each other and share their
(can)
간접의문문 (「의문사 + 주어 + 동사」의 어순)   동사 1   동사 2
lives with one another].
서로

Humanitas는 어떻게 다른 나이대의 사람들이 서로 도우며 삶을 공유할 수 있는지의 좋은 예이다.

50 The older residents gain a more youthful perspective on life, while the younger residents receive
반면에 (접속사)
valuable life lessons.

학생 거주자들은 소중한 인생 교훈을 얻는 반면, 노인 거주자들은 삶에 대한 더 젊은 관점을 얻는다.

점점 더 많은
51 More and more care homes around Europe are now trying intergenerational living, [bringing the
주어   동사 (현재진행형)   분사구문 <동시동작>
young and old together in harmony].

유럽 전역의 점점 더 많은 요양원들이 젊은 사람들과 노인들을 조화롭게 결속시키면서 세대 간 생활을 시도하고 있다.

교과서 본문 익히기 ❶ 옳은 어법·어휘 고르기

♣ 다음 네모 안에서 옳은 것을 고르시오.

01 Humanitas is a yellow brick house locating / located in the city of Deventer, the Netherlands.

02 It is a care center that houses more than 160 elderly residents who / which require assistance.

03 Along with its supportive environment, Humanitas offers something unusual / unusual something : young neighbors.

04 This unique "intergenerational living" project began in 2012, after budget cuts reduced the amount / number of money care homes in the Netherlands received.

05 This funding reduction led to the lose / loss of many essential elderly care programs, including social, educational, and counseling services.

06 Humanitas needed to seek an affordable solution to fill the gap left / leaving by the removal of these services.

07 Since the building had numerous empty rooms available, the director decided offering / to offer local university students free accommodations in return for spending time with the elderly residents.

08 Many students were struggling to afford the area's high rents, so / because the proposal was a true win-win situation.

09 Hi! My name is Jacob Jansen, and I've been living at Humanitas for / during over two years.

10 As / Like a live-in student, I'm required to spend at least 30 hours per month with my elderly neighbors in exchange for free accommodations.

11 In reality, however, we spend a lot more time together as / than that.

12 Sometimes I teach them things, such as how / what to use social media, and other times I just hang out with them.

13 We have meals together, play games, and go shopping / to shop .

14 Humanitas doesn't sound / feel like a care home to me.

15 Instead, I consider it a community what / that I am a part of.

16   When I have a problem, they always have useful advice / advices to share.

17   With so much experience gathering / gathered over a lifetime, they possess knowledge that I have yet to acquire.

18   They also teach me lots of little but important things, often without realize / realizing it.

19   For example, I've learned the value of / for having a casual chat over a cup of coffee from them.

20   It's a really great way to take a break from pushing / rushing around all the time.

21   I used to / am used to feel sorry for the elderly because I focused only on the things they *can't* do.

22   Obviously, Humanitas provides me with much / very more than a free place to stay.

23   I've made deep, meaning / meaningful friendships that I'll never forget here.

24   I intend to stay at Humanitas for at little / least one more year.

25   Living here has changed my life in ways I never thought possible / possibly, and I'm really grateful for this transformative experience.

26   I have learned so much from my neighbors already, but I'm sure there is still a lot / a lot of more that they can teach me.

27   I have been living at Humanitas for the past 15 years, so I remember when / where we were first informed that we would have young people as neighbors.

28   Believe me, not everyone was / were happy about it!

29   They make us laugh and create / to create a joyful mood.

30   Humanitas was already a decent place to live before / after the students arrived, but it has become a lot more fun since they moved in / out.

31   Recently, the students joined / held a pajama party and invited us to join them.

32   They taught us how / what to play some new games, and we all had a great time.

33 It's a small matter comparing / compared to what they've brought to our lives.

34 I'm grateful every day that / what they have become part of our community.

35 Speaking / Spoken of my young neighbor, she has been here for more than two years now.

36 Last year, she went through a difficult time of grief after she lost her father, so I did that / what came naturally.

37 I stayed with her, held her hands when she cried, and listened to which / what she said.

38 She later told me that I was a great comfort during that difficult time, that / which made me feel very good.

39 It always feels nice / nicely to be reminded that I'm still capable of doing things for others.

40 I understand that my knees aren't going to get any worse / better.

41 There is nothing / anything much the doctors can do about the pain.

42 But have / having young, vibrant people around helps me forget / forgetting about the pain and enjoy my life!

43 There are currently six students living at Humanitas, with a long waiting list of others hoping to offer / be offered a spot.

44 Humanitas is a great example of how people of different ages can help each other and share their life / lives with one another.

45 The older residents gain a more youthful perspective on life, when / while the younger residents receive valuable life lessons.

46 More and more care homes around Europe is / are now trying intergenerational living, bringing the young and old together in harmony / conflict.

✤ 다음 밑줄 친 부분이 옳으면 ○표 하고, 틀리면 바르게 고쳐 쓰시오.

01 Humanitas is a yellow brick house <u>locating</u> in the city of Deventer, the Netherlands.

02 It is a care center that houses more than 160 elderly residents <u>who require</u> assistance.

03 Along with its supportive environment, Humanitas offers <u>unusual something</u>: young neighbors.

04 At Humanitas, <u>elderly residents</u> share their living space with university students.

05 This unique "intergenerational living" project began in 2012, after budget cuts reduced the <u>number</u> of money care homes in the Netherlands received.

06 This funding reduction <u>led to</u> the loss of many essential elderly care programs, including social, educational, and counseling services.

07 Humanitas needed to seek an affordable solution <u>filling the gap</u> left by the removal of these services.

08 Since the building had numerous empty rooms available, the director decided to offer local university students free accommodations <u>in return for</u> spending time with the elderly residents.

09 Many students were struggling to afford the area's high rents, <u>because</u> the proposal was a true win-win situation.

10 Hi! My name is Jacob Jansen, and <u>I've been living</u> at Humanitas for over two years.

11 As a live-in student, I'm required to spend <u>at little</u> 30 hours per month with my elderly neighbors in exchange for free accommodations.

12 In reality, however, we spend a lot more time together <u>as that</u>.

13 Sometimes I teach them things, such as <u>how to use</u> social media, and other times I just hang out with them.

14 We have meals together, play games, and <u>go to shop</u>.

15 Instead, I consider it a community that I am <u>a part</u>.

16 When I have a problem, they always have <u>useful advice</u> to share.

17 With so <u>many experience</u> gathered over a lifetime, they possess knowledge that I have yet to acquire.

18 They also teach me lots of <u>little and important</u> things, often without realizing it.

19 For example, I've learned the value <u>of</u> having a casual chat over a cup of coffee from them.

20   It's a really great way <u>to take a break</u> from rushing around all the time.

21   I <u>was used to</u> feel sorry for the elderly because I focused only on the things they *can't* do.

22   Obviously, Humanitas provides me with <u>very</u> more than a free place to stay.

23   I intend to stay at Humanitas <u>during</u> at least one more year.

24   <u>Living here has changed</u> my life in ways I never thought <u>possibly</u>, and I'm really grateful for this transformative experience.

25   I have learned so much from my neighbors already, but I'm sure there is still <u>a lot of</u> more that they can teach me.

26   I have been living at Humanitas for the past 15 years, so I remember <u>when</u> we were first informed that we would have young people as neighbors.

27   They make us <u>laughing</u> and create a joyful mood.

28   Humanitas was already a decent place to live before the students arrived, but it has become a lot <u>much</u> fun since they moved in.

29   Recently, the students held a pajama party and <u>invite</u> us to join them.

30   They taught us <u>how to play</u> some new games, and we all had a great time.

31   It's a small matter <u>comparing</u> to what they've brought to our lives.

32   I'm grateful every day that they <u>have became</u> part of our community.

33   <u>Spoken</u> of my young neighbor, she has been here for more than two years now.

34   Last year, she went through a difficult time of grief after she lost her father, so I did <u>that</u> came naturally.

35   I stayed with her, held her hands when she cried, and listened to <u>what she said</u>.

36   She later told me that I was a great comfort <u>for</u> that difficult time, <u>which</u> made me feel very good.

37   It always <u>feels nicely</u> to be reminded that I'm still capable of doing things <u>for other</u>.

38   I understand that my knees aren't going to get any <u>well</u>.

39   There is <u>nothing much</u> the doctors can do about the pain.

40   But having young, vibrant people around <u>help</u> me forget about the pain and <u>enjoying</u> my life!

41 There are currently six students <u>living</u> at Humanitas, with a long waiting list of others hoping to <u>offer</u> a spot.

42 Humanitas is a great example of <u>how can people of different ages help</u> each other and share their lives with one another.

43 The older residents gain a more youthful perspective on life, <u>while</u> the younger residents receive valuable life lessons.

44 More and more care homes around Europe <u>are now trying</u> intergenerational living, <u>bring</u> the young and old together in harmony.

교과서 **본문 익히기** ③ 빈칸 완성하기

♣ 다음 우리말과 일치하도록 빈칸에 알맞은 말을 쓰시오.

Humanitas is a yellow brick house (1) _____ _____ the city of Deventer, the Netherlands.

Humanitas는 네덜란드의 데벤터르시에 위치한 노란 벽돌집이다.

It is a care center that (2) _____ _____ _____ 160 elderly residents who require assistance.

그것은 도움이 필요한 160명 이상의 노인 거주자들을 수용하고 있는 요양 시설이다.

(3) _____ _____ its supportive environment, Humanitas (4) _____ _____ _____ :
young neighbors.

Humanitas는 그곳의 지원적인 환경과 함께, 젊은 이웃이라는 특이한 요소를 제공한다.

At Humanitas, (5) _____ _____ _____ their living space with university students.

Humanitas에서 노인 거주자들은 그들의 생활공간을 대학생들과 공유한다.

This unique "intergenerational living" project began in 2012, after budget cuts (6) _____ _____
_____ _____ _____ care homes in the Netherlands received.

이 독특한 '세대 간 생활' 프로젝트는 네덜란드의 요양원이 받았던 돈이 예산 삭감으로 줄어든 후였던 2012년에 시작되었다.

This funding reduction (7) _____ _____ _____ _____ of many essential elderly care
programs, including social, educational, and counseling services.

이 자금 삭감은 사회, 교육, 그리고 상담 서비스를 포함한 여러 가지 필수적인 노인 돌봄 프로그램의 손실로 이어졌다.

Humanitas needed to (8) _____ _____ _____ _____ to fill the gap left by the removal of
these services.

Humanitas는 이 서비스들이 사라지면서 남은 공백을 메우기 위해 적당한 해결책을 찾아야 했다.

Since the building (9) _____ _____ _____ _____ _____ , the director decided to
offer local university students free accommodations in return for spending time with the elderly residents.

그 건물에는 사용 가능한 빈 방이 많았기 때문에, 시설장은 지역 대학생들에게 노인 거주자들과 함께 시간을 보내는 것의 대가로 무료 거처를 제공하기로 결정했다.

Many students (10) _____ _____ _____ _____ the area's high rents, so the proposal was a
true win-win situation.

많은 학생들이 그 지역의 높은 임대료를 감당하기 어려워하고 있었고, 그래서 그 제안은 진정으로 모두에게 유리한 상황이었다.

Now, let's hear more (11) _____ _____ _____ _____ from two of the residents.

이제 두 명의 주민으로부터 이 흥미진진한 공간에 대해 더 들어보자.

More Than a Free Place to Stay
무료로 머무를 수 있는 곳, 그 이상

Hi! My name is Jacob Jansen, and (12) _____ _____ _____ at Humanitas for over two years. I've really enjoyed my time here.

안녕하세요! 제 이름은 Jacob Jansen이고, 2년 넘게 Humanitas에서 살고 있어요. 저는 이곳에서 정말 즐겁게 지내고 있어요.

As a live-in student, I'm required to spend at least 30 hours per month with my elderly neighbors (13) _____ _____ _____ _____ _____.

입주 학생으로서, 저는 무료 거처에 대한 대가로 한 달에 최소 30시간을 노인 이웃들과 함께 보내야 하죠.

(14) _____ _____, however, we spend a lot more time together than that.

하지만 실제로 우린 그것보다 훨씬 더 많은 시간을 함께 보내요.

Sometimes I teach them things, such as (15) _____ _____ _____ _____ _____, and other times I just hang out with them.

전 때로는 그분들에게 소셜 미디어를 사용하는 법과 같은 것들을 가르쳐 주고, 다른 때에는 그저 함께 시간을 보내요.

We (16) _____ _____ _____, play games, and go shopping.

우리는 밥을 같이 먹고, 게임도 하고, 쇼핑을 가기도 하죠.

Humanitas doesn't (17) _____ _____ _____ _____ _____ to me.

Humanitas는 제게 요양원처럼 느껴지지 않아요.

Instead, I (18) _____ _____ _____ _____ that I am a part of.

대신, 저는 그곳을 제가 속한 공동체라고 생각해요.

Every time I come home, I (19) _____ _____ _____ about my day.

집에 올 때마다, 저는 이웃들에게 저의 하루에 대해 이야기하죠.

When I have a problem, they always have (20) _____ _____ _____ _____.

제가 고민이 있을 때, 그분들은 항상 공유해 줄 수 있는 유용한 조언이 있어요.

(21) _____ _____ _____ _____ gathered over a lifetime, they possess knowledge that I have yet to acquire.

평생 동안 쌓은 많은 경험과 함께, 그분들은 제가 아직 얻지 못한 지식을 가지고 있어요.

They also teach me lots of (22) _____ _____ _____ _____, often without realizing it.

또한 그분들은 모르는 사이에 사소하지만 중요한 것들을 제게 많이 가르쳐 줘요.

For example, I've learned the value of (23) _____ _____ _____ _____ over a cup of coffee from them.

예를 들어, 저는 그분들에게서 커피 한 잔과 함께 가볍게 이야기를 나누는 것의 가치를 배웠어요.

It's a really great way to take a break (24) _____ _____ _____ all the time.

그건 항상 분주하게 돌아다니던 것에서 벗어나 잠시 휴식을 취할 수 있는 정말 좋은 방법이에요.

I (25) _____ _____ _____ _____ _____ the elderly because I focused only on the things they *can't* do.

저는 어르신들이 할 수 없는 일들에만 초점을 맞추었기 때문에, 그분들에 대해 안타까움을 느끼곤 했어요.

When I look at them now, however, I (26) _____ _____ _____ _____ they *can* do.

하지만 이제 그분들을 볼 때, 그분들이 할 수 있는 모든 것들이 보여요.

Obviously, Humanitas provides me with (27) _____ _____ _____ a free place to stay.

확실히 Humanitas는 제게 무료로 머물 수 있는 공간 이상의 많은 것을 제공해 줘요.

I've made deep, (28) _____ _____ that I'll never forget here.

여기서 절대로 잊지 못할 깊고 의미 있는 우정을 쌓았죠.

I (29) _____ _____ _____ _____ Humanitas for at least one more year.

저는 Humanitas에서 적어도 1년은 더 지내려고 해요.

Living here has changed my life in ways I never thought possible, and I'm (30) _____ _____ _____ this transformative experience.

여기서 사는 것은 제가 가능하다고 생각하지 못했던 방식으로 제 삶을 변화시켰고, 이러한 변화의 경험에 정말 감사함을 느껴요.

I (31) _____ _____ _____ _____ from my neighbors already, but I'm sure there is still a lot more that they can teach me.

제 이웃들에게 이미 많은 것을 배웠지만, 그분들이 제게 가르쳐 줄 수 있는 것이 아직 훨씬 더 많다고 확신해요.

A Breath of Fresh Air
신선한 공기의 숨결

My name is Helena Smit, and I am 93 years old. I have been living at Humanitas for the past 15 years, so I remember (32) _____ _____ _____ _____ that we would have young people as neighbors.

제 이름은 Helena Smit이고, 93살이에요. 저는 지난 15년간 Humanitas에서 살아왔기에, 젊은이들이 이웃으로 온다는 것을 처음 알게 되었을 때를 기억해요.

Believe me, not everyone was happy about it! But that quickly changed (33) _____ _____ _____ _____.

정말로, 모든 사람들이 다 그것을 반기지는 않았어요! 하지만 그들이 입주하자마자, 그것은 빠르게 바뀌었죠.

The students here are energetic, friendly, and caring. They (34) _____ _____ _____ _____ a joyful mood.

이곳의 학생들은 활기차고, 친절하고, 배려심이 많아요. 그들은 우리를 웃게 하고 즐거운 분위기를 만들죠.

Humanitas was already (35) _____ _____ _____ _____ _____ before the students arrived, but it has become a lot more fun since they moved in.

Humanitas는 학생들이 오기 전에도 이미 살기 괜찮은 곳이었지만, 그들이 입주하고 나서 훨씬 더 즐거워졌어요.

Recently, the students (36) _____ _____ _____ _____ and invited us to join them.

최근에 학생들은 잠옷 파티를 열었고, 그들과 함께 하자고 우리를 초대했어요.

They (37) _____ _____ _____ _____ _____ some new games, and we all had a great time. It was like we were in our 20s again.

그들은 우리에게 새로운 게임을 하는 방법도 가르쳐 주었고, 우린 모두 즐거운 시간을 보냈죠. 마치 우리가 다시 20대로 돌아간 기분이었어요.

I sometimes (38) _____ _____ _____ _____ my young next-door neighbor's apartment, but that is okay.

가끔은 옆집 젊은 이웃의 아파트에서 큰 음악 소리가 들리긴 하지만, 괜찮아요.

It's a small matter (39) _____ _____ what they've brought to our lives.

그것은 그들이 우리 인생에 가져다준 것에 비해서는 사소한 문제거든요.

I'm grateful every day that they (40) _____ _____ _____ _____ _____ _____.

그들이 우리 공동체의 일원이 된 것에 저는 매일 감사해요.

(41) _____ _____ my young neighbor, she has been here for more than two years now.

제 젊은 이웃에 대해 이야기하자면, 그녀는 이제 여기서 2년 넘게 지내왔어요.

Last year, she (42) _____ _____ _____ _____ _____ of grief after she lost her father, so I did what came naturally.

그녀는 작년에 아버지를 여의고 나서 힘든 슬픔의 시간을 겪었고, 저는 자연스럽게 하게 되는 일을 했어요.

I stayed with her, held her hands when she cried, and (43) _____ _____ _____ _____ _____.

저는 그녀와 함께 있어 주었고, 그녀가 울 때 손을 잡아주었고, 그녀가 말하는 것을 들어주었죠.

She later told me that I was a great comfort during that difficult time, (44) _____ _____ _____ _____ very good.

나중에 그녀는 그 힘든 시기에 제가 큰 위로가 되었다고 말해주었는데, 그 사실이 저를 매우 기분 좋게 해주었어요.

It always feels nice to be reminded that I'm still (45) _____ _____ _____ _____ for others.

제가 아직 다른 사람을 위해 무언가 할 수 있다는 것이 생각날 땐 항상 기분이 좋아요.

I am nearly 100 years old, and I (46) _____ _____ _____. I understand that my knees aren't going to (47) _____ _____ _____.

저는 거의 100살이고, 무릎이 좋지 않아요. 저의 무릎이 더는 좋아지지 않을 거라는 것을 잘 알죠.

(48) _____ _____ _____ _____ the doctors can do about the pain.

이 통증에 관해서 의사가 해줄 수 있는 것이 별로 없어요.

But having young, vibrant people around (49) _____ _____ _____ about the pain and enjoy my life!

하지만 젊고 활기찬 사람들을 곁에 두는 것은 이 통증을 잊고 제 삶을 즐길 수 있게 도와준답니다!

There are currently six students living at Humanitas, with a long waiting list of others (50) _____ _____ _____ _____ a spot.

현재 Humanitas에 살고 있는 여섯 명의 학생들이 있고, 한 자리를 얻길 원하는 다른 학생들의 긴 대기 목록도 있다.

Humanitas is a great example of how people of different ages can help each other and (51) _____ _____ _____ _____ _____ _____.

Humanitas는 어떻게 다른 나이대의 사람들이 서로 도우며 삶을 공유할 수 있는지의 좋은 예이다.

The older residents (52) _____ _____ _____ _____ _____ on life, while the younger residents receive valuable life lessons.

학생 거주자들은 소중한 인생 교훈을 얻는 반면, 노인 거주자들은 삶에 대한 더 젊은 관점을 얻는다.

More and more care homes around Europe are now trying intergenerational living, (53) _____ _____ _____ _____ _____ _____ in harmony.

유럽 전역의 점점 더 많은 요양원들이 젊은 사람들과 노인들을 조화롭게 결속시키면서 세대 간 생활을 시도하고 있다.

01 밑줄 친 부분 중, 문맥상 낱말의 쓰임이 적절하지 않은 것은?

Humanitas is a yellow brick house located in the city of Deventer, the Netherlands. It is a care center that houses more than 160 elderly residents who require ① assistance. Along with its supportive environment, Humanitas offers something ② usual: young neighbors. At Humanitas, elderly residents ③ share their living space with university students.

This unique "intergenerational living" project began in 2012, after ④ budget cuts reduced the amount of money care homes in the Netherlands received. This funding reduction led to the ⑤ loss of many essential elderly care programs, including social, educational, and counseling services.

02 (A), (B), (C)의 각 네모 안에서 문맥에 맞는 낱말로 가장 적절한 것은?

Humanitas needed to seek an affordable (A) problem / solution to fill the gap left by the removal of these services. Since the building had numerous empty rooms available, the director decided to offer local university students (B) free / expensive accommodations in return for spending time with the elderly residents. Many students were struggling to afford the area's high rents, so the (C) proposal / refusal was a true win-win situation. Now, let's hear more about this intriguing place from two of the residents.

	(A)	(B)	(C)
①	problem	⋯ free	⋯ proposal
②	problem	⋯ expensive	⋯ refusal
③	solution	⋯ free	⋯ refusal
④	solution	⋯ free	⋯ proposal
⑤	solution	⋯ expensive	⋯ proposal

03 밑줄 친 부분 중, 문맥상 낱말의 쓰임이 적절하지 않은 것은?

Hi! My name is Jacob Jansen, and I've been living at Humanitas ① for over two years. I've really ② enjoyed my time here. As a live-in student, I'm ③ required to spend at least 30 hours per month with my elderly neighbors in exchange for ④ expensive accommodations. In reality, however, we spend a lot more time together than that. Sometimes I teach them things, such as how to use social media, and other times I just ⑤ hang out with them. We have meals together, play games, and go shopping.

04 (A), (B), (C)의 각 네모 안에서 문맥에 맞는 낱말로 가장 적절한 것은?

I used to feel (A) sorry / grateful for the elderly because I focused only on the things they *can't* do. When I look at them now, however, I see all the things they *can* do. Obviously, Humanitas provides me with much more than a free place to stay. I've made deep, meaningful friendships that I'll never forget here.

I (B) intend / pretend to stay at Humanitas for at least one more year. Living here has changed my life in ways I never thought possible, and I'm really grateful for this (C) conservative / transformative experience. I have learned so much from my neighbors already, but I'm sure there is still a lot more that they can teach me.

	(A)	(B)	(C)
①	sorry	⋯ pretend	⋯ transformative
②	sorry	⋯ intend	⋯ conservative
③	sorry	⋯ intend	⋯ transformative
④	grateful	⋯ intend	⋯ transformative
⑤	grateful	⋯ pretend	⋯ conservative

05 밑줄 친 부분 중, 문맥상 낱말의 쓰임이 적절하지 <u>않은</u> 것은?

Humanitas doesn't feel like a care home to me. Instead, I consider it a ①community that I am a part of. Every time I come home, I tell my ②neighbors about my day. When I have a problem, they always have useful ③advice to share. With so much ④experience gathered over a lifetime, they possess knowledge that I have yet to acquire. They also teach me lots of little but important things, often without realizing it. For example, I've learned the value of having a ⑤serious chat over a cup of coffee from them. It's a really great way to take a break from rushing around all the time.

06 밑줄 친 부분 중, 문맥상 낱말의 쓰임이 적절하지 <u>않은</u> 것은?

My name is Helena Smit, and I am 93 years old. I have been living at Humanitas for the past 15 years, so I remember when we were first informed that we would have young people as ①neighbors. Believe me, not everyone was happy about it! But that quickly changed once they moved in. The students here are energetic, friendly, and caring. They make us laugh and create a ②joyful mood.

Humanitas was already a ③decent place to live before the students arrived, but it has become a lot more fun since they moved in. Recently, the students ④held a pajama party and invited us to join them. They taught us how to play some new games, and we all had a great time. It was like we were in our 20s again.

I sometimes hear ⑤calm music from my young next-door neighbor's apartment, but that is okay. It's a small matter compared to what they've brought to our lives. I'm grateful every day that they have become part of our community.

07 밑줄 친 부분 중, 문맥상 낱말의 쓰임이 적절하지 <u>않은</u> 것은?

Speaking of my young neighbor, she has been here for more than two years now. Last year, she went through a difficult time of ①grief after she lost her father, so I did what came naturally. I stayed with her, held her hands when she cried, and listened to what she said. She later told me that I was a great ②discomfort during that difficult time, which made me feel very good. It always feels nice to be reminded that I'm still ③capable of doing things for others.

I am nearly 100 years old, and I have bad knees. I understand that my knees aren't going to get any better. There is ④nothing much the doctors can do about the pain. But having young, ⑤vibrant people around helps me forget about the pain and enjoy my life!

08 (A), (B), (C)의 각 네모 안에서 문맥에 맞는 낱말로 가장 적절한 것은?

There are currently six students living at Humanitas, with a long waiting list of others hoping to be offered a spot. Humanitas is a great example of how people of (A) similar / different ages can help each other and share their lives with one another. The older residents gain a more youthful (B) experience / perspective on life, while the younger residents receive valuable life lessons. More and more care homes around Europe are now trying (C) international / intergenerational living, bringing the young and old together in harmony.

	(A)		(B)		(C)
①	similar	⋯	perspective	⋯	intergenerational
②	similar	⋯	experience	⋯	international
③	different	⋯	perspective	⋯	international
④	different	⋯	perspective	⋯	intergenerational
⑤	similar	⋯	experience	⋯	intergenerational

01 (A), (B), (C)의 각 네모 안에서 어법에 맞는 표현으로 가장 적절한 것은?

Humanitas is a yellow brick house (A) locating / located in the city of Deventer, the Netherlands. It is a care center that houses more than 160 elderly residents (B) who / which require assistance. Along with its supportive environment, Humanitas offers (C) something unusual / unusual something : young neighbors. At Humanitas, elderly residents share their living space with university students.

	(A)		(B)		(C)
①	locating	⋯	who	⋯	something unusual
②	located	⋯	who	⋯	something unusual
③	locating	⋯	which	⋯	unusual something
④	located	⋯	who	⋯	unusual something
⑤	located	⋯	which	⋯	something unusual

02 (A), (B), (C)의 각 네모 안에서 어법에 맞는 표현으로 가장 적절한 것은?

Humanitas needed to seek an affordable solution to fill the gap (A) leaving / left by the removal of these services. Since the building had numerous empty rooms available, the director decided to offer local university students free accommodations in return for (B) spending / spent time with the elderly residents. Many students were struggling (C) affording / to afford the area's high rents, so the proposal was a true win-win situation. Now, let's hear more about this intriguing place from two of the residents.

	(A)		(B)		(C)
①	leaving	⋯	spent	⋯	affording
②	leaving	⋯	spending	⋯	to afford
③	left	⋯	spending	⋯	to afford
④	left	⋯	spending	⋯	affording
⑤	left	⋯	spent	⋯	to afford

03 (A), (B), (C)의 각 네모 안에서 어법에 맞는 표현으로 가장 적절한 것은?

Hi! My name is Jacob Jansen, and I've been living at Humanitas for over two years. I've really (A) enjoying / enjoyed my time here. As a live-in student, I'm required to spend at least 30 hours per month with my elderly neighbors in exchange for free accommodations. In reality, however, we spend (B) very / a lot more time together than that. Sometimes I teach them things, such as (C) how / what to use social media, and other times I just hang out with them. We have meals together, play games, and go shopping.

	(A)		(B)		(C)
①	enjoying	⋯	very	⋯	what
②	enjoying	⋯	a lot	⋯	how
③	enjoyed	⋯	very	⋯	how
④	enjoyed	⋯	a lot	⋯	what
⑤	enjoyed	⋯	a lot	⋯	how

04 다음 글의 밑줄 친 부분 중, 어법상 틀린 것은?

Humanitas doesn't feel like a care home to me. Instead, I consider it a community that I am a part of. Every time I come home, I tell my neighbors about my day. When I have a problem, they always have useful advice ①to share. With so much experience ②gathering over a lifetime, they possess knowledge that I have yet to acquire. They also teach me lots of little but important things, often without ③realizing it. For example, I've learned the value of ④having a casual chat over a cup of coffee from them. It's a really great way ⑤to take a break from rushing around all the time.

05 다음 글의 밑줄 친 부분 중, 어법상 틀린 것은?

I ① was used to feel sorry for the elderly because I focused only on the things they *can't* do. When I look at them now, however, I see all the things they *can* do. Obviously, Humanitas provides me with much more than a free place ②to stay. I've made deep, meaningful friendships that I'll never forget here.

I intend to stay at Humanitas for ③at least one more year. ④Living here has changed my life in ways I never thought possible, and I'm really grateful for this transformative experience. I have learned so much from my neighbors already, but I'm sure there is still ⑤a lot more that they can teach me.

06 다음 글의 밑줄 친 부분 중, 어법상 틀린 것은?

My name is Helena Smit, and I am 93 years old. I ①have been living at Humanitas for the past 15 years, so I remember when we were first informed that we would have young people as neighbors. Believe me, not everyone was happy about it! But that quickly changed once they moved in. The students here are energetic, friendly, and caring. They make us ②to laugh and create a joyful mood.

Humanitas was already a decent place to live before the students arrived, but it has become ③a lot more fun since they moved in. Recently, the students held a pajama party and invited us to join them. They taught us ④how to play some new games, and we all had a great time. It was like we were in our 20s again.

I sometimes hear loud music from my young next-door neighbor's apartment, but that is okay. It's a small matter ⑤compared to what they've brought to our lives. I'm grateful every day that they have become part of our community.

07 다음 글의 밑줄 친 부분 중, 어법상 틀린 것은?

①Speaking of my young neighbor, she has been here for more than two years now. Last year, she went through a difficult time of grief after she lost her father, so I did ②what came naturally. I stayed with her, held her hands when she cried, and listened to what she said. She later told me that I was a great comfort during that difficult time, ③which made me feel very good. It always feels ④nice to be reminded that I'm still capable of doing things for others.

I am nearly 100 years old, and I have bad knees. I understand that my knees aren't going to get any better. There is nothing much the doctors can do about the pain. But having young, vibrant people around ⑤help me forget about the pain and enjoy my life!

08 (A), (B), (C)의 각 네모 안에서 어법에 맞는 표현으로 가장 적절한 것은?

There are currently six students living at Humanitas, with a long waiting list of others hoping to (A) offer / be offered a spot. Humanitas is a great example of how people of different ages can help each other and share their lives with one another. The older residents gain a (B) more / most youthful perspective on life, while the younger residents receive valuable life lessons. More and more care homes around Europe (C) is / are now trying intergenerational living, bringing the young and old together in harmony.

	(A)	(B)	(C)
①	offer	⋯ most ⋯	is
②	be offered	⋯ more ⋯	are
③	offer	⋯ more ⋯	are
④	be offered	⋯ most ⋯	are
⑤	be offered	⋯ more ⋯	is

01 다음 대화 후 두 사람이 할 일로 가장 적절한 것은?

> **B** That was an exciting game, wasn't it?
> **G** Yes, it really was. But it's disappointing to see all this trash left behind at the stadium.
> **B** Yeah, it's a mess. I wish people had been more considerate and cleaned up after themselves.
> **G** Why don't we help out? Let's pick up some trash before we head to the subway station.
> **B** Sure. I will go and get some bags.

① 경기 관람하기   ② 쓰레기 줍기
③ 화장실 찾기   ④ 가방 사러 가기
⑤ 지하철역으로 가기

[02~03] 다음 글을 읽고, 물음에 답하시오.

> Humanitas is a yellow brick house located in the city of Deventer, the Netherlands. It is a care center that houses more than 160 elderly residents who require assistance. Along with its supportive environment, Humanitas offers something unusual: young _____. At Humanitas, elderly residents share their living space with university students.
>
> This unique "intergenerational living" project began in 2012, after budget cuts reduced the amount of money care homes in the Netherlands received. This funding reduction led to the loss of many essential elderly care programs, including social, educational, and counseling services.

02 윗글의 빈칸에 들어갈 말로 가장 적절한 것은?

① directors   ② employees   ③ neighbors
④ teachers   ⑤ patients

03 윗글의 밑줄 친 This unique "intergenerational living" project가 의미하는 바를 우리말로 쓰시오. (40자 이내)

_____

_____

[04~05] 다음 글을 읽고, 물음에 답하시오.

> Humanitas needed to seek an affordable solution to fill the gap ⓐleave by the removal of these services. Since the building had numerous empty rooms available, the director decided to offer local university students free accommodations in return for ⓑspend time with the elderly residents. Many students were struggling ⓒafford the area's high rents, so the proposal was a true win-win situation. Now, let's hear more about this intriguing place from two of the residents.

04 윗글의 밑줄 친 ⓐ~ⓒ를 어법상 알맞은 형태로 바꿔 쓰시오. (필요시 단어를 추가할 것)

ⓐ _____

ⓑ _____

ⓒ _____

05 윗글의 내용과 일치하지 않는 것은?

① Humanitas는 서비스가 중단된 후 해결책을 모색했다.
② Humanitas에는 사용할 수 있는 빈 방이 많이 있었다.
③ 지역의 대학생들은 높은 임대료 때문에 어려움을 겪고 있었다.
④ Humanitas의 생활은 노인과 대학생 모두에게 이익이 되었다.
⑤ 대학생들은 노인들과 시간을 보내는 대가로 급여를 받았다.

[06~08] 다음 글을 읽고, 물음에 답하시오.

Humanitas doesn't feel like a care home to me. Instead, I consider it ①a community that I am a part of. Every time I come home, I tell my neighbors about my day. When I have a problem, they always have useful advice to share. With so much ②experience gathered over a lifetime, they possess knowledge that I have yet to acquire. They also teach me lots of little but important things, often without realizing it. For example, I've learned ③the value of having a casual chat over a cup of coffee from them. It's a really great way to take a break from rushing around all the time.

I ④used to feel sorry for the elderly because I focused only on the things they *can't* do. When I look at them now, however, I see all the things they *can* do. Obviously, Humanitas provides me with much more than a free place to stay. I've made deep, meaningful friendships that I'll never forget here.

I intend to stay at Humanitas for ⑤at least one more year. Living here has changed my life in ways I never thought possible, and I'm really grateful for this transformative experience. I have learned so much from my neighbors already, but I'm sure there is still a lot more that they can teach me.

06 윗글의 필자가 처음에 어르신들에 대해 느꼈을 심경으로 가장 적절한 것은?

① 감사함   ② 죄송함   ③ 안타까움
④ 두려움   ⑤ 실망스러움

07 윗글의 밑줄 친 they가 가리키는 것을 찾아 쓰시오.

_____

08 윗글의 밑줄 친 ①~⑤ 중, 우리말 해석이 옳지 <u>않은</u> 것은?

① 내가 속한 공동체
② 평생 동안 쌓은 경험
③ 가볍게 이야기를 나누는 것의 가치
④ 안타까움을 느끼곤 했다
⑤ 많아야 1년 더

[09~10] 다음 글을 읽고, 물음에 답하시오.

Dumplin' is an inspiring story ①writing by Julie Murphy. It tells the story of a teenage girl named Willowdean Dickson. Willowdean is overweight, but she is proud of who is she. She decides ②to enter a beauty contest, and, along the way, she learns to stand up for ③what she believes in. This book will keep you ④inspired and teach you an important lesson about self-acceptance. I recommend this book to anyone ⑤who enjoys reading humorous and moving stories.

09 윗글의 밑줄 친 ①~⑤ 중, 어법상 <u>틀린</u> 것은?

①   ②   ③   ④   ⑤

10 윗글의 밑줄 친 문장에서 어법상 <u>틀린</u> 부분을 찾아 바르게 고쳐 쓰시오.

_____

[11~12] 다음 글을 읽고, 물음에 답하시오.

Hi! My name is Jacob Jansen, and I've been living at Humanitas (A) for / during over two years. I've really enjoyed my time here. As a live-in student, I'm (B) requiring / required to spend at least 30 hours per month with my elderly neighbors in exchange for free accommodations. In reality, however, we spend a lot more time together than that. Sometimes I teach them things, such as 소셜 미디어를 사용하는 방법, and (C) other / another times I just hang out with them. We have meals together, play games, and go shopping.

11 (A), (B), (C)의 각 네모 안에서 어법에 맞는 표현으로 가장 적절한 것은?

	(A)		(B)		(C)
①	for	…	required	…	other
②	for	…	requiring	…	other
③	for	…	required	…	another
④	during	…	requiring	…	another
⑤	during	…	required	…	other

12 윗글의 밑줄 친 우리말과 일치하도록 주어진 조건에 맞게 영작하시오.

조건
• 「의문사+to부정사」 구문을 사용할 것
• 사용할 표현: social media

[13~14] 다음 글을 읽고, 물음에 답하시오.

My name is Helena Smit, and I am 93 years old. I have been living at Humanitas for the past 15 years, so I remember when we were first informed that we would have young people as neighbors. Believe me, not everyone was happy about ⓐ it! But that quickly changed once they moved in. The students here are energetic, friendly, and caring. They make us laugh and create a joyful mood.

Humanitas was already a decent place to live before the students arrived, but it has become a lot more fun since they moved in. Recently, the students held a pajama party and invited us to join them. They taught us how to play some new games, and we all had a great time. It was like we were in our 20s again.

I sometimes hear loud music from my young next-door neighbor's apartment, but that is okay. It's a small matter compared to ⓑ what they've brought to our lives. I'm grateful every day that they have become part of our community.

13 윗글의 밑줄 친 ⓐ it이 의미하는 바를 우리말로 쓰시오.

_____

14 윗글의 밑줄 친 ⓑ what과 쓰임이 같은 것을 모두 고르면?

① He explained what happened during the meeting.
② Can you explain what this word means?
③ What they discovered surprised everyone.
④ I can't decide what to cook for her birthday.
⑤ What do you think is the best way to learn a new language quickly?

(A) <u>Spoken of my young neighbor, she has been here for more than two years now.</u> Last year, she went through a difficult time of <u>grief</u> after she lost her father, so I did what came naturally. I stayed with her, held her hands when she cried, and listened to what she said. She later told me that I was a great comfort during that difficult time, which made me feel very good. It always feels nice to be reminded that I'm still capable of doing things for others.

I am nearly 100 years old, and I have bad knees. I understand that my knees aren't going to get any better. There is nothing much the doctors can do about the pain. (B) <u>But having young, vibrant people around help me forget about the pain and enjoy my life!</u>

15 윗글의 밑줄 친 (A), (B)에서 어법상 틀린 부분을 찾아 바르게 고쳐 쓰시오.

(A) _____

_____

(B) _____

_____

16 윗글의 밑줄 친 grief의 영어 뜻풀이로 가장 적절한 것은?

① a point of view on a particular topic
② intense sorrow caused by the loss of someone
③ a feeling of encouragement and support
④ advice and support for personal, social, or psychological problems
⑤ the act of giving help or support, or the help that is given

B Susan, how was the movie yesterday?
G The movie was better than I expected, but I was annoyed with someone at the theater.
B Why? Did someone spoil the twist?
G No. There was a guy who kept texting during the movie. The light from his phone was distracting.
B Oh, that was really rude. I hate it when people do that in a theater. They should respect others.
G Yes, it's important _____.
Anyway, the movie itself was really well-made. I highly recommend it.
B Okay, I will watch it this weekend. I hope no one uses their phone during it.

17 위 대화의 빈칸에 들어갈 말로 가장 적절한 것은?

① to enjoy snacks during the movie
② to prepare for the movie experience
③ to leave the theater before the credits
④ to watch movies without company
⑤ to follow etiquette in public places

18 위 대화의 내용과 일치하지 <u>않는</u> 것은?

① Susan은 영화가 기대했던 것보다 좋다고 생각했다.
② Susan은 영화관에서 누군가의 행동에 짜증이 났다.
③ 누군가의 휴대폰 사용이 Susan의 영화 관람을 방해했다.
④ 누군가가 Susan에게 영화의 반전을 미리 말해주었다.
⑤ 남학생은 주말에 Susan이 본 영화를 볼 계획이다.

[01~02] 다음 글을 읽고, 물음에 답하시오.

(A) Humanitas is a yellow brick house locating in the city of Deventer, the Netherlands. It is a care center that houses more than 160 elderly residents who require ① assistance. (B) Along with its supportive environment, Humanitas offers unusual something: young neighbors. At Humanitas, elderly residents ② share their living space with university students.

This ③ unique "intergenerational living" project began in 2012, after budget cuts reduced the ④ amount of money care homes in the Netherlands received. This funding ⑤ growth led to the loss of many essential elderly care programs, including social, educational, and counseling services.

01 윗글의 밑줄 친 ①~⑤ 중, 문맥상 낱말의 쓰임이 적절하지 않은 것은?

①   ②   ③   ④   ⑤

02 윗글의 밑줄 친 (A), (B)에서 어법상 틀린 부분을 찾아 바르게 고쳐 쓰시오.

(A) _____

_____

(B) _____

_____

[03~04] 다음 글을 읽고, 물음에 답하시오.

Humanitas needed to seek an affordable solution to fill the gap left by the (A) removal / approval of these services. Since the building had numerous empty rooms (B) available / unavailable, the director decided to offer local university students free accommodations in return for spending time with the elderly residents. Many students were (C) struggling / planning to afford the area's high rents, so the proposal was a true win-win situation. Now, let's hear more about this intriguing place from two of the residents.

03 (A), (B), (C)의 각 네모 안에서 문맥에 맞는 낱말로 가장 적절한 것은?

    (A)   (B)   (C)
① removal ··· unavailable ··· struggling
② removal ··· available ··· struggling
③ approval ··· available ··· struggling
④ approval ··· unavailable ··· planning
⑤ removal ··· available ··· planning

04 윗글의 밑줄 친 affordable의 영어 뜻풀이로 가장 적절한 것은?

① providing help and encouragement
② feeling or showing appreciation
③ full of energy and life
④ having a cost that isn't too high; being reasonable in terms of price
⑤ having importance or value

05 글의 흐름으로 보아, 주어진 문장이 들어갈 위치로 가장 적절한 곳은?

> In reality, however, we spend a lot more time together than that.

> Hi! My name is Jacob Jansen, and I've been living at Humanitas for over two years. (①) I've really enjoyed my time here. (②) As a live-in student, I'm required to spend at least 30 hours per month with my elderly neighbors in exchange for free accommodations. (③) Sometimes I teach them things, such as how to use social media, and other times I just hang out with them. (④) We have meals together, play games, and go shopping. (⑤)

①   ②   ③   ④   ⑤

[06~08] 다음 글을 읽고, 물음에 답하시오.

> Humanitas doesn't feel like a care home to me. Instead, I consider it a community that I am a part of. Every time I come home, I tell my neighbors about my day. When I have a problem, they always have useful advice to share. With so much experience gathered over a lifetime, they possess knowledge that I have yet to acquire. They also teach me lots of little but important things, often without realizing it. For example, (A) 저는 그분들에게서 커피 한 잔과 함께 가볍게 이야기를 나누는 것의 가치를 배웠어요. It's a really great way to take a break from rushing around all the time.
>
> I used to feel sorry for the elderly because I focused only on the things they *can't* do. When I look at them now, however, I see all the things they *can* do. Obviously, Humanitas provides me with much more than a free place to stay. I've made deep, meaningful friendships that I'll never forget here.

> I intend to stay at Humanitas for at least one more year. (B) 여기서 사는 것은 제가 가능하다고 생각하지 못했던 방식으로 제 삶을 변화시켰고, and I'm really grateful for this transformative experience. I have learned so much from my neighbors already, but I'm sure there is still a lot more that they can teach me.

06 윗글의 밑줄 친 우리말 (A)와 일치하도록 <조건>에 맞게 문장을 완성하시오.

> **조건**
> • 사용할 표현: value, of, have a casual chat
> • 필요시 어형을 변형하거나 단어를 추가할 것

I've learned _____
over a cup of coffee from them.

07 윗글의 밑줄 친 우리말 (B)와 일치하도록 <보기>에 주어진 말을 배열하시오.

> **보기**
> my life / here / has / never / changed / in / thought / living / ways / I / possible

_____

_____

08 윗글의 내용과 일치하는 것은?

① 필자는 개인적인 문제를 노인들과 공유한다.
② 필자는 일 년 이내에 Humanitas를 떠날 계획이다.
③ 필자는 노인들이 가르쳐 줄 수 있는 모든 것을 이미 배웠다고 생각한다.
④ 필자는 노인들이 할 수 없는 것들에 대해 계속 안타까움을 느끼고 있다.
⑤ 필자는 노인들과의 세대 차이를 극복하는 데는 한계가 있다고 생각한다.

[09~10] 다음 글을 읽고, 물음에 답하시오.

My name is Helena Smit, and I am 93 years old. I have been living at Humanitas for the past 15 years, so I remember when we were first informed that we would have young people as neighbors. Believe me, not everyone was happy about it! But that quickly changed once they moved in. The students here are energetic, friendly, and caring. They make us ⓐ laugh and create a joyful mood.

Humanitas was already a decent place ⓑ live before the students arrived, but it has become a lot more fun since they moved in. Recently, the students held a pajama party and invited us to join them. They taught us how to play some new games, and we all had a great time. It was like we were in our 20s again.

I sometimes hear loud music from my young next-door neighbor's apartment, but that is okay. It's a small matter ⓒ compare to what they've brought to our lives. I'm grateful every day that they have become part of our community.

09 윗글의 밑줄 친 ⓐ~ⓒ를 알맞은 형태로 바꿔 쓰시오. (필요시 단어를 추가하고, 변형이 필요 없는 경우 그대로 쓸 것)

ⓐ _____

ⓑ _____

ⓒ _____

10 윗글의 내용과 일치하는 것은?

① Helena Smit는 93세에 Humanitas에 입주했다.

② Humanitas는 입주 후 15년 동안 거주할 수 있다.

③ 처음 젊은이들이 이웃으로 온다고 했을 때 모두가 좋아했다.

④ 학생들이 들어온 후, 분위기가 밝아지고 재미있어졌다.

⑤ Helena Smit가 가장 싫어한 것은 학생들이 들려주는 큰 음악소리였다.

[11~12] 다음 글을 읽고, 물음에 답하시오.

Speaking of my young neighbor, she has been here for more than two years now. Last year, she went through a difficult time of grief after she lost her father, so I did what came naturally. I stayed with her, held her hands when she cried, and listened to what she said. She later told me that I was a great comfort during that difficult time, which made me feel very good. It always feels nice to be reminded that I'm still capable of doing things for others.

I am nearly 100 years old, and I have bad knees. I understand that my knees aren't going to get any better. There is nothing much the doctors can do about the pain. But having young, vibrant people around helps me forget about the pain and enjoy my life!

11 다음 영어 뜻풀이에 해당하는 단어를 윗글에서 찾아 쓰시오.

a feeling of encouragement and support

→ _____

12 윗글의 밑줄 친 that difficult time이 의미하는 바를 우리말로 쓰시오. (30자 이내)

_____

13 다음 글의 밑줄 친 우리말 (A), (B)를 각각 3단어의 영어로 쓰시오.

To whom it may concern,
I recently purchased a computer from your store, and I am disappointed with its quality. I don't know (A) 무엇을 해야 할지, as it makes too much noise and the screen keeps turning off. Also, some of my data was lost, and I have no idea (B) 어떻게 복구해야 할지 it. Please let me know where to get it fixed.
Thank you,
Ryan Adams

(A) _____   (B) _____

On a tough day, Amy went inside a café for some coffee. After picking up her order, 그녀는 누군가에 의해 컵에 쓰인 메시지를 발견했다: "You make the world a better place." That unexpected warm gesture from a stranger deeply moved her. She said, "That little thing made the rest of my day."

People who perform a random act of kindness tend to underestimate its power. However, the recipients consider the gesture to be meaningful because they appreciate the fact that someone did something nice for them. So try to do one small act of kindness every day. If you are not sure how to start, begin with a smile. It is universal and costs nothing! Smile and greet people who you meet warmly and see their faces turn bright with your small gesture of kindness!

14 윗글의 주제로 가장 적절한 것은?

① appropriate ways to express gratitude
② useful tips for writing inspiring messages
③ the power of random acts of kindness
④ the surprising effect of a cup of coffee
⑤ how friendly service makes customers happy

15 윗글의 밑줄 친 우리말과 일치하도록 보기 에 주어진 단어를 배열하여 문장을 완성하시오.

보기

written / noticed / a message / on / she / the cup

→ After picking up her order, _____
_____ by someone:

April 28 is a special day. It's Pay It Forward Day, a worldwide celebration of kindness. You don't need to wear special clothes or eat special food on this day. All you need to do is be kind to other people! This day was inspired by a 1999 novel by Catherine Ryan Hyde called *Pay It Forward*. Pay It Forward Day started in Australia in 2007, and it has now spread to over 80 countries. It is a day for people to do acts of kindness for others so that the recipients can keep passing them on. It sends the message that one person's small act of kindness can create a chain reaction of good deeds. Let's think about what we can do on Pay It Forward Day. How about volunteering at a local charity? We can also say nice things about someone or pay for someone's cup of coffee. The possibilities are endless! And here's the most important part. We don't need to wait until April 28 to do any of these things. Small acts of kindness are appropriate and meaningful on any day!

16 윗글의 밑줄 친 recipients가 의미하는 바를 구체적으로 쓰시오.

_____

17 Pay It Forward Day에 할 수 있는 친절한 행동의 예로 윗글에서 언급되지 않은 것을 모두 고르면?

① eating special food
② volunteering at a local charity
③ saying nice things about someone
④ wearing special clothes
⑤ paying for someone's cup of coffee

[01~02] 다음 글을 읽고, 물음에 답하시오.

Humanitas is ①a yellow brick house located in the city of Deventer, the Netherlands. It is a care center ②that houses more than 160 elderly residents who require assistance. Along with its supportive environment, Humanitas offers something unusual: young neighbors. At Humanitas, elderly residents ③share their living space with university students.

This unique "intergenerational living" project began in 2012, after budget cuts ④reduced the amount of money care homes in the Netherlands received. This funding reduction ⑤led to the loss of many essential elderly care programs, including social, educational, and counseling services.

01 다음 영어 뜻풀이에 해당하는 단어를 윗글에서 찾아 쓰시오.

the amount of money that is available for or assigned to a certain purpose

→ _____

02 윗글의 밑줄 친 ①~⑤ 중, 잘못 설명한 것은?

① a yellow brick house가 주어이고 located가 동사이다.
② that 이하는 a care center를 수식하는 주격 관계대명사절이다.
③ share A with B는 'A를 B와 공유하다'라는 의미이다.
④ the amount of ~는 '~의 양'이라는 의미로 셀 수 없는 명사의 양을 나타내는 표현이다.
⑤ lead to는 '~으로 이어지다'라는 뜻이다.

[03~04] 다음 글을 읽고, 물음에 답하시오.

Humanitas needed to seek an affordable solution to fill the gap left by the removal of these services. Since the building had numerous empty rooms available, the director decided to offer local university students free _____ in return for spending time with the elderly residents. Many students were struggling to afford the area's high rents, so the proposal was a true win-win situation. Now, let's hear more about this intriguing place from two of the residents.

03 윗글의 빈칸에 들어갈 말로 가장 적절한 것은?

① meals   ② advice   ③ books
④ money   ⑤ accommodations

04 윗글의 주제로 가장 적절한 것은?

① 빈 방을 활용한 세대 간 상생 프로그램
② 노인 복지 시설의 재정 확보 방법
③ 대학생을 위한 저렴한 주거 공간 제공
④ 지역 사회의 자원봉사 활성화 방안
⑤ 지역 대학생들의 학업 성취도 향상 방안

05 자연스러운 대화가 되도록 (A)~(D)를 배열하시오.

That was an exciting game, wasn't it?
(A) Yeah, it's a mess. I wish people had been more considerate and cleaned up after themselves.
(B) Yes, it really was. But it's disappointing to see all this trash left behind at the stadium.
(C) Why don't we help out? Let's pick up some trash before we head to the subway station.
(D) Sure. I will go and get some bags.

[06~07] 다음 글을 읽고, 물음에 답하시오.

Hi! My name is Jacob Jansen, and I've been living at Humanitas ① for over two years. I've really enjoyed my time here. As a live-in student, I'm required to spend ② at least 30 hours per month with my elderly neighbors ③ in exchange for free accommodations. In reality, however, we spend a lot more time together than that. Sometimes I teach them things, such as ④ how to use social media, and other times I just ⑤ hang out with them. We have meals together, play games, and go shopping.

06 윗글의 밑줄 친 ①~⑤ 중, 우리말 해석이 바르지 <u>않은</u> 것은?

① 2년이 넘는 동안
② 한 달에 많아야 30시간
③ 무료 거처에 대한 대가로
④ 소셜 미디어를 사용하는 법
⑤ 그들과 시간을 보내다

07 윗글의 밑줄 친 As와 쓰임이 같은 것끼리 묶은 것은?

ⓐ As technology advances, our lives become easier.
ⓑ As I entered the room, everyone turned to look at me.
ⓒ Lucas was chosen as the team captain.
ⓓ As the weather was bad, the flight was delayed.
ⓔ Ms. Davis served as a mentor to many young students.

① ⓐ, ⓑ   ② ⓐ, ⓒ   ③ ⓑ, ⓒ, ⓓ
④ ⓒ, ⓔ   ⑤ ⓒ, ⓓ, ⓔ

08 다음 글의 빈칸에 들어갈 말로 가장 적절한 것은?

There are currently six students living at Humanitas, with a long waiting list of others hoping to be offered a spot. Humanitas is a great example of how people of different ages can help each other and share their lives with one another. The older residents gain a more youthful perspective on life, _____ the younger residents receive valuable life lessons. More and more care homes around Europe are now trying intergenerational living, bringing the young and old together in harmony.

① but   ② if   ③ while
④ because   ⑤ although

09 다음 편지를 쓴 목적으로 가장 적절한 것은?

Dear Hyerin,
I hope you are doing well. I want to thank you for helping me make new friends this year. As I am a shy and quiet person, I usually find it difficult to introduce myself to new classmates at the beginning of every semester. Thankfully, you approached me and asked me to hang out with some of your friends after school. With your help, I was able to easily adapt to the new environment and make more connections with other students. I truly appreciate what you did for me, and I'm so glad to have an amazing friend like you! Thank you again, and please feel free to text or call me anytime!
Best regards,
Taemin

① to suggest a new activity
② to thank a friend for their help
③ to invite a friend to a party
④ to apologize for being shy
⑤ to ask for advice on making friends

[10~11] 다음 글을 읽고, 물음에 답하시오.

Humanitas doesn't feel like a care home to me. Instead, I consider it a community that I am a part of. Every time I come home, I tell my neighbors about my day. When I have a problem, they always have useful advice to share. (A) With / Without so much experience gathered over a lifetime, they possess knowledge that I have yet to acquire. They also teach me lots of little but important things, often without ①realizing it. For example, I've learned the (B) plan / value of having a casual chat over a cup of coffee from them. It's a really great way ②to take a break from rushing around all the time.

I ③used to feel (C) sorry / disappointed for the elderly because I focused only on the things they *can't* do. When I look at them now, however, I see all the things they *can* do. Obviously, Humanitas provides me with ④much more than a free place to stay. I've made deep, meaningful friendships that I'll never forget here.

I intend to stay at Humanitas for ⑤at least one more year. Living here has changed my life in ways I never thought possible, and I'm really grateful for this transformative experience. I have learned so much from my neighbors already, but I'm sure there is still a lot more that they can teach me.

10 (A), (B), (C)의 각 네모 안에서 문맥에 맞는 낱말로 가장 적절한 것은?

	(A)		(B)		(C)
①	With	…	plan	…	sorry
②	Without	…	value	…	sorry
③	With	…	value	…	disappointed
④	Without	…	plan	…	disappointed
⑤	With	…	value	…	sorry

11 윗글의 밑줄 친 ①~⑤ 중, 설명이 잘못된 것은?

① 전치사 without의 목적어 역할을 하는 동명사이다.
② way를 수식하는 형용사적 용법의 to부정사이다.
③ '~하는 데 익숙하다'라는 의미의 관용 표현이다.
④ much는 비교급 more를 수식하는 부사이다.
⑤ '적어도, 최소한'이라는 의미의 관용 표현이다.

[12~13] 다음 대화를 읽고, 물음에 답하시오.

A It is important to follow proper etiquette in public places.
B You're right. It is annoying when people don't.
A Speaking of etiquette, what rules should we keep in mind while using the subway?
B We need to wait for passengers to exit before entering the train car.
A I agree. What else should we do to show consideration for others?
B We should make sure we don't sit in _____ seats reserved for certain people.
A Oh, that's also important. We should respect others by following those rules.

12 위 대화의 빈칸에 들어갈 말로 가장 적절한 것은?

① aisle   ② corner   ③ window
④ priority   ⑤ front

13 위 대화에서 지하철 에티켓으로 언급된 것 두 가지를 우리말로 쓰시오.

(1) _____

(2) _____

My name is Helena Smit, and I am 93 years old. I have been living at Humanitas for the past 15 years, so ① I remember when we were first informed that we would have young people as neighbors. Believe me, not everyone was happy about it! But that quickly changed once they moved in. The students here are energetic, friendly, and caring. ② They make us laugh and create a joyful mood.

Humanitas was already a decent place to live before the students arrived, but ③ it has become a lot more fun since they moved in. Recently, the students held a pajama party and invited us to join them. ④ They taught us how we play some new games, and we all had a great time. It was like we were in our 20s again.

I sometimes hear loud music from my young next-door neighbor's apartment, but that is okay. ⑤ It's a small matter compared to what they've brought to our lives. I'm grateful every day that they have become part of our community.

14 윗글의 밑줄 친 ①~⑤ 중, 어법상 틀린 문장을 찾아 바르게 고쳐 쓰시오.

_____ → _____

_____

15 윗글의 내용과 일치하지 <u>않는</u> 것은?

① Helena는 15년 동안 Humanitas에 살고 있다.
② 학생들은 웃음을 주고 즐거운 분위기를 만든다.
③ 학생들이 오기 전에도 Humanitas는 살기 좋은 곳이었다.
④ 학생들은 Helena Smit에게 새로운 게임을 어떻게 하는지 가르쳐 주었다.
⑤ Helena Smit은 학생들이 시끄러운 음악을 틀어 불편하다고 생각한다.

(A) Speaking / Spoken of my young neighbor, she has been here for more than two years now. Last year, she went through a difficult time of grief after she lost her father, so I did what came naturally. I stayed with her, held her hands when she cried, and listened to what she said. She later told me that I was a great comfort during that difficult time, (B) that / which made me feel very good. It always feels nice to be reminded that I'm still capable of doing things for others.

I am nearly 100 years old, and I have bad knees. I understand that my knees aren't going to get any better. There is nothing much the doctors can do about the pain. But having young, vibrant people around (C) help / helps me forget about the pain and enjoy my life!

16 윗글에 드러난 'I'의 성격으로 적절한 것은?

① shy　　　　② selfish　　　③ generous
④ energetic　　⑤ impersonal

17 (A), (B), (C)의 각 네모 안에서 어법에 맞는 표현으로 가장 적절한 것은?

	(A)		(B)		(C)
①	Spoken	…	that	…	helps
②	Speaking	…	that	…	helps
③	Speaking	…	which	…	help
④	Speaking	…	which	…	helps
⑤	Spoken	…	which	…	help

Humanitas needed to seek an affordable solution to fill the gap left by the removal of these services. Since the building had numerous empty rooms available, the director decided to offer local university students free accommodations in return for spending time with the elderly residents. Many students were struggling to afford the area's high rents, so the proposal was a true win-win situation. Now, let's hear more about this intriguing place from two of the residents.

[01~02] 다음 글을 읽고, 물음에 답하시오.

Humanitas is a yellow brick house (A) locating / located in the city of Deventer, the Netherlands. It is a care center that houses more than 160 elderly residents (B) who / which require assistance. Along with its supportive environment, Humanitas offers something unusual: young neighbors. At Humanitas, elderly residents share their living space with university students.

This unique "intergenerational living" project began in 2012, after budget cuts reduced the (C) number / amount of money care homes in the Netherlands received. This funding reduction led to the loss of many essential elderly care programs, including social, educational, and counseling services.

03 윗글의 다음에 이어질 내용으로 가장 적절한 것은?

① 대학생들이 주거 비용 부담으로 겪는 어려움의 실례
② Humanitas의 서비스 축소가 가져온 여파
③ Humanitas의 변화된 주거 환경에 대한 주거민의 소회
④ 노인들과 시간을 보낼 때 주의해야 할 점
⑤ Humanitas의 변화를 계획한 관리자와의 인터뷰

01 (A), (B), (C)의 각 네모 안에서 어법에 맞는 표현으로 가장 적절한 것은?

	(A)	(B)	(C)
①	locating	… who	… amount
②	located	… who	… amount
③	located	… who	… number
④	located	… which	… amount
⑤	locating	… which	… number

04 윗글의 내용과 일치하도록 할 때, 빈칸에 들어갈 말로 가장 적절한 것은?

Many students were struggling to afford the area's high rents, so the proposal was a true win-win situation. _____, both the elderly and the students benefited from this arrangement.

① In contrast   ② As a result
③ Nevertheless   ④ For example
⑤ On the other hand

02 윗글의 밑줄 친 "intergenerational living" project에 관한 설명으로 내용과 일치하지 <u>않는</u> 것은?

① 노인들이 대학생들과 생활 공간을 공유하는 프로그램이다.
② 세대 간의 이해와 소통을 위해 마련된 프로그램이다.
③ 2012년에 시작된 프로젝트이다.
④ 요양원이 받았던 예산 삭감을 계기로 시작되었다.
⑤ 네덜란드 전역의 모든 요양원에서 시행되고 있다.

[05~06] 다음 글을 읽고, 물음에 답하시오.

Hi! My name is Jacob Jansen, and I ① have been lived at Humanitas for over two years. I've really enjoyed my time here. As a live-in student, I'm required ② to spend at least 30 hours per month with my elderly neighbors in exchange for free accommodations. In reality, however, we spend ③ a lot more time together than that. Sometimes I teach them things, such as ④ how to use social media, and other times I just hang out with them. We have meals together, play games, and ⑤ go shopping.

05 윗글의 밑줄 친 ①~⑤ 중, 어법상 틀린 것은?

①   ②   ③   ④   ⑤

06 Jacob Jansen에 관한 설명으로 바르지 않은 것은?

① 2년 넘게 Humanitas에서 지내고 있다.
② 노인 이웃들과 한 달에 최소 30시간을 보내야 한다.
③ 실제로는 정해진 시간보다 훨씬 더 많은 시간을 함께 보낸다.
④ Humanitas에서 무료 숙소를 제공받고 있다.
⑤ 노인들에게 소셜 미디어 사용법을 배우고 있다.

[07~09] 다음 글을 읽고, 물음에 답하시오.

(A) I used to ① feeling sorry for the elderly because I focused only on the things they *can't* do. When I look at them now, however, I see all the things they *can* do. Obviously, Humanitas provides me with much more than a free place to stay. I've made deep, meaningful friendships that I'll never forget here.

(B) I intend to stay at Humanitas for at least one more year. ② Living here has changed my life in ways I never thought possible, and I'm really grateful for this transformative experience. I have learned so much from my neighbors already, but I'm sure there is still a lot more that they can teach me.

(C) Humanitas doesn't feel like a care home to me. Instead, I consider it a community that I am a part of. Every time I come home, I tell my neighbors about my day. When I have a problem, they always have useful advice to share. With so much experience _____ over a lifetime, they possess knowledge that I have yet to acquire. They also teach me lots of little but important things, often without ③ realizing it. For example, I've learned the value of ④ having a casual chat over a cup of coffee from them. It's a really great way to take a break from ⑤ rushing around all the time.

07 윗글의 빈칸에 들어갈 말로 가장 적절한 것은?

① wasted   ② gathered   ③ ignored
④ divided   ⑤ shared

08 윗글의 밑줄 친 ①~⑤ 중, 어법상 틀린 것은?

①   ②   ③   ④   ⑤

09 자연스러운 흐름이 되도록 (A)~(C)를 바르게 배열한 것은?

① (A) – (B) – (C)   ② (A) – (C) – (B)
③ (B) – (A) – (C)   ④ (B) – (C) – (A)
⑤ (C) – (A) – (B)

[10~11] 다음 글을 읽고, 물음에 답하시오.

My name is Helena Smit, and I am 93 years old. (①) I have been living at Humanitas for the past 15 years, so I remember when we were first informed that we would have young people as neighbors. (②) But that quickly changed once they moved in. (③) The students here are energetic, friendly, and caring. (④) They make us laugh and create a joyful mood. (⑤)

Humanitas was already a decent place to live before the students arrived, but it has become (A) a lot / a lot of more fun since they moved in. Recently, the students held a pajama party and invited us to join them. They taught us (B) what / how to play some new games, and we all had a great time. It was like we were in our 20s again.

I sometimes hear loud music from my young next-door neighbor's apartment, but that is okay. It's a small matter compared to (C) that / what they've brought to our lives. I'm grateful every day that they have become part of our community.

10 글의 흐름으로 보아, 주어진 문장이 들어가기에 가장 적절한 곳은?

Believe me, not everyone was happy about it!

①   ②   ③   ④   ⑤

11 (A), (B), (C)의 각 네모 안에서 어법에 맞는 표현으로 가장 적절한 것은?

	(A)	(B)	(C)
①	a lot	what	that
②	a lot	how	that
③	a lot of	how	what
④	a lot	how	what
⑤	a lot of	what	that

[12~13] 다음 글을 읽고, 물음에 답하시오.

Speaking of my young neighbor, she has been here for more than two years now. Last year, she went through a difficult time of _____ after she lost her father, so I did what came naturally. I stayed with her, held her hands when she cried, and listened to what she said. She later told me that I was a great (A) comfort / conflict during that difficult time, which made me feel very good. It always feels nice to be reminded that I'm still (B) careful / capable of doing things for others.

I am nearly 100 years old, and I have bad knees. I understand that my knees aren't going to get any better. There is nothing much the doctors can do about the pain. But having young, (C) vibrant / violent people around helps me forget about the pain and enjoy my life!

12 윗글의 빈칸에 들어갈 말로 가장 적절한 것은?

① wonder   ② grief   ③ relief
④ excitement   ⑤ disappointment

13 (A), (B), (C)의 각 네모 안에서 문맥에 맞는 낱말로 가장 적절한 것은?

	(A)	(B)	(C)
①	comfort	capable	vibrant
②	comfort	careful	vibrant
③	comfort	capable	violent
④	conflict	capable	vibrant
⑤	conflict	careful	violent

Dear Hyerin,

I hope you are doing well. I want to thank you for helping me make new friends this year. As I am a shy and quiet person, I usually find it difficult to introduce myself to new classmates at the beginning of every semester. Thankfully, you approached me and asked me to hang out with some of your friends after school. With your help, I was able to easily adapt to the new environment and make more connections with other students. I truly appreciate what you did for me, and I'm so glad to have an amazing friend like you! Thank you again, and please feel free to text or call me anytime!

Best regards,

Taemin

14 윗글에서 태민이 혜린이에 대해 느끼는 감정으로 가장 적절한 것은?

① worried ② annoyed ③ indifferent
④ grateful ⑤ disappointed

15 윗글의 요지로 가장 적절한 것은?

① Being quiet is better than being outgoing.
② Making new friends is always easy.
③ It is important to do activities after school.
④ Asking for help is important in school.
⑤ A friend's kindness can help someone overcome shyness.

Hello, everyone. I'm Kevin Lowell, and I'm here to give you a small life lesson today. Many of us often hesitate to perform acts of kindness. Perhaps that is because we don't realize how much acts of kindness are appreciated by others. The result of an interesting experiment recently revealed this to be true. At an ice rink in Chicago on a cold day, researchers handed ①participants a cup of hot chocolate. They were told to keep it for themselves or give it to a stranger. Those who chose to give it to a stranger were then asked to ②rate on a scale of one to ten how much they thought their act of kindness was appreciated. Surprisingly, when the ③recipients of the hot chocolate were asked to rate how much they actually appreciated the act, their scores were consistently ④lower than what the givers had expected. It turns out that people easily underestimate how much their acts of kindness are appreciated. So let's all acknowledge how ⑤powerful small acts of kindness can be and find ways to do more of them!

16 윗글의 제목으로 가장 적절한 것은?

① Acts of Kindness Are Key to Bringing People Together
② Why We Often Hesitate to Be Kind to Others
③ The Power of Kindness: Stronger Than You Think
④ What a Cup of Hot Chocolate Can Teach Us About Kindness
⑤ How Performing Acts of Kindness Affects Our Brain

17 윗글의 밑줄 친 ①~⑤ 중, 문맥상 적절하지 <u>않은</u> 것은?

① ② ③ ④ ⑤

01 다음 글의 밑줄 친 문장에서 어법상 틀린 부분을 두 군데 찾아 바르게 고쳐 쓰시오.

> Humanitas is a yellow brick house located in the city of Deventer, the Netherlands. It is a care center that house more than 160 elderly residents which require assistance. Along with its supportive environment, Humanitas offers something unusual: young neighbors. At Humanitas, elderly residents share their living space with university students.

_____

_____

02 다음을 읽고, 노인 세대와 함께 사는 것의 장단점을 구분하여 해당하는 칸에 기호를 쓰시오.

> ⓐ We can learn from their wisdom and life experience.
> ⓑ Having different communication styles can sometimes lead to misunderstandings.
> ⓒ It can be hard to manage differences in lifestyle and values.
> ⓓ We can get emotional support while living with them.

Living Together with Older People	
(1) 장점	(2) 단점

03 다음 빈칸에 들어갈 말로 알맞은 것을 보기 에서 골라 쓰시오.

> 보기
> in exchange for   hang out with
> go through   rush around

(1) Lisa는 자신의 꿈을 이루기 위해 많은 어려움을 겪어야 했다.
   → Lisa had to _____ a lot of challenges to achieve her dreams.

(2) 그들은 약간의 돈을 받는 대가로 설거지를 했다.
   → They did the dishes _____ a small amount of money.

(3) Tim은 정말 인기가 많았고, 모든 사람이 그와 함께 시간을 보내고 싶어 했다.
   → Tim was really popular, and everyone wanted to _____ him.

(4) 그녀는 아이들을 돌보느라 하루 종일 분주하게 뛰어다니곤 했다.
   → She used to _____ all day taking care of her children.

[04~05] 다음 글을 읽고, 물음에 답하시오.

> Humanitas doesn't feel like a care home to me. Instead, I consider it a community that I am a part of. Every time I come home, I tell my neighbors about my day. When I have a problem, they always have useful advice to share. (1) (so much / with / gathered / experience / over a lifetime), they possess knowledge that I have yet to acquire. They also teach me lots of little but important things, often without realizing it. For example, I've learned (2) (a casual chat / of / the value / over / having / a cup of coffee) from them. 그것은 항상 분주하게 돌아다니던 것에서 벗어나 잠시 휴식을 취할 수 있는 정말 좋은 방법이에요.

04 윗글의 (1), (2)에 주어진 단어를 바르게 배열하시오.

(1) _____

(2) _____

05 윗글의 밑줄 친 우리말과 일치하도록 조건에 맞게 문장을 완성하시오.

> 조건
> • 사용할 표현: take a break, rush around, all the time
> • 필요시 단어를 추가하거나 어형을 변형할 것

It's a really great way _____
_____.

06 다음 글을 읽고, 노인들에 대한 필자의 생각이 어떻게 변화했는지 쓰시오.

> I used to feel sorry for the elderly because I focused only on the things they *can't* do. When I look at them now, however, I see all the things they *can* do. Obviously, Humanitas provides me with much more than a free place to stay. I've made deep, meaningful friendships that I'll never forget here.
>
> I intend to stay at Humanitas for at least one more year. Living here has changed my life in ways I never thought possible, and I'm really grateful for this transformative experience. I have learned so much from my neighbors already, but I'm sure there is still a lot more that they can teach me.

_____

_____

07 다음 글의 빈칸에 공통으로 들어갈 말을 주어진 단어의 형태를 바꿔 쓰시오. (복수형으로 쓸 것)

> There are currently six students living at Humanitas, with a long waiting list of others hoping to be offered a spot. Humanitas is a great example of how people of different ages can help each other and share their lives with one another. The older _____ gain a more youthful perspective on life, while the younger _____ receive valuable life lessons.

reside → _____

[08~09] 다음 글을 읽고, 물음에 답하시오.

> My name is Helena Smit, and I am 93 years old. I have been living at Humanitas ___(A)___ the past 15 years, so I remember when we were first informed that we would have young people ___(B)___ neighbors. Believe me, not everyone was happy ___(C)___ it! But that quickly changed once they moved in. The students here are energetic, friendly, and caring. (1) They make us to laugh and create a joyful mood.
>
> Humanitas was already a decent place to live before the students arrived, but it has become a lot more fun since they moved in. Recently, the students held a pajama party and invited us to join them. (2) They taught us how to playing some new games, and we all had a great time. It was like we were ___(D)___ our 20s again.

08 윗글의 빈칸 (A)~(D)에 들어갈 전치사로 알맞은 것을 보기에서 찾아 쓰시오.

> 보기
> as   in   of   from   for   about

(A) _____   (B) _____

(C) _____   (D) _____

09 윗글의 밑줄 친 (1), (2)에서 어법상 틀린 부분을 찾아 바르게 고쳐 쓰시오.

(1) _____

(2) _____

[10~11] 다음 글을 읽고, 물음에 답하시오.

①Speaking of my young neighbor, she has been here for more than two years now. Last year, she went through a difficult time of grief after she lost her father, so ②I did what came naturally. I stayed with her, held her hands when she cried, and listened to what she said. She later told me that I was a great comfort during that difficult time, ③which made me to feel very good. ④It always feels nice to be reminded that I'm still capable of doing things for others.

I am nearly 100 years old, and I have bad knees. I understand that my knees aren't going to get any better. There is nothing much the doctors can do about the pain. ⑤But having young, vibrant people around help me forget about the pain and enjoy my life!

10 다음 영어 뜻풀이에 해당하는 단어를 윗글에서 찾아 쓰시오.

(1) _____ : intense sorrow caused by the loss of someone

(2) _____ : a feeling of encouragement and support

(3) _____ : full of energy and life

11 윗글의 밑줄 친 ①~⑤ 중, 어법상 틀린 것을 두 개 찾아 바르게 고쳐 쓰고 이유를 쓰시오.

번호	고친 것	이유

[12~13] 다음 글을 읽고, 물음에 답하시오.

April 28 is a special day. It's Pay It Forward Day, a worldwide celebration of kindness. You don't need to wear special clothes or eat special food on this day. All you need to do is be kind to other people! This day was inspired by a 1999 novel by Catherine Ryan Hyde called *Pay It Forward*. Pay It Forward Day started in Australia in 2007, and it has now spread to over 80 countries. It is a day for people to do acts of kindness for others so that the recipients can keep passing them on. It sends the message that one person's small act of kindness can create a chain reaction of good deeds. Let's think about what we can do on Pay It Forward Day. How about volunteering at a local charity? We can also say nice things about someone or pay for someone's cup of coffee. The possibilities are endless! And here's the most important part. We don't need to wait until April 28 to do any of these things. Small acts of kindness are appropriate and meaningful on any day!

12 윗글의 밑줄 친 a chain reaction이 의미하는 바를 우리말로 쓰시오. (30자 이내)

_____

13 Pay It Forward Day에 사람들이 할 수 있는 구체적인 친절의 예시를 세 가지 찾아 우리말로 쓰시오.

(1)	
(2)	
(3)	

[01~02] 다음 글을 읽고, 물음에 답하시오.

Welcome to the exhibition! My name is Amy Martinez, and I will be your guide for today. Before we start the tour, I'd like to remind you of some rules you need to follow in the gallery. First, to prevent damage, please make sure _____. Second, please remember that you are not allowed to bring any food or drinks inside the gallery. Third, loud conversations and phone calls are not permitted. Please put your phone on silent mode so as not to disturb other visitors. It is important to maintain a peaceful and respectful environment. If you'd like to take pictures, you are welcome to do so. However, please keep some distance from the artworks so that there is enough room for everyone to appreciate them. All right, now let's start the tour. Follow me this way!

01 윗글의 목적으로 가장 적절한 것은?

① to explain the history of the gallery
② to remind visitors of the gallery's rules
③ to inform visitors of a temporary closure
④ to promote the new exhibition opening
⑤ to give information about the artworks on display

02 윗글의 빈칸에 들어갈 말로 가장 적절한 것은?

① you don't keep your belongings in your bag
② you don't talk with your friends
③ you don't touch any of the artworks
④ you don't speak rudely to others
⑤ you move the artworks to a better place

03 주어진 단어를 괄호 안의 지시대로 바꿔 쓰시오.

(1) use (형용사형) → _____
(2) explore (명사형) → _____
(3) remove (명사형) → _____
(4) harmful (반의어) → _____
(5) reside (사람을 나타내는 명사형) → _____
(6) value (형용사형) → _____
(7) propose (명사형) → _____
(8) participate (사람을 나타내는 명사형) → _____

04 다음 우리말과 일치하도록 보기 에서 알맞은 말을 골라 쓰시오.

보기	draw	generate	share
	pursue	possess	seek

(1) 우리는 현재 은행 산업에 대한 광범위한 지식을 가진 지원자들을 찾고 있다.
→ We are currently looking for applicants who _____ extensive knowledge of the banking industry.

(2) 노란색은 일반적으로 운전자들의 주의를 끌기 위해 경고 표지판에 사용된다.
→ The color yellow is typically used in warning signs to _____ the attention of drivers.

(3) 제조업자는 생산 문제에 대한 해결책을 계속해서 찾았다.
→ The manufacturer continued to _____ a solution to the production problem.

(4) 태양광과 바람은 우리가 전기를 생산하는 데 사용하는 재생 가능한 에너지 자원이다.
→ Sunlight and wind are renewable energy sources we use to _____ electricity.

[05~06] 다음 글을 읽고, 물음에 답하시오.

Good habits make our lives better. However, many people ①fail to form new habits because it takes time and effort. Fortunately, there is a trick to doing this quickly and easily. It's called "habit stacking." How do you do it? Start by ②identifying a habit you already have. Then simply "stack" a new habit on top of it. The basic formula is "After I do the ③current habit, I will do the new habit." Suppose you decide to start stretching every morning. Think about what you normally do in the morning. If you check your email after you wake up, that is your current habit. Therefore, your formula will be "After I check my email, I will stretch for five minutes." By doing this, you make your existing habit a ④trigger for your new habit. This works well because your current habits are already established. Add a new activity to your daily routine and see how ⑤difficult it is to turn that activity into a habit. Give habit stacking a try. If it works for you, keep adding more good habits to your life. You won't regret it!

05 윗글의 제목으로 가장 적절한 것은?

① 하루 일과를 기록하는 방법
② 새로운 습관을 만드는 데 드는 비용
③ 습관을 깨는 것이 어려운 이유
④ 좋은 습관을 형성하는 데 도움이 되는 방법
⑤ 아침에 이메일을 확인하는 습관의 문제점

06 윗글의 밑줄 친 ①~⑤ 중, 문맥상 낱말의 쓰임이 적절하지 않은 것은?

①   ②   ③   ④   ⑤

[07~08] 다음 글을 읽고, 물음에 답하시오.

Jacques Cousteau is a French ocean explorer, inventor, and filmmaker. He ①dedicated his life to exploring and documenting the wonders of the underwater world. As a young man, he ②dreamed of becoming a pilot, but then he broke both of his arms in a terrible car accident. As part of his physical therapy, Cousteau began swimming. He ③became intrigued by the mysteries of the ocean, and he wanted to explore further. However, the diving equipment available at that time was insufficient. Instead of giving up, Cousteau decided to create his own equipment. After a long series of failed attempts, he finally ④succeeded to develop a portable breathing device, which he called the "Aqua-Lung." Cousteau shared his underwater experiences with the world in a compelling documentary film released in 1956. It transformed people's perceptions of the ocean and promoted the need for marine conservation.

Cousteau's curiosity ⑤drove him to constantly challenge himself in new areas, and his passion enabled him to make the impossible a reality.

07 윗글의 밑줄 친 ①~⑤ 중, 어법상 틀린 것은?

①   ②   ③   ④   ⑤

08 Jacques Cousteau에 관한 설명으로 글의 내용과 일치하지 않는 것은?

① 프랑스의 해양 탐험가, 발명가이자 영화 제작자이다.
② 교통사고로 인해 다리 부상을 입었고 운동선수의 꿈을 포기했다.
③ 물리 치료로 시작한 수영을 통해 바다에 호기심을 가지게 되었다.
④ 오랜 실패 끝에 마침내 휴대용 호흡 기계를 개발했다.
⑤ 다큐멘터리 영화로 바다에 대한 사람들의 인식을 변화시켰고, 해양 보존의 필요성을 알렸다.

다음 중 영어 뜻풀이가 적절하지 <u>않은</u> 것을 고르시오.

09

① validity: the quality of correctness or being sound
② diagnose: to identify an illness or the cause of a problem
③ alert: without much thought
④ opportunity: a situation that makes it possible to do or achieve something
⑤ calculation: the process of finding an answer using mathematics

10

① investigate: to look further into something
② reliable: appropriate or rational
③ grief: intense sorrow caused by the loss of someone
④ resident: someone who lives somewhere permanently or for a long time
⑤ persistence: the quality that allows somebody to keep doing something even if it is difficult

[11~13] 다음 글을 읽고, 물음에 답하시오.

Kim Sang-jin was the first Korean animator to work for Walt Disney Animation Studios. Beyond the fact that he worked for a world-famous company, I admire him for pursuing his dream despite the difficulties he faced. From a young age, Kim was enthusiastic about drawing. _____(A)_____, his dream of studying art in college was disrupted when he was diagnosed with color vision deficiency during high school. Surprisingly, he didn't allow this misfortune to discourage him. _____(B)_____, he simply viewed his condition as a minor issue that could happen to anyone.

_____(C)_____ he graduated with a degree in economics, he searched for a job related to art that wouldn't involve working with colors. He found out that some animators work only in pencil, so he sent his portfolio to all the animation studios in Korea. One of them gave him an opportunity, and he was finally able to start his career. <u>His hard work and talent eventually led him to a position at Disney at the age of 37.</u>

11 윗글의 주제로 가장 적절한 것은?

① 애니메이터가 되기 위한 조건
② 색각 이상이 예술가의 진로에 미치는 영향
③ 디즈니 애니메이션의 발전 과정
④ 경제학 전공자의 미술계 진출
⑤ 역경을 극복하고 꿈을 이룬 애니메이터의 도전

12 윗글의 빈칸 (A), (B), (C)에 들어갈 말로 가장 적절한 것은?

	(A)	(B)	(C)
①	However	Instead	Although
②	Nevertheless	Meanwhile	Because
③	Therefore	For example	Since
④	Furthermore	Thus	After
⑤	Otherwise	Similarly	Unless

13 윗글의 밑줄 친 문장을 〈조건〉에 맞게 고쳐 쓰시오.

〈조건〉
• 「It was ~ that ....」 강조구문을 사용할 것
• 주어를 강조할 것

_____

_____

[14~15] 다음 글을 읽고, 물음에 답하시오.

We make about 35,000 decisions every day without realizing it, and it is (A) possible / impossible to make every one of these consciously. So it's quite reasonable and (B) effective / ineffective) for the brain to be a bit lazy sometimes. ⓐHave a lazy brain allows us to save energy for critical tasks that require our focus and attention. However, it is dangerous when this becomes a habit. If your brain ⓑwill become too reliant on System 1, it will not be able to apply System 2 when you confront a problem that requires intense concentration. System 2 is essential for exercising human intelligence, so the ⓒlittle you use it, the more likely you are to become a lazy thinker. Those who have an overly lazy brain frequently make errors and bad decisions. They can also develop a habit of ⓓaccept things to be true even though they have never been proven. Therefore, it can be (C) harmful / harmless to develop lazy brain habits.

14 윗글의 밑줄 친 ⓐ~ⓓ를 어법에 맞게 고쳐 쓰시오.

ⓐ Have → _____

ⓑ will become → _____

ⓒ little → _____

ⓓ accept → _____

15 (A), (B), (C)의 각 네모 안에서 문맥에 맞는 낱말로 가장 적절한 것은?

	(A)	(B)	(C)
①	possible	⋯ effective	⋯ harmful
②	possible	⋯ ineffective	⋯ harmless
③	impossible	⋯ effective	⋯ harmless
④	impossible	⋯ effective	⋯ harmful
⑤	impossible	⋯ ineffective	⋯ harmful

16 주어진 문장 다음에 이어질 글의 순서로 가장 적절한 것은?

My future goal is to become a veterinarian.

(A) After graduation, I would like to enroll in a veterinary school. I will study relevant subjects like medicine and surgery to gain valuable knowledge in this field.

(B) When I finally become a veterinarian, I will help animals that are brought to my clinic. I plan to keep studying and expanding my expertise.

(C) In my first year of high school, I regularly volunteered at an animal shelter. Through this experience, I discovered my passion for animals and their welfare.

① (A) – (B) – (C)   ② (A) – (C) – (B)
③ (B) – (A) – (C)   ④ (C) – (A) – (B)
⑤ (C) – (B) – (A)

17 다음 중 어법상 틀린 문장을 두 개 골라 바르게 고쳐 쓰고, 이유를 쓰시오.

ⓐ The smell of homemade bread was so nice that it made my mouth water.

ⓑ She asked me play badminton with her after breakfast.

ⓒ Some of the information on the website was proven wrong.

ⓓ The instruction sheet provides information about how to install the program.

ⓔ If you will leave earlier, you will be able to avoid the traffic.

ⓕ She has a high chance of winning the award due to her incredible performance.

(1) _____ : _____ → _____
틀린 이유: _____

(2) _____ : _____ → _____
틀린 이유: _____

18 다음 글의 ①~⑤ 중, 전체 흐름과 무관한 문장은?

Hi! My name is Jacob Jansen, and I've been living at Humanitas for over two years. I've really enjoyed my time here. ① As a live-in student, I'm required to spend at least 30 hours per month with my elderly neighbors in exchange for free accommodations. ② In reality, however, we spend a lot more time together than that. ③ Many students find it challenging to balance their studies with part-time jobs. ④ Sometimes I teach them things, such as how to use social media, and other times I just hang out with them. ⑤ We have meals together, play games, and go shopping.

①　　　②　　　③　　　④　　　⑤

19 다음 글의 밑줄 친 they가 가리키는 것으로 가장 적절한 것은?

Humanitas doesn't feel like a care home to me. Instead, I consider it a community that I am a part of. Every time I come home, I tell my neighbors about my day. When I have a problem, they always have useful advice to share. With so much experience gathered over a lifetime, they possess knowledge that I have yet to acquire. They also teach me lots of little but important things, often without realizing it. For example, I've learned the value of having a casual chat over a cup of coffee from them. It's a really great way to take a break from rushing around all the time.

① Jacob의 가족　　　② Humanitas의 직원들
③ Jacob의 이웃들　　　④ Jacob의 친구들
⑤ Humanitas에 사는 학생들

[20~21] 다음 글을 읽고, 물음에 답하시오.

System 2 is responsible for our reasoning and deeper decision-making processes. Our brains use this system when we compare the prices and ①features of products, check the validity of an argument, or encounter difficult questions like "238×79×451=?". It controls ②conscious mental activities when we need to focus or make careful choices. However, while System 2 is more ③reliable, its application requires time and effort. If you got the right answer to the notebook and pen question after taking a few seconds to ④reflect, then your brain used System 2 to check System 1's initial response. However, our brains tend to rely heavily on taking mental shortcuts with System 1. That is why it's common for people to answer the question ⑤correctly at first.

20 윗글의 밑줄 친 부분 중, 문맥상 낱말의 쓰임이 적절하지 않은 것은?

①　　　②　　　③　　　④　　　⑤

21 윗글의 어조로 가장 적절한 것은?

① creative and imaginative
② critical and logical
③ informative and explanatory
④ hopeful and optimistic
⑤ descriptive and narrative

[22~23] 다음 글을 읽고, 물음에 답하시오.

My name is Helena Smit, and I am 93 years old. I have been living at Humanitas for the past 15 years, so I remember when we were first informed that we would have young people as neighbors. Believe me, not everyone was happy about it! But that quickly changed once they moved in. The students here are energetic, friendly, and caring. They make us laugh and create a joyful mood.

Humanitas was already a decent place to live before the students arrived, but it has become a lot more fun since they moved in. Recently, the students held a pajama party and invited us to join them. They taught us how to play some new games, and we all had a great time. It was like we were in our 20s again.

22 윗글의 내용과 일치하도록 할 때, 빈칸에 들어갈 말로 가장 적절한 것은?

Thanks to her interactions with the students, Helena Smit felt that life at Humanitas became _____.

① lonelier
② more boring
③ more lively
④ more uncomfortable
⑤ more dangerous

23 윗글의 내용과 일치하지 <u>않는</u> 것은?

① Helena Smit는 Humanitas에 15년 동안 거주했다.
② 학생들이 처음 이사 왔을 때 모든 노인들이 기뻐했다.
③ 학생들은 노인들에게 새로운 게임을 가르쳐주었다.
④ 학생들과의 교류로 Humanitas의 분위기가 더 즐거워졌다.
⑤ 학생들이 파자마 파티를 열고 노인들을 초대했다.

[24~25] 다음 글을 읽고, 물음에 답하시오.

To "pay it forward" means to perform an act of kindness for someone after someone else has done something kind for you. For example, if a man who lives next door helps you (A) move / moving some heavy boxes, you can give him some cookies in return, or you can "pay it forward" by helping other neighbors in need.

In the movie *Pay It Forward*, based on the novel of the same name, a boy (B) naming / named Trevor comes up with an idea to change the world. He suggests doing a nice thing for three people and (C) asks / asking them to pay it forward to three others in need. In this way, a wave of kindness spreads, leading to a national "pay it forward" movement.

24 윗글의 제목으로 가장 적절한 것은?

① A Guide to Making New Friends
② How to Return a Favor Directly
③ The History of Kindness in Movies
④ The Power of *Paying It Forward*
⑤ Why Kindness Should Be Kept Secret

25 (A), (B), (C)의 각 네모 안에서 어법에 맞는 표현으로 가장 적절한 것은?

	(A)	(B)	(C)
①	move	naming	asks
②	moving	naming	asking
③	move	named	asks
④	moving	named	asking
⑤	move	named	asking

04

Spark Your Creativity

Functions

▶ 충고 구하기
Could you give me some advice on how to start?

▶ 제안하기
I suggest you start with something simple.

Structures

▶ **When viewed** normally, it is just an ordinary still life of vegetables in a bowl.

▶ By **doing so**, we are turning the ordinary into something extraordinary.

교과서 어휘

Words

□ extraordinary	형 비상한 (↔ ordinary 평범한)
□ instantly	부 즉시
□ divide	동 나누다
□ belief	명 믿음
□ object	명 물건
□ depict	동 묘사하다
□ standard	형 일반적인, 보통의
□ portrait	명 초상화
□ unconventional	형 색다른
□ striking	형 눈에 띄는
□ originality	명 독창성 (original 형 독창적인)
□ arrange	동 배열하다
□ mulberry	명 오디
□ representative	명 대표, 전형
□ signature	형 특징적인
□ composite	형 합성의
□ reversible	형 뒤집을 수 있는
□ flip	동 휙 뒤집다, 젖히다
□ adjustment	명 수정, 조정
□ examination	명 검사, 조사
□ interactive	형 상호작용을 하는
□ element	명 요소
□ visual	형 시각의
□ typical	형 보통의, 일반적인
□ potential	명 잠재력, 가능성
□ innovative	형 혁신적인
□ approach	명 접근법
□ collection	명 무리, 더미

□ clothesline	명 빨랫줄
□ witty	형 재치 있는, 익살맞은
□ amusing	형 재미있는
□ creation	명 창작물
□ playful	형 웃기는, 재미나는
□ illusion	명 환각, 착각
□ force	동 ～을 하게 만들다
□ confirm	동 확인하다
□ household	형 가정(용)의
□ surrealism	명 초현실주의
□ laundry	명 세탁물
□ clothespin	명 빨래집게
□ sweatshirt	명 운동복 상의
□ highlight	동 강조하다, 돋보이다
□ astonishing	형 정말 놀라운
□ edible	형 먹을 수 있는
□ respectively	부 (말한 순서대로) 각각
□ concept	명 발상
□ observation	명 관찰 (observe 동 관찰하다)
□ stare	동 빤히 쳐다보다
□ admit	동 인정[시인]하다
□ acceptable	형 용인되는
□ keen	형 예리한
□ exceptional	형 특출난
□ exclusive	형 한정적인, 독점적인
□ display	동 드러내다
□ adapt	동 조정하다
□ rearrange	동 재배열하다

Phrases

□ upside down	거꾸로
□ take a look at	～을 보다
□ come up with	(생각이) 떠오르다
□ nothing more than	～에 불과한

□ put together	만들다
□ belong to	～에 속하다
□ give a glance	힐끗 보다

교과서 어휘 익히기

❖ 다음 영어는 우리말로, 우리말은 영어로 쓰시오.

01 depict	동	
02 originality	명	
03 stare	동	
04 instantly	부	
05 unconventional	형	
06 witty	형	
07 highlight	동	
08 signature	형	
09 household	형	
10 confirm	동	
11 take a look at		
12 respectively	부	
13 display	동	
14 standard	형	
15 reversible	형	
16 adapt	동	
17 concept	명	
18 striking	형	
19 put together		
20 creation	명	
21 exceptional	형	
22 flip	동	
23 representative	명	
24 sweatshirt	명	
25 playful	형	

26 명 잠재력, 가능성		
27 형 혁신적인		
28 형 비상한		
29 명 초상화		
30 명 환각, 착각		
31 형 한정적인, 독점적인		
32 명 세탁물		
33 동 배열하다		
34 명 수정, 조정		
35 명 요소		
36 명 믿음		
37 형 먹을 수 있는		
38 형 시각의		
39 거꾸로		
40 형 상호작용을 하는		
41 명 관찰		
42 동 인정[시인]하다		
43 형 예리한		
44 형 용인되는		
45 ~에 속하다		
46 명 검사, 조사		
47 형 합성의		
48 명 초현실주의		
49 힐끗 보다		
50 명 접근법		

교과서 핵심 문법

POINT 1 부사절의 「주어 + be동사」 생략

예제	**Although tired**, they continued to work on the science project. = Although they were tired 비록 피곤했지만, 그들은 과학 프로젝트를 계속 준비했다.
교과서	**When viewed** normally, it is just an ordinary still life of vegetables in a bowl. = When it is viewed 정상적으로 보면 그것은 그릇에 담긴 채소를 그린 평범한 정물화일 뿐이다.

▶ 부사절의 주어가 <mark>주절의 주어와 같고 동사가 be동사일 때</mark> 「주어+be동사」를 생략할 수 있다.
▶ 이때 부사절에는 「접속사+분사」 또는 「접속사+형용사」만 남을 수 있다.

Study Point 🍊

1 시간을 나타내는 부사절

- While we were watching the documentary, we learned about ancient Chinese history.
  _{부사절의 주어 be동사   주절의 주어}
  → **While watching** the documentary, we learned about ancient Chinese history.

  다큐멘터리를 보며 우리는 고대 중국의 역사에 관해 알게 되었다.

- Sue finally felt calm and happy when she was left alone.
  _{주절의 주어   부사절의 주어 be동사}
  → Sue finally felt calm and happy **when left** alone.

  혼자 남겨지자 Sue는 마침내 고요하고 행복한 기분이 들었다.

2 조건, 양보를 나타내는 부사절

- You are not allowed to enter the room unless you are permitted.
  _{주절의 주어   부사절의 주어 be동사}
  → You are not allowed to enter the room **unless permitted**.

  허락을 받지 않았다면 당신은 그 방에 들어갈 수 없다.

- Though I was busy, I helped the old lady find her way to the station.
  _{부사절의 주어 be동사   주절의 주어}
  → **Though busy**, I helped the old lady find her way to the station.

  비록 바빴지만 나는 그 노부인이 역까지 가는 길을 찾는 걸 도와드렸다.

Q 다음 네모 안에서 어법상 알맞은 것을 고르시오.

1 While [read / reading] a detective novel, I tried to anticipate the criminal's next move.

2 [Though / Since] disappointed, Kevin tried his best until the final match.

3 When [asking / asked] about her whereabouts, her parents kept silent.

Check-up 🍑

01 다음 문장의 밑줄 친 부분을 보기 와 같이 바꿔 쓰시오.

> 보기 When he was asked the question, he posted his opinion on social media.
> → When asked the question, he posted his opinion on social media.

(1) Do not move your seat <u>unless you are given permission</u>.

→ Do not move your seat _____.

(2) <u>While he was young</u>, my uncle traveled around the world by himself.

→ _____, my uncle traveled around the world by himself.

(3) <u>Although they were exhausted</u>, the players practiced hard for the soccer game.

→ _____, the players practiced hard for the soccer game.

(4) The needle should be disposed of <u>once it is used</u>.

→ The needle should be disposed of _____.

02 다음 두 문장이 같은 뜻이 되도록 밑줄 친 부분을 보기 와 같이 바꿔 쓰시오.

> 보기 <u>Though poor</u>, Ted lived a happy life with his grandparents.
> → <u>Though he was poor</u>, Ted lived a happy life with his grandparents.

(1) <u>While walking</u> down the street, I saw my mother's car.

→ _____ down the street, I saw my mother's car.

(2) <u>If given a chance</u>, they would travel around the country.

→ _____, they would travel around the country.

(3) <u>Though uncertain</u> of the future, we tried to remain optimistic.

→ _____ of the future, we tried to remain optimistic.

(4) <u>Since feeling tired</u>, she decided not to attend the meeting.

→ _____, she decided not to attend the meeting.

03 (A), (B), (C)의 각 네모 안에서 어법에 맞는 표현을 고르시오. (교과서 103쪽)

> Welcome aboard, passengers. We kindly request that you pay attention to the following announcements. First, you must keep your seat belt fastened while (A) seating / seated . Second, for your safety, please cooperate with our flight attendants (B) when / though asked to do something. Our flight is expected to arrive in Chicago as (C) schedule / scheduled , in two hours. Enjoy your flight!

(A) _____   (B) _____   (C) _____

(**POINT 2**) 대동사 do를 이용한 표현

예제	When they were asked to help the animals, they **did so** without hesitating. = helped the animals 동물들을 도와달라고 요청받자, 그들은 망설이지 않고 그렇게 했다.
교과서	By **doing so**, we are turning the ordinary into something extraordinary. = using creativity 그렇게 함으로써 우리는 평범한 것을 비상한 것으로 바꾸고 있다.

▶ 일반동사를 대신하는 대동사 do와 '그렇게'라는 의미의 so가 쓰여 '그렇게 하다'라는 의미로 앞에 나온 표현의 반복을 피해 사용된다.
▶ 문장에서의 역할에 따라 do[does] so, doing so, done so 등의 다양한 형태로 쓰인다.

Study Point 🍊

1 대동사 do

일반동사의 반복을 피하기 위해 do를 대신 쓸 수 있다.

- My sister *plays basketball* better than I **do**. 내 여동생은 나보다 농구를 더 잘한다.
  = play basketball
- I really wanted to *learn* Spanish when young, so I **did** it. 나는 어려서 스페인어를 정말 배우고 싶어서 그렇게 했다.
  = learned

2 do so

대동사 do 뒤에 '그렇게'라는 의미의 부사 so를 함께 쓰면 일반동사와 그에 동반하는 목적어 또는 보어를 대신하는 역할을 한다.

- He was told to *add some cheese* to the soup, but he made the soup without **doing so**.
  = adding some cheese
  그는 수프에 치즈를 좀 넣으라고 들었지만, 그렇게 하지 않고 수프를 만들었다.

- My dad promised to *call me* as soon as he arrived at the airport. He must have forgotten to **do so**.
  = call me
  아빠는 공항에 도착하자마자 내게 전화하겠다고 약속했다. 그는 그렇게 하는 것을 잊었음이 틀림없다.

- Daisy *handed in the report on time* since she was supposed to **do so**.
  = hand in the report on time
  Daisy는 그렇게 하기로 되어 있었으므로 보고서를 제시간에 제출했다.

Q 다음 네모 안에서 어법상 알맞은 것을 고르시오.

1 Keep safety rules in mind. Do / Doing so will help you in an emergency.

2 We wanted to watch the baseball game on TV, but we couldn't do / did so.

3 When asked to tell the truth, he did so / such without hesitation.

Check-up 🍎

01 다음 문장의 밑줄 친 부분이 가리키는 것을 쓰시오.

(1) If you want to try on the clothes at the store, feel free to <u>do so</u>.

→ _____

(2) Why don't you book the hotel in advance? <u>Doing so</u> will save time and money.

→ _____

(3) We planned to build some birdhouses in the forest, and we <u>did so</u> last Sunday.

→ _____

(4) You should apply for a passport if you haven't <u>done so</u> yet.

→ _____

02 우리말과 일치하도록 괄호 안에 주어진 표현을 활용하여 문장을 완성하시오.

(1) Jake는 내게 코트를 입으라고 충고했지만, 나는 그렇게 하지 않았다. (do so)

→ Jake advised me to put on my coat, but _____.

(2) 매일 개를 산책시켜라. 그렇게 하지 않으면 개가 공격적으로 될 수 있다. (unless, do so)

→ Walk your dog every day. _____, it may become aggressive.

(3) 나는 엄마가 그렇게 해달라고 요청해서 그 노래를 틀었다. (request, do so)

→ I played the song because my mom _____.

(4) 영어 신문 기사를 읽어라. 그렇게 함으로써 당신의 영어 실력이 향상될 것이다. (by, do so)

→ Read English news articles. _____, your English skills will improve.

03 다음 글에서 밑줄 친 (A)와 (B)가 가리키는 것을 찾아 쓰시오. (교과서 103쪽)

> Basic Yoga for Beginners
> ⟨1⟩ Child's Pose
>   • Start by sitting on your knees. Then gently lean forward, lowering your upper body.
>   • Rest your forehead on the floor and relax your entire body. (A) <u>Doing so</u> will relieve any back pain you might have.
> ⟨2⟩ Tree Pose
>   • Stand tall with your feet together. Shift your weight onto your right leg and slowly lift your left foot off the ground.
>   • Maintain your balance. Pressing your standing foot firmly into the ground will help you (B) <u>do so</u>.

(A) _____

(B) _____

교과서 본문 분석

Seeing the Extraordinary in the Ordinary
평범한 것에서 비상한 것을 발견하기

01 Creativity. [When you hear this word], what instantly pops into your mind?
부사절 〈시간〉   pop into one's mind: 갑자기 떠오르다

창의력. 이 단어를 들었을 때 무엇이 즉시 당신의 마음에 떠오르는가?

02 You may think it is a quality [that only artists and writers possess]— some special talent [you are
(that)   목적격 관계대명사절   dash(—)로 부연 설명
either born with or without].
either A or B: A 또는 B 중 하나

당신은 그것이 예술가나 작가만이 가지고 있는 특성, 즉 타고나거나 타고나지 않는 어떤 특별한 재능이라고 생각할 수도 있다.

03 Many people accept the idea that we can be divided into two groups: those [who are creative] and
동격의 that   ~으로 나뉘어지다   주격 관계대명사절
those [who are not].
(creative)

많은 사람들이 우리가 창의적인 사람과 그렇지 않은 사람의 두 그룹으로 나뉠 수 있다는 생각을 받아들인다.

04 This common belief, however, is far from the truth.
전혀 ~이 아닌

그러나 이 일반적인 생각은 사실과 거리가 멀다.

05 Everyone has the ability [to be creative].
형용사적 용법

누구나 창의력을 발휘할 수 있는 능력을 갖추고 있다.

06 [Finding creativity inside yourself] just takes a little effort.
주어 (동명사구)   동사

내면에 있는 창의력을 발견하는 것에 약간의 노력이 필요할 뿐이다.

07 Some artists, for example, spark their creativity by looking closely at ordinary objects.
by v-ing: ~함으로써

예를 들어, 일부 예술가들은 평범한 사물을 자세히 관찰함으로써 창의력을 발휘한다.

08 They try to discover the beauty [hidden within these common objects] and then turn them into
과거분사구   병렬 구조   (to)   = these common objects
works of art.

그들은 이러한 평범한 사물 속에 숨겨진 아름다움을 발견하고 예술 작품으로 승화시키려고 노력한다.

Giuseppe Arcimboldo

09 Look at these two paintings.

이 두 그림을 보아라.

10 Believe it or not, they both depict the same person, Holy Roman Emperor Rudolf II.
믿거나 말거나, 믿기 힘들겠지만

믿기 어렵겠지만, 이 두 작품은 모두 같은 인물인 신성 로마 제국의 황제 루돌프 2세를 묘사한다.

11 The one [on the left] might look familiar, as it is a standard style of portrait [that you would see in
전치사구   ~ 때문에 (접속사)   목적격 관계대명사절
a gallery or an art book].

왼쪽에 있는 그림은 미술관이나 미술책에서 볼 수 있는 일반적인 스타일의 초상화이기 때문에 익숙해 보일 수도 있다.

12 However, the one [on the right], called *Vertumnus*, is very unconventional.
                                      〈삽입구〉

그렇지만 오른쪽에 있는 〈Vertumnus〉라는 그림은 매우 색다르다.

13 Created by a 16th-century Italian painter [named Giuseppe Arcimboldo], the painting shows
                                              과거분사구
striking creativity and originality.

Giuseppe Arcimboldo라는 16세기 이탈리아 화가가 그린 이 그림은 눈에 띄는 창의력과 독창성을 보여준다.

14 Fruits, flowers, and vegetables are arranged like the pieces of a puzzle to create a human head.
                                        수동태   부사적 용법 〈목적〉

과일, 꽃, 그리고 채소가 사람의 머리를 만들기 위해 퍼즐 조각처럼 배열되어 있다.

15 주어 (복수)   주어 (복수)
A cherry and a mulberry become the dark eyes, while an apple and a peach act as the pink cheeks.
                          동사   ~과 동시에 (접속사)   동사

체리와 오디는 짙은 눈이 되고 사과와 복숭아는 분홍빛 뺨이 된다.

16 This painting is representative of the artist's signature style of "composite portraits."

이 그림은 작가의 특징적인 스타일인 '합성 초상화'를 대표하는 작품이다.

17 He used plants, animals, and other objects to create many other portraits like this.
                                          부사적 용법 〈목적〉   = Vertumnus

그는 이와 같은 많은 초상화를 만들기 위해 식물, 동물, 그리고 다른 사물들을 활용했다.

18 Another good example of Arcimboldo's unique creativity can be found in *The Gardener*, [one of
his "reversible" paintings].
수동태   =
뒤집을 수 있는

Arcimboldo의 독특한 창의력의 또 다른 좋은 예는 그의 '뒤집을 수 있는' 그림 중 하나인 〈The Gardener〉에서 발견할 수 있다.

19 (it is)
[When viewed normally,] it is just an ordinary still life of vegetables in a bowl.
정물화

정상적으로 보면 그것은 그릇에 담긴 채소를 그린 평범한 정물화일 뿐이다.

20 (it is)
However, [when flipped upside down], it is magically transformed into a smiling face!
거꾸로   수동태   현재분사

하지만 거꾸로 뒤집으면 마법처럼 웃는 얼굴로 변한다!

21 Experts have studied this painting, along with Arcimboldo's other reversible ones.
현재완료   ~과 함께   = paintings

전문가들은 이 그림을 Arcimboldo의 다른 뒤집을 수 있는 그림들과 함께 연구했다.

22 명사절 (showed의 목적어)
Their research showed [that he first painted them as still life paintings and then turned them
동사 1   동사 2
upside down and made some adjustments to create faces].
동사 3   부사적 용법 〈목적〉

그들의 연구는 그가 먼저 정물화로 그 그림들을 그렸고, 그러고 나서 그것들을 거꾸로 뒤집고 얼굴을 만들기 위해 약간의 수정을 했다는 것을 보여주
었다.

23 X-ray examination revealed [that he sometimes changed the positions of some of the fruits and
명사절 (revealed의 목적어)
vegetables].

엑스레이 검사는 그가 때때로 일부 과일과 채소의 위치를 바꾼 것을 밝혀냈다.

24 Why did he make his paintings reversible?

그는 왜 그림을 뒤집을 수 있도록 만들었을까?

25 It was probably because he wanted to add an interactive element to his work by doing so.
add A to B: A를 B에 더하다   = making his paintings reversible

아마도 그렇게 함으로써 자신의 작품에 상호작용적 요소를 더하고 싶었기 때문일 것이다.

26 Viewers feel as if they are playing a visual game, [which brings them a sense of pleasure].
마치 ~인 것처럼   계속적 용법의 주격 관계대명사절

(그림을) 보는 사람들은 마치 시각적인 게임을 하는 것처럼 느끼게 되는데, 이는 즐거움을 가져다준다.

27
Each of Arcimboldo's works is a careful study of everyday objects.
each of + 복수명사 + 단수동사

각각의 Arcimboldo의 작품은 일상적인 사물에 대한 세심한 연구이다.

28
[When he looked at typical objects, such as a bowl of vegetables], he saw the artistic and
부사절 〈시간〉   ~과 같은
imaginative potential in them.
= typical objects

채소 한 그릇과 같은 일반적인 사물을 볼 때, 그는 그 안에 담긴 예술적이고 창의적인 잠재력을 보았다.

29
His innovative approach to art inspired many great artists [who came after him], including Pablo
come after: ~의 뒤를 잇다 ~을 포함하여 (전치사)
Picasso, Salvador Dalí, and René Magritte.

예술에 대한 그의 혁신적인 접근법은 Pablo Picasso, Salvador Dalí, René Magritte를 포함하여 그의 뒤를 이은 많은 위대한 예술가들에게 영감을 주었다.

Helga Stentzel

30
Take a look at this picture.

이 사진을 보아라.

31
Do you see a horse [standing in a field]?
현재분사구

들판에 서 있는 말이 보이는가?

32
Or is it simply a collection of clothes [hanging on a clothesline]?
현재분사구

아니면 그것은 단순히 빨랫줄에 걸려 있는 옷가지들인가?

33
This witty and amusing creation is actually a work of art [created by the visual artist Helga
Stentzel].
과거분사구

이 재치 있고 재미있는 창작물은 사실 시각 예술가 Helga Stentzel이 만든 예술 작품이다.

34 Using everyday items, she creates playful visual illusions [that force you to look twice in order to confirm {what you have just seen}].

주격 관계대명사절
force + 목적어 + to-v: ~이 … 하게 (강요)하다
선행사를 포함하는 관계대명사

그녀는 일상적인 물건을 사용하여 당신이 방금 본 것을 확인하기 위해 두 번 보게 하는 재미난 착시를 만들어 낸다.

35 Her unique style has been called "household surrealism."

현재완료 수동태

그녀의 독특한 스타일은 '집 안의 초현실주의'라고 불려왔다.

36 Stentzel is perhaps best known for her *Clothesline Animals* series.

be known for: ~으로 알려져 있다

Stentzel은 아마 그녀의 〈빨랫줄 동물들〉 시리즈로 가장 잘 알려져 있을 것이다.

37 She got inspiration for the series while she was hanging her laundry.

~하는 동안 (접속사)
과거진행형

그녀는 빨래를 널다가 이 시리즈에 대한 영감을 얻었다.

38 By simply adding some colorful clothespins and a dish towel, she was able to transform her black sweatshirt and dark grey pants into a horse.

by v-ing: ~함으로써
transform A into B: A를 B로 변화시키다

그녀는 단순히 알록달록한 빨래집게 몇 개와 행주 하나를 추가함으로써 검정 운동복 상의와 짙은 회색 바지를 말로 변신시킬 수 있었다.

39 Other creations followed, including a brown cow [standing on some hills] and a zebra [crossing the desert].

현재분사구
현재분사구

언덕 위에 서 있는 갈색 소와 사막을 횡단하는 얼룩말을 포함한 다른 작품도 뒤이어 나왔다.

40 All of these works were created from nothing more than laundry and household items.

수동태
nothing more than: ~에 불과한

이 작품들은 모두 세탁물과 가정용품에 불과한 것으로 만들어졌다.

41 [Another series {that highlights Stentzel's astonishing creativity}] is *Edible Creatures*.

주어 (단수)
주격 관계대명사절
동사

Stentzel의 놀라운 창의력이 돋보이는 또 다른 시리즈는 〈먹을 수 있는 존재들〉이다.

42 For this series, she arranges food items [you can find in any kitchen] to create cute animals.
(that) 목적격 관계대명사절

이 시리즈에서 그녀는 어느 주방에서든지 흔히 찾을 수 있는 식재료를 배열하여 귀여운 동물을 만들어 낸다.

43 The stars of the series are *Brad Pet* and *Crunchie*, a pair of puppies [made of sliced bread and lettuce respectively].
과거분사구
(말한 순서대로) 각각

이 시리즈의 주인공은 각각 자른 빵과 양상추로 만든 한 쌍의 강아지 Brad Pet과 Crunchie이다.

44 Stentzel says she came up with the concept of *Crunchie* [while putting together a salad for her family].
(that)
접속사를 생략하지 않은: 분사구문 〈시간〉

Stentzel은 가족을 위해 샐러드를 만들다가 Crunchie의 발상을 떠올렸다고 말한다.

45 What do you think her secret is?

그녀의 비결이 무엇이라고 생각하는가?

46 명사절 (says의 목적어)
Stentzel says [that it is her active observation skills that allow her to make magic out of the ordinary].
「it is[was] ~ that」 강조 구문   allow + 목적어 + to-v: ~이 …하게 하다

Stentzel은 평범함 속에서 마법을 만들게 하는 것은 바로 그녀의 적극적인 관찰 기술이라고 말한다.

47 ~하곤 했다
As a child, she would spend time staring at the patterns in the wood of her bed, [trying to find different animal shapes].
spend time v-ing: ~하면서 시간을 보내다   분사구문 〈동시동작〉

어릴 때 그녀는 다양한 동물 모양을 찾으려고 하면서 침대의 나무 무늬를 바라보며 시간을 보내곤 했다.

48 She admits [that even today she stares at things longer than is acceptable in society].
명사절 (admits의 목적어)   용인되는

그녀는 지금도 사회에서 용인되는 시간보다 더 오래 사물을 바라본다고 인정한다.

49 선행사를 포함한 관계대명사절
This keen observation is [what enables her to continuously produce creative and imaginative works of art].
enable + 목적어 + to-v: ~이 …할 수 있게 하다

이러한 예리한 관찰력이 그녀가 창의적이고 상상력이 풍부한 예술 작품을 계속해서 만들어낼 수 있게 하는 것이다

50 Creativity is not some kind of exceptional skill [that belongs to exclusive groups of people].

주격 관계대명사절

belong to: ~에 속하다

창의력은 한정된 집단에만 있는 특출난 기술이 아니다.

51 It is actually a part of our daily lives, a power [that we can display anytime we choose to].

= Creativity

동격의 콤마

목적격 관계대명사절

창의력은 사실 우리 일상생활의 일부이며, 우리가 마음만 먹으면 언제든 드러낼 수 있는 힘이다.

52 부사절 〈양보〉

[Whether we realize it or not], we are constantly using our creativity to adapt, adjust, and rearrange the things around us.

현재진행형

병렬 구조

인식하든 인식하지 못하든, 우리는 우리 주변의 것들을 조정하고, 맞추고, 재배열하기 위해 끊임없이 창의력을 발휘하고 있다.

53 – using our creativity

By doing so, we are turning the ordinary into something extraordinary—something [that has never been seen before].

주격 관계대명사절

has been seen: 현재완료 수동태

그렇게 함으로써 우리는 평범한 것을 비상한 것, 즉 이전에는 볼 수 없었던 무언가로 바꾸고 있다.

54 Take a look at the things around you, but don't just give them a quick glance.

give A a glance: A를 힐끗 보다

당신 주변의 사물들을 둘러보되, 그저 힐끗 보기만 하지 말아라.

55 Look carefully, and you might discover something [that sparks your own imagination and creativity].

주격 관계대명사절

주의 깊게 살펴보면 당신만의 상상력과 창의력을 자극하는 무언가를 발견할지도 모른다.

교과서 본문 익히기 ❶ 옳은 어법·어휘 고르기

♣ 다음 네모 안에서 옳은 것을 고르시오.

01 Creativity. When you hear this word, how / what instantly pops into your mind?

02 You may think it is a quality / quantity that only artists and writers possess—some special talent you are either born with nor / or without.

03 Many people accept the idea that / which we can be divided into two groups: that / those who are creative and those who are not.

04 This common belief, however / therefore, is far from the truth.

05 Finding creativity inside yourself just take / takes a little effort.

06 Some artists, for example, spark their creative / creativity by looking closely at ordinary objects.

07 They try to discover the beauty hiding / hidden within these common objects and then turn them into works of art.

08 Believe it or no / not, they both depict the same person, Holy Roman Emperor Rudolf II.

09 The one on the left might look familiar / familiarly, as it is a standard style of portrait that you would see in a gallery or an art book.

10 However, the one on the right, calling / called *Vertumnus*, is very unconventional.

11 Creating / Created by a 16th-century Italian painter named Giuseppe Arcimboldo, the painting shows strike / striking creativity and originality.

12 Fruits, flowers, and vegetables arrange / are arranged like the pieces of a puzzle to create a human head.

13 A cherry and a mulberry become the dark eyes, though / while an apple and a peach act as the pink cheeks.

14 This painting is representation / representative of the artist's signature style of "composite portraits."

15 He used plants, animals, and other objects / objectives to create many other portraits like this.

16 Another / The other good example of Arcimboldo's unique creativity can be found in *The Gardener*, one of his "reversible" paintings.

17 When viewed normally, it is just an ordinary still life of vegetables in a ball / bowl.

18 However, when flipped upside down / out , it is magically transformed into a smiling face!

19 Experts have studied this painting, along to / with Arcimboldo's other reversible ones.

20 Their research showed that he first painted them as still / static life paintings and then turned them upside down and make / made some adjustments to create faces.

21 It was probably because / why he wanted to add an interactive element to his work by do / doing so.

22 Viewers feel as if they are playing a visual game, that / which brings them a sense of pleasure.

23 Each of Arcimboldo's works are / is a careful study of everyday objects.

24 When he looked at typical objects, such as a bowl of vegetables, he saw the artistic and imaginary / imaginative potential in them.

25 His innovative approach to art inspired many great artists who / whom came after him, including Pablo Picasso, Salvador Dalí, and René Magritte.

26 Make / Take a look at this picture.

27 Or is it simply a collection of clothes hang / hanging on a clothesline?

28 This witty and amusing creation is actually a work of art created by / from the visual artist Helga Stentzel.

29 Using everyday items, she creates playful visual illusions that force you look / to look twice in order to confirm what you have just seen.

30 Her unique style has called / been called "household surrealism."

31 Stentzel is perhaps best / most known for her *Clothesline Animals* series.

32 She got inspiration for the series since / while she was hanging her laundry.

33 By simply add / adding some colorful clothespins and a dish towel, she was able to transform her black sweatshirt and dark grey pants into / with a horse.

34 Other creations followed, including a brown cow standing on some hills and a zebra cross / crossing the desert.

35 All of these works were created from nothing / something more than laundry and household items.

36   Another series that highlights Stentzel's astonishing creativity / creation is *Edible Creatures*.

37   For this series, she arranges food items you can find / look for in any kitchen to create cute animals.

38   The stars of the series are *Brad Pet* and *Crunchie*, a pair of puppy / puppies made of sliced bread and lettuce respectively.

39   Stentzel says she came up with the concept of *Crunchie* while put / putting together a salad for her family.

40   How / What do you think her secret is?

41   Stentzel says that it is her active observation skills that / which allow her to make magic out of the ordinary.

42   As a child, she would spend time staring / to stare at the patterns in the wood of her bed, trying to find different animal shapes.

43   She admits that even today she stares at / to things longer than is acceptable in society.

44   This keen observation is that / what enables her to continuously produce creative and imaginative works of art.

45   Creativity is not some kind of exceptional skill that belongs to inclusive / exclusive groups of people.

46   It is actually a part of our daily lives, a power if / that we can display anytime we choose to.

47   Though / Whether we realize it or not, we are constantly using our creativity to adapt, adjust, and rearrange the things around us.

48   By doing so / such, we are turning the ordinary into something extraordinary—something that has never been seen before.

49   Take a look at the things around you, but don't just give them a quick glance / glare.

50   Look carefully, and you might / must discover something that sparks your own imagination and creativity.

✤ 다음 밑줄 친 부분이 옳으면 ○표 하고, 틀리면 바르게 고쳐 쓰시오.

01 You may think it is a quality that only artists and writers possess—some special talent you are <u>neither born with nor without</u>.

02 Many people accept the idea <u>which we can divide</u> into two groups: those who are creative and those who are not.

03 This common belief, however, is <u>far to</u> the truth.

04 Everyone has the ability <u>to creative</u>.

05 Finding creativity inside yourself just <u>takes a little effort</u>.

06 Some artists, for example, spark their creativity <u>by look</u> closely at ordinary objects.

07 They try to discover the beauty <u>hiding</u> within these common objects and then turn them into works of art.

08 Believe it or not, they <u>both depicts</u> the same person, Holy Roman Emperor Rudolf II.

09 The one on the left might look familiar, as it is a standard style of portrait <u>that you would see</u> in a gallery or an art book.

10 <u>Creating by</u> a 16th-century Italian painter named Giuseppe Arcimboldo, the painting shows striking creativity and originality.

11 He used plants, animals, and <u>another object</u> to create many other portraits like this.

12 Another good example of Arcimboldo's unique creativity can be found in *The Gardener*, one of his "reversible" <u>painting</u>.

13 <u>When view</u> normally, it is just an ordinary still life of vegetables in a bowl.

14 However, when flipped upside down, it is magically <u>transforming for</u> a smiling face!

15 Experts have studied this painting, along with Arcimboldo's other reversible <u>one</u>.

16 Their research showed that he first painted them as still life paintings and then turned them upside down and <u>make</u> some adjustments to create faces.

17 It was probably because he wanted to add an interactive element to his work by <u>do so</u>.

18 Viewers feel as if they are playing a visual game, <u>which brings them</u> a sense of pleasure.

19 Each of Arcimboldo's <u>works are</u> a careful study of everyday objects.

20 When he looked at typical objects, such as a bowl of vegetables, he saw the artistic and imaginative <u>potential in them</u>.

21 His innovative approach to art inspired many great artists <u>who come after</u> him, including Pablo Picasso, Salvador Dalí, and René Magritte.

22 Do you see a horse <u>standing</u> in a field?

23 Using everyday items, she creates playful visual illusions that force <u>you look</u> twice in order to confirm <u>that</u> you have just seen.

24 Her unique style <u>has been calling</u> "household surrealism."

25 Stentzel is perhaps <u>best know by</u> her *Clothesline Animals* series.

26 She got inspiration for the series <u>though</u> she was hanging her laundry.

27 <u>In simply add</u> some colorful clothespins and a dish towel, she was able to transform her black sweatshirt and dark grey pants into a horse.

28 Other creations followed, including a brown cow standing on some hills and a zebra <u>cross</u> the desert.

29 All of these works were created from <u>something more than</u> laundry and household items.

30 Another series <u>that highlight</u> Stentzel's astonishing creativity is *Edible Creatures*.

31 For this series, she arranges food items <u>you can find</u> in any kitchen to create cute animals.

32 The stars of the series are *Brad Pet* and *Crunchie*, a pair of puppies <u>make of slice</u> bread and lettuce respectively.

33 Stentzel says she came up with the concept of *Crunchie* <u>while put</u> together a salad for her family.

34   What do you think <u>is her secret</u>?

35   Stentzel says that it is her active observation skills that allow <u>her make</u> magic out of the ordinary.

36   As a child, she would spend time staring at the patterns in the wood of her bed, <u>try</u> to find different animal shapes.

37   She admits that even today she stares at things <u>longer than is</u> acceptable in society.

38   This keen observation is what enables her <u>continuously produce</u> creative and imaginative works of art.

39   Creativity is not some kind of exceptional skill <u>that belong</u> to exclusive groups of people.

40   It is actually a part of our daily lives, a power that we can display anytime <u>to choose</u> to.

41   <u>Whether we realize it or not</u>, we are constantly using our creativity to adapt, adjust, and rearrange the things around us.

42   By doing so, we are turning the ordinary into <u>extraordinary something</u>—something that has never been seen before.

43   Take a look at the things around you, but don't just <u>give it</u> a quick glance.

44   Look carefully, and you might discover something <u>which spark</u> your own imagination and creativity.

교과서 **본문 익히기** ③ 빈칸 완성하기

✤ 다음 우리말과 일치하도록 빈칸에 알맞은 말을 쓰시오.

Creativity. When you hear this word, what (1) _____ _____ _____ _____ _____ ?

창의력. 이 단어를 들었을 때 무엇이 즉시 당신의 마음에 떠오르는가?

You may think it is a quality (2) _____ _____ _____ _____ _____ _____

—some special talent you are either born with or without.

당신은 그것이 예술가나 작가만이 가지고 있는 특성, 즉 타고나거나 타고나지 않는 어떤 특별한 재능이라고 생각할 수도 있다.

Many people (3) _____ _____ _____ _____ we can be divided into two groups: those

who are creative and (4) _____ _____ _____ _____ .

많은 사람들이 우리가 창의적인 사람과 그렇지 않은 사람의 두 그룹으로 나뉠 수 있다는 생각을 받아들인다.

(5) _____ _____ _____ , however, is far from the truth.

그러나 이 일반적인 생각은 사실과 거리가 멀다.

Everyone has (6) _____ _____ _____ _____ _____ .

누구나 창의력을 발휘할 수 있는 능력을 갖추고 있다.

Finding creativity inside yourself (7) _____ _____ _____ _____ _____ .

내면에 있는 창의력을 발견하는 것에 약간의 노력이 필요할 뿐이다.

Some artists, for example, (8) _____ _____ _____ by looking closely at ordinary objects.

예를 들어, 일부 예술가들은 평범한 사물을 자세히 관찰함으로써 창의력을 발휘한다.

They try to discover the beauty (9) _____ _____ _____ _____ _____ and then turn

them into works of art.

그들은 이러한 평범한 사물 속에 숨겨진 아름다움을 발견하고 예술 작품으로 승화시키려고 노력한다.

Giuseppe Arcimboldo

(10) _____ _____ these two paintings.

이 두 그림을 보아라.

(11) _____ _____ _____ _____ , they both depict the same person, Holy Roman Emperor

Rudolf II.

믿기 어렵겠지만, 이 두 작품은 모두 같은 인물인 신성 로마 제국의 황제 루돌프 2세를 묘사한다.

The one on the left might look familiar, (12) _____ _____ _____ _____ _____

_____ of portrait that you would see in a gallery or an art book.

왼쪽에 있는 그림은 미술관이나 미술책에서 볼 수 있는 일반적인 스타일의 초상화이기 때문에 익숙해 보일 수도 있다.

However, the one on the right, called *Vertumnus*, (13) _____ _____ _____.

그렇지만 오른쪽에 있는 〈Vertumnus〉라는 그림은 매우 색다르다.

Created by a 16th-century Italian painter named Giuseppe Arcimboldo, the painting shows (14) _____
_____ _____ _____.

Giuseppe Arcimboldo라는 16세기 이탈리아 화가가 그린 이 그림은 눈에 띄는 창의력과 독창성을 보여준다.

Fruits, flowers, and vegetables are arranged (15) _____ _____ _____ _____
_____ to create a human head.

과일, 꽃, 그리고 채소가 사람의 머리를 만들기 위해 퍼즐 조각처럼 배열되어 있다.

A cherry and a mulberry become the dark eyes, while an apple and a peach (16) _____ _____
_____ _____ _____.

체리와 오디는 짙은 눈이 되고 사과와 복숭아는 분홍빛 뺨이 된다.

This painting is representative of (17) _____ _____ _____ _____ of "composite portraits."

이 그림은 작가의 특징적인 스타일인 '합성 초상화'를 대표하는 작품이다.

He used plants, animals, and other objects (18) _____ _____ _____ _____ _____
like this.

그는 이와 같은 많은 초상화를 만들기 위해 식물, 동물, 그리고 다른 사물들을 활용했다.

(19) _____ _____ _____ of Arcimboldo's unique creativity can be found in *The Gardener*, one of
his "reversible" paintings.

Arcimboldo의 독특한 창의력의 또 다른 좋은 예는 그의 '뒤집을 수 있는' 그림 중 하나인 〈The Gardener〉에서 발견할 수 있다.

(20) _____ _____ _____, it is just an ordinary still life of vegetables in a bowl.

정상적으로 보면 그것은 그릇에 담긴 채소를 그린 평범한 정물화일 뿐이다.

However, (21) _____ _____ _____ _____, it is magically transformed into a smiling face!

하지만 거꾸로 뒤집으면 마법처럼 웃는 얼굴로 변한다!

Experts (22) _____ _____ _____ _____, along with Arcimboldo's other reversible ones.

전문가들은 이 그림을 Arcimboldo의 다른 뒤집을 수 있는 그림들과 함께 연구했다.

Their research showed that he first painted them as still life paintings and then turned them upside down and
(23) _____ _____ _____ _____ _____ _____ _____.

그들의 연구는 그가 먼저 정물화로 그 그림들을 그렸고, 그러고 나서 그것들을 거꾸로 뒤집고 얼굴을 만들기 위해 약간의 수정을 했다는 것을 보여주었다.

X-ray examination revealed that he (24) _____ _____ _____ _____ of some of the fruits
and vegetables.

엑스레이 검사는 그가 때때로 일부 과일과 채소의 위치를 바꾼 것을 밝혀냈다.

(25) _____ _____ _____ _____ his paintings reversible?

그는 왜 그림을 뒤집을 수 있도록 만들었을까?

It was probably (26) _____ _____ _____ _____ _____ an interactive element to his work by doing so.

아마도 그렇게 함으로써 자신의 작품에 상호작용적 요소를 더하고 싶었기 때문일 것이다.

Viewers feel (27) _____ _____ _____ _____ _____ a visual game, which brings them a sense of pleasure.

(그림을) 보는 사람들은 마치 시각적인 게임을 하는 것처럼 느끼게 되는데, 이는 즐거움을 가져다준다.

Each of Arcimboldo's works (28) _____ _____ _____ _____ of everyday objects.

각각의 Arcimboldo의 작품은 일상적인 사물에 대한 세심한 연구이다.

When he looked at typical objects, (29) _____ _____ _____ _____ _____ _____, he saw the artistic and imaginative potential in them.

채소 한 그릇과 같은 일반적인 사물을 볼 때, 그는 그 안에 담긴 예술적이고 창의적인 잠재력을 보았다.

(30) _____ _____ _____ _____ art inspired many great artists who came after him, including Pablo Picasso, Salvador Dalí, and René Magritte.

예술에 대한 그의 혁신적인 접근법은 Pablo Picasso, Salvador Dalí, René Magritte를 포함하여 그의 뒤를 이은 많은 위대한 예술가들에게 영감을 주었다.

Helga Stentzel

(31) _____ _____ _____ _____ this picture.

이 사진을 보아라.

Do you see a horse (32) _____ _____ _____ _____?

들판에 서 있는 말이 보이는가?

Or is it simply a collection of clothes (33) _____ _____ _____ _____?

아니면 그것은 단순히 빨랫줄에 걸려 있는 옷가지들인가?

This (34) _____ _____ _____ _____ is actually a work of art created by the visual artist Helga Stentzel.

이 재치 있고 재미있는 창작물은 사실 시각 예술가 Helga Stentzel이 만든 예술 작품이다.

(35) _____ _____ _____, she creates playful visual illusions that (36) _____ _____ _____ _____ in order to confirm what you have just seen.

그녀는 일상적인 물건을 사용하여 당신이 방금 본 것을 확인하기 위해 두 번 보게 하는 재미난 착시를 만들어 낸다.

Her unique style (37) _____ _____ _____ "household surrealism."

그녀의 독특한 스타일은 '집 안의 초현실주의'라고 불려왔다.

Stentzel is perhaps (38) _____ _____ _____ her *Clothesline Animals* series.

Stentzel은 아마 그녀의 〈빨랫줄 동물들〉 시리즈로 가장 잘 알려져 있을 것이다.

She got inspiration for the series (39) _____ _____ _____ _____

_____.

그녀는 빨래를 널다가 이 시리즈에 대한 영감을 얻었다.

(40) _____ _____ _____ some colorful clothespins and a dish towel, (41) _____

_____ _____ _____ _____ her black sweatshirt and dark grey pants into a horse.

그녀는 단순히 알록달록한 빨래집게 몇 개와 행주 하나를 추가함으로써 검정 운동복 상의와 짙은 회색 바지를 말로 변신시킬 수 있었다.

Other creations followed, including a brown cow (42) _____ _____ _____ and a

zebra (43) _____ _____ _____.

언덕 위에 서 있는 갈색 소와 사막을 횡단하는 얼룩말을 포함한 다른 작품도 뒤이어 나왔다.

All of these works were created from (44) _____ _____ _____ laundry and household items.

이 작품들은 모두 세탁물과 가정용품에 불과한 것으로 만들어졌다.

(45) _____ _____ _____ _____ Stentzel's astonishing creativity is *Edible Creatures*.

Stentzel의 놀라운 창의력이 돋보이는 또 다른 시리즈는 〈먹을 수 있는 존재들〉이다.

For this series, she arranges food items (46) _____ _____ _____ _____ _____

_____ to create cute animals.

이 시리즈에서 그녀는 어느 주방에서든지 흔히 찾을 수 있는 식재료를 배열하여 귀여운 동물을 만들어 낸다.

The stars of the series are *Brad Pet* and *Crunchie*, (47) _____ _____ _____ _____

_____ _____ sliced bread and lettuce respectively.

이 시리즈의 주인공은 각각 자른 빵과 양상추로 만든 한 쌍의 강아지 Brad Pet과 Crunchie이다.

Stentzel says (48) _____ _____ _____ _____ _____ of *Crunchie* while

putting together a salad for her family.

Stentzel은 가족을 위해 샐러드를 만들다가 Crunchie의 발상을 떠올렸다고 말한다.

What (49) _____ _____ _____ her secret is?

그녀의 비결이 무엇이라고 생각하는가?

Stentzel says that (50) _____ _____ her active observation skills (51) _____ _____

_____ _____ _____ magic out of the ordinary.

Stentzel은 평범함 속에서 마법을 만들게 하는 것은 바로 그녀의 적극적인 관찰 기술이라고 말한다.

As a child, she (52) _____ _____ _____ _____ _____ the patterns in the wood of her bed, trying to find different animal shapes.

어릴 때 그녀는 다양한 동물 모양을 찾으려고 하면서 침대의 나무 무늬를 바라보며 시간을 보내곤 했다.

She admits that even today she stares at things (53) _____ _____ _____ _____ in society.

그녀는 지금도 사회에서 용인되는 시간보다 더 오래 사물을 바라본다고 인정한다.

This keen observation is (54) _____ _____ _____ _____ _____ _____ creative and imaginative works of art.

이러한 예리한 관찰력이 그녀가 창의적이고 상상력이 풍부한 예술 작품을 계속해서 만들어낼 수 있게 하는 것이다

Creativity is not some kind of (55) _____ _____ _____ _____ to exclusive groups of people.

창의력은 한정된 집단에만 있는 특출난 기술이 아니다.

It is actually a part of our daily lives, a power that we can display (56) _____ _____ _____ _____ .

창의력은 사실 우리 일상생활의 일부이며, 우리가 마음만 먹으면 언제든 드러낼 수 있는 힘이다.

(57) _____ _____ _____ _____ _____ _____ , we are constantly using our creativity to adapt, adjust, and rearrange the things around us.

인식하든 인식하지 못하든, 우리는 우리 주변의 것들을 조정하고, 맞추고, 재배열하기 위해 끊임없이 창의력을 발휘하고 있다.

(58) _____ _____ _____ , we are turning the ordinary into something extraordinary—something that (59) _____ _____ _____ _____ _____ .

그렇게 함으로써 우리는 평범한 것을 비상한 것, 즉 이전에는 볼 수 없었던 무언가로 바꾸고 있다.

Take a look at the things around you, (60) _____ _____ _____ _____ _____ a quick glance.

당신 주변의 사물들을 둘러보되, 그저 힐끗 보기만 하지 말아라.

Look carefully, and you might (61) _____ _____ _____ _____ your own imagination and creativity.

주의 깊게 살펴보면 당신만의 상상력과 창의력을 자극하는 무언가를 발견할지도 모른다.

01 밑줄 친 부분 중, 문맥상 낱말의 쓰임이 적절하지 <u>않은</u> 것은?

Creativity. When you hear this word, what instantly pops into your mind? You may think it is a quality that only artists and writers possess—some special talent you are ①either born with or without. Many people ②doubt the idea that we can be divided into two groups: those who are creative and those who are not. This ③common belief, however, is far from the truth. Everyone has the ability to be creative. Finding creativity inside yourself just takes a ④little effort. Some artists, for example, ⑤spark their creativity by looking closely at ordinary objects.

02 밑줄 친 부분 중, 문맥상 낱말의 쓰임이 적절하지 <u>않은</u> 것은?

Look at these two paintings. Believe it or not, they both depict the same person, Holy Roman Emperor Rudolf II. The one on the left might look familiar, as it is a ①standard style of portrait that you would see in a gallery or an art book. However, the one on the right, called *Vertumnus*, is very ②conventional. Created by a 16th-century Italian painter named Giuseppe Arcimboldo, the painting shows striking creativity and ③originality. Fruits, flowers, and vegetables are arranged like the pieces of a puzzle to ④create a human head. A cherry and a mulberry become the dark eyes, while an apple and a peach act as the pink cheeks. This painting is ⑤representative of the artist's signature style of "composite portraits."

03 밑줄 친 부분 중, 문맥상 낱말의 쓰임이 적절하지 <u>않은</u> 것은?

Another good example of Arcimboldo's unique creativity can be found in *The Gardener*, one of his "reversible" paintings. When viewed ①normally, it is just an ordinary still life of vegetables in a bowl. However, when flipped upside down, it is magically ②transformed into a smiling face! Experts have studied this painting, along with Arcimboldo's other ③reversible ones. Their research showed that he first painted them as ④static life paintings and then turned them upside down and made some ⑤adjustments to create faces. X-ray examination revealed that he sometimes changed the positions of some of the fruits and vegetables.

04 (A), (B), (C)의 각 네모 안에서 문맥에 맞는 낱말로 가장 적절한 것은?

Why did he make his paintings reversible? It was probably because he wanted to add an (A) interactive / international element to his work by doing so. Viewers feel as if they are playing a visual game, which brings them a sense of pleasure.

Each of Arcimboldo's works is a careful study of everyday objects. When he looked at (B) typical / unique objects, such as a bowl of vegetables, he saw the artistic and imaginative potential in them. His innovative (C) approach / aspect to art inspired many great artists who came after him, including Pablo Picasso, Salvador Dalí, and René Magritte.

	(A)	(B)	(C)
①	interactive	⋯ typical	⋯ approach
②	interactive	⋯ unique	⋯ approach
③	interactive	⋯ typical	⋯ aspect
④	international	⋯ unique	⋯ aspect
⑤	international	⋯ typical	⋯ aspect

05 (A), (B), (C)의 각 네모 안에서 문맥에 맞는 낱말로 가장 적절한 것은?

Using everyday items, she creates playful visual illusions that force you to look twice in order to (A) confirm / conform what you have just seen. Her unique style has been called "household surrealism."

Stentzel is perhaps best known for her *Clothesline Animals* series. She got (B) inspiration / interest for the series while she was hanging her laundry. By simply adding some colorful clothespins and a dish towel, she was able to (C) transfer / transform her black sweatshirt and dark grey pants into a horse.

	(A)		(B)		(C)
①	confirm	⋯	inspiration	⋯	transfer
②	confirm	⋯	interest	⋯	transfer
③	confirm	⋯	inspiration	⋯	transform
④	conform	⋯	interest	⋯	transform
⑤	conform	⋯	inspiration	⋯	transform

06 (A), (B), (C)의 각 네모 안에서 문맥에 맞는 낱말로 가장 적절한 것은?

Another series that highlights Stentzel's (A) amused / astonishing creativity is *Edible Creatures*. For this series, she arranges food items you can find in any kitchen to create cute animals. The stars of the series are *Brad Pet* and *Crunchie*, a (B) fair / pair of puppies made of sliced bread and lettuce (C) respectfully / respectively. Stentzel says she came up with the concept of *Crunchie* while putting together a salad for her family.

	(A)		(B)		(C)
①	amused	⋯	fair	⋯	respectfully
②	amused	⋯	pair	⋯	respectfully
③	astonishing	⋯	fair	⋯	respectfully
④	astonishing	⋯	pair	⋯	respectively
⑤	astonishing	⋯	fair	⋯	respectively

07 (A), (B), (C)의 각 네모 안에서 문맥에 맞는 낱말로 가장 적절한 것은?

What do you think her secret is? Stentzel says that it is her (A) active / passive observation skills that allow her to make magic out of the ordinary. As a child, she would spend time staring at the patterns in the wood of her bed, trying to find different animal shapes. She (B) admits / permits that even today she stares at things longer than is acceptable in society. This keen observation is what enables her to continuously (C) consume / produce creative and imaginative works of art.

	(A)		(B)		(C)
①	active	⋯	admits	⋯	consume
②	active	⋯	admits	⋯	produce
③	active	⋯	permits	⋯	consume
④	passive	⋯	permits	⋯	produce
⑤	passive	⋯	permits	⋯	consume

08 밑줄 친 부분 중, 문맥상 낱말의 쓰임이 적절하지 <u>않은</u> 것은?

Creativity is not some kind of exceptional skill that ①belongs to exclusive groups of people. It is actually a part of our daily lives, a power that we can display anytime we choose to. Whether we realize it or not, we are ②constantly using our creativity to adapt, adjust, and rearrange the things around us. By doing so, we are turning the ordinary into something ③extraordinary — something that has never been seen before. Take a look at the things around you, but don't just give them a ④thorough glance. Look carefully, and you might discover something that ⑤sparks your own imagination and creativity.

01 다음 글의 밑줄 친 부분 중, 어법상 틀린 것은?

Creativity. When you hear this word, ① what instantly pops into your mind? You may think it is a quality ② that only artists and writers possess — some special talent you are either born with or without. Many people accept the idea ③ which we can be divided into two groups: those who are creative and those who are not. This common belief, however, is far from the truth. Everyone has the ability to be creative. Finding creativity inside yourself just ④ takes a little effort. Some artists, for example, spark their creativity by ⑤ looking closely at ordinary objects.

02 다음 글의 밑줄 친 부분 중, 어법상 틀린 것은?

Look at these two paintings. Believe it or not, they both ① depict the same person, Holy Roman Emperor Rudolf II. The one on the left might look familiar, as it is a standard style of portrait that you would see in a gallery or an art book. However, the one on the right, ② calling *Vertumnus*, is very unconventional. Created by a 16th-century Italian painter ③ named Giuseppe Arcimboldo, the painting shows striking creativity and originality. Fruits, flowers, and vegetables ④ are arranged like the pieces of a puzzle to create a human head. A cherry and a mulberry become the dark eyes, while an apple and a peach act as the pink cheeks. This painting is representative of the artist's signature style of "composite portraits." He used plants, animals, and other objects ⑤ to create many other portraits like this.

03 다음 글의 밑줄 친 부분 중, 어법상 틀린 것은?

Experts have studied this painting, along with Arcimboldo's other reversible ① one. Their research showed that he first painted them as still life paintings and then turned them upside down and made some adjustments to create faces. X-ray examination revealed ② that he sometimes changed the positions of some of the fruits and vegetables. Why did he make his paintings ③ reversible? It was probably because he wanted to add an interactive element to his work by ④ doing so. Viewers feel as if they are playing a visual game, ⑤ which brings them a sense of pleasure.

04 (A), (B), (C)의 각 네모 안에서 어법에 맞는 표현으로 가장 적절한 것은?

Take a look at this picture. Do you see a horse (A) standing / stood in a field? Or is it simply a collection of clothes hanging on a clothesline? This witty and amusing creation is actually a work of art created by the visual artist Helga Stentzel. Using everyday items, she creates playful visual illusions that force you (B) look / to look twice in order to confirm what you have just seen. Her unique style has (C) called / been called "household surrealism."

	(A)		(B)		(C)
①	standing	⋯	look	⋯	called
②	stood	⋯	look	⋯	called
③	standing	⋯	to look	⋯	called
④	stood	⋯	to look	⋯	been called
⑤	standing	⋯	to look	⋯	been called

05 (A), (B), (C)의 각 네모 안에서 어법에 맞는 표현으로 가장 적절한 것은?

Another series that (A)[highlight / highlights] Stentzel's astonishing creativity is *Edible Creatures*. For this series, she arranges food items you can find in any kitchen to create cute animals. The stars of the series are *Brad Pet* and *Crunchie*, a pair of puppies (B)[making / made] of sliced bread and lettuce respectively. Stentzel says she came up with the concept of *Crunchie* while (C)[put / putting] together a salad for her family.

	(A)		(B)		(C)
①	highlight	⋯	making	⋯	put
②	highlight	⋯	made	⋯	put
③	highlights	⋯	making	⋯	put
④	highlights	⋯	made	⋯	putting
⑤	highlights	⋯	making	⋯	putting

06 다음 글의 밑줄 친 부분 중, 어법상 틀린 것은?

What do you think ① her secret is? Stentzel says that it is her active observation skills ② which allow her to make magic out of the ordinary. As a child, she would spend time ③ staring at the patterns in the wood of her bed, trying to find different animal shapes. She admits that even today she stares at things longer than ④ is acceptable in society. This keen observation is ⑤ what enables her to continuously produce creative and imaginative works of art.

07 다음 글의 밑줄 친 부분 중, 어법상 틀린 것은?

Creativity is not some kind of exceptional skill ① that belongs to exclusive groups of people. It is actually a part of our daily lives, a power that we can display anytime ② we choose to. Whether we realize it or not, we are constantly using our creativity to adapt, adjust, and rearrange the things around us. ③ By doing so, we are turning the ordinary into something extraordinary—something that ④ has never seen before. Take a look at the things around you, but don't just give them a quick glance. Look carefully, and you might discover ⑤ something that sparks your own imagination and creativity.

08 (A), (B), (C)의 각 네모 안에서 어법에 맞는 표현으로 가장 적절한 것은?

While it is well known that exercise is essential for our physical health, not many people know that (A)[it / they] can also boost our creativity. This is because physical activity can enhance our mood and reduce negative emotions, (B)[what / which] are factors that restrict creativity. Also, exercise increases blood flow to the brain, providing it with the nutrients it needs to function better. When at its best, the brain can generate more creative ideas. Moreover, exercise often leads us to go outside and (C)[visit / visiting] different places. By doing so, we can expose ourselves to new sources of inspiration and alter the way we think.

	(A)		(B)		(C)
①	it	⋯	what	⋯	visit
②	it	⋯	which	⋯	visit
③	it	⋯	what	⋯	visiting
④	they	⋯	which	⋯	visiting
⑤	they	⋯	what	⋯	visiting

[01~02] 다음 대화를 읽고, 물음에 답하시오.

> G Sean, what are you doing?
>
> B I'm doing a daily creative challenge. Have you heard about it?
>
> G No, I haven't. What is it?
>
> B It is an activity that cultivates creativity by challenging you to do something creative every day. You can write a poem, play a musical instrument, or craft something!
>
> G Sounds interesting! So what is your challenge?
>
> B I do a drawing challenge. (①) I've been drawing different things every day for a month now.
>
> G I'd like to start a challenge too! (②) Could you give me some advice on how to start?
>
> B (③) If you choose something too complicated, you may not be able to complete the challenge every day.
>
> G Hmm… (④) I'm still not sure what to do.
>
> B Well, how about trying a photo challenge? (⑤) You can easily take a picture with your phone every day.

01 위 대화의 주제로 가장 적절한 것은?

① how to improve drawing skills
② advice on a daily creative challenge
③ benefits of doing simple tasks every day
④ how to make complicated works simple
⑤ tips on taking pictures with your phone

02 대화의 흐름으로 보아, 주어진 문장이 들어가기에 가장 적절한 곳은?

> I suggest you start with something simple.

①   ②   ③   ④   ⑤

[03~04] 다음 글을 읽고, 물음에 답하시오.

> Creativity. When you hear this word, what instantly pops _____ your mind? You may think it is a quality that only artists and writers possess — some special talent you are either born with or without. Many people accept the idea that we can be divided into two groups: those who are creative and those who are not. This common belief, however, is far from <u>the truth</u>. Everyone has the ability to be creative. Finding creativity inside yourself just takes a little effort. Some artists, for example, spark their creativity by looking closely at ordinary objects. They try to discover the beauty hidden within these common objects and then turn them _____ works of art.

03 윗글의 밑줄 친 the truth가 가리키는 내용을 글에서 찾아 한 문장으로 쓰시오.

→ _____

04 윗글의 빈칸에 공통으로 들어갈 말로 가장 적절한 것은?

① into   ② from   ③ with
④ on   ⑤ through

[05~06] 다음 글을 읽고, 물음에 답하시오.

Look at these two paintings. Believe it or not, they both depict the same person, Holy Roman Emperor Rudolf II. The one on the left might look familiar, as it is a standard style of portrait that you would see in a gallery or an art book. However, the one on the right, called *Vertumnus*, is very unconventional. Created by a 16th-century Italian painter named Giuseppe Arcimboldo, the painting shows striking creativity and originality. Fruits, flowers, and vegetables are arranged like the pieces of a puzzle to create a human head. A cherry and a mulberry become the dark eyes, while an apple and a peach act as the pink cheeks. This painting is representative of the artist's signature style of "composite portraits." He used plants, animals, and other objects to create many other portraits like this.

05 윗글의 밑줄 친 these two paintings에 관한 설명으로 바르지 않은 것은?

① 모두 신성 로마 제국의 황제인 루돌프 2세의 초상화이다.
② 모두 Arcimboldo가 그린 작품이다.
③ 두 작품은 상반되는 화풍으로 제작되었다.
④ 왼쪽에 있는 그림은 친숙해 보이는 초상화이다.
⑤ 오른쪽에 있는 그림은 과일로 얼굴을 표현하였다.

06 윗글에서 주어진 영어 뜻풀이에 해당하는 단어를 찾아 쓰시오.

(1) to show somebody or something in a picture
(2) the quality of being new and different in an unusual way

(1) _____

(2) _____

[07~08] 다음 글을 읽고, 물음에 답하시오.

Experts have studied this painting, along with Arcimboldo's other reversible ones. Their research showed that he first painted them as still life paintings and then turned them ⓐ거꾸로 and made some adjustments to create faces. X-ray examination revealed that he sometimes changed the positions of some of the fruits and vegetables. Why did he make his paintings reversible? It was probably because he wanted to add an interactive element to his work by ⓑdoing so. Viewers feel as if they are playing a visual game, which brings them a sense of pleasure.

07 윗글의 밑줄 친 ⓐ의 우리말과 일치하도록 알맞은 표현을 쓰시오. (두 단어)

ⓐ 거꾸로 → _____

08 윗글의 밑줄 친 ⓑ doing so가 가리키는 내용으로 가장 적절한 것은?

① making his paintings reversible
② changing the positions of some objects
③ creating still life paintings
④ examining his paintings
⑤ bringing viewers joy and pleasure

[09~10] 다음 글을 읽고, 물음에 답하시오.

Another series that highlights Stentzel's astonishing creativity is *Edible Creatures*. For this series, she arranges food items you can find in any kitchen to create cute animals. The stars of the series are *Brad Pet* and *Crunchie*, a pair of puppies made of sliced bread and lettuce respectively. Stentzel says she came up with the concept of *Crunchie* while putting together a salad for her family.

What do you think her secret is? <u>Stentzel says that her active observation skills allow her to make magic out of the ordinary.</u> As a child, she would spend time staring at the patterns in the wood of her bed, trying to find different animal shapes. She admits that even today she stares at things longer than is acceptable in society. This keen observation is what enables her to continuously produce creative and imaginative works of art.

09 윗글을 읽고 Stentzel에 관해 답할 수 있는 질문이 **아닌** 것은?

① What is used to create *Edible Creatures*?
② What was she doing when she came up with the idea *Crunchie*?
③ How long did it take to complete *Brad Pet*?
④ How did she show active observation skills as a child?
⑤ What enabled her to create imaginative artworks?

10 윗글의 밑줄 친 문장을 주어진 **조건**에 맞게 바꿔 쓰시오.

> **조건**
> • 다음 표현을 강조할 것: her active observation skills
> • it is ~ that 구문을 활용할 것

→ Stentzel says that _____
_____ .

[11~12] 다음 글을 읽고, 물음에 답하시오.

Creativity is not some kind of exceptional skill that belongs to exclusive groups of people.

(A) By doing so, we are turning the ordinary into something extraordinary — something that has never been seen before.
(B) Take a look at the things around you, but don't just give them a quick glance. Look carefully, and you might discover something that sparks your own imagination and creativity.
(C) It is actually a part of our daily lives, a power that we can display anytime we choose to. Whether we realize it or not, we are constantly using our creativity to adapt, adjust, and rearrange the things around us.

11 주어진 문장 다음에 이어질 글의 순서로 가장 적절한 것은?

① (A) – (B) – (C)　　② (A) – (C) – (B)
③ (B) – (A) – (C)　　④ (B) – (C) – (A)
⑤ (C) – (A) – (B)

12 윗글의 요지로 가장 적절한 것은?

① 창의력은 주변을 주의 깊게 관찰함으로써 발휘될 수 있는 우리 모두가 지닌 능력이다.
② 창의력을 발휘하기 위해서는 특별한 노력이 필요하다.
③ 비범한 상상력과 창의력을 가진 사람들에 의해 예술과 과학이 발전해 왔다.
④ 여러 가지 특별한 경험을 하는 것이 창의력을 키우는 데 도움이 된다.
⑤ 우리는 끊임 없이 주변의 것들을 조정하거나 재배열하고 있다.

[13~14] 다음 글을 읽고, 물음에 답하시오.

Students throw away a lot of books at the end of each school year. This is a problem because it has a negative effect on the environment by (A) generate / generating a huge amount of waste. I'd like to propose two solutions to this problem. First, we can organize a school event (B) which / where students can buy, sell, and trade books. This way, we can decrease the number of discarded books and buy books at cheaper prices. Second, I suggest collecting unwanted books and (C) donating / to donate them to our local library. By doing so, we can increase the life span of these books and help our community at the same time. I hope the problem of throwing away books can be solved effectively with these two solutions.

13 (A), (B), (C)의 각 네모 안에서 어법에 맞는 표현으로 가장 적절한 것은?

	(A)		(B)		(C)
①	generate	⋯	which	⋯	donating
②	generate	⋯	which	⋯	to donate
③	generate	⋯	where	⋯	donating
④	generating	⋯	where	⋯	to donate
⑤	generating	⋯	where	⋯	donating

14 윗글의 밑줄 친 these two solutions가 가리키는 내용을 우리말로 쓰시오.

(1) _____

(2) _____

[15~16] 다음 글을 읽고, 물음에 답하시오.

While it is well known that exercise is essential for our physical health, not many people know that it can also boost our creativity. This is because physical activity can enhance our mood and reduce negative emotions, which _____. Also, exercise increases blood flow to the brain, providing it with the nutrients it needs to function better. When at its best, the brain can generate more creative ideas. Moreover, exercise often leads us to go outside and visit different places. By doing so, we can expose ourselves to new sources of inspiration and alter the way we think.

15 윗글의 내용을 요약할 때 빈칸에 알맞은 말을 글에서 찾아 쓰시오.

(1) _____ is good for your body and can also make you more creative. It boosts your mood, helps your brain work better due to more (2) _____ flow, and exposes you to new ideas.

16 윗글의 빈칸에 들어갈 말로 가장 적절한 것은?

① can boost creativity
② are factors that restrict creativity
③ are the main causes of stronger relationships
④ can be prevented with increased stress
⑤ should be avoided for the mental wellness

[01~02] 다음 글을 읽고, 물음에 답하시오.

As a content creator, I'm always in need of fresh ideas, and I recently read about an interesting experiment. A researcher conducted a study to investigate the effects of walking on creativity. Participants had to come up with as many different ways to use everyday objects as they could. For example, a car key could be used as a bottle opener and a box cutter. The results were surprising. The people who took the test while walking on a treadmill generated almost twice as many ideas as those who took the test while sitting! This means that taking a walk can help you enhance your creativity and develop new ideas. 그러니 다음에 당신이 창의력이 필요한 과업에 직면한다면, 산책하는 것을 추천합니다. You'll be surprised to see how it helps boost your creativity!

01 윗글의 내용을 요약할 때 빈칸에 알맞은 말을 글에서 찾아 쓰시오.

A study found that walking on a(n)
(1) _____ doubled the number of creative ideas generated compared to sitting. Therefore, walking can effectively enhance (2) _____.

02 윗글의 밑줄 친 우리말과 일치하도록 주어진 조건에 맞게 문장을 완성하시오.

조건
• next time을 사용할 것
• 사용할 표현 : faced with, require, suggest

→ So _____,
_____ you take a walk.

[03~04] 다음 글을 읽고, 물음에 답하시오.

Creativity. When you hear this word, what instantly pops into your mind? You may think it is a quality ⓐthat only artists and writers possess — some special talent you are either born with or without. Many people accept the idea ⓑthat we can be divided into two groups: those who are creative and those who are not. This common belief, however, is far from the truth. Everyone has the ability to be creative. Finding creativity inside yourself just takes a little effort. Some artists, for example, spark their creativity by looking closely at ordinary objects. They try to discover the beauty hidden within these common objects and then turn them into works of art.

03 윗글의 요지로 가장 적절한 것은?

① 예술가에게 창의력은 필수적인 자격 요건이다.
② 창의력을 지니고 있는가는 태생적인 요인이 매우 크다.
③ 일상적인 것에서 예술적 영감을 얻을 수 있다.
④ 노력을 통해 누구나 창의성을 발휘할 수 있다.
⑤ 창의력을 키울 방법에 대한 다양한 연구가 진행 중이다.

04 윗글의 밑줄 친 ⓐ, ⓑ that과 쓰임이 같은 것을 모두 골라 기호를 쓰시오.

(A) It was at 6:00 p.m. that I saw the accident.
(B) We had a strong belief that she would come back safely.
(C) The story that he told proved false.
(D) It seems that Tony can be the school president.
(E) My sister is the only student that walks to school.

ⓐ → _____

ⓑ → _____

[05~06] 다음 글을 읽고, 물음에 답하시오.

Another good example of Arcimboldo's unique creativity can be found in *The Gardener*, one of his "reversible" paintings. When viewed normally, it is just an ordinary still life of vegetables in a bowl. However, when flipped upside down, it is magically transformed into a smiling face! (①) Experts have studied this painting, along with Arcimboldo's other reversible ones. (②) Their research showed that he first painted them as still life paintings and then turned them upside down and made some adjustments to create faces. (③) X-ray examination revealed that he sometimes changed the positions of some of the fruits and vegetables. (④) It was probably because he wanted to add an interactive element to his work by doing so. (⑤) Viewers feel as if they are playing a visual game, which brings them a sense of pleasure.

05 윗글의 앞에 언급되었을 내용으로 가장 적절한 것은?

① 우리에게 친숙한 '뒤집을 수 있는 그림' 작품들
② Arcimboldo가 자신의 작품에 사용한 독특한 기법
③ 창의력과 상상력이 두드러진 16세기 화가들
④ Archimboldo의 창의성이 드러나는 예술 작품
⑤ 과일, 채소, 꽃을 작품의 소재로 사용한 예술가들

06 글의 흐름으로 보아, 주어진 문장이 들어가기에 가장 적절한 곳은?

Why did he make his paintings reversible?

①   ②   ③   ④   ⑤

[07~09] 다음 글을 읽고, 물음에 답하시오.

Take a look at ⓐ this picture. Do you see a horse standing in a field? Or is it simply a collection of clothes hanging on a clothesline? This witty and amusing creation is actually a work of art created by the visual artist Helga Stentzel. Using everyday items, she creates playful visual illusions that force you to look twice in order to confirm what you have just seen. Her unique style has been called "household surrealism."

Stentzel is perhaps best known for her *Clothesline Animals* series. She got inspiration for the series ⓑ while she was hanging her laundry. By simply adding some colorful clothespins and a dish towel, she was able to transform her black sweatshirt and dark grey pants into a horse. Other creations followed, including a brown cow standing on some hills and a zebra crossing the desert. All of these works were created from ＿＿＿＿＿＿＿ laundry and household items.

07 윗글의 밑줄 친 ⓐ this picture에 관해 글의 내용과 일치하지 <u>않는</u> 것은?

① 사막을 횡단하는 얼룩말처럼 보인다.
② 빨랫줄에 걸린 옷가지처럼 보인다.
③ Helga Stentzel에 의해 창작된 작품이다.
④ 검정색 운동복 상의를 사용하여 창작되었다.
⑤ '집 안의 초현실주의' 작품이다.

08 윗글의 밑줄 친 ⓑ와 바꿔 쓸 수 있는 표현으로 적절한 것은?

① while she was hung her laundry
② while hanging her laundry
③ while she hanging her laundry
④ while hung her laundry
⑤ while was hanging her laundry

09 윗글의 빈칸에 들어갈 말로 가장 적절한 것은?

① better than   ② at least
③ nothing more than   ④ no sooner than
⑤ not so much as

[10~11] 다음 글을 읽고, 물음에 답하시오.

Another series that highlights Stentzel's astonishing creativity is *Edible Creatures*. For this series, she arranges food items you can find in any kitchen to create cute animals. The stars of the series are *Brad Pet* and *Crunchie*, a pair of puppies made of sliced bread and lettuce respectively. Stentzel says she came up with the concept of *Crunchie* while putting together a salad for her family.

What do you think her secret is? Stentzel says that it is her active observation skills that allow her to make magic out of the ordinary. As a child, she would spend time staring at the patterns in the wood of her bed, trying to find different animal shapes. She admits that even today she stares at things longer than is acceptable in society. This keen observation is what enables her to continuously produce creative and imaginative works of art.

10 윗글의 밑줄 친 cute animals의 예를 글에서 찾아 쓰시오.

→ _____

11 윗글의 내용과 일치하도록 주어진 질문에 대한 답을 글에서 찾아 쓰시오. (두 단어)

What allows Stentzel to generate creative and imaginative works of art?

→ _____

[12~13] 다음 글을 읽고, 물음에 답하시오.

Creativity is not some kind of exceptional skill that belongs to exclusive groups of people. It is actually a part of our daily lives, a power that we can display anytime we choose to. (A) Whether / While we realize it or not, we are constantly using our creativity to adapt, adjust, and rearrange the things around us. By (B) being / doing so, we are turning the ordinary into something extraordinary — something that has never been seen before. Take a look at the things around you, but don't _____.
Look carefully, and you might discover something that (C) spark / sparks your own imagination and creativity.

12 윗글의 빈칸에 들어갈 말로 가장 적절한 것은?

① make your daily lives special
② constantly use your creativity
③ just give them a quick glance
④ try to make something extraordinary
⑤ think of yourself as a creative person

13 (A), (B), (C)의 각 네모 안에서 어법에 맞는 표현으로 가장 적절한 것은?

	(A)	(B)	(C)
①	Whether	being	spark
②	While	being	spark
③	Whether	doing	spark
④	While	doing	sparks
⑤	Whether	doing	sparks

When we talk about "creativity," you might think of a painter, an author, or a movie director. In other words, you might think of people who actually make artistic "creations." What are the differences between "creation" and "creativity"? "Creation" is the act of bringing something into existence. It is mainly focused on the outcome of one's efforts to produce something. ⓐIt can often be the result of someone's artistic expression or thinking. The word "creativity" means the ability to generate something new or original. ⓑIt includes not only using one's imagination for artistic purposes, but also coming up with fresh ideas or solutions to problems. It emphasizes the quality of being innovative and original regardless of the field. We should remember this broader definition of creativity.

14 윗글의 제목으로 가장 적절한 것은?

① Creation vs. Creativity: Beyond the Art
② Broader Understanding of Creation
③ How to Come Up with Fresh Ideas
④ What Is the Purpose of the Art?
⑤ Various Fields of Creation

15 윗글의 밑줄 친 ⓐ, ⓑ It이 가리키는 것을 글에서 찾아 쓰시오.

ⓐ It → _____

ⓑ It → _____

Students throw away a lot of books at the end of each school year. This is a problem because it has a negative effect on the environment by generating a huge amount of waste. I'd like to propose two solutions to this problem. First, we can organize a school event where students can buy, sell, and trade books. This way, we can decrease the number of discarded books and buy books at cheaper prices. Second, I suggest collecting unwanted books and donating them to our local library. By doing so, we can increase the life span of these books and help our community at the same time. I hope the problem of throwing away books can be solved effectively with these two solutions.

16 윗글의 필자와 주장하는 바가 다른 사람은?

① Josh: We discard too many books when we finish the semester.
② Theo: The thrown-away books generate a lot of trash.
③ Caryn: Let's donate the used books to the library.
④ Minji: We can organize a flea market and trade the used books.
⑤ Hojun: I suggest we pass down our used books to our juniors.

17 윗글의 밑줄 친 doing so가 가리키는 내용을 글에서 찾아 쓰시오.

→ _____
_____

[01~02] 다음 대화를 읽고, 물음에 답하시오.

G Sean, what are you doing?

B I'm doing a daily creative challenge. Have you heard about it?

G No, I haven't. What is it?

B It is an activity that cultivates creativity by challenging you to do something creative every day. You can write a poem, play a musical instrument, or craft something!

G Sounds interesting! So what is your challenge?

B I do a drawing challenge. I've been drawing different things every day for a month now.

G I'd like to start a challenge too! Could you give me some advice on how to start?

B I suggest you start with something simple. If you choose something too complicated, you _____.

G Hmm… I'm still not sure what to do.

B Well, how about trying a photo challenge? You can easily take a picture with your phone every day.

01 위 대화의 내용과 일치하지 <u>않는</u> 것은?

① 남학생은 일일 창의적 도전 활동을 한 달째 하고 있다.

② 여학생은 창의적 도전 활동에 대해 들어본 적이 없다.

③ 여학생은 창의적 도전 활동을 직접 해 보고 싶어 한다.

④ 시를 쓰거나 악기를 연주하는 것 등이 창의적 도전 활동에 해당한다.

⑤ 남학생은 여학생에게 그림 그리기를 해보라고 제안한다.

02 위 대화의 빈칸에 들어갈 말로 가장 적절한 것은?

① can easily cultivate creativity

② are not good at taking pictures

③ may be tired of doing same things every day

④ may not be able to complete the challenge every day

⑤ would be able to grow your skills to create something

[03~04] 다음 글을 읽고, 물음에 답하시오.

As a content creator, I'm always in need of fresh ideas, and I recently read about an interesting (A) experience / experiment . A researcher conducted a study to investigate the effects of walking on creativity. (B) Participants / Participation had to come up with as many different ways to use everyday objects as they could. For example, a car key could be used as a bottle opener and a box cutter. The results were surprising. The people who took the test while walking on a treadmill generated almost twice as many ideas as those who took the test while sitting! This means that taking a walk can help you (C) enhance / enable your creativity and develop new ideas. So next time you're faced with a task that requires creativity, I suggest _____. You'll be surprised to see how it helps boost your creativity!

03 (A), (B), (C)의 각 네모 안에서 문맥에 맞는 낱말로 가장 적절한 것은?

	(A)		(B)		(C)
①	experience	···	Participants	···	enhance
②	experiment	···	Participants	···	enhance
③	experience	···	Participants	···	enable
④	experiment	···	Participation	···	enable
⑤	experience	···	Participation	···	enable

04 윗글의 빈칸에 들어갈 말로 가장 적절한 것은?

① you take a walk

② you watch my video

③ you try making online content

④ you generate as many ideas as possible

⑤ you use everyday objects in different ways

[05~06] 다음 글을 읽고, 물음에 답하시오.

Creativity. When you hear this word, what instantly pops into your mind? (①) You may think it is a quality that only artists and writers possess — some special talent you are either born with or without. (②) This common belief, however, is far from the truth. (③) Everyone has the ability to be creative. (④) Finding creativity inside yourself just takes a little effort. (⑤) Some artists, for example, spark their creativity by looking closely at ordinary objects. They try to discover the beauty hidden within these common objects and then turn them into works of art.

05 글의 흐름으로 보아, 주어진 문장이 들어가기에 가장 적절한 곳은?

Many people accept the idea that we can be divided into two groups: those who are creative and those who are not.

①   ②   ③   ④   ⑤

06 윗글에서 다음 영어 뜻풀이에 해당하는 단어를 찾아 쓰시오.

a feeling of being sure that something exists or is true

→ _____

[07~08] 다음 글을 읽고, 물음에 답하시오.

Look at these two paintings. Believe it or not, they both depict the same person, Holy Roman Emperor Rudolf II. The one on the left might look familiar, as it is a standard style of portrait that you would see in a gallery or an art book. However, the one on the right, called *Vertumnus*, is very unconventional. Created by a 16th-century Italian painter named Giuseppe Arcimboldo, the painting shows striking creativity and originality. 과일, 꽃, 채소가 사람의 머리를 만들기 위해 퍼즐 조각처럼 배열되어 있다. A cherry and a mulberry become the dark eyes, while an apple and a peach act as the pink cheeks. This painting is representative of the artist's signature style of "composite portraits." He used plants, animals, and other objects to create many other portraits like this.

07 윗글의 그림 〈Vertumnus〉에 사용된 과일이 <u>아닌</u> 것은?

① a cherry   ② a mulberry
③ an apple   ④ a plum
⑤ a peach

08 윗글의 밑줄 친 우리말과 일치하도록 주어진 조건 에 맞게 문장을 완성하시오.

> 조건
> • 다음 표현을 주어로 문장을 시작할 것: Fruits, flowers, and vegetables
> • 사용할 단어 : arrange, puzzle, create, human

→ _____
    _____

[09~11] 다음 글을 읽고, 물음에 답하시오.

Another good example of Arcimboldo's unique creativity can be found in ⓐ *The Gardener*, one of his "reversible" paintings. When ⓑ view normally, it is just an ordinary still life of vegetables in a bowl. However, when ⓒ flip upside down, it is magically transformed into a smiling face! Experts have studied this painting, along with Arcimboldo's other reversible _____. Their research showed that he first painted them as still life paintings and then turned them upside down and made some adjustments to create faces. X-ray examination revealed that he sometimes changed the positions of some of the fruits and vegetables.

09 윗글의 밑줄 친 ⓐ The Gardener에 관해 글의 내용과 일치하지 않는 것은?

① Arcimboldo가 만든 작품이다.
② 그릇에 담긴 채소를 그린 정물화이다.
③ 거꾸로 뒤집으면 웃는 얼굴이 나타난다.
④ 전문가들이 Arcimboldo의 다른 그림들과 함께 엑스레이 검사를 시행했다.
⑤ 똑바로 보았을 때와 거꾸로 뒤집었을 때 사물의 위치는 동일하다.

10 윗글의 밑줄 친 ⓑ와 ⓒ를 알맞은 형태로 바꿔 쓰시오.

ⓑ view → _____

ⓒ flip → _____

11 윗글의 빈칸에 들어갈 말로 가장 적절한 것은?

① it   ② one   ③ those
④ ones   ⑤ painting

[12~13] 다음 글을 읽고, 물음에 답하시오.

Take a look at this picture. Do you see a horse standing in a field? Or is it simply a collection of clothes hanging on a clothesline? This witty and amusing creation is actually a work of art (A) creating / created by the visual artist Helga Stentzel. Using everyday items, she creates playful visual illusions that force you to look twice in order to confirm (B) that / what you have just seen. Her unique style has been called "household surrealism."

Stentzel is perhaps best known for her *Clothesline Animals* series. She got inspiration for the series while she was hanging her laundry. By simply adding some colorful clothespins and a dish towel, she was able to transform her black sweatshirt and dark grey pants into a horse. Other creations followed, including a brown cow standing on some hills and a zebra (C) cross / crossing the desert. All of these works were created from nothing more than laundry and household items.

12 윗글의 밑줄 친 this picture에 관해 주어진 질문에 대한 답을 모두 찾아 쓰시오.

What objects are used to create this picture?

→ _____

_____

13 (A), (B), (C)의 각 네모 안에서 어법에 맞는 표현으로 가장 적절한 것은?

	(A)	(B)	(C)
①	creating	that	cross
②	creating	what	cross
③	creating	that	crossing
④	created	what	crossing
⑤	created	that	crossing

Creativity is not some kind of exceptional skill that belongs to exclusive groups of people. It is actually a part of our daily lives, a power that we can display anytime we choose to. Whether we realize it or not, we are constantly using our creativity to adapt, adjust, and rearrange the things around us. By doing so, we are turning the ordinary into something extraordinary — _____. Take a look at the things around you, but don't just give them a quick glance. Look carefully, and you might discover something that sparks your own imagination and creativity.

14 윗글의 내용과 일치하도록 다음 문장의 빈칸에 알맞은 말을 글에서 찾아 쓰시오.

Though we may not (1) _____ it, we keep using our creativity. Thus we should (2) _____ watch the things around us and find what inspires our creativity.

15 윗글의 빈칸에 들어갈 말을 보기 에 주어진 단어를 바르게 배열하여 쓰시오.

보기
that / something / been / before / never / has / seen

→ _____

Students throw away a lot of books at the end of each school year. This is a problem because it has a negative effect on the environment by generating a huge amount of waste. I'd like to propose two solutions to this problem. First, we can organize a school event where students can buy, sell, and trade books. This way, we can decrease the number of discarded books and buy books at cheaper prices. Second, I suggest collecting unwanted books and donating them to our local library. By doing so, we can increase the life span of these books and help our community at the same time. I hope the problem of throwing away books can be solved effectively with these two solutions.

16 윗글의 어조로 가장 적절한 것은?

① persuasive   ② humorous
③ hopeful   ④ critical
⑤ sympathetic

17 윗글의 밑줄 친 this problem의 구체적인 내용을 우리말로 쓰시오.

→ _____

[01~02] 다음 글을 읽고, 물음에 답하시오.

As a content creator, I'm always in need of fresh ideas, and I recently read about an interesting experiment. A researcher ①conducted a study to investigate the effects of walking on creativity. Participants had to come up with as many different ways to use ②everyday objects as they could. For example, a car key could be used as a bottle opener and a box cutter. The ③results were surprising. The people who took the test while walking on a treadmill generated almost twice as many ideas as those who took the test while sitting! This means that taking a walk can help you ④enhance your creativity and develop new ideas. So next time you're faced with a task that ⑤restricts creativity, I suggest you take a walk. You'll be surprised to see how it helps boost your creativity!

01 윗글의 요지로 가장 적절한 것은?

① The most important qualification for a content creator is generating ideas.
② Those who walk a lot live healthier lives than those who don't.
③ The best way to come up with ideas is to think twice.
④ Research shows that outdoor activities are good for mental health.
⑤ Walking can significantly enhance creativity and the ability to generate new ideas.

02 윗글의 밑줄 친 부분 중, 문맥상 낱말의 쓰임이 적절하지 않은 것은?

①   ②   ③   ④   ⑤

[03~04] 다음 글을 읽고, 물음에 답하시오.

Creativity. When you hear this word, what instantly pops into your mind? You may think it is a quality that only artists and writers possess—some special talent you are either born with or without. Many people accept the idea that _____ : those who are creative and those who are not. This common belief, however, is far from the truth. Everyone has the ability to be creative. Finding creativity inside yourself just takes a little effort. Some artists, for example, spark their creativity by looking closely at ordinary objects. They try to discover the beauty hidden within these common objects and then turn them into works of art.

03 윗글의 요약문을 완성할 때 빈칸 (A), (B)에 들어갈 말이 바르게 짝지어진 것은?

Creativity is an innate ability everyone ___(A)___ . By making a conscious effort, anyone can unlock their creative potential and ___(B)___ ordinary things into something artistic.

	(A)		(B)
①	asks	⋯	create
②	belongs	⋯	generate
③	aspires	⋯	change
④	inherited	⋯	enhance
⑤	possesses	⋯	transform

04 윗글의 빈칸에 들어갈 말로 가장 적절한 것은?

① only artists and writers have creativity
② we can be divided into two groups
③ everyone has potential to be creative
④ finding hidden creativity takes time
⑤ close observation helps grow creativity

[05~06] 다음 글을 읽고, 물음에 답하시오.

Look at these two paintings. Believe it or not, they ① both depicts the same person, Holy Roman Emperor Rudolf II. The one on the left might look familiar, as it is a standard style of portrait ② that you would see in a gallery or an art book. However, the one on the right, called *Vertumnus*, is very unconventional. ③ Created by a 16th-century Italian painter named Giuseppe Arcimboldo, the painting shows striking creativity and originality. Fruits, flowers, and vegetables ④ are arranged like the pieces of a puzzle to create a human head. A cherry and a mulberry become the dark eyes, while an apple and a peach act as the pink cheeks. This painting is representative of the artist's signature style of "composite portraits." He used plants, animals, and other objects ⑤ to create many other portraits like this.

05 윗글의 〈Vertumnus〉에 관한 설명으로 글의 내용과 일치하지 않는 것은?

① It is the portrait of Holy Roman Emperor Rudolf II.
② It looks unconventional to the viewers.
③ It was painted by Giuseppe Arcimboldo.
④ The man in the picture is eating fruit.
⑤ It represents the artist's style of "composite portraits."

06 윗글의 밑줄 친 부분 중, 어법상 틀린 것은?

① ② ③ ④ ⑤

[07~08] 다음 글을 읽고, 물음에 답하시오.

Experts have studied this painting, along with Arcimboldo's other reversible ones. ① Their research showed that he first painted them as still life paintings and then turned them upside down and made some adjustments to create faces. ② X-ray examination revealed that he sometimes changed the positions of some of the fruits and vegetables. ③ The research suggests that viewers of Arcimboldo's reversible paintings felt a sense of confusion. ④ Why did he make his paintings reversible? ⑤ It was probably because he wanted to add an interactive element to his work by doing so. Viewers feel as if they are playing a visual game, which brings them a sense of pleasure.

07 윗글의 ①~⑤ 중에서 전체 흐름과 관계 없는 문장은?

① ② ③ ④ ⑤

08 윗글의 제목으로 가장 적절한 것은?

① The Life of Italian Artist, Arcimboldo
② The Still Life Art of 16th-Century Italy
③ The Scientific Analysis of Artistic Masterpieces
④ The Reversible Art of Arcimboldo: From Still Life to Portrait
⑤ The Artistic Techniques for Painting Detailed Fruits and Vegetables

[09~10] 다음 글을 읽고, 물음에 답하시오.

Take a look at this picture. Do you see a horse standing in a field? Or is it simply a collection of clothes hanging on a clothesline? This witty and amusing creation is actually a work of art created by the visual artist Helga Stentzel. Using everyday items, she creates playful visual (A) allusions / illusions that force you to look twice in order to confirm what you have just seen. Her unique style has been called "household surrealism."

Stentzel is perhaps best known for her *Clothesline Animals* series. She got inspiration for the series _____. By simply adding some colorful clothespins and a dish towel, she was able to (B) transfer / transform her black sweatshirt and dark grey pants into a horse. Other creations followed, including a brown cow standing on some hills and a zebra crossing the (C) desert / dessert. All of these works were created from nothing more than laundry and household items.

09 윗글의 빈칸에 들어갈 말로 가장 적절한 것은?

① while hanging her laundry
② at her kitchen table
③ when she visited the zoo
④ by watching animals carefully
⑤ to create "household surrealism"

10 (A), (B), (C)의 각 네모 안에서 문맥에 맞는 낱말로 가장 적절한 것은?

	(A)		(B)		(C)
①	allusions	⋯	transfer	⋯	desert
②	allusions	⋯	transfer	⋯	dessert
③	allusions	⋯	transform	⋯	desert
④	illusions	⋯	transform	⋯	dessert
⑤	illusions	⋯	transform	⋯	desert

[11~12] 다음 글을 읽고, 물음에 답하시오.

Another series that highlights Stentzel's astonishing creativity is *Edible Creatures*. For this series, she arranges food items you can find in any kitchen to create cute animals. The stars of the series are *Brad Pet* and *Crunchie*, a pair of puppies made of sliced bread and lettuce respectively. (①) Stentzel says she came up with the concept of *Crunchie* while putting together a salad for her family.

What do you think her secret is? (②) As a child, she would spend time staring at the patterns in the wood of her bed, trying to find different animal shapes. (③) She admits that even today she stares at things longer than is acceptable in society. (④) This keen observation is what enables her to continuously produce creative and imaginative works of art. (⑤)

11 글의 흐름으로 보아, 주어진 문장이 들어가기에 가장 적절한 곳은?

Stentzel says that it is her active observation skills that allow her to make magic out of the ordinary.

①   ②   ③   ④   ⑤

12 윗글의 내용과 일치하지 않는 것은?

① One of Stentzel's well-known series is *Edible Creatures*.
② *Crunchie* is made of sliced bread and lettuce.
③ Stentzel got the inspiration for *Edible Creatures* from her kitchen.
④ Young Stentzel spent time staring at things around her.
⑤ Stentzel believes her creativity comes from her observation skills.

When we talk about "creativity," you might think of a painter, an author, or a movie director. _____, you might think of people who actually make artistic "creations." What are the differences between "creation" and "creativity"?

(A) The word "creativity" means the ability to generate something new or original.

(B) "Creation" is the act of bringing something into existence. It is mainly focused on the outcome of one's efforts to produce something. It can often be the result of someone's artistic expression or thinking.

(C) It emphasizes the quality of being innovative and original regardless of the field. We should remember this broader definition of creativity.

(D) It includes not only using one's imagination for artistic purposes, but also coming up with fresh ideas or solutions to problems.

13 주어진 문장 다음에 이어질 글의 순서로 가장 적절한 것은?

① (A) – (C) – (B) – (D)
② (B) – (A) – (D) – (C)
③ (B) – (D) – (C) – (A)
④ (C) – (B) – (A) – (D)
⑤ (D) – (A) – (C) – (B)

14 윗글의 빈칸에 들어갈 말로 가장 적절한 것은?

① For example
② In consequence
③ On the other hand
④ In other words
⑤ What is more

While it is well known that exercise is essential for our physical health, not many people know that it can also boost our creativity. This is because physical activity can enhance our mood and (A) reduce / reduces negative emotions, which are factors that restrict creativity. Also, exercise increases blood flow to the brain, (B) provide / providing it with the nutrients it needs to function better. When at its best, the brain can generate more creative ideas. Moreover, exercise often leads us to go outside and visit different places. By (C) doing / done so, we can expose ourselves to new sources of inspiration and alter the way we think.

15 윗글의 제목으로 가장 적절한 것은?

① Go Outside and Find Inspiration for Your Art
② The Importance of Physical Activities
③ When Does Your Brain Work Best?
④ How Exercise Boosts Creativity
⑤ Exercise and Mental Health

16 (A), (B), (C)의 각 네모 안에서 어법에 맞는 표현으로 가장 적절한 것은?

	(A)		(B)		(C)
①	reduce	…	provide	…	doing
②	reduce	…	providing	…	doing
③	reduce	…	provide	…	done
④	reduces	…	providing	…	done
⑤	reduces	…	provide	…	done

[01~02] 다음 글을 읽고, 물음에 답하시오.

Creativity. When you hear this word, what instantly pops into your mind? You may think it is a quality that only artists and writers possess — _____ . Many people accept the idea that we can be divided into two groups: those who are creative and those who are not. This common belief, however, is far from the truth. Everyone has the ability to be creative. Finding creativity inside yourself just ⓐ<u>take</u> a little effort. Some artists, for example, spark their creativity by looking closely at ordinary objects. They try to discover the beauty ⓑ<u>hide</u> within these common objects and then turn them into works of art.

01 윗글의 빈칸에 들어갈 말을 보기 에 주어진 표현을 바르게 배열하여 쓰시오.

보기

either / you / or / born / with / without / are / some special talent

→ _____

02 윗글의 밑줄 친 ⓐ, ⓑ의 동사를 알맞은 형태로 바꿔 쓰시오.

ⓐ take → _____

ⓑ hide → _____

[03~04] 다음 글을 읽고, 물음에 답하시오.

Look at these two paintings. Believe it or not, they both depict the same person, Holy Roman Emperor Rudolf II. The one on the left might look familiar, as it is a standard style of portrait that you would see in a gallery or an art book. However, the one on the right, called ⓐ*Vertumnus*, is very unconventional. ⓑGiuseppe Arcimboldo라는 이름의 16세기 이탈리아 화가에 의해 창작되어, the painting shows striking creativity and originality. Fruits, flowers, and vegetables are arranged like the pieces of a puzzle to create a human head. A cherry and a mulberry become the dark eyes, while an apple and a peach act as the pink cheeks. This painting is representative of the artist's signature style of "composite portraits." He used plants, animals, and other objects to create many other portraits like this.

03 윗글의 밑줄 친 ⓐ Vertumnus에 사용된 과일을 모두 찾아 쓰시오.

→ _____

04 윗글의 밑줄 친 ⓑ의 우리말과 일치하도록 주어진 조건 에 맞게 문장을 완성하시오.

조건

• 과거분사로 문장을 시작할 것
• 사용할 단어: create, name

→ _____

Giuseppe Arcimboldo, the painting shows striking creativity and originality.

[05~06] 다음 글을 읽고, 물음에 답하시오.

Another good example of Arcimboldo's unique creativity can be found in *The Gardener*, one of his "reversible" paintings. When viewing normally, it is just an ordinary still life of vegetables in a bowl. However, when flipped upside down, it is magically transformed into a smiling face! Experts have studied this painting, along with Arcimboldo's other reversible ones. Their research showed that he first painted them as still life paintings and then turned them upside down and made some adjustments to create faces. X-ray examination revealed that he sometimes changed the positions of some of the fruits and vegetables. Why did he make his paintings reversible? It was probably because he wanted to add an interactive element to his work by doing so. Viewers feel as if they are playing a visual game, which brings them a sense of pleasure.

05 윗글의 밑줄 친 his "reversible" paintings의 구체적인 제작 방식을 나타낸 문장을 글에서 찾아 쓰시오.

→ _____

_____

06 윗글의 내용과 일치하도록 주어진 질문에 대한 답을 완성하시오.

What was the reason Arcimboldo created reversible paintings?

→ It was probable that _____

_____ .

[07~09] 다음 글을 읽고, 물음에 답하시오.

Another series that highlights Stentzel's astonishing creativity is *Edible Creatures*. For this series, she arranges food items you can find in any kitchen to create cute animals. The stars of the series are *Brad Pet* and *Crunchie*, a pair of puppies made of sliced bread and lettuce respectively. Stentzel says she came up with the concept of *Crunchie* ⓐwhile she was putting together a salad for her family.

What do you think her secret is? Stentzel says that it is her active observation skills that allow her to make magic out of the ordinary. As a child, she would spend time staring at the patterns in the wood of her bed, trying to find different animal shapes. She admits that even today she stares at things longer than is acceptable in society. ⓑ이러한 예리한 관찰력이 그녀가 창의적이고 상상력이 풍부한 예술 작품을 계속해서 만들어낼 수 있게 하는 것이다.

07 윗글의 내용과 일치하도록 다음 문장의 빈칸에 알맞은 말을 글에서 찾아 쓰시오.

Stentzel created *Brad Pet* with (1) _____ bread, which is the (2) _____ of her *Edible Creatures* series.

08 윗글의 밑줄 친 ⓐ에서 생략할 수 있는 부분을 찾아 바꿔 쓰시오.

→ Stentzel says she came up with the concept of *Crunchie* _____ .

09 윗글의 밑줄 친 ⓑ의 우리말과 일치하도록 주어진 조건에 맞게 문장을 완성하시오.

조건
• 관계대명사 what을 사용할 것
• 사용할 단어: enable, produce, imaginative

→ This keen observation is _____

_____ .

[10~11] 다음 글을 읽고, 물음에 답하시오.

Creativity is not some kind of exceptional skill that belongs to exclusive groups of people. It is actually a part of our daily lives, a power that we can display anytime we choose to. ⓐ우리가 그것을 인식하든 인식하지 못하든, we are constantly using our creativity to adapt, adjust, and rearrange the things around us. ⓑ그렇게 함으로써, we are turning the ordinary into something _____ —something that has never been seen before. Take a look at the things around you, but don't just give them a quick glance. Look carefully, and you might discover something that sparks your own imagination and creativity.

10 윗글의 밑줄 친 ⓐ, ⓑ의 우리말과 일치하도록 보기 에 주어진 표현을 활용하여 쓰시오.

> **보기**
>
> whether, realize, by, do

ⓐ → _____

ⓑ → _____

11 윗글의 빈칸에 알맞은 말을 주어진 조건 에 맞게 쓰시오.

> **조건**
> • 한 단어의 형용사로 쓸 것
> • 글에서 쓰인 단어의 반의어로 나타낼 것

→ _____

[12~13] 다음 글을 읽고, 물음에 답하시오.

While it is well known that exercise is essential for our physical health, not many people know that ⓐit can also boost our creativity. This is because physical activity can enhance our mood and reduce negative emotions, which are factors that restrict creativity. Also, exercise increases blood flow to the brain, providing ⓑit with the nutrients it needs to function better. When at its best, the brain can generate more creative ideas. Moreover, exercise often leads us to go outside and visit different places. By doing so, we can expose ourselves to new sources of inspiration and alter the way we think.

12 윗글의 밑줄 친 ⓐ, ⓑ it이 가리키는 것을 글에서 찾아 쓰시오.

ⓐ it → _____

ⓑ it → _____

13 윗글에서 언급된 신체 활동(exercise)의 기능 세 가지를 우리 말로 쓰시오. (각 10단어 내외)

(1) _____

(2) _____

(3) _____

05

Rise Above Challenges

Functions

▶ 능력 표현하기
I was able to talk to people without much difficulty thanks to the app.

▶ 놀람 표현하기
It's surprising that we can communicate in a language we don't know.

Structures

▶ She started looking for a coach in Berlin who could **help** her **reach** her full potential.
▶ She eventually met Sven Spannekrebs and **asked if** he could be her coach.

교과서 **어휘** ────────────────────

Words

☐ journey	몡 여행, 여정	☐ disappear	통 사라지다 (↔ appear 나타나다)
☐ former	혱 과거의, 이전의	☐ drift	통 표류하다
☐ professional	혱 전문적인	☐ shore	몡 해안, 해변
☐ compete	통 참가하다, 경쟁하다 (competition 몡 경쟁)	☐ distance	몡 거리
☐ represent	통 대표하다	☐ border	몡 국경, 경계
☐ international	혱 국제적인	☐ exhausted	혱 지친, 기진맥진한
☐ risky	혱 위험한 (risk 몡 위험)	☐ overwhelming	혱 압도적인 (overwhelm 통 압도하다)
☐ chaos	몡 혼란, 혼돈	☐ settle	통 정착하다
☐ fateful	혱 운명적인 (fate 몡 운명)	☐ refugee	몡 난민
☐ bomb	몡 폭탄	☐ hardship	몡 어려움, 고난
☐ explode	통 터지다 (explosion 몡 폭발)	☐ adversity	몡 역경
☐ incident	몡 사건	☐ undergo	통 (안 좋은 일을) 겪다 (undergo−underwent−undergone)
☐ horrifying	혱 무서운 (horrify 통 몸서리치게 하다)	☐ outstanding	혱 뛰어난
☐ flee	통 달아나다, 도망치다 (flee−fled−fled)	☐ persistent	혱 끈질긴
☐ destination	몡 목적지	☐ excellence	몡 탁월함 (excellent 혱 뛰어난)
☐ board	통 (배, 기차 등에) 타다	☐ instruction	몡 지도, 가르침
☐ strike	통 발생하다	☐ hesitant	혱 망설이는 (hesitate 통 망설이다)
☐ sink	통 가라앉다	☐ pity	몡 연민
☐ panic	통 겁에 질려 어쩔 줄 모르다	☐ athlete	몡 (운동)선수
☐ desperate	혱 필사적인	☐ determined	혱 굳게 결심한
☐ possessions	몡 소지품, 재산	☐ pour	통 붓다
☐ heartbroken	혱 비통해 하는	☐ alongside	전 ~과 함께
☐ treasure	통 소중히 여기다	☐ statement	몡 성명, 진술
☐ belongings	몡 소지품, 재산	☐ remark	통 언급하다

Phrases

☐ center around	~에 중점을 두다	☐ feel at home	마음이 편하다
☐ come true	실현되다	☐ have no choice but to-v	~하지 않을 수 없다
☐ break out	발발하다	☐ take up	시작하다
☐ cling to	~에 매달리다	☐ day and night	주야로, 끊임없이
☐ wake-up call	정신을 차리게 하는 신호	☐ pay off	성과를 내다
☐ make up one's mind	결심하다 (= decide)	☐ turn down	거절하다 (= refuse)

교과서 어휘 익히기

♣ 다음 영어는 우리말로, 우리말은 영어로 쓰시오.

01 adversity ㊅ _____	26 ㊅ 난민 _____
02 represent ㊊ _____	27 ㊅ 혼란, 혼돈 _____
03 risky ㊌ _____	28 ㊅ 국경, 경계 _____
04 alongside ㊓ _____	29 ㊌ 망설이는 _____
05 flee ㊊ _____	30 ㊅ 여행, 여정 _____
06 settle ㊊ _____	31 ㊊ 소중히 여기다 _____
07 horrifying ㊌ _____	32 결심하다 _____
08 panic ㊊ _____	33 ㊌ 압도적인 _____
09 belongings ㊅ _____	34 ㊌ 끈질긴 _____
10 come true _____	35 ㊅ 연민 _____
11 instruction ㊅ _____	36 ㊊ 터지다 _____
12 heartbroken ㊌ _____	37 ㊌ 과거의, 이전의 _____
13 bomb ㊅ _____	38 ㊊ (안 좋은 일을) 겪다 _____
14 board ㊊ _____	39 거절하다 _____
15 hardship ㊅ _____	40 ㊊ 표류하다 _____
16 statement ㊅ _____	41 ㊌ 운명적인 _____
17 possessions ㊅ _____	42 ㊅ 탁월함 _____
18 strike ㊊ _____	43 ㊊ 가라앉다 _____
19 determined ㊌ _____	44 발발하다 _____
20 cling to _____	45 ㊌ 지친, 기진맥진한 _____
21 incident ㊅ _____	46 ㊅ (운동)선수 _____
22 remark ㊊ _____	47 ㊊ 참가하다, 경쟁하다 _____
23 outstanding ㊌ _____	48 ㊌ 국제적인 _____
24 professional ㊌ _____	49 ㊌ 필사적인 _____
25 pay off _____	50 ㊅ 목적지 _____

POINT 1 help + 목적어 + 동사원형

예제 This application can **help** people **(to) gain** confidence in speaking English.
        목적어   목적격 보어
이 앱은 사람들이 영어 말하기에 자신감을 가지도록 도와줄 수 있다.

교과서 She started looking for a coach in Berlin who could **help** her **(to) reach** her full potential.
                                                     목적어   목적격 보어
그녀는 베를린에서 자신의 최대 잠재력에 도달할 수 있도록 도와줄 코치를 찾기 시작했다.

▶ 동사 help는 준사역동사로 「동사＋목적어＋목적격 보어」의 5형식 문장으로 많이 쓰이며, '(목적어)가 ~하는 것을 돕다'라는 의미이다.
▶ 목적격 보어 자리에 동사원형이나 to부정사 둘 다 올 수 있으며, 보통 동사원형 형태로 더 많이 쓰인다.

Study Point 🏅

1 help + 목적어 + 목적격 보어

- Can you **help me (to) finish** my science project this weekend?
  이번 주말에 내가 과학 프로젝트 완성하는 걸 도와줄 수 있니?

- It was her brother who **helped her (to) learn** how to ride a bike.
  그녀가 자전거 타는 법을 배우도록 도와준 사람은 바로 그녀의 오빠였다.

- I **helped my grandma (to) get** tickets for her favorite singer's concert online.
  나는 할머니가 좋아하는 가수의 콘서트 표를 온라인으로 사는 것을 도와드렸다.

2 help를 사용한 여러 관용 표현

- Tommy **could not help laughing** at the man's ridiculous remark.
  <u>cannot help v-ing: ~하지 않을 수 없다 (= cannot help but + 동사원형)</u>
  Tommy는 그 남자의 어처구니 없는 말에 웃을 수밖에 없었다.

- She approached the table and **helped herself to** the sandwiches and cookies.
  <u>help oneself to: ~을 마음껏 먹다[쓰다]</u>
  그녀는 식탁으로 다가가서 샌드위치와 과자를 맘껏 먹었다.

Q 다음 네모 안에서 어법상 알맞은 것을 고르시오.

1 Ms. Briton helped her daughter follow / follows her dream.

2 The coach helped the athletes improved / to improve their skills.

3 Regular exercise can help / allow people stay healthy.

Check-up 🍊

01 우리말과 일치하도록 괄호 안에 주어진 표현을 활용하여 문장을 완성하시오.

(1) 음악을 듣는 것은 당신이 스트레스를 줄이는 데에 도움이 될 수 있다. (help, relieve)

→ Listening to music _____ .

(2) 도서관의 프로그램은 학생들이 독서 습관을 키우는 데 도움이 될 것이다. (help, cultivate)

→ The library program _____ .

(3) 수학을 배우는 것은 우리가 논리적으로 사고하는 데에 도움이 된다. (help, logically)

→ Learning math _____ .

(4) 그의 개는 그가 덜 외롭게 느끼도록 도와주었다. (help, lonely)

→ His dog _____ .

02 다음 문장에서 어법상 <u>어색한</u> 부분을 찾아 바르게 고쳐 쓰시오.

(1) The scientists helped the baby elephant survives in the forest.

→ _____

(2) The director of the movie wanted to help people understanding the environmental crisis.

→ _____

(3) Michel helped me learned French during my stay in Paris.

→ _____

(4) Self-confidence will make you to face challenges in your life.

→ _____

03 다음 글을 읽고, Power Clean에 대한 설명으로 바르지 <u>않은</u> 것을 고르시오. 교과서 129쪽

> Are you tired of trying to get dirty stains out of your clothes? Try Power Clean! This brand-new product will help your clothes regain their original brightness and colors. With Power Clean, your clothes can always look as good as new! Also, Power Clean contains special ingredients that help clothes smell fresh and clean for a longer period of time. Try our product and witness the difference!

① 옷에 묻은 얼룩을 지워준다.　　　　　　② 원래 옷의 밝기와 색깔을 되찾아 준다.

③ 옷을 새것처럼 보이게 해준다.　　　　　④ 빠르게 땀을 배출하게 도와준다.

⑤ 상쾌하고 깨끗한 냄새가 나게 해준다.

POINT 2 의문문의 화법 전환

예제	He **asked whether** he could get a free ticket for the baseball game.

↳ "Can I get a free ticket for the baseball game?"

그는 야구 경기의 공짜 표를 구할 수 있는지 물었다.

교과서	She eventually met Sven Spannekrebs and **asked if** he could be her coach.

↳ "Can you be my coach?"

그녀는 결국 Sven Spannekrebs를 만났고, 그에게 그녀의 코치가 되어줄 수 있는지 물어봤다.

▶ 의문사가 없는 의문문을 간접화법으로 바꿀 때에는 동사 **ask**를 사용한다.
▶ 의문문은 접속사 **if나 whether**를 사용하여 연결하며, 평서문의 어순으로 바꾼다.

Study Point 🍑

1 의문사가 없는 의문문의 화법 전환

간접의문문 앞에 접속사 if나 whether를 사용하고 어순은 「주어+동사」로 바꾼 후, 동사의 시제와 인칭대명사를 알맞게 전환한다.

• Tony asked, "Are you a vegetarian?"

→ Tony **asked if[whether]** I was a vegetarian. Tony는 내가 채식주의자인지 물었다.

• We asked, "Does she like dancing?"

→ We **asked if[whether]** she liked dancing. 우리는 그녀가 춤을 좋아하는지 물었다.

2 의문사가 있는 의문문의 화법 전환

간접의문문에 쓰인 의문사가 접속사의 역할을 한다. 어순은 「주어+동사」로 바꾼 후, 동사의 시제와 인칭대명사를 알맞게 전환한다.

• Kevin asked, "What do you do for exercise?"

→ Kevin **asked what** I did for exercise. Kevin은 내가 운동으로 무엇을 하는지 물었다.

Q 다음 네모 안에서 어법상 알맞은 것을 고르시오.

1 Joan asked ⎡what / where⎤ I had bought the flowers.

2 They said ⎡that / whether⎤ he was their older brother.

3 The teacher asked ⎡if / that⎤ we had any questions about the project.

4 He asked whether I ⎡have / had⎤ read the Harry Potter series.

Check-up 🍅

01 우리말과 일치하도록 괄호 안에 주어진 표현을 활용하여 문장을 완성하시오.

(1) 그들은 내가 그들과 같이 축구를 하고 싶은지 물었다. (play soccer)

→ They asked _____ with them.

(2) 나는 그녀가 몇 시에 학교에 가는지 물었다. (go to school)

→ I asked _____.

(3) 엄마는 누가 그녀의 컵을 깨뜨렸는지 물었다. (break)

→ Mom asked _____.

(4) 그녀는 그들이 과제를 끝냈는지 물었다. (finish the project)

→ She asked _____.

02 다음 문장을 보기와 같이 바꿔 쓰시오.

> 보기 The doctor asked, "Do you usually sleep well?"
> → The doctor asked if I usually slept well.

(1) I asked, "Does she work at this restaurant?"

→ I _____.

(2) The teacher asked, "Are you ready for the math test?"

→ The teacher _____.

(3) She asked, "Have you ever been to Paris?"

→ She _____.

(4) We asked, "Why did the singer cancel her concert?"

→ We _____.

03 다음 글의 밑줄 친 부분을 간접화법으로 바꿔 쓰시오. 교과서 129쪽

> To the shop manager,
> I want to express my deepest appreciation for the exceptional service provided by one of your employees. Last week, I stopped by your store to buy a scarf for my daughter and left my phone there. To my surprise, as soon as I got back to the store, he remembered me and (1) asked, "Did you leave something behind?" I told him I had forgotten my phone and (2) asked, "Did you see it?" He kindly asked the other employees about my phone, and I got it back from one of them. I would have been disappointed if I had lost my phone, so his kindness made my day.

(1) _____ (2) _____

A Journey from War to the Olympics
전쟁에서 올림픽까지의 여정

01 When Yusra Mardini was a young girl [growing up in Damascus, Syria], her life centered around
현재분사구   center around: ~에 중점을 두다
swimming.

Yusra Mardini가 시리아의 다마스쿠스에서 자라는 어린 소녀였을 때, 그녀의 삶은 수영을 중심으로 돌아갔다.

02 Her father was a former professional swimmer, and she started learning how to swim from a young
how to-v: ~하는 방법
age.

그녀의 아버지는 전직 프로 수영 선수였고, 그래서 그녀는 어릴 때부터 수영하는 방법을 배우기 시작했다.

03 [When she was nine years old], she was already faster than many older swimmers.
부사절 <시간>

아홉 살 때 이미 그녀는 나이가 더 많은 다른 수영 선수들보다 더 빨랐다.

04 It was clear [that she had a special talent], and she fell in love with the sport.
가주어   진주어   = swimming

그녀에게 특별한 재능이 있는 것이 분명했고, 그녀는 그 스포츠와 사랑에 빠졌다.

05 동명사 (enjoyed의 목적어)
She enjoyed watching Olympic swimming events with her father, [which led her to dream about
계속적 용법의 주격 관계대명사절
competing in the Olympics].

그녀는 자신의 아버지와 함께 올림픽 수영 경기를 보는 것을 즐겼고, 이는 그녀가 올림픽에 참가하는 것을 꿈꾸게 했다.

06 형용사적 용법
She got the chance [to represent Syria in an international swimming championship], and it seemed
seem like: ~처럼 보이다
like her Olympic dream might someday come true.
실현되다

그녀는 국제 수영 선수권 대회에서 시리아를 대표할 기회를 얻었고, 올림픽에 대한 그녀의 꿈이 언젠가 실현될 것처럼 보였다.

07 However, Yusra had no idea that her life would soon be turned upside down by the horrors of the
대과거(had p.p.)   수동태
Syrian civil war, [which had broken out in 2011].
계속적 용법의 주격 관계대명사절

하지만, Yusra는 시리아 내전의 공포로 인해 그녀의 삶이 곧 뒤집어질 것이라고 전혀 생각하지 못했는데, 그것(시리아 내전)은 2011년에 발발했다.

08 Over the next few years, normal activities [like going to school] became risky.
전치사구

이후 몇 년간, 학교에 가는 것과 같은 평범한 활동이 위험해졌다.

09 Through all of this chaos, she clung to her dream and kept swimming.
동사 1 — cling to: ~에 매달리다
동사 2 — keep v-ing: 계속해서 ~하다

이 모든 혼란 속에서도 그녀는 자신의 꿈에 매달렸고, 계속 수영을 했다.

10 However, even this became dangerous.
= swimming

그럴지만 이것조차도 위험해졌다.

11 One fateful day, a bomb fell in the pool [where she was training].
관계부사절

어느 운명적인 날, 그녀가 훈련하고 있던 수영장에 폭탄이 떨어졌다.

12 Although it did not explode, this incident was horrifying enough to be a wake-up call for Yusra
= a bomb
형용사[부사] + enough to-v: ~할 만큼 충분히 …한[하게]
and her sister Sara.

비록 그것이 폭발하지는 않았지만, 이 사건은 Yusra와 그녀의 언니 Sara의 정신을 차리게 하는 신호가 될 만큼 충분히 무서운 일이었다.

13 They realized [that they could no longer stay in their home country], and they made up their
명사절 (realized의 목적어)
동사 1 — 더 이상 ~하지 않는 — 동사 2
minds to flee Syria and go to Germany [to avoid the war].
(to) — 부사적 용법 〈목적〉

그들은 더 이상 조국에 머물 수 없다는 것을 깨달았고, 전쟁을 피해 시리아에서 달아나 독일로 가기로 결심했다.

14 If they reached Europe, the rest of the family would follow.
전치사 to가 필요 없는 타동사

그들이 유럽에 도착하면, 나머지 가족도 뒤따라오기로 했다.

15 The decision was not an easy one, but Yusra knew [that it was her only option {if she wanted to
명사절 (knew의 목적어)
부사절 〈조건〉
pursue her dream and live without fear}].
(to)

그것은 쉽지 않은 결정이었지만, Yusra는 자신의 꿈을 추구하고 두려움 없이 살고 싶다면 그것이 유일한 선택지라는 것을 알고 있었다.

16 In August, 2015, the sisters began their dangerous journey by making their way to their first
<u>make one's way: 나아가다</u>
destination, Türkiye.
동격의 콤마

2015년 8월, 자매는 그들의 첫 번째 목적지인 튀르키예로 향하면서 그들의 위험한 여정을 시작했다.

17 There, along with 18 other people, including children and babies, they boarded a tiny boat [designed
~과 함께   <삽입구>   과거분사구
for seven passengers].

그곳에서 그들은 어린이들과 아기들을 포함한 18명의 다른 사람들과 함께 7명의 승객이 탑승할 수 있도록 만들어진 작은 보트에 탔다.

18 They were heading across the sea towards Greece [when disaster struck].
과거진행형   부사절 <시간>

재앙이 닥쳤을 때, 그들은 그리스를 향해 바다를 건너는 중이었다.

19 The boat's engine failed in the middle of the open sea, and the weather rapidly grew worse.
~의 한가운데에   grow + 형용사(비교급): ~해지다

보트의 엔진이 망망대해 한가운데서 멈췄고, 날씨가 급격히 나빠졌다.

20 The heavy boat began to sink, and the panicked, desperate passengers had no choice but to throw
have no choice but to-v: ~할 수밖에 없다
their possessions into the sea.

무거운 보트는 가라앉기 시작했고, 겁에 질린 필사적인 승객들은 자신의 소지품을 바다로 던질 수밖에 없었다.

21 부사절 (~하면서)
Yusra felt heartbroken [as she watched people's treasured belongings disappear under the waves].
watch(지각동사) + 목적어 + 동사원형: ~이 …하는 것을 보다

Yusra는 사람들의 소중한 소지품들이 물결 아래로 사라지는 것을 보며 비통함을 느꼈다.

22 However, she had no time to reflect.
형용사적 용법

하지만, 그녀는 깊이 생각할 시간이 없었다.

23 in order to-v: ~하기 위해
She had to take action immediately in order to save herself and the other passengers.
조치를 취하다, 행동에 옮기다   재귀대명사 (재귀용법)

그녀는 자신과 다른 승객들을 구하기 위해 즉시 조치를 취해야 했다.

24 She jumped into the water along with Sara and two others, and the four of them guided the
~과 함께
drifting boat.
현재분사

그녀는 Sara와 다른 두 명과 함께 물속으로 뛰어들었고, 넷은 표류하는 보트를 이끌었다.

25 They swam for three and a half hours until they arrived safely with all the other passengers on the
~까지 (접속사)
shore of a Greek island.

그들은 다른 모든 승객과 함께 그리스 섬 해안에 안전하게 도착할 때까지 세 시간 반 동안 헤엄쳤다.

26 Next, Yusra and Sara had to travel through Macedonia, Serbia, Hungary, and Austria.
~을 거쳐 (전치사)

이후에 Yusra와 Sara는 마케도니아, 세르비아, 헝가리, 그리고 오스트리아를 거쳐 이동해야 했다.

27 They walked great distances, and even though they caught rides in small cars and crowded buses
비록 ~일지라도 (접속사)   catch a ride: (탈것에) 타다   과거분사
from time to time, they had to cross every border on foot.
가끔   걸어서

그들은 어마어마한 거리를 걸었고, 가끔 작은 차나 붐비는 버스를 타기도 했지만, 모든 국경을 걸어서 건너야했다.

28 No matter how exhausted they were, they kept moving.
아무리 ~하더라도

아무리 지쳐도 그들은 계속 움직였다.

29 At the end of this overwhelming 25-day journey, they finally made it to Germany and settled at a
현재분사   make it to: ~에 도달하다
refugee center in Berlin.

25일간의 엄청난 여정 끝에, 그들은 마침내 독일에 도착하여 베를린의 한 난민 센터에 정착했다.

30
~에도 불구하고 (전치사)   (that[which])
Despite all the hardships and adversities [she underwent], Yusra's passion for swimming never left
                                                          목적격 관계대명사절
her.

그녀가 겪은 모든 어려움과 역경에도 불구하고, Yusra의 수영에 대한 열정은 그녀를 떠나지 않았다.

31
                                    (that)
In fact, it was the only thing [she could do] to feel at home in this foreign land.
= swimming   부사적 용법 <목적>

사실, 그것은 그녀가 이국땅에서 편안함을 느끼기 위해 할 수 있는 유일한 일이었다.

32 She decided to take up training again, and she started looking for a coach in Berlin [who could help her reach her full potential].
시작하다
help + 목적어 + 동사원형: ~이 …하는 것을 돕다

그녀는 다시 훈련을 시작하기로 결심했고, 베를린에서 자신의 최대 잠재력에 도달할 수 있도록 도와줄 코치를 찾기 시작했다.

33 She eventually met Sven Spannekrebs at a swimming club [near the refugee center] and asked [if he could be her coach].
동사1 / 전치사구 / 동사 2
간접의문문 (평서문의 어순)

그녀는 결국 난민 센터 근처의 수영 클럽에서 Sven Spannekrebs를 만났고, 그에게 그녀의 코치가 되어줄 수 있는지 물어봤다.

34 When he saw her swim, he immediately recognized her outstanding talent and agreed to do so.
동사1 / 동사 2
see(지각동사) + 목적어 + 동사원형

그녀가 수영하는 모습을 봤을 때, 그는 즉시 그녀의 뛰어난 재능을 알아봤고 그렇게 하기로 승낙했다.

35 Sven helped Yusra stay focused and persistent in her efforts [to pursue excellence].
help + 목적어 + 동사원형: ~이 …하는 것을 돕다 / 형용사적 용법

Sven은 Yusra가 탁월함을 추구하고자 하는 그녀의 노력에 집중하고 끈질기게 노력할 수 있도록 도왔다.

36 Following his instructions, Yusra trained hard day and night, [hoping her efforts would pay off one day].
(that)
밤낮으로 / 분사구문

Yusra는 자신의 노력이 언젠가 성과를 내길 바라며 그의 가르침에 따라 밤낮으로 열심히 훈련했다.

37 Yusra soon received a chance [to make her dream a reality] when she was invited to join the first ever refugee team at the 2016 Summer Olympic Games in Rio de Janeiro.
형용사적 용법 / 수동태

Yusra는 곧 2016 리우데자네이루 하계 올림픽에서 사상 최초의 난민 올림픽 선수단에 합류할 것을 요청받아 그녀의 꿈을 실현할 수 있는 기회를 얻었다.

38 [Although it seemed like a great opportunity], Yusra was hesitant.
부사절 〈양보〉

그것은 좋은 기회처럼 보였지만, Yusra는 망설였다.

39 If she joined the refugee team, she thought, people might view her with pity instead of [seeing her
〈삽입절〉   동명사구 (전치사
as a serious athlete].
instead of의 목적어)

그녀가 난민 올림픽 선수단에 합류하면, 사람들이 그녀를 진지한 운동선수로 보는 대신 연민을 가지고 바라볼 수도 있다고 생각했다.

40 She almost turned down the invitation, but she decided to accept it [after she realized that she
                                                                                부사절 (~한 후에)
turn down: 거절하다   = the invitation   접속사
could inspire hope in millions of other refugees {facing similar challenges}].
                                                    현재분사구

그녀는 초대를 거절할 뻔했지만, 비슷한 어려움에 처한 수백만 명의 다른 난민들에게 희망을 심어줄 수 있다는 사실을 깨달은 후에 그것을 수락하기로
결정했다.

41 At the Games, Yusra competed in both the 100-meter butterfly and the 100-meter freestyle events.
                                                            (수영의) 접영   (수영의) 자유형
                                          both A and B: A와 B 둘 다

올림픽 경기에서 Yusra는 접영 100m와 자유형 100m에 모두 출전했다.

42 When she stepped onto the starting blocks, she was determined to pour everything [she had] into
                                                                                    (that)
the competition.   목적격 관계대명사절

출발대에 섰을 때, 그녀는 가지고 있는 모든 것을 경기에 쏟아붓기로 굳게 결심했다.

43 She came in 41st out of 45 competitors in the butterfly event and 45th out of 46 in the freestyle
              ~ 중에서
event.

그녀는 접영에서는 45명 중 41위, 자유형에서는 46명 중 45위를 기록했다.

44 Even though she left the Olympics without a medal, she was proud to have made history alongside
비록 ~이지만 (접속사)   완료부정사   ~과 함께
her teammates.

비록 메달을 따지 못한 채로 올림픽을 떠났지만, 그녀는 팀 동료들과 함께 새로운 역사를 만들었다는 것에 자부심을 느꼈다.

45 The time on the scoreboard did not matter.
                                        중요하다

점수판에 있는 기록은 중요하지 않았다.

46 In one interview, when a reporter asked if she could make a statement, she remarked, "I want
진술하다
everyone to stay strong for their goals in life, because if you have your goals in front of your eyes,
want의 목적격 보어   (that)   (do)
you will do everything [you can]; and I think even if I fail, I will try again. …
설령 ~할지라도

한 인터뷰에서 기자가 한마디 해줄 수 있냐고 요청했을 때 그녀는 말했다. "저는 모두가 자기 인생의 목표를 위하여 굳세게 버텨내길 바랍니다. 왜냐하면 여러분의 눈앞에 목표가 있으면, 여러분이 할 수 있는 모든 것을 할 것이기 때문입니다. 그리고 설령 제가 실패하더라도, 저는 다시 도전할 거라고 생각해요. …

47 명사절 (show의 직접목적어)
I want to show everybody [that it's hard to arrive at your dreams, but it's not impossible].
가주어   진주어

저는 꿈에 도달하는 것은 어렵지만 불가능하지 않다는 것을 모두에게 보여주고 싶습니다.

48 You can do it; everyone can do it."

여러분은 할 수 있고, 모두가 할 수 있습니다."

교과서 **본문 익히기** ❶ 옳은 어법·어휘 고르기

❖ 다음 네모 안에서 옳은 것을 고르시오.

01 When Yusra Mardini was a young girl growing up in Damascus, Syria, her life centered / was centered around swimming.

02 Her father was a former professional swimmer, and she started learning how / what to swim from a young age.

03 It was clear if / that she had a special talent, and she fell in love with the sport.

04 She enjoyed watching Olympic swimming events with her father, that / which led her to dream about competing in the Olympics.

05 She got the chance to represent Syria in an international swimming championship, and it seemed like her Olympic dream might someday come true / truly.

06 However, Yusra had no idea that her life would soon be turned inside / upside down by the horrors of the Syrian civil war, which had broken out / up in 2011.

07 Over the next few years, normal activities like going to school became risk / risky.

08 Through all of this chaos, she clings / clung to her dream and kept swimming.

09 One fateful day, a bomb fell in the pool where / which she was training.

10 Although it did not explode, this incident was horrifying enough / too to be a wake-up call for Yusra and her sister Sara.

11 They realized that they could no longer stay in their home country, and they made / took up their minds to flee Syria and go to Germany avoiding / to avoid the war.

12 If they reached Europe, the rest of the family will / would follow.

13 The decision was not an easy one, but Yusra knew that it was her only option if / whether she wanted to pursue her dream and live without fear.

14 In August, 2015, the sisters began their dangerous journey by making their way to their first destiny / destination, Türkiye.

15 There, along with 18 other people, including children and babies, they boarded a tiny boat designing / designed for seven passengers.

16 They were heading across the sea towards Greece when / where disaster struck.

17 The heavy boat began to sink, and the panicked, desperate / determined passengers had no choice but to throw / throwing their possessions into the sea.

18 Yusra felt heartbroken as she watched people's treasured belongings disappear / disappeared under the waves.

19 She had to take action immediately in order to save herself and another / the other passengers.

20 They swam during / for three and a half hours until they arrived safely with all the other passengers on the shore of a Greek island.

21 They walked great distances, and even though they caught rides in small cars and crowded buses for / from time to time, they had to cross every border by / on foot.

22 No matter how exhausted they did / were , they kept moving.

23 At the end of this overwhelming 25-day journey, they finally made it to Germany and set / settled at a refugee center in Berlin.

24 Despite / Though all the hardships and adversities she underwent, Yusra's passion for swimming never left her.

25 In fact, it was the only thing she could do to feel at home / house in this foreign land.

26 She decided taking / to take up training again, and she started looking for a coach in Berlin who could help her reach / reaching her full potential.

27 She eventually met Sven Spannekrebs at a swimming club near the refugee center and asked if could he / he could be her coach.

28 When he saw her swim, he immediately found / recognized her outstanding talent and agreed to do so.

29 Sven helped Yusra stay focused and consistent / persistent in her efforts to pursue excellence.

30 Following his instructions, Yusra trained hard day and night, hoping her efforts would lay / pay off one day.

31 Yusra soon received a chance to make her dream a reality / realization when she was invited to join the first ever refugee / refuse team at the 2016 Summer Olympic Games in Rio de Janeiro.

32 Although it seemed like a great opportunity, Yusra was hesitate / hesitant .

33 If she joined the refugee team, she thought, people might view her with pity in spite of / instead of seeing her as a serious athlete.

34 She almost turned down / off the invitation, but she decided to accept it after she realized that she could aspire / inspire hope in millions of other refugees facing similar challenges.

35 At the Games, Yusra competed in both / either the 100-meter butterfly and the 100-meter freestyle events.

36 When she stepped onto the starting blocks, she was decided / determined to pour everything she had into the competition.

37 She came / made in 41st out of 45 competitors in the butterfly event and 45th out of 46 in the freestyle event.

38 Even though she left the Olympics with / without a medal, she was proud to have made history alongside her teammates.

39 In one interview, when a reporter asked if she could make a statement, she remarked, "I want everyone to stay strong for their goals in life, because if you have / will have your goals in front of your eyes, you will do everything you can; and I think because / even if I fail, I will try again. …

40 I want to show everybody that it's / that's hard to arrive at your dreams, but it's not impossible.

❖ 다음 밑줄 친 부분이 옳으면 ○표 하고, 틀리면 바르게 고쳐 쓰시오.

01 When Yusra Mardini was a young girl growing up in Damascus, Syria, her life <u>centered around</u> swimming.

02 Her father was a former professional swimmer, and she started learning <u>how swim</u> from a young age.

03 It was clear <u>what</u> she had a special talent, and she fell in love with the sport.

04 She enjoyed watching Olympic swimming events with her father, <u>that led</u> her to dream about competing in the Olympics.

05 She got the chance to represent Syria in an international swimming championship, and it <u>seems as</u> her Olympic dream might someday come true.

06 However, Yusra had no <u>idea of</u> her life would soon be turned upside down by the horrors of the Syrian civil war, which had broken out in 2011.

07 Through all of this chaos, she <u>clings to</u> her dream and kept swimming.

08 One fateful day, a bomb fell in the pool <u>which</u> she was training.

09 Although it did not explode, this incident was <u>enough horrifying</u> to be a wake-up call for Yusra and her sister Sara.

10 They realized that they could no longer stay in their home country, and <u>making up</u> their minds to flee Syria and go to Germany to avoid the war.

11 If they <u>reached to</u> Europe, the rest of the family <u>will follow</u>.

12 The decision was not an easy one, but Yusra knew that it was her only option if she wanted to pursue her dream and <u>live without fear</u>.

13 In August, 2015, the sisters began their dangerous journey <u>by make</u> their way to their first destination, Türkiye.

14 There, along with 18 other people, including children and babies, they boarded a tiny boat <u>designing</u> for seven passengers.

15 The boat's engine failed in the middle of the open sea, and the weather rapidly <u>were grown worse</u>.

16 The heavy boat began to sink, and the panicked, desperate passengers <u>had not choice but throwing</u> their possessions into the sea.

17   Yusra felt heartbroken as she watched people's treasured belongings <u>to disappear</u> under the waves.

18   She had to take action immediately in order to save <u>her</u> and the other passenger.

19   They swam for three and a half hours <u>after they arrived</u> safely with all the other passengers on the shore of a Greek island.

20   They walked great distances, and even though they caught rides in small cars and crowded buses from time to time, they <u>have to cross every borders</u> on foot.

21   <u>No matter what</u> exhausted they were, they kept moving.

22   At the end of this overwhelming 25-day journey, they finally <u>made it Germany</u> and settled at a refugee center in Berlin.

23   Despite all the hardships and adversities she <u>undergone</u>, Yusra's passion for swimming never left her.

24   In fact, it was the only thing she could do <u>feeling at home</u> in this foreign land.

25   She decided to take up training again, and she started looking for a coach in Berlin <u>where</u> could help her reach her full potential.

26   She eventually met Sven Spannekrebs at a swimming club near the refugee center and asked <u>that he could be</u> her coach.

27   When he saw her swim, he immediately recognized her outstanding talent and <u>agreeed to do so</u>.

28   Sven helped Yusra <u>stay focus</u> and persistent in her efforts to pursue excellence.

29   Following his instructions, Yusra trained hard <u>the day and the night</u>, hoping her efforts would pay off one day.

30   Yusra soon received a chance to <u>make her dream a reality</u> when she was invited to join the first ever refugee team at the 2016 Summer Olympic Games in Rio de Janeiro.

31   <u>Since it seemed</u> like a great opportunity, Yusra was hesitant.

32 If she joined the refugee team, she thought, people might view her with pity <u>instead seeing</u> her as a serious athlete.

33 She almost turned down the invitation, but she decided to accept it after she realized that she could inspire hope in millions of <u>other refugee faced</u> similar challenges.

34 At the Games, Yusra competed in both the 100-meter butterfly <u>or</u> the 100-meter freestyle events.

35 When she stepped onto the starting blocks, she <u>was determined to pour</u> everything she had into the competition.

36 Even though she left the Olympics without a medal, she was proud <u>to have made history</u> alongside her teammates.

37 The time on the scoreboard <u>was not matter</u>.

38 In one interview, when a reporter asked <u>if she could make a statement</u>, she remarked, "I want everyone to stay strong for their goals in life, because if you <u>will have</u> your goals in front of your eyes, you will do everything you can; and I think even if I fail, I will try again. …

39 I want to show everybody that it's hard to arrive at your dreams, but it's not <u>possible</u>.

✤ 다음 우리말과 일치하도록 빈칸에 알맞은 말을 쓰시오.

When Yusra Mardini was a young girl growing up in Damascus, Syria, her life ⁽¹⁾ _____ _____

_____ .

Yusra Mardini가 시리아의 다마스쿠스에서 자라는 어린 소녀였을 때, 그녀의 삶은 수영을 중심으로 돌아갔다.

Her father was a former professional swimmer, and she started learning ⁽²⁾ _____ _____ _____

_____ a young age.

그녀의 아버지는 전직 프로 수영 선수였고, 그래서 그녀는 어릴 때부터 수영하는 방법을 배우기 시작했다.

⁽³⁾ _____ _____ _____ _____ _____ _____ , she was already faster than

many older swimmers.

아홉 살 때 이미 그녀는 나이가 더 많은 다른 수영 선수들보다 더 빨랐다.

⁽⁴⁾ _____ _____ _____ _____ she had a special talent, and she fell in love with the sport.

그녀에게 특별한 재능이 있는 것이 분명했고, 그녀는 그 스포츠와 사랑에 빠졌다.

She enjoyed watching Olympic swimming events with her father, ⁽⁵⁾ _____ _____ _____

_____ _____ _____ competing in the Olympics.

그녀는 자신의 아버지와 함께 올림픽 수영 경기를 보는 것을 즐겼고, 이는 그녀가 올림픽에 참가하는 것을 꿈꾸게 했다.

She got ⁽⁶⁾ _____ _____ _____ _____ Syria in an international swimming championship,

and it seemed like her Olympic dream ⁽⁷⁾ _____ _____ _____ _____ .

그녀는 국제 수영 선수권 대회에서 시리아를 대표할 기회를 얻었고, 올림픽에 대한 그녀의 꿈이 언젠가 실현될 것처럼 보였다.

However, Yusra ⁽⁸⁾ _____ _____ _____ _____ her life would soon be turned upside down

by the horrors of the Syrian civil war, which ⁽⁹⁾ _____ _____ _____ _____ _____ .

하지만, Yusra는 시리아 내전의 공포로 인해 그녀의 삶이 곧 뒤집어질 것이라고 전혀 생각하지 못했는데, 그것(시리아 내전)은 2011년에 발발했다.

⁽¹⁰⁾ _____ _____ _____ _____ _____ , normal activities like going to school

became risky.

이후 몇 년간, 학교에 가는 것과 같은 평범한 활동이 위험해졌다.

Through all of this chaos, she clung to her dream and ⁽¹¹⁾ _____ _____ .

이 모든 혼란 속에서도 그녀는 자신의 꿈에 매달렸고, 계속 수영을 했다.

⁽¹²⁾ _____ , _____ _____ became dangerous.

그렇지만 이것조차도 위험해졌다.

One fateful day, a bomb fell in the pool (13) _____ _____ _____ _____.

어느 운명적인 날, 그녀가 훈련하고 있던 수영장에 폭탄이 떨어졌다.

Although it did not explode, this incident was (14) _____ _____ _____ a wake-up call for Yusra and her sister Sara.

비록 그것이 폭발하지는 않았지만, 이 사건은 Yusra와 그녀의 언니 Sara의 정신을 차리게 하는 신호가 될 만큼 충분히 무서운 일이었다.

They realized that they could no longer stay in their home country, and they (15) _____ _____ _____ _____ to flee Syria and go to Germany (16) _____ _____ _____ _____.

그들은 더 이상 조국에 머물 수 없다는 것을 깨달았고, 전쟁을 피해 시리아에서 달아나 독일로 가기로 결심했다.

(17) _____ _____ _____ _____, the rest of the family would follow.

그들이 유럽에 도착하면, 나머지 가족도 뒤따라오기로 했다.

The decision was not an easy one, but Yusra knew that it was (18) _____ _____ _____ if she wanted to pursue her dream and (19) _____ _____ _____.

그것은 쉽지 않은 결정이었지만, Yusra는 자신의 꿈을 추구하고 두려움 없이 살고 싶다면 그것이 유일한 선택지라는 것을 알고 있었다.

In August, 2015, the sisters (20) _____ _____ _____ _____ by making their way to their first destination, Türkiye.

2015년 8월, 자매는 그들의 첫 번째 목적지인 튀르키예로 향하면서 그들의 위험한 여정을 시작했다.

There, along with 18 other people, (21) _____ _____ _____ _____, they boarded a tiny boat designed for seven passengers.

그곳에서 그들은 어린이들과 아기들을 포함한 18명의 다른 사람들과 함께 7명의 승객이 탑승할 수 있도록 만들어진 작은 보트에 탔다.

They were heading (22) _____ _____ _____ _____ Greece when disaster struck.

재앙이 닥쳤을 때, 그들은 그리스를 향해 바다를 건너는 중이었다.

The boat's engine failed in the middle of the open sea, and (23) _____ _____ _____ _____ _____.

보트의 엔진이 망망대해 한가운데서 멈췄고, 날씨가 급격히 나빠졌다.

The heavy boat began to sink, and the panicked, desperate passengers (24) _____ _____ _____ _____ _____ _____ their possessions into the sea.

무거운 보트는 가라앉기 시작했고, 겁에 질린 필사적인 승객들은 자신의 소지품을 바다로 던질 수밖에 없었다.

Yusra (25) _____ _____ as she watched people's treasured belongings disappear under the waves.

Yusra는 사람들의 소중한 소지품들이 물결 아래로 사라지는 것을 보며 비통함을 느꼈다.

However, she had (26) _____ _____ _____ _____.

하지만, 그녀는 깊이 생각할 시간이 없었다.

She had to take action immediately (27) _____ _____ _____ _____ _____ and the other passengers.

그녀는 자신과 다른 승객들을 구하기 위해 즉시 조치를 취해야 했다.

She jumped into the water along with Sara and two others, and the four of them (28) _____ _____ _____ _____.

그녀는 Sara와 다른 두 명과 함께 물속으로 뛰어들었고, 넷은 표류하는 보트를 이끌었다.

They swam (29) _____ _____ _____ _____ _____ until they arrived safely with all the other passengers on the shore of a Greek island.

그들은 다른 모든 승객과 함께 그리스 섬 해안에 안전하게 도착할 때까지 세 시간 반 동안 헤엄쳤다.

Next, Yusra and Sara (30) _____ _____ _____ Macedonia, Serbia, Hungary, and Austria.

이후에 Yusra와 Sara는 마케도니아, 세르비아, 헝가리, 그리고 오스트리아를 거쳐 이동해야 했다.

They walked great distances, and (31) _____ _____ _____ _____ _____ in small cars and crowded buses from time to time, they had to cross every border on foot.

그들은 어마어마한 거리를 걸었고, 가끔 작은 차나 붐비는 버스를 타기도 했지만, 모든 국경을 걸어서 건너야했다.

(32) _____ _____ _____ _____ they were, they kept moving.

아무리 지쳐도 그들은 계속 움직였다.

At the end of this overwhelming 25-day journey, (33) _____ _____ _____ _____ _____ Germany and settled at a refugee center in Berlin.

25일간의 엄청난 여정 끝에, 그들은 마침내 독일에 도착하여 베를린의 한 난민 센터에 정착했다.

(34) _____ _____ _____ _____ and adversities she underwent, Yusra's passion for swimming never left her.

그녀가 겪은 모든 어려움과 역경에도 불구하고, Yusra의 수영에 대한 열정은 그녀를 떠나지 않았다.

In fact, it was the only thing she could do (35) _____ _____ _____ _____ in this foreign land.

사실, 그것은 그녀가 이국땅에서 편안함을 느끼기 위해 할 수 있는 유일한 일이었다.

She (36) _____ _____ _____ _____ _____ again, and she started looking for a coach in Berlin who could help her reach her full potential.

그녀는 다시 훈련을 시작하기로 결심했고, 베를린에서 자신의 최대 잠재력에 도달할 수 있도록 도와줄 코치를 찾기 시작했다.

She eventually met Sven Spannekrebs at a swimming club near the refugee center and asked (37) _____
_____ _____ _____ _____ _____.

그녀는 결국 난민 센터 근처의 수영 클럽에서 Sven Spannekrebs를 만났고, 그에게 그녀의 코치가 되어줄 수 있는지 물어봤다.

When he saw her swim, (38) _____ _____ _____ her outstanding talent and agreed to do so.

그녀가 수영하는 모습을 봤을 때, 그는 즉시 그녀의 뛰어난 재능을 알아봤고 그렇게 하기로 승낙했다.

Sven helped Yusra (39) _____ _____ _____ _____ in her efforts to pursue excellence.

Sven은 Yusra가 탁월함을 추구하고자 하는 그녀의 노력에 집중하고 끈질기게 노력할 수 있도록 도왔다.

Following his instructions, Yusra trained hard (40) _____ _____ _____, hoping her efforts would pay off one day.

Yusra는 자신의 노력이 언젠가 성과를 내길 바라며 그의 가르침에 따라 밤낮으로 열심히 훈련했다.

Yusra soon received a chance (41) _____ _____ _____ _____
when she was invited to join the first ever refugee team at the 2016 Summer Olympic Games in Rio de Janeiro.

Yusra는 곧 2016 리우데자네이루 하계 올림픽에서 사상 최초의 난민 올림픽 선수단에 합류할 것을 요청받아 그녀의 꿈을 실현할 수 있는 기회를 얻었다.

(42) _____ _____ _____ _____ a great opportunity, Yusra was hesitant.

그것은 좋은 기회처럼 보였지만, Yusra는 망설였다.

If she joined the refugee team, she thought, people (43) _____ _____ _____ _____
_____ instead of seeing her as a serious athlete.

그녀가 난민 올림픽 선수단에 합류하면, 사람들이 그녀를 진지한 운동선수로 보는 대신 연민을 가지고 바라볼 수도 있다고 생각했다.

She almost (44) _____ _____ _____ _____, but she decided to accept it after she realized that she could inspire hope in millions of other refugees (45) _____ _____ _____.

그녀는 초대를 거절할 뻔했지만, 비슷한 어려움에 처한 수백만 명의 다른 난민들에게 희망을 심어줄 수 있다는 사실을 깨달은 후에 그것을 수락하기로 결정했다.

At the Games, Yusra competed in both (46) _____ _____ _____ and the 100-meter freestyle events.

올림픽 경기에서 Yusra는 접영 100m와 자유형 100m에 모두 출전했다.

(47) _____ _____ _____ _____ the starting blocks, she was determined to pour everything she had into the competition.

출발대에 섰을 때, 그녀는 가지고 있는 모든 것을 경기에 쏟아붓기로 굳게 결심했다.

She came in **(48)** _____ _____ _____ _____ _____ in the butterfly event and 45th out of 46 in the freestyle event.

그녀는 접영에서는 45명 중 41위, 자유형에서는 46명 중 45위를 기록했다.

Even though she left the Olympics without a medal, she was **(49)** _____ _____ _____ _____ history alongside her teammates.

비록 메달을 따지 못한 채로 올림픽을 떠났지만, 그녀는 팀 동료들과 함께 새로운 역사를 만들었다는 것에 자부심을 느꼈다.

The time on the scoreboard **(50)** _____ _____ _____.

점수판에 있는 기록은 중요하지 않았다.

In one interview, when a reporter asked if she could make a statement, she remarked, "I want everyone to stay **(51)** _____ _____ _____ _____ in life, because if you have your goals in front of your eyes, you will do everything you can; and I think **(52)** _____ _____ _____ _____, I will try again. ...

한 인터뷰에서 기자가 한마디 해줄 수 있냐고 요청했을 때 그녀는 말했다. "저는 모두가 자기 인생의 목표를 위하여 굳세게 버텨내길 바랍니다. 왜냐하면 여러분의 눈앞에 목표가 있으면, 여러분이 할 수 있는 모든 것을 할 것이기 때문입니다. 그리고 설령 제가 실패하더라도, 저는 다시 도전할 거라고 생각해요. ⋯

I want to show everybody that **(53)** _____ _____ _____ _____ at your dreams, but it's not impossible.

저는 꿈에 도달하는 것은 어렵지만 불가능하지 않다는 것을 모두에게 보여주고 싶습니다.

You can do it; **(54)** _____ _____ _____ _____."

여러분은 할 수 있고, 모두가 할 수 있습니다."

01 밑줄 친 부분 중, 문맥상 낱말의 쓰임이 적절하지 <u>않은</u> 것은?

When Yusra Mardini was a young girl growing up in Damascus, Syria, her life centered around swimming. Her father was a former ①professional swimmer, and she started learning how to swim from a young age. When she was nine years old, she was already faster than many older swimmers. It was ②clear that she had a special ③talent, and she fell in love with the sport. She enjoyed watching Olympic swimming events with her father, which led her to dream about ④completing in the Olympics. She got the chance to ⑤represent Syria in an international swimming championship, and it seemed like her Olympic dream might someday come true.

02 밑줄 친 부분 중, 문맥상 어구의 쓰임이 적절하지 <u>않은</u> 것은?

However, Yusra had no idea that her life would soon be turned ①upside down by the horrors of the Syrian civil war, which had ②broken up in 2011. Over the next few years, normal activities like going to school became risky. Through all of this chaos, she ③clung to her dream and kept swimming. However, even this became dangerous. One fateful day, a bomb fell in the pool where she was training. Although it did not explode, this incident was horrifying enough to be a ④wake-up call for Yusra and her sister Sara. They realized that they could no longer stay in their home country, and they ⑤made up their minds to flee Syria and go to Germany to avoid the war.

03 (A), (B), (C)의 각 네모 안에서 문맥에 맞는 낱말로 가장 적절한 것은?

In August, 2015, the sisters began their dangerous journey by making their way to their first (A) destination / destiny , Türkiye. There, along with 18 other people, including children and babies, they boarded a tiny boat designed for seven passengers. They were heading across the sea (B) forwards / towards Greece when disaster struck. The boat's engine failed in the middle of the open sea, and the weather rapidly grew worse. The heavy boat began to sink, and the panicked, desperate passengers had no choice but to throw their (C) possesses / possessions into the sea.

	(A)	(B)	(C)
①	destination	forwards	possesses
②	destiny	forwards	possesses
③	destination	forwards	possessions
④	destiny	towards	possessions
⑤	destination	towards	possessions

04 (A), (B), (C)의 각 네모 안에서 문맥에 맞는 낱말로 가장 적절한 것은?

Yusra felt heartbroken as she watched people's treasured belongings (A) appear / disappear under the waves. However, she had no time to (B) refer / reflect . She had to take action immediately in order to save herself and the other passengers. She jumped into the water along with Sara and two others, and the four of them guided the (C) drafting / drifting boat. They swam for three and a half hours until they arrived safely with all the other passengers on the shore of a Greek island.

	(A)	(B)	(C)
①	appear	refer	drafting
②	appear	reflect	drafting
③	appear	refer	drifting
④	disappear	reflect	drifting
⑤	disappear	refer	drifting

05 (A), (B), (C)의 각 네모 안에서 문맥에 맞는 낱말로 가장 적절한 것은?

Next, Yusra and Sara had to travel through Macedonia, Serbia, Hungary, and Austria. They walked great distances, and even though they caught rides in small cars and (A) clouded / crowded buses from time to time, they had to cross every border on foot. No matter how (B) excited / exhausted they were, they kept moving. At the end of this overwhelming 25-day journey, they finally made it to Germany and settled at a refugee center in Berlin. Despite all the hardships and (C) adversaries / adversities she underwent, Yusra's passion for swimming never left her. In fact, it was the only thing she could do to feel at home in this foreign land.

	(A)	(B)	(C)
①	clouded	excited	adversaries
②	clouded	exhausted	adversaries
③	clouded	excited	adversities
④	crowded	exhausted	adversities
⑤	crowded	excited	adversities

06 밑줄 친 부분 중, 문맥상 낱말의 쓰임이 적절하지 않은 것은?

She decided to take up training again, and she started looking for a coach in Berlin who could help her reach her full ①potential. She eventually met Sven Spannekrebs at a swimming club near the ②refugee center and asked if he could be her coach. When he saw her swim, he immediately recognized her ③outstanding talent and agreed to do so. Sven helped Yusra stay focused and ④persistent in her efforts to pursue excellence. Following his ⑤constructions, Yusra trained hard day and night, hoping her efforts would pay off one day.

07 (A), (B), (C)의 각 네모 안에서 문맥에 맞는 낱말로 가장 적절한 것은?

Yusra soon received a chance to make her dream a reality when she was invited to join the first ever refugee team at the 2016 Summer Olympic Games in Rio de Janeiro. Although it seemed like a great opportunity, Yusra was (A) hesitant / persistent. If she joined the refugee team, she thought, people might view her with (B) pity / respect instead of seeing her as a serious athlete. She almost turned down the invitation, but she decided to accept it after she realized that she could inspire (C) hope / horror in millions of other refugees facing similar challenges.

	(A)	(B)	(C)
①	hesitant	pity	hope
②	hesitant	pity	horror
③	hesitant	respect	hope
④	persistent	respect	horror
⑤	persistent	respect	hope

08 밑줄 친 부분 중, 문맥상 낱말의 쓰임이 적절하지 않은 것은?

At the Games, Yusra ①competed in both the 100-meter butterfly and the 100-meter freestyle events. When she stepped onto the starting blocks, she was determined to ②pour everything she had into the competition. She came in 41st out of 45 competitors in the butterfly event and 45th out of 46 in the freestyle event. Even though she left the Olympics ③without a medal, she was proud to have made history alongside her teammates. The time on the scoreboard did not ④work. In one interview, when a reporter asked if she could make a statement, she ⑤remarked, "I want everyone to stay strong for their goals in life, because if you have your goals in front of your eyes, you will do everything you can. ... You can do it; everyone can do it."

01 다음 글의 밑줄 친 부분 중, 어법상 틀린 것은?

Natural disasters are an unavoidable part of life. However, not every country has enough resources or expertise ①to deal with serious disasters. Fortunately, people around the world often cooperate to help disaster victims ②recover and rebuild. This happened when a massive earthquake struck Türkiye and Syria in 2023. Nearly 60,000 people died, and countless buildings were destroyed. Millions of people lost their homes and ③left in danger due to a lack of food and water. However, over 100 countries and organizations quickly responded to the disaster ④by sending multiple forms of aid. They sent rescue teams to search for survivors. They also offered financial support ⑤so that people could purchase food, clothes, and necessary supplies.

02 다음 글의 밑줄 친 부분 중, 어법상 틀린 것은?

When Yusra Mardini was a young girl ①growing up in Damascus, Syria, her life centered around swimming. Her father was a former professional swimmer, and she started learning ②how to swim from a young age. When she was nine years old, she was already faster than many older swimmers. ③It was clear that she had a special talent, and she fell in love with the sport. She enjoyed watching Olympic swimming events with her father, ④that led her to dream about competing in the Olympics. She got the chance to represent Syria in an international swimming championship, and it ⑤seemed like her Olympic dream might someday come true.

03 (A), (B), (C)의 각 네모 안에서 어법에 맞는 표현으로 가장 적절한 것은?

However, Yusra had no idea that her life would soon be turned upside down by the horrors of the Syrian civil war, which had broken out in 2011. Over the next few years, normal activities like going to school became risky. Through all of this chaos, she clung to her dream and kept (A) swimming / to swim . However, even this became dangerous. One fateful day, a bomb fell in the pool (B) where / which she was training. Although it did not explode, this incident was horrifying enough to be a wake-up call for Yusra and her sister Sara. They realized that they could no longer stay in their home country, and they made up their minds to flee Syria and go to Germany to avoid the war. If they (C) reach / reached Europe, the rest of the family would follow.

	(A)		(B)		(C)
①	swimming	...	where	...	reach
②	swimming	...	where	...	reached
③	swimming	...	which	...	reach
④	to swim	...	which	...	reached
⑤	to swim	...	which	...	reach

04 (A), (B), (C)의 각 네모 안에서 어법에 맞는 표현으로 가장 적절한 것은?

In August, 2015, the sisters began their dangerous journey by making their way to their first destination, Türkiye. There, along with 18 other people, including children and babies, they boarded a tiny boat (A) designing / designed for seven passengers. They were heading across the sea towards Greece when disaster struck. The boat's engine failed in the middle of the open sea, and the weather rapidly grew worse. The heavy boat began to sink, and the panicked, desperate passengers had no choice but to (B) throw / throwing their possessions into the sea. Yusra felt heartbroken as she watched people's treasured belongings (C) disappear / to disappear under the waves.

	(A)	(B)	(C)
①	designing	… throw	… disappear
②	designing	… throwing	… disappear
③	designed	… throw	… disappear
④	designed	… throwing	… to disappear
⑤	designed	… throw	… to disappear

05 (A), (B), (C)의 각 네모 안에서 어법에 맞는 표현으로 가장 적절한 것은?

She decided to take up training again, and she started looking for a coach in Berlin (A) where / who could help her reach her full potential. She eventually met Sven Spannekrebs at a swimming club near the refugee center and asked (B) if / that he could be her coach. When he saw her swim, he immediately recognized her outstanding talent and agreed to do so. Sven helped Yusra stay focused and persistent in her efforts to pursue excellence. (C) Following / Followed his instructions, Yusra trained hard day and night, hoping her efforts would pay off one day.

	(A)	(B)	(C)
①	where	… if	… Following
②	where	… if	… Followed
③	who	… if	… Following
④	who	… that	… Followed
⑤	who	… that	… Following

06 다음 글의 밑줄 친 부분 중, 어법상 틀린 것은?

Yusra soon received a chance ①to make her dream a reality when she was invited to join the first ever refugee team at the 2016 Summer Olympic Games in Rio de Janeiro. ②Although it seemed like a great opportunity, Yusra was hesitant. If she joined the refugee team, she thought, people ③might view her with pity instead of seeing her as a serious athlete. She almost turned down the invitation, but she decided ④to accept it after she realized that she could inspire hope in millions of other refugees ⑤faced similar challenges.

07 다음 글의 밑줄 친 부분 중, 어법상 틀린 것은?

Even though she left the Olympics without a medal, she was proud ①to have made history alongside her teammates. The time on the scoreboard did not matter. In one interview, when a reporter ②asked if she could make a statement, she remarked, "I want everyone ③stay strong for their goals in life, because if you have your goals in front of your eyes, you will do everything you can; and I think ④even if I fail, I will try again. … I want to show everybody that it's hard ⑤to arrive at your dreams, but it's not impossible. You can do it; everyone can do it."

08 (A), (B), (C)의 각 네모 안에서 어법에 맞는 표현으로 가장 적절한 것은?

One of the biggest difficulties that I used to face (A) was / were my fear of public speaking. Last year, I had to speak in front of the whole school. I was so nervous that I made a lot of mistakes. I thought I might never be able to speak in front of others again. However, I wanted to get over my fear, so I decided to join the speech club. My fellow club members gave me great advice, and I practiced many different speeches. After a while, I got used to (B) make / making eye contact with the audience and speaking confidently in a loud, clear voice. As a result, I was able to give a successful speech at the next school event. This experience taught me (C) if / that I can overcome difficulties through persistent effort.

	(A)	(B)	(C)
①	was	… make	… if
②	were	… make	… if
③	was	… making	… if
④	were	… making	… that
⑤	was	… making	… that

[01~02] 다음 대화를 읽고, 물음에 답하시오.

G Yesterday, I met a group of Spanish tourists and helped them find a hotel.

B That was very kind of you. But I didn't know you spoke Spanish.

G I don't. I used a translation app on my phone.

B Oh, I've never used one before.

G ①This one is quite easy to use. Just open the app and speak into the phone in your own language. Then ②it will translate what you've said into the language you select!

B That sounds like it would be useful in many situations.

G Yes, it is. I used ③it when I went to France last year. I was able to talk to people without much difficulty thanks to the app.

B Wow! ④It's surprising that we can communicate in a language we don't know. I'm going to download ⑤it!

01 위 대화의 내용과 일치하지 <u>않는</u> 것은?

① 여학생은 어제 스페인 여행객들에게 도움을 주었다.
② 여학생은 번역 앱을 사용해 여행객들과 대화했다.
③ 여학생이 사용한 앱은 전화기에 말을 하면 원하는 언어로 번역해 줄 수 있다.
④ 여학생은 프랑스 여행 시 언어로 어려움을 겪었다.
⑤ 남학생은 번역 앱을 다운로드하려 한다.

02 위 대화의 밑줄 친 부분 중, 가리키는 대상이 나머지와 <u>다른</u> 것은?

①   ②   ③   ④   ⑤

[03~05] 다음 글을 읽고, 물음에 답하시오.

When Yusra Mardini was a young girl growing up in Damascus, Syria, her life centered around swimming. Her father was a former professional swimmer, and she started learning how to swim from a young age. When she was nine years old, she was already faster than many older swimmers. It was clear that she had a special talent, and she fell in love with the sport. <u>She enjoyed to watch Olympic swimming events with her father, what led her to dream about competing in the Olympics.</u> She got the chance to represent Syria in an international swimming championship, and it seemed like her Olympic dream might someday come true.

03 윗글의 분위기로 가장 적절한 것은?

① cheerful and festive   ② gloomy and sad
③ tense and desperate   ④ hopeful and optimistic
⑤ critical and sarcastic

04 윗글을 읽고 Yusra Mardini에 관해 답할 수 있는 질문이 <u>아닌</u> 것은?

① What is her home country?
② What was her father's job?
③ At what age did she start swimming?
④ With whom did she enjoy watching Olympic swimming games?
⑤ What was her dream as a child?

05 윗글의 밑줄 친 문장에서 어법상 어색한 부분을 <u>두 군데</u> 찾아 바르게 고쳐 쓰시오.

→ She _____

_____

in the Olympics.

[06~07] 다음 글을 읽고, 물음에 답하시오.

However, Yusra had no idea that her life would soon be turned ①upside down by the horrors of the Syrian civil war, which had ②broken out in 2011. Over the next few years, normal activities like going to school became risky. Through all of this chaos, she ③clung to her dream and kept swimming. (A) However, even this became dangerous. (B) Although it did not explode, this incident was horrifying enough to be ④a wake-up call for Yusra and her sister Sara. (C) They realized that they could no longer stay in their home country, and they ⑤made up their minds to flee Syria and go to Germany to avoid the war. (D) If they reached Europe, the rest of the family would follow. (E) The decision was not an easy one, but Yusra knew that it was her only option if she wanted to pursue her dream and live without fear.

06 글의 흐름으로 보아, 주어진 문장이 들어가기에 가장 적절한 곳은?

One fateful day, a bomb fell in the pool where she was training.

① (A)　　② (B)　　③ (C)　　④ (D)　　⑤ (E)

07 윗글의 밑줄 친 부분을 우리말로 바르게 옮기지 <u>않은</u> 것은?

① upside down: 거꾸로
② broken out: 발발했다
③ clung to: ~에 매달렸다
④ a wake-up call: 정신을 차리게 하는 신호
⑤ made up their minds: 생각을 바꿨다

[08~10] 다음 글을 읽고, 물음에 답하시오.

In August, 2015, the sisters began their dangerous journey by making their way to their first destination, Türkiye. There, ①along with 18 other people, including children and babies, they boarded a tiny boat designed for seven passengers. They were ②heading across the sea towards Greece when disaster struck. The boat's engine failed in the middle of the open sea, and the weather rapidly grew worse. The heavy boat began to sink, and the panicked, desperate passengers had ③no choice but to throw their possessions into the sea. Yusra felt _____ as she watched people's treasured belongings disappear under the waves. However, she had no time to reflect. She had to ④do action immediately in order to save herself and ⑤the other passengers. She jumped into the water along with Sara and two others, and the four of them guided the drifting boat. They swam for three and a half hours until they arrived safely with all the other passengers on the shore of a Greek island.

08 윗글의 내용과 일치하지 <u>않는</u> 것은?

① Yusra와 언니 Sara는 2015년 작은 보트를 타고 그리스로 향했다.
② 일곱 명이 정원인 보트에는 18명의 성인이 타고 있었다.
③ 항해 중 기상이 악화되고 보트의 엔진이 작동을 멈추었다.
④ Yusra와 Sara는 다른 두 명의 승객과 함께 바다에 뛰어들어 보트를 끌었다.
⑤ 세 시간 반 동안의 사투 끝에 무사히 그리스 섬의 해안에 도착했다.

09 윗글의 빈칸에 들어갈 말로 가장 적절한 것은?

① excited　　　　　② disappointed
③ nervous　　　　　④ disgusted
⑤ heartbroken

10 윗글의 밑줄 친 부분 중, 문맥상 어구의 쓰임이 적절하지 <u>않은</u> 것은?

①　　　　②　　　　③　　　　④　　　　⑤

[11~12] 다음 글을 읽고, 물음에 답하시오.

Next, Yusra and Sara had to travel through Macedonia, Serbia, Hungary, and Austria. They walked great distances, and even though they caught rides in small cars and crowded buses ① from time to time, they had to cross every border on foot. ② No matter how exhausted they were, they kept moving. At the end of this overwhelming 25-day journey, they finally ③ made it to Germany and settled at a refugee center in Berlin. ④ Despite all the hardships and adversities she underwent, Yusra's passion for swimming never ⑤ left her. In fact, it was the only thing she could do _____.

11 윗글의 밑줄 친 부분과 바꿔 쓸 표현으로 적절하지 <u>않은</u> 것은?

① from time to time: occasionally
② No matter how: However
③ made it to: found
④ Despite: In spite of
⑤ left her: disappeared

12 윗글의 빈칸에 들어갈 말로 가장 적절한 것은?

① to compete in the Olympic swimming events
② to get back to her homeland as early as possible
③ to stay in the country
④ to feel at home in this foreign land
⑤ to help the other Syrians in Berlin

[13~14] 다음 글을 읽고, 물음에 답하시오.

She decided to take up training again, and she started looking for a coach in Berlin who could ① help her reach her full potential. She eventually met Sven Spannekrebs at a swimming club near the refugee center and ② asked that he could be her coach. When he saw ③ her swim, he immediately recognized her outstanding talent and agreed to do so. Sven은 Yusra가 탁월함을 추구하고자 하는 그녀의 노력에 집중하고 끈질기게 노력할 수 있도록 도왔다. Following his instructions, Yusra trained hard day and night, ④ hoping her efforts would pay off one day.

Yusra soon received a chance to make her dream a reality when she ⑤ was invited to join the first ever refugee team at the 2016 Summer Olympic Games in Rio de Janeiro.

13 윗글의 밑줄 친 부분 중, 어법상 <u>틀린</u> 것은?

① ② ③ ④ ⑤

14 윗글의 밑줄 친 우리말과 일치하도록 주어진 조건에 맞게 문장을 완성하시오.

조건
• 동사 help를 사용할 것
• 사용할 단어: focused, persistent, excellence

→ Sven _____ _____.

[15~16] 다음 글을 읽고, 물음에 답하시오.

At the Games, Yusra competed in both the 100-meter butterfly and the 100-meter freestyle events. When she stepped onto the starting blocks, she was determined to pour everything she had into the competition. She came in 41st out of 45 competitors in the butterfly event and 45th out of 46 in the freestyle event. Even though she left the Olympics without a medal, she was proud to have made history alongside her teammates. The time on the scoreboard did not matter. In one interview, when a reporter asked if she could make a statement, she remarked, "I want everyone to stay strong for their goals in life, because if you have your goals in front of your eyes, you will do everything you can; and I think even if I fail, I will try again. ... I want to show everybody that it's hard to arrive at your dreams, but it's not impossible. You can do it; everyone can do it."

15 윗글의 내용을 요약할 때 빈칸에 알맞은 말을 글에서 찾아 쓰시오.

Although Yusra failed to win a(n) (1) _____ in the Olympics, she was proud of herself since she did her best and she knew she could reach her (2) _____.

16 윗글의 밑줄 친 it이 가리키는 것을 글에서 찾아 쓰시오.

→ _____

[17~18] 다음 글을 읽고, 물음에 답하시오.

On average, about 6,800 natural disasters, including earthquakes, floods, and hurricanes, happen worldwide each year. The restoration costs of a disaster usually exceed the resources and capabilities of the affected countries. In these cases, international aid and cooperation are essential for those countries to recover from the damage. _____(A)_____, disaster survivors are often in need of food, shelter, and medical support. International aid can provide them with urgent supplies and help rebuild core facilities like power plants, public transportation, and hospitals. _____(B)_____, countries can cooperate by sharing knowledge in disaster situations. By doing so, more countries can develop early warning systems and invest in risk reduction. These efforts help global communities respond better to future disasters. By working together, we will be able to ensure that no one is left behind.

17 윗글의 빈칸 (A), (B)에 들어갈 말이 바르게 짝지어진 것은?

(A)	(B)
① In other words	··· Therefore
② For example	··· Furthermore
③ However	··· To make matters worse
④ Meanwhile	··· On the other hand
⑤ In short	··· However

18 윗글의 밑줄 친 doing so가 가리키는 것을 글에서 찾아 쓰시오.

→ _____

[01~02] 다음 대화를 읽고, 물음에 답하시오.

M Thanks for joining us! Today, psychologist Carla Jensen is here to share her insights on the ideal mindset for overcoming challenges and achieving success. Welcome, Dr. Jensen!

W Thanks for having me!

M So, Doctor, what mindsets do people have when facing challenges?

W There are two mindsets that people can have. The first one is a fixed mindset. People with this mindset believe their abilities cannot be developed any further. Therefore, they often feel discouraged when facing a difficult task and are not motivated to pursue their goals.

M I guess they are afraid to experience failure.

W Exactly. _____, some people have a growth mindset. They believe that their knowledge and abilities can be improved through effort.

M That sounds more like the kind of mindset we need to cultivate in order to succeed.

01 위 대화의 주제로 가장 적절한 것은?

① 성공적인 삶을 위해 필요한 요소
② 정신 건강과 육체 건강의 상관 관계
③ 의사소통 능력이 성공에 미치는 영향
④ 성공에 도움이 되는 바람직한 사고방식
⑤ 문제 해결 능력을 키우는 데 도움이 되는 일상의 습관

02 위 대화의 빈칸에 들어갈 말로 가장 적절한 것은?

① For example   ② On the other hand
③ In other words   ④ In short
⑤ In that case

[03~05] 다음 글을 읽고, 물음에 답하시오.

A massive earthquake struck Türkiye and Syria in 2023. Nearly 60,000 people died, and ① countless buildings were destroyed. (A) Millions of people lost their homes and were left in danger due to a lack of food and water. (B) They sent rescue teams to search for ② survivors. (C) They also offered financial support so that people could ③ purchase food, clothes, and necessary supplies. (D) Many organizations provided vital medical support and ④ psychological assistance to the victims through mobile clinic services. (E) Meanwhile, citizens from across the globe ⑤ received money and goods. Some even did volunteer work at the disaster sites. The suffering and loss of life caused by this earthquake were terrible. However, the situation would have been a lot worse _____.

03 글의 흐름으로 보아, 주어진 문장이 들어가기에 가장 적절한 곳은?

However, over 100 countries and organizations quickly responded to the disaster by sending multiple forms of aid.

① (A)   ② (B)   ③ (C)   ④ (D)   ⑤ (E)

04 윗글의 밑줄 친 부분 중, 문맥상 낱말의 쓰임이 적절하지 않은 것은?

①   ②   ③   ④   ⑤

05 윗글의 빈칸에 들어갈 말로 가장 적절한 것은?

① without the global relief effort
② with natural disasters increasing
③ without disaster prediction systems
④ with the help of international assistance
⑤ if it had not been for the medical support

[06~07] 다음 글을 읽고, 물음에 답하시오.

However, Yusra had no idea that her life would soon be turned upside down by the horrors of the Syrian civil war, which had broken out in 2011. Over the next few years, normal activities like going to school became risky. Through all of this chaos, she clung to her dream and kept swimming. However, even this became dangerous. One fateful day, a bomb fell in the pool where she was training. Although ⓐit did not explode, this incident was horrifying enough to be a wake-up call for Yusra and her sister Sara. They realized that they could no longer stay in their home country, and they made up their minds to flee Syria and go to Germany to avoid the war. If they reached Europe, the rest of the family would follow. The decision was not an easy one, but Yusra knew that ⓑit was her only option if she wanted to pursue her dream and live without fear.

06 윗글의 내용과 일치하는 것은?

① 2001년 시리아 내전이 발발했다.
② 내전으로 인해 Yusra는 학교와 수영장에 갈 수 없었다.
③ Yusra가 다니던 수영장이 폭탄 투하로 파괴되었다.
④ Yusra의 가족은 다 함께 시리아를 탈출하기로 계획했다.
⑤ Yusra는 독일에서 꿈을 추구하기로 결심했다.

07 윗글의 밑줄 친 ⓐ, ⓑ it이 가리키는 것을 쓰시오.

ⓐ it → _____

ⓑ it → _____

[08~09] 다음 글을 읽고, 물음에 답하시오.

Next, Yusra and Sara had to travel through Macedonia, Serbia, Hungary, and Austria. They walked great distances, and even though they caught rides in small cars and crowded buses from time to time, they had to cross every border on foot. 아무리 지쳐도 그들은 계속 움직였다. At the end of this overwhelming 25-day journey, they finally made it to Germany and settled at a refugee center in Berlin. Despite all the hardships and adversities she underwent, Yusra's passion for swimming never left her. In fact, it was the only thing she could do to feel at home in this foreign land.

08 윗글의 내용과 일치하지 <u>않는</u> 것은?

① Yusra와 언니는 마케도니아로부터 오스트리아까지 거쳐 이동했다.
② 그들은 여정 내내 걸어서 이동해야만 했다.
③ 그들의 여정은 25일 정도가 걸렸다.
④ 그들은 독일의 난민 센터에 정착했다.
⑤ Yusra는 수영을 통해 마음의 평안을 찾고자 했다.

09 윗글의 밑줄 친 우리말과 일치하도록 주어진 **조건**에 맞게 문장을 완성하시오.

조건
• No matter로 문장을 시작할 것
• 사용할 단어: exhausted, move

→ _____

[10~11] 다음 글을 읽고, 물음에 답하시오.

> She decided to ①take up training again, and she started looking for a coach in Berlin who could help her ②reach her full potential. She eventually met Sven Spannekrebs at a swimming club near the refugee center and asked, "Can you be my coach?" When he saw her swim, he immediately recognized her outstanding talent and agreed to do so. Sven helped Yusra stay focused and persistent in her efforts to ③pursue excellence. Following his instructions, Yusra trained hard ④day and night, hoping her efforts would ⑤pay off one day.

10 윗글의 밑줄 친 부분을 우리말로 바르게 옮기지 <u>않은</u> 것은?

① take up: 시작하다
② reach her full potential: 최대 잠재력에 도달하다
③ pursue excellence: 탁월함을 갖추다
④ day and night: 밤낮으로
⑤ pay off: 성과를 내다

11 윗글의 밑줄 친 부분을 간접화법으로 바꿔 쓰시오.

→ She eventually met Sven Spannekrebs at a swimming club near the refugee center and _____ _____.

[12~13] 다음 글을 읽고, 물음에 답하시오.

> Yusra soon received a chance (A) making / to make her dream a reality when she was invited to join the first ever refugee team at the 2016 Summer Olympic Games in Rio de Janeiro. (B) Although / Since it seemed like a great opportunity, Yusra was hesitant. If she joined the refugee team, she thought, people might view her with pity instead of seeing her as a serious athlete. She almost turned down the invitation, but she decided to accept it after she realized (C) that / what she could inspire hope in millions of other refugees facing similar challenges.

12 (A), (B), (C)의 각 네모 안에서 어법에 맞는 표현으로 가장 적절한 것은?

	(A)	(B)	(C)
①	making	··· Although	··· that
②	making	··· Since	··· that
③	to make	··· Although	··· that
④	to make	··· Since	··· what
⑤	to make	··· Although	··· what

13 윗글의 밑줄 친 accept와 반대의 뜻을 가진 표현을 글에서 찾아 쓰시오. (필요시 형태를 바꿀 것)

→ _____

At the Games, Yusra competed in both the 100-meter butterfly and the 100-meter freestyle events. When she stepped onto the starting blocks, she was determined to pour everything she had into the competition. She came in 41st out of 45 competitors in the butterfly event and 45th out of 46 in the freestyle event. Even though she left the Olympics without a medal, she was proud to have made history alongside her teammates. _____ did not matter. In one interview, when a reporter asked if she could make a statement, she remarked, "I want everyone to stay strong for their goals in life, because if you have your goals in front of your eyes, you will do everything you can; and I think even if I fail, I will try again. … I want to show everybody that 꿈에 도달하는 것은 어렵지만 불가능하지는 않다. You can do it; everyone can do it."

14 윗글의 빈칸에 들어갈 말로 가장 적절한 것은?

① The number of competitors
② Interviews with reporters
③ The time on the scoreboard
④ The competition at Olympic events
⑤ Everything she poured into the games

15 윗글의 밑줄 친 우리말과 일치하도록 주어진 조건 에 맞게 문장을 완성하시오.

조건
• 가주어 it으로 절을 시작할 것
• 사용할 표현: arrive at, impossible

→ I want to show everybody that _____
_____ .

One of the biggest difficulties that I used to ⓐface was my fear of public speaking. Last year, I had to speak in front of the whole school. I was so nervous that I ⓑmade a lot of mistakes. I thought I might never be able to speak in front of others again. However, I wanted to get over my fear, so I decided ⓒto join the speech club. My fellow club members gave me great advice, and I ⓓpracticed many different speeches. After a while, I got used to making eye contact with the audience and ⓔspeak confidently in a loud, clear voice. As a result, I was able to give a successful speech at the next school event. This experience taught me ⓕthat I can overcome difficulties through persistent effort.

16 윗글에서 유추할 수 있는 필자의 심경 변화로 가장 적절한 것은?

① excited → disappointed
② frustrated → proud
③ anxious → furious
④ worried → relieved
⑤ anticipating → nervous

17 윗글의 밑줄 친 부분 중 어법상 바르지 않은 것을 찾아 기호를 쓰고, 바르게 고쳐 쓰시오.

_____ → _____

[01~02] 다음 대화를 읽고, 물음에 답하시오.

> G Yesterday, I met a group of Spanish tourists and helped them find a hotel.
>
> B That was very kind of you. But I didn't know you spoke Spanish.
>
> G I don't. (①) I used a translation app on my phone.
>
> B Oh, I've never used one before.
>
> G This one is quite easy to use. (②) Just open the app and speak into the phone in your own language. Then it will translate what you've said into the language you select!
>
> B That sounds like it would be useful in many situations. (③)
>
> G Yes, it is. I used it when I went to France last year. (④)
>
> B Wow! (⑤) It's surprising that we can communicate in a language we don't know. I'm going to download it!

01 대화의 흐름으로 보아, 주어진 문장이 들어가기에 가장 적절한 곳은?

> I was able to talk to people without much difficulty thanks to the app.

①   ②   ③   ④   ⑤

02 대화가 끝나고 남학생이 할 일로 가장 적절한 것은?

① 스페인어를 배울 것이다.
② 영어 말하기를 연습할 것이다.
③ 관광객들을 안내할 것이다.
④ 여학생이 소개한 애플리케이션을 내려받을 것이다.
⑤ 여학생에게 애플리케이션을 보여 줄 것이다.

[03~04] 다음 글을 읽고, 물음에 답하시오.

> When Yusra Mardini was a young girl ⓐgrow up in Damascus, Syria, her life centered around swimming. Her father was a former professional swimmer, and she started learning how to swim from a young age. When she was nine years old, she was already faster than many older swimmers. It was clear that _____, and she fell in love with the sport. She enjoyed watching Olympic swimming events with her father, which led her to dream about competing in the Olympics. She got the chance ⓑrepresent Syria in an international swimming championship, and it seemed like her Olympic dream might someday come true.

03 윗글의 빈칸에 들어갈 말로 가장 적절한 것은?

① she had a special talent
② people in Syria loved swimming
③ her father was an Olympic medalist
④ she would win the Olympic games
⑤ she loved watching swimming events

04 윗글의 밑줄 친 ⓐ와 ⓑ를 알맞은 형태로 바꿔 쓰시오. (필요시 단어를 추가할 것)

ⓐ grow → _____

ⓑ represent → _____

[05~06] 다음 글을 읽고, 물음에 답하시오.

In August, 2015, the sisters began their dangerous journey by making their way to their first destination, Türkiye. There, along with 18 other people, including children and babies, they boarded a tiny boat designed for seven passengers.

(A) The heavy boat began to sink, and the panicked, desperate passengers had no choice but to throw their _____ into the sea.

(B) They swam for three and a half hours until they arrived safely with all the other passengers on the shore of a Greek island.

(C) They were heading across the sea towards Greece when disaster struck. The boat's engine failed in the middle of the open sea, and the weather rapidly grew worse.

(D) Yusra jumped into the water along with Sara and two others, and the four of them guided the drifting boat.

05 윗글의 주어진 문장 다음에 이어질 글의 순서로 가장 적절한 것은?

① (A) – (C) – (D) – (B)
② (B) – (A) – (D) – (C)
③ (B) – (C) – (D) – (A)
④ (C) – (A) – (D) – (B)
⑤ (D) – (A) – (C) – (B)

06 윗글의 빈칸에 알맞은 단어를 다음 영어 뜻풀이를 참고하여 쓰시오.

the things that are owned, held, or controlled by someone

→ _____

[07~08] 다음 글을 읽고, 물음에 답하시오.

Next, Yusra and Sara had to travel through Macedonia, Serbia, Hungary, and Austria. They walked great distances, and _____(A)_____ they caught rides in small cars and crowded buses from time to time, they had to cross every border on foot. No matter how exhausted they were, they kept moving. At the end of this overwhelming 25-day journey, they finally made it to Germany and settled at a refugee center in Berlin. _____(B)_____ all the hardships and adversities she underwent, Yusra's passion for swimming never left her. In fact, it was the only thing she could do to feel at home in this foreign land.

07 윗글을 읽고 Yusra에 관해 알 수 있는 내용이 <u>아닌</u> 것은?

① how many countries she crossed
② where she reached and settled
③ how long it took for her to get to the refugee center
④ what she did to comfort herself
⑤ where in Berlin she started swimming

08 윗글의 빈칸 (A), (B)에 들어갈 말이 바르게 짝지어진 것은?

	(A)		(B)
①	since	···	With
②	in case	···	By
③	while	···	Through
④	even though	···	Despite
⑤	because	···	But for

[09~10] 다음 글을 읽고, 물음에 답하시오.

She decided to take up training again, and she started looking for a coach in Berlin ___(A)___ could help her reach her full potential. She eventually met Sven Spannekrebs at a swimming club near the refugee center and asked ___(B)___ he could be her coach. <u>When he saw her to swim, he immediately recognized her outstanding talent and agree to do so.</u> Sven helped Yusra stay focused and persistent in her efforts to pursue excellence. Following his instructions, Yusra trained hard day and night, hoping her efforts would pay off one day.

09 윗글의 빈칸 (A), (B)에 알맞은 말을 보기에서 골라 쓰시오.

보기

| but | if | what | where | which | who |

(A) _____

(B) _____

10 윗글의 밑줄 친 문장에서 어법상 어색한 부분을 두 군데 찾아 바르게 고쳐 쓰시오.

→ When _____

_____ .

[11~12] 다음 글을 읽고, 물음에 답하시오.

Yusra soon received a chance to make her dream a reality when she was invited to join the first ever refugee team at the 2016 Summer Olympic Games in Rio de Janeiro. Although it seemed like a great opportunity, Yusra was hesitant. If she joined the refugee team, she thought, people might view her with pity instead of seeing her as a serious athlete. She almost turned down the invitation, but she decided to accept <u>it</u> after she realized that she could inspire hope in millions of other refugees facing similar challenges.

11 윗글의 내용과 일치하는 것은?

① Yusra는 2016 하계 올림픽에 시리아 대표로 참석했다.
② 리우 올림픽에서 최초로 난민 올림픽 선수단이 결성되었다.
③ 올림픽 출전 제안을 받고 Yusra는 즉시 수용했다.
④ 리우 올림픽 기간 동안 난민 올림픽 선수단은 동정을 받았다.
⑤ 수많은 사람들이 그녀를 설득한 뒤에 Yusra는 출전을 결심했다.

12 윗글의 밑줄 친 it이 가리키는 내용으로 가장 적절한 것은?

① the refugee team
② the invitation
③ a great opportunity
④ the pity from the audience
⑤ the hope for refugees

One of the biggest difficulties that I used to face was my fear of public speaking. Last year, I had to speak in front of the whole school. 나는 너무 긴장돼서 많은 실수를 저질렀다. I thought I might never be able to speak in front of others again. However, I wanted to get over my fear, so I decided to join the speech club. My fellow club members gave me great advice, and I practiced many different speeches. After a while, I got used to making eye contact with the audience and speaking confidently in a loud, clear voice. As a result, I was able to give a successful speech at the next school event. This experience taught me that I can overcome difficulties through persistent effort.

13 윗글의 교훈을 나타낸 격언으로 가장 적절한 것은?

① Practice makes perfect.
② A stitch in time saves nine.
③ A rolling stone gathers no moss.
④ Speech is silver, but silence is gold.
⑤ When in Rome, do as Romans do.

14 윗글의 밑줄 친 우리말과 일치하도록 주어진 조건 에 맞게 문장을 완성하시오.

조건
• so ~ that 구문을 사용하여 문장을 만들 것
• 사용할 표현: nervous, make a mistake

→ I _____ .

On average, about 6,800 natural disasters, including earthquakes, floods, and hurricanes, happen worldwide each year. The restoration costs of a disaster usually exceed the resources and capabilities of the affected countries. In these cases, international aid and cooperation are essential for those countries to recover from the damage. For example, disaster survivors are often in need of food, shelter, and medical support. International aid can provide them with urgent supplies and help rebuild core facilities like power plants, public transportation, and hospitals. Furthermore, countries can cooperate by sharing knowledge in disaster situations. By doing so, more countries can develop early warning systems and invest in risk reduction. These efforts help global communities respond better to future disasters. By working together, we will be able to ensure that no one is left behind.

15 윗글의 내용과 일치하지 <u>않는</u> 것은?

① 전세계에서 6천 건이 넘는 자연재해가 매년 발생한다.
② 재난 복구 비용은 보통 피해 국가의 자원과 능력을 넘어선다.
③ 재난 피해 시 식량, 대피소, 의료 자원이 긴급히 필요하다.
④ 피해 국가의 핵심 시설 재건은 스스로의 노력으로 이루어져야 한다.
⑤ 조기 재난 경보 시스템 구축을 통해 미래 재난에 대응할 수 있다.

16 윗글의 밑줄 친 them이 가리키는 것을 글에서 찾아 쓰시오. (두 단어)

→ _____

[01~02] 다음 글을 읽고, 물음에 답하시오.

People with a fixed mindset and people with a growth mindset will react to the same situation differently.

(A) For example, when getting a poor grade on a math exam, people with a fixed mindset might feel frustrated and give up on studying math.

(B) On the other hand, people with a growth mindset might be motivated to try harder at math.

(C) What kind of mindset do you have? If you have a fixed mindset, why don't you try to adopt a growth mindset?

(D) They might also say, "I am just not good at math. I can't improve my math skills."

(E) They might say, "I'm sure I can get a much better grade next time if I work harder."

01 윗글의 주어진 문장 다음에 이어질 글의 순서로 가장 적절한 것은?

① (A) – (B) – (D) – (C) – (E)
② (A) – (D) – (B) – (E) – (C)
③ (B) – (C) – (E) – (D) – (A)
④ (C) – (E) – (A) – (D) – (B)
⑤ (D) – (A) – (E) – (C) – (B)

02 윗글의 어조로 가장 적절한 것은?

① skeptical ② humorous
③ encouraging ④ complaining
⑤ appreciative

[03~04] 다음 글을 읽고, 물음에 답하시오.

Natural disasters are an unavoidable part of life. However, not every ① country has enough resources or expertise to deal with serious disasters. Fortunately, people around the world often cooperate to help disaster victims ② recover and rebuild. This happened when a massive earthquake struck Türkiye and Syria in 2023. Nearly 60,000 people died, and countless buildings were destroyed. Millions of people lost their homes and were left in danger due to a lack of food and water. However, over 100 countries and organizations ③ were quickly responded to the disaster by sending multiple forms of aid. They sent rescue teams to search for survivors. They also offered financial support ④ so that people could purchase food, clothes, and necessary supplies. Many organizations provided vital medical support and psychological assistance to the victims through mobile clinic services. Meanwhile, citizens from across the globe donated money and goods. Some even did volunteer work at the disaster sites. The suffering and loss of life ⑤ caused by this earthquake were terrible. However, the situation would have been a lot worse without the global relief effort.

03 윗글의 제목으로 가장 적절한 것은?

① Growing Natural Disasters Worldwide
② Global Solidarity in the Face of Disaster
③ The Importance of Earthquake Prediction
④ International Aid for Those Who Suffer from Hunger
⑤ The Impact of Türkiye-Syria Earthquake in 2023

04 윗글의 밑줄 친 부분 중 어법상 틀린 것은?

① ② ③ ④ ⑤

[05~06] 다음 글을 읽고, 물음에 답하시오.

However, Yusra had no idea that her life would soon be turned upside down by the horrors of the Syrian civil war, which had broken out in 2011. Over the next few years, normal activities like going to school became risky. Through all of this chaos, she clung to her dream and kept swimming. However, even this became dangerous. One fateful day, a bomb fell in the pool where she was training. Although it did not explode, this incident was horrifying enough to be a wake-up call for Yusra and her sister Sara. They realized that _____, and they made up their minds to flee Syria and go to Germany to avoid the war. If they reached Europe, the rest of the family would follow. The decision was not an easy one, but Yusra knew that it was her only option if she wanted to pursue her dream and live without fear.

05 윗글의 분위기로 가장 적절한 것은?

① calm and peaceful
② urgent and desperate
③ humorous and exciting
④ indifferent and detached
⑤ cheerful and festive

06 윗글의 빈칸에 들어갈 말로 가장 적절한 것은?

① a civil war would soon break out
② they had to visit countries in Europe
③ they should look for new swimming pools
④ they could no longer stay in their home country
⑤ their dream to compete in the Olympics would never come true

[07~08] 다음 글을 읽고, 물음에 답하시오.

In August, 2015, the sisters began their dangerous journey by making their way to their first destination, Türkiye. There, along with 18 other people, including children and babies, they boarded a tiny boat designed for seven passengers. They were heading across the sea towards Greece when disaster (A) struck / was struck . The boat's engine failed in the middle of the open sea, and the weather rapidly grew worse. The heavy boat began to sink, and the panicked, desperate passengers had no choice but to throw their possessions into the sea. Yusra felt heartbroken as she watched people's treasured belongings (B) disappear / to disappear under the waves. However, she had no time to reflect. She had to take action immediately in order to save (C) her / herself and the other passengers. She jumped into the water along with Sara and two others, and the four of them guided the drifting boat. They swam for three and a half hours until they arrived safely with all the other passengers on the shore of a Greek island.

07 윗글의 내용과 일치하는 것은?

① Yusra started her journey in the spring of 2015.
② There were eighteen passengers on the boat.
③ The boat was heading for Türkiye.
④ The passengers had to give up their belongings as the boat sank.
⑤ Yusra and four other passengers pulled the boat to shore.

08 (A), (B), (C)의 각 네모 안에서 어법에 맞는 표현으로 가장 적절한 것은?

	(A)	(B)	(C)
①	struck	disappear	her
②	struck	disappear	herself
③	struck	to disappear	her
④	was struck	to disappear	herself
⑤	was struck	to disappear	her

[09~10] 다음 글을 읽고, 물음에 답하시오.

Next, Yusra and Sara had to travel through Macedonia, Serbia, Hungary, and Austria. They walked great distances, and even though they caught rides in small cars and crowded buses from time to time, they had to cross every (A) board / border on foot. No matter how exhausted they were, they kept moving. At the end of this overwhelming 25-day journey, they finally made it to Germany and (B) battled / settled at a refugee center in Berlin. Despite all the hardships and adversities she (C) understood / underwent, Yusra's passion for swimming never left her. In fact, it was the only thing she could do to feel at home in this foreign land.

09 윗글의 주제로 가장 적절한 것은?

① the geography of Syria and Europe
② refugee policies in European countries
③ the benefits of swimming for physical health
④ the cultural differences between Syria and Germany
⑤ a refugee journey and an enduring passion for swimming

10 (A), (B), (C)의 각 네모 안에서 문맥에 맞는 낱말로 가장 적절한 것은?

	(A)	(B)	(C)
①	board	battled	understood
②	board	settled	understood
③	border	battled	understood
④	border	settled	underwent
⑤	border	battled	underwent

[11~12] 다음 글을 읽고, 물음에 답하시오.

① Yusra soon received a chance to make her dream a reality when she was invited to join the first ever refugee team at the 2016 Summer Olympic Games in Rio de Janeiro. ② Although it seemed like a great opportunity, Yusra was hesitant. If she joined the refugee team, she thought, people might view her with pity instead of seeing her as _____. ③ Her Olympic dream eventually came true. ④ She almost turned down the invitation, but she decided to accept it after she realized that she could inspire hope in millions of other refugees facing similar challenges. ⑤ At the Games, Yusra competed in both the 100-meter butterfly and the 100-meter freestyle events.

11 윗글의 ①~⑤ 중에서 전체 흐름과 관계 <u>없는</u> 문장은?

①   ②   ③   ④   ⑤

12 윗글의 빈칸에 들어갈 말로 가장 적절한 것은?

① a teen swimmer   ② a serious athlete
③ Syrian refugee   ④ an Olympic medalist
⑤ an anti-war activist

One of the biggest difficulties that I used to face was my fear of public speaking. Last year, I had to speak in front of the whole school. I was so nervous that I made a lot of mistakes. I thought I might never be able to speak in front of others again. However, I wanted to get over my fear, so I decided to join the speech club. My fellow club members gave me great advice, and I practiced many different speeches. After a while, I got used to making eye contact with the audience and speaking confidently in a loud, clear voice. _____, I was able to give a successful speech at the next school event. This experience taught me that I can overcome difficulties through persistent effort.

13 윗글의 내용을 요약할 때 빈칸에 들어갈 말이 바르게 짝지어진 것은?

Overcoming a ___(A)___ of public speaking through joining a club, practicing, and ___(B)___ effort led to a successful speech and a valuable lesson in perseverance.

	(A)		(B)
①	fear	…	persistent
②	skill	…	insufficient
③	fear	…	common
④	skill	…	persistent
⑤	knowledge	…	common

14 윗글의 빈칸에 들어갈 말로 가장 적절한 것은?

① In short   ② That is
③ As a result   ④ For example
⑤ On the other hand

On average, about 6,800 natural disasters, including earthquakes, floods, and hurricanes, happen worldwide each year. (①) The restoration costs of a disaster usually exceed the resources and capabilities of the affected countries. (②) In these cases, international aid and cooperation are essential for those countries to recover from the damage. (③) For example, disaster survivors are often in need of food, shelter, and medical support. (④) Furthermore, countries can cooperate by sharing knowledge in disaster situations. (⑤) By doing so, more countries can develop early warning systems and invest in risk reduction. These efforts help global communities respond better to future disasters. By working together, we will be able to ensure that no one is left behind.

15 글의 흐름으로 보아, 주어진 문장이 들어가기에 가장 적절한 곳은?

International aid can provide them with urgent supplies and help rebuild core facilities like power plants, public transportation, and hospitals.

①   ②   ③   ④   ⑤

16 윗글의 밑줄 친 These efforts로 글에서 언급되지 <u>않은</u> 것은?

① 재난 피해자들에게 식량과 대피 시설을 제공한다.
② 국제적 원조로 핵심시설의 재건을 돕는다.
③ 국가 간에 재난 상황에서의 지식을 공유한다.
④ 재난 생존자의 자활을 돕는 국제기구를 설립한다.
⑤ 조기 재난 경보 시스템을 구축한다.

[01~02] 다음 글을 읽고, 물음에 답하시오.

People with a fixed mindset and people with a growth mindset will react to the same situation differently. For example, when getting a poor grade on a math exam, people with a fixed mindset might feel frustrated and give up on studying math. They might also say, "I am just not good at math. I can't improve my math skills." On the other hand, people with a growth mindset might be motivated to try harder at math. They might say, "_____" What kind of mindset do you have? If you have a fixed mindset, why don't you try to adopt a growth mindset?

01 윗글의 내용과 일치하도록 다음 질문에 알맞은 답을 글에서 찾아 쓰시오.

What would people with a fixed mindset say when they get a poor math grade?

→ They would say, "_____
_____"

02 윗글의 빈칸에 들어갈 말을 보기 에 주어진 표현을 바르게 배열하여 쓰시오.

보기

next time / I'm sure / can / I / a much better / harder / I / get / work / grade / if

→ _____
_____

[03~04] 다음 글을 읽고, 물음에 답하시오.

However, ⓐYusra는 시리아 내전의 공포로 인해 그녀의 삶이 곧 뒤집어질 것이라고 전혀 생각하지 못했는데, 그것은 2011년에 발발했다. Over the next few years, normal activities like going to school became risky. Through all of this chaos, she clung to her dream and kept swimming. However, even this became dangerous. One fateful day, a bomb fell in the pool where she was training. Although it did not explode, this incident was horrifying enough to be a wake-up call for Yusra and her sister Sara. They realized that they could no longer stay in their home country, and they made up their minds to flee Syria and go to Germany to avoid the war. If they reached Europe, the rest of the family would follow. ⓑThe decision was not an easy one, but Yusra knew that it was her only option if she wanted to pursue her dream and live without fear.

03 윗글의 밑줄 친 ⓐ의 우리말과 일치하도록 주어진 조건 에 맞게 문장을 완성하시오.

조건

• 관계대명사 which를 사용할 것
• 동사의 시제에 주의할 것
• 사용할 표현: have no idea, upside down, break out

→ However, _____
_____ by the horrors of the Syrian civil war, _____ in 2011.

04 윗글의 밑줄 친 ⓑThe decision이 가리키는 것을 글에서 찾아 쓰시오.

→ _____

[05~07] 다음 글을 읽고, 물음에 답하시오.

In August, 2015, the sisters began their dangerous journey ⓐ by making their way to their first destination, Türkiye. There, along with 18 other people, including children and babies, they boarded a tiny boat ⓑ designed for seven passengers. They were heading across the sea towards Greece when disaster struck. The boat's engine failed in the middle of the open sea, and the weather rapidly ⓒ grew worse. The heavy boat began to sink, and the panicked, desperate passengers had no choice but ⓓ to throwing their possessions into the sea. Yusra felt heartbroken as she watched people's treasured belongings ⓔ to disappear under the waves. However, she had no time to reflect. She had to take action immediately ⓕ in order to save herself and the other passengers. She jumped into the water along with Sara and two others, and the four of them guided the drifting boat. They swam for three and a half hours until ⓖ they arrived safely with all the other passengers on the shore of a Greek island.

05 윗글에서 Yusra와 다른 승객들이 느꼈을 심경을 나타내는 단어를 모두 찾아 쓰시오.

→ _____

06 윗글의 내용과 일치하도록 다음 문장의 빈칸에 알맞은 말을 글에서 찾아 쓰시오.

The tiny boat Yusra and her sister boarded along with other ⁽¹⁾_____ passengers began to ⁽²⁾_____ in the middle of the ocean. The sisters jumped into the sea and ⁽³⁾_____ the boat to shore.

07 윗글의 밑줄 친 ⓐ~ⓖ 중 어법상 틀린 것을 두 개 찾아 기호를 쓰고, 바르게 고쳐 쓰시오.

(1) _____ → _____

(2) _____ → _____

[08~09] 다음 글을 읽고, 물음에 답하시오.

Next, Yusra and Sara had to travel through Macedonia, Serbia, Hungary, and Austria. They walked great distances, and even though they caught rides in small cars and crowded buses from time to time, they had to cross every border on foot. _____
At the end of this overwhelming 25-day journey, they finally made it to Germany and settled at a refugee center in Berlin. Despite all the hardships and adversities she underwent, Yusra's passion for swimming never left her. In fact, it was the only thing she could do to feel at home in this foreign land.

08 윗글의 내용과 일치하도록 주어진 질문에 대한 답을 완성하시오.

(1) Which countries did Yusra cross to get to Germany?
→ _____

(2) How long did it take for Yusra to get to Germany?
→ _____

09 윗글의 빈칸에 알맞은 말을 보기에 주어진 표현을 바르게 배열하여 쓰시오.

보기

how / they / no / moving / exhausted / they / kept / matter / were

→ _____
_____

10 다음 글의 빈칸 (A), (B)에 주어진 영어 뜻풀이에 해당하는 말을 쓰시오.

She decided to take up training again, and she started looking for a coach in Berlin who could help her reach her full potential. She eventually met Sven Spannekrebs at a swimming club near the refugee center and asked if he could be her coach. When he saw her swim, he immediately recognized her   (A)   talent and agreed to do so. Sven helped Yusra stay focused and   (B)   in her efforts to pursue excellence. Following his instructions, Yusra trained hard day and night, hoping her efforts would pay off one day.

(A) much better than average
(B) determined to continue doing something even when it's difficult

(A) _____

(B) _____

11 다음 글에서 밑줄 친 부분의 이유를 우리말로 쓰시오. (40자 내외)

Yusra soon received a chance to make her dream a reality when she was invited to join the first ever refugee team at the 2016 Summer Olympic Games in Rio de Janeiro. Although it seemed like a great opportunity, <u>Yusra was hesitant</u>. If she joined the refugee team, she thought, people might view her with pity instead of seeing her as a serious athlete. She almost turned down the invitation, but she decided to accept it after she realized that she could inspire hope in millions of other refugees facing similar challenges.

→ _____
_____

[12~13] 다음 글을 읽고, 물음에 답하시오.

On average, about 6,800 natural disasters, including earthquakes, floods, and hurricanes, happen worldwide each year. The restoration costs of a disaster usually exceed the resources and capabilities of the affected countries. In these cases, international aid and cooperation are essential for those countries to recover from the damage. For example, disaster survivors are often in need of food, shelter, and medical support. International aid can provide them with urgent supplies and help rebuild core facilities like power plants, public transportation, and hospitals. Furthermore, countries can cooperate by sharing knowledge in disaster situations. By doing so, more countries can develop early warning systems and invest in risk reduction. 이러한 노력은 국제 사회가 미래의 재난에 더 잘 대응하도록 돕는다. By working together, we will be able to ensure that no one is left behind.

12 윗글의 내용과 일치하도록 주어진 질문에 대한 답을 완성하시오.

(1) How many natural disasters occur worldwide each year?
→ _____
worldwide each year.

(2) What things are most urgently needed for disaster survivors?
→ _____
are most urgently needed.

13 윗글의 밑줄 친 우리말과 일치하도록 주어진 조건에 맞게 문장을 완성하시오.

조건
• 동사 help를 사용할 것
• 사용할 표현: efforts, global communities, respond

→ _____
_____

Special Lesson

The Open Window

교과서 어휘

Words

☐ confident	형 자신감 있는
☐ meanwhile	명 그동안
☐ flatter	동 추켜세우다, 아첨하다
☐ niece	명 (여자) 조카
☐ doubt	동 의심하다
☐ stranger	명 낯선 사람
☐ cure	동 낫게 하다
☐ nervousness	명 신경과민(증)
☐ rural	형 시골의 (↔ urban 도시의)
☐ silent	형 침묵을 지키는, 말 없는
☐ distinct	형 명확한, 뚜렷한
☐ regret	명 후회
☐ practically	부 사실상
☐ widowed	형 과부가 된
☐ undefinable	형 표현하기 힘든
☐ tragedy	명 비극 (tragic 형 비극의)
☐ peaceful	형 평화로운
☐ lawn	명 잔디밭
☐ swamp	명 늪
☐ muddy	형 진창인, 진흙투성이인
☐ tremble	동 (몸을) 떨다
☐ waterproof	형 방수의
☐ bound	동 껑충껑충 달리다
☐ tease	동 놀리다
☐ creepy	형 으스스한, 오싹한
☐ relieved	형 안도하는
☐ apologize	동 사과하다 (apology 명 사과)

☐ amuse	동 즐겁게 하다
☐ mind	동 신경 쓰다, 싫어하다
☐ mess	명 엉망진창인 상태
☐ dreadful	형 끔찍한
☐ upsetting	형 속상하게 하는
☐ unfortunate	형 운이 없는 (↔ fortunate 운 좋은)
☐ coincidence	명 우연의 일치
☐ anniversary	명 기념일
☐ mistakenly	부 잘못하여
☐ illness	명 병
☐ barely	부 간신히
☐ yawn	명 하품
☐ delight	명 기쁨
☐ slightly	부 약간
☐ sympathy	명 동정
☐ direction	명 방향
☐ figure	명 (사람의) 형체
☐ grab	동 잡아채다
☐ notice	동 의식하다
☐ bush	명 덤불
☐ crash	동 충돌하다
☐ cemetery	명 묘지
☐ grave	명 무덤
☐ bark	동 짖다
☐ furiously	부 맹렬하게
☐ elaborate	형 정교한, 공을 들인
☐ speciality	명 전문 (분야), 특기

Phrases

☐ put up with	~을 참고 견디다
☐ as far as	~하는 한
☐ get on one's nerves	신경에 거슬리게 하다

☐ hold back	누르다, 참다
☐ run away	도망치다
☐ dash off	급히 떠나다

교과서 어휘 익히기

♣ 다음 영어는 우리말로, 우리말은 영어로 쓰시오.

01	swamp	명 _____	26	형 시골의	_____
02	unfortunate	형 _____	27	명 잔디밭	_____
03	sympathy	명 _____	28	동 (몸을) 떨다	_____
04	flatter	동 _____	29	명 하품	_____
05	cemetery	명 _____	30	형 방수의	_____
06	tease	동 _____	31	~하는 한	_____
07	barely	부 _____	32	동 의심하다	_____
08	anniversary	명 _____	33	동 잡아채다	_____
09	mistakenly	부 _____	34	명 그동안	_____
10	hold back	_____	35	명 (여자) 조카	_____
11	furiously	부 _____	36	형 명확한, 뚜렷한	_____
12	nervousness	명 _____	37	명 비극	_____
13	apologize	동 _____	38	동 껑충껑충 달리다	_____
14	crash	동 _____	39	명 엉망진창인 상태	_____
15	practically	부 _____	40	도망치다	_____
16	speciality	명 _____	41	명 우연의 일치	_____
17	cure	동 _____	42	명 (사람의) 형체	_____
18	creepy	형 _____	43	명 덤불	_____
19	notice	동 _____	44	명 무덤	_____
20	get on one's nerves	_____	45	형 정교한, 공을 들인	_____
21	dreadful	형 _____	46	동 짖다	_____
22	widowed	형 _____	47	형 자신감 있는	_____
23	mind	동 _____	48	명 후회	_____
24	undefinable	형 _____	49	명 병	_____
25	put up with	_____	50	형 진창인, 진흙투성이인	_____

교과서 **본문 분석**

01 "My aunt will be down soon, Mr. Nuttel," said the very confident 15-year old girl.

"이모가 곧 내려오실 거예요, Nuttel 씨," 매우 자신감 넘치는 열다섯 살의 소녀가 말했다.

02 "In the meanwhile, you must put up with me."
　　　　그동안　　　　　　　　　　　참고 견디다

"그동안 저를 참고 견디셔야겠네요."

03 　　　　　　　　　　　　　　　　　　↓　　　　　　주격 관계대명사절
Framton Nuttel tried to say something [that would flatter the niece] without making it seem like

he was focusing on her rather than her aunt, who had yet to come down.
　　　과거진행형　　　　　　　　　～보다　　　　　계속적 용법의 주격 관계대명사

Framton Nuttel은 이모보다 조카에게 집중하는 것처럼 보이지 않으면서도, 조카를 추켜세울만한 뭔가를 말하려고 노력했고, 이모는 아직 내려오지 않았다.

04 　　　　　　　명사절 (doubted의 목적어)
He doubted [whether these formal visits to the homes of total strangers would do much to help
　　　　　　　　　　　　　　　　　　　　　　　　　　　　　　　　　　　큰 기여를 하다, 보탬이 되다
cure his nervousness].
　　　신경과민(증)

그는 완전히 낯선 사람의 집에 공식적으로 방문하는 것이 그의 신경과민증을 치료하는 데 큰 도움이 될지 확신하지 못했다.

05 　　　　　　　　　　　　　　　　　　　　　　　　　　부사절 <시간>
"I know [how it will be]," his sister had said [when he was preparing to move to this rural area].
　　　　　　간접의문문 (의문사 + 주어 + 동사)　　과거완료 (대과거)

"나는 어떻게 될지 알아," 그가 이 시골 지역으로 이사할 준비를 하고 있었을 때 그의 누나가 말했다.

06 　　　　　　　　　　　　　　　　　　　(will)
"You will hide yourself down there and not speak to anyone.
　　　　동사 1　　　　　　　　　　　　　　　　동사 2

"넌 거기서 몸을 숨기고 아무에게도 말하지 않을 거야.

07 Then your nervousness will be worse than ever.
　　　　　　　　　　　　　　　　한층 심하게

그러면 네 신경과민증은 그 어느 때보다 더 심해지겠지.

08 　　　　　　　　(that)　　목적격 관계대명사절
I will tell all the people [I know there] that you're coming.
　　　　간접목적어　　　　　　　　직접목적어

그곳에서 내가 아는 모든 사람들에게 네가 간다고 말할 거야.

09 Some of them, as far as I can remember, were quite nice."
　　　　　　　　～하는 한

내가 기억하는 한 그들 중 몇몇은 꽤 친절했거든."

10 Framton wondered [whether Mrs. Sappleton, the woman {he was now visiting}, belonged in the
　　　　　　　　명사절 (wondered의 목적어)　　동격의 콤마　　　목적격 관계대명사절
"nice" category].

Framton은 그가 지금 방문하고 있는 Sappleton 부인이 '친절한' 범주에 속하는지 궁금했다.

11 "Do you know many of the people around here?" asked the niece [when she decided that they had
부사절 〈시간〉 접속사 과거완료
stayed silent for long enough].

"이 주변의 사람들을 많이 아세요?" 조카가 그들이 충분히 오랫동안 침묵하고 있었다고 판단했을 때 물었다.

12 "Hardly anyone," said Framton. "My sister stayed here four years ago, and she gave me [the
거의 ~ 않다 간접목적어 직접목적어
names of some of the people {she wants me to meet}]."
목적격 관계대명사절

"거의 몰라," Framton이 말했다. "누나가 4년 전에 여기 살았는데, 내가 만났으면 하는 몇몇 사람들의 이름을 알려주긴 했어."

13 He made the last statement in a tone of distinct regret.

그는 뚜렷한 후회가 묻어나는 어조로 마지막 말을 했다.

14 "Then you know practically nothing about my aunt?" asked the confident young lady.
사실상

"그러면 제 이모에 대해서 사실상 아무것도 모르시는 거네요?" 자신감 넘치는 소녀가 물었다.

15 "Only her name and address," admitted Framton.

"오직 이름과 주소만 알지," Framton이 인정했다.

16 He was wondering [whether Mrs. Sappleton was married or widowed].
명사절 (was wondering의 목적어) 과부가 된
그는 Sappleton 부인이 기혼인지 또는 과부인지 궁금해하고 있었다.

17 Something undefinable about the room suggested [that a man lived there].
(-thing으로 끝나는 대명사: 형용사가 뒤에서 수식) 명사절 (suggested의 목적어)
그 방에서 표현할 수 없는 무언가가 거기에 남자가 산다는 것을 암시했다.

18 "A great tragedy happened just three years ago," said the girl. "It was after your sister left."

"불과 3년 전에 엄청난 비극이 일어났어요," 소녀가 말했다. "아저씨의 누나가 떠난 후였어요."

19 "A tragedy?" asked Framton.

"비극?" Framton이 물었다.

20 Somehow, tragedies seemed out of place in such a calm and peaceful countryside.
맞지 않는, 부적절한 such + a(n) + 형용사 + 명사: 그토록 ~한 (명사)
왠지 이 고요하고 평화로운 시골에 비극은 어울리지 않는 것 같았다.

21 간접의문
"You may wonder [why we have left that window wide open on an October afternoon]," said the
leave + 목적어 + 목적격 보어(형용사): ~을 …한 상태로 두다
niece, [pointing to a French window {that opened onto a lawn}].
분사구문 〈동시동작〉 주격 관계대명사절
"저희가 10월의 오후에 왜 저 유리문을 활짝 열어놓았는지 궁금하실지도 모르겠네요." 조카가 잔디밭 쪽으로 열린 유리문을 가리키며 말했다.

22 "Well, it is quite warm for this time of the year," said Framton.
비인칭 주어 / 이맘때

"글쎄, 이 시기치고 꽤 따뜻하긴 하구나," Framton이 말했다.

23 "But does that window have anything to do with the tragedy?"
have something to do with: ~과 관련이 있다 (의문문에서 something 대신 anything 사용)

"하지만 저 유리문이 그 비극과 관련이 있니?"

24 "Three years ago today, her husband and her two younger brothers went off on a hunting trip
go off: (~을 하러) 자리를 뜨다
through that window. They never came back.

"3년 전 오늘, 이모의 남편과 두 남동생이 저 유리문을 통해 사냥 여행을 떠났어요. 그들은 다시 돌아오지 못했어요.

25 [While crossing the woods to their favorite hunting spot], they fell into a swamp.
(they were) / 부사절 <시간>

숲을 가로질러 가장 좋아하는 사냥터로 가던 중, 그들은 늪에 빠졌어요.

26 It had been very wet and muddy that summer, you know.
과거완료

아시다시피, 그해 여름은 매우 습하고 진창이었어요.

27 Places [that had been safe in other years] suddenly became dangerous.
주격 관계대명사절

다른 해에는 안전했던 장소가 갑자기 위험해졌어요.

28 Their bodies were never found. That was the worst part of this story."
수동태 / 앞문장을 가리키는 지시대명사

그들의 시신은 결국 발견되지 않았어요. 그게 이 이야기의 최악인 부분이죠."

29 Here the girl's voice lost its confident tone and began to tremble.
동사 1 / 동사 2

여기서 소녀의 목소리는 자신감 넘치는 어조를 잃고 떨리기 시작했다.

30 "My poor aunt still thinks that they will come back someday, along with the little brown dog [that
접속사 / ~과 같이 / 주격 관계대명사절
was lost with them], [walking in through that window just as they used to do].
분사구문 <동시동작> / 꼭 ~ 처럼 / used to-v: ~하곤 했다

"우리 불쌍한 이모는 여전히 그들이 언젠가 그들과 같이 사라진 작은 갈색 강아지와 함께 예전에 그랬던 것처럼 저 유리문을 통해 걸어 들어오며 돌아올 것이라고 생각하세요.

31 That is why the window is kept open every day until sunset.
~까지 (전치사)

그게 매일 해 질 녘까지 유리문이 열려 있는 이유예요.

32 My aunt often told me [how they left].
간접의문문

이모는 자주 제게 그들이 어떻게 떠났는지 말해주셨어요.

33 Her husband had his white waterproof coat over his arm, and Ronnie, her youngest brother, was
singing 'Bertie, why do you bound?' as he always did to tease her, [because she said it got on her
nerves].

get on one's nerves: 신경에 거슬리게 하다

그녀의 남편은 그의 흰색 방수 코트를 팔에 걸치고 있었고, 그녀의 막내 남동생 Ronnie는 그녀를 놀리기 위해 늘 하던 대로 'Bertie, why do you bound?'를 부르고 있었는데, 그건 그 노래가 신경에 거슬린다고 그녀가 말했기 때문이죠.

34 Sometimes on still, quiet evenings like this, I almost get a creepy feeling that they will all walk in
through that window—"

가끔 이렇게 고요하고 조용한 저녁이면, 저는 그들이 모두 저 유리문으로 걸어 들어올 것만 같은 으스스한 느낌이 들어요—"

35 She stopped speaking suddenly and shook a little.

stop v-ing: ~하는 것을 멈추다

그녀는 갑자기 말을 멈추고 살짝 떨었다.

36 Framton was relieved [when the aunt rushed into the room and apologized for being late].

이모가 방으로 급하게 달려와 늦은 것에 대해 사과했을 때 Framton은 안도했다.

37 "I hope Vera has been amusing you," she said.

현재완료 진행형

"Vera가 당신을 즐겁게 해주고 있었길 바라요," 그녀가 말했다.

38 "She has been very interesting," said Framton.

"그녀는 매우 재미있었어요," Framton이 말했다.

39 "I hope you don't mind the open window," said Mrs. Sappleton.

신경 쓰다, 싫어하다

"열린 유리문은 신경 쓰지 마시길 바라요," Sappleton 부인이 말했다.

40 "My husband and brothers will soon be back from hunting, and they always come in this way.

"제 남편과 동생들이 곧 사냥에서 돌아오는데, 그들은 항상 여기를 통해 들어와요.

41 They've been out in the forest today, so they'll make a mess of my poor carpets.

현재완료

오늘 종일 숲에 있었으니, 그들은 제 불쌍한 카펫을 엉망으로 만들 거예요.

42 Men always do that sort of thing, don't they?"

부가의문

남자들은 항상 그런 짓을 하잖아요, 그렇죠?"

43 She talked cheerfully about hunting and the lack of birds in the area.

그녀는 사냥과 그 지역에 새가 부족하다는 것에 대해 쾌활하게 이야기했다.

44

To Framton, it was dreadful [to listen to her].
　　　　가주어　　　　　　진주어

Framton에게 그녀의 이야기를 듣는 것은 끔찍한 일이었다.

45

He made a partially successful effort [to change the subject to a less upsetting topic].
　　　　　　　　　　　　　　　　　　　　　　　　 형용사적 용법

그는 주제를 덜 속상한 주제로 바꾸려는, 부분적으로 성공적인 노력을 했다.

46

He was conscious that Mrs. Sappleton was giving him only a small part of her attention.
　　　　　　　　　　　 접속사　　　　　　　　　　　　　　 간접목적어　직접목적어

그는 Sappleton 부인이 자신에게 아주 작은 관심만을 기울이고 있다는 것을 알고 있었다.

47

Her eyes were constantly moving past him to the open window and the lawn beyond.

그녀의 시선은 거듭해서 그를 지나 열려있는 유리문과 그 너머에 있는 잔디밭을 향해 움직이고 있었다.

48

It was an unfortunate coincidence [that he had visited her on such a tragic anniversary].
가주어　　　　　　　　　　　　　　　 진주어　　과거완료　　　　　　「such + a(n) + 형용사 + 명사」의 어순

그가 그런 비극적인 기일에 그녀를 방문했다는 것은 불행한 우연의 일치였다.

49

　　　　　　　　　　　　　　　　　　　　　 「both A and B: A와 B 둘 다」
"My doctors ordered me to rest and to avoid both excitement and physical exercise," said
　　　　　 order + 목적어 + to-v: ~에게 …하라고 지시하다
Framton, [who mistakenly believed that strangers were interested in his illnesses, as well as their
　　　　　계속적 용법의 주격 관계대명사절　　 접속사　　　　　　　　　　　　　　　　　 ~ 뿐만 아니라　 = illnesses
causes and cures].

"제 의사들은 제가 휴식을 취하고 흥분과 운동을 자제할 것을 지시했어요,"라고 Framton이 말했는데, 그는 낯선 사람들이 자신의 병에 더하여 그
원인과 치료법에 대해서도 관심 있어 한다고 잘못 생각했다.

50

"However, they are not so much in agreement on [what exactly my diet should be]," he continued.
　　　　　　　　　　　　　　　　　　　　　　　　　　　　　　 간접의문문

"하지만, 제 식단이 정확히 어떻게 되어야 하는지에 대해서는 의견이 별로 잘 맞진 않았어요," 그는 말을 이어갔다.

51

　　　　　　　　　　　　　　　　　 분사구문 〈동시동작〉
"No?" asked Mrs. Sappleton, [barely holding back a yawn at the last moment].
　　　　　　　　　　　　　　　　 간신히　 hold back: 누르다, 참다

"그렇지 않았다고요?" Sappleton 부인이 마지막 순간에 하품을 간신히 참으며 물었다.

52

Then she suddenly smiled and sat up straight—but it was not because of [what Framton was
　　　　　　　　　　　　　　　　　　　　　　　　　　　　　　　　　 명사절 (because of의 목적어)
saying].

그리고 그녀는 갑자기 웃으며 허리를 펴고 앉았다—그러나 그것은 Framton이 이야기하던 것 때문은 아니었다.

53

"Here they are at last!" she cried in delight. "Just in time for tea.
　　　　　　　　 마침내　　　　　　　　　　　　　　 알맞은 때에

"마침내 그들이 왔어요!" 그녀가 기쁘게 외쳤다. "차 마실 시간에 딱 맞춰 왔네요.

54

But they look as if they were in the mud up to their eyes!"
　　　　　 as if + 주어 + 동사의 과거형: 마치 ~인 것처럼

그렇지만 마치 눈까지 진흙 속에 빠진 것처럼 보여요!"

55 Framton trembled slightly and turned towards the niece with a look [that expressed sympathy for
동사 1   동사 2   주격 관계대명사절
her aunt's condition].

Framton은 살짝 떨고는, 이모의 상태에 대해 동정을 표하는 표정으로 조카를 향해 고개를 돌렸다.

56 The girl was staring out through the open window with horror in her eyes.

소녀는 공포에 질린 눈으로 유리문 밖을 바라보고 있었다.

분사구문 <동시동작>
57 [Suddenly feeling fear in his stomach], Framton turned around in his seat and looked in the same
동사 1   동사 2
direction.

갑자기 두려움을 느끼면서, Framton은 앉은 채로 돌아서 같은 방향을 바라보았다.

58 In the evening darkness, three figures were walking across the lawn towards the window.
figure: (사람의) 형체

저녁 어둠 속에서, 세 사람의 형체가 잔디밭을 지나 유리문을 향해 걸어오고 있었다.

59 They all carried guns under their arms, and one of them had a white coat over his shoulders.

그들은 모두 겨드랑이에 총을 끼고 있었고, 그중 한 사람은 어깨에 흰 코트를 걸치고 있었다.

60 A tired brown dog walked at their feet.

지친 갈색 강아지가 그들의 발치에서 걸었다.

61 They silently neared the house, and then a young voice began to sing in the dark, "Bertie, why do
near(동사): 가까워지다, 다가오다
you bound?"

그들은 조용히 집으로 가까이 다가왔고, 어둠 속에서 젊은 목소리가 'Bertie, why do you bound?'라고 노래 부르기 시작했다.

62 Framton grabbed wildly for his umbrella and hat.

Framton은 그의 우산과 모자를 거칠게 잡아챘다.

63 He barely noticed the driveway and the front gate [as he ran away from the house].
거의 ~않다   부사절 <때>
그는 집에서 달아나면서 진입로와 대문도 거의 의식하지 못했다.

64 A man [riding his bike along the road] had to ride into a bush [to avoid crashing into him].
현재분사구   부사적 용법 <목적>
길에서 자전거를 타고 가던 한 남자는 그와 부딪히는 것을 피하기 위해 덤불 속으로 자전거를 몰아야 했다.

65 "Here we are, my dear," said the man with the white coat, [coming in through the open window].
분사구문 <동시동작>
"우리 왔소, 여보." 흰 코트를 입은 남자가 열린 유리문으로 들어오며 말했다.

66　"Our clothes got a bit muddy, but they're mostly dry now.

　　　조금, 약간

　　　"우리 옷에 진흙이 조금 묻긴 했는데, 이제 거의 말랐소.

67　Who was that [who just ran out of the room as we arrived]?"

　　　　　　　　　　　　　　　주격 관계대명사절

　　　의문사　지시대명사　　　　　　　　　　　　　　　～할 때 (접속사)

　　　우리가 도착했을 때 방에서 뛰어나간 저 사람은 누구였소?"

68　"An unusual man [named Mr. Nuttel]," said Mrs. Sappleton.

　　　　　　　　　　　　　　　과거분사구

　　　"Nuttel 씨라는 특이한 남자예요," Sappleton 부인이 말했다.

69　"He talked only about his illnesses and dashed off without saying goodbye or apologizing when

　　　　　　　　　　　동사 1　　　　　　　　　　　　　동사 2　　　　　　　　　　병렬 구조

　　　you arrived. It was like he had seen a ghost."

　　　　　　　　　　　　　　　　과거완료

　　　"그는 자기 병에 대해서만 이야기하다가, 당신이 도착했을 때 작별 인사나 사과도 없이 급히 떠났어요. 마치 유령을 보기라도 한 것처럼요."

70　"I think it was the dog," said the niece calmly. "He told me he was scared of dogs.

　　　　　　　　　　　　　　　　　　　　　　　　　　　　　(that)

　　　"제가 생각했을 땐 개 때문인 것 같아요," 조카가 차분하게 말했다. "그가 개를 무서워한다고 제게 말했거든요.

71　He was once hunted into a cemetery somewhere along the banks of the Ganges by a pack of wild

　　　　　　　　수동태　　　　　　묘지　　　　　　　　　　　　　　　　　갠지스 강　　　　　한 무리의

　　　dogs and had to spend the night in a newly dug grave with the creatures barking furiously just

　　　　　　　　　　　　　　　　　　　　　　과거분사

　　　above him.

　　　한번은 들개 떼에게 쫓겨 갠지스강둑 따라 어딘가에 있는 묘지로 들어가서, 새로 파놓은 무덤 속에서 바로 위에서 맹렬하게 짖는 개들과 함께 밤을 지새워야 했다고 해요.

72　That would be enough to make anyone lose their nerve."

　　　　　　　　　enough to-v: ～하기에 충분한　　lose one's nerve: 겁먹다

　　　누구라도 겁먹게 하기 충분한 상황이죠."

73　[Coming up with elaborate tales on short notice] was her speciality.

　　　주어 (동명사구)　　　　　　　　　　　예고 없이, 순식간에　　동사

　　　순식간에 정교한 이야기를 지어내는 것은 그 소녀의 특기였다.

교과서 본문 익히기 ❶ 옳은 어법·어휘 고르기

✤ 다음 네모 안에서 옳은 것을 고르시오.

01   "My aunt will be down soon, Mr. Nuttel," said the very confidence / confident 15-year old girl.

02   In the meanwhile, you must put on / up with me.

03   Framton Nuttel tried to say something that would flatter the niece without making it seem like he was focusing on her rather than her aunt, which / who had yet to come down.

04   He doubted whether these formal visits to the homes of total strangers would be / do much to help cure his nervousness.

05   "I know how it will / will it be," his sister had said when he was preparing to move to this rural area.

06   You will hide yourself down there and not speak / speaking to anyone.

07   I will tell all the people I know there that / where you're coming.

08   Framton wondered that / whether Mrs. Sappleton, the woman he was now visiting, belonged in the "nice" category.

09   "Do you know many of the people around here?" asked the niece when she decided that they had stayed silent / silently for long enough.

10   He made the last statement in a tone of distant / distinct regret.

11   He was wondering whether Mrs. Sappleton was marrying / married or widowed.

12   "You may wonder how / why we have left that window wide open on an October afternoon," said the niece, pointing to a French window that opened onto a lawn.

13   But does that window have anything / something to do with the tragedy?

14   While cross / crossing the woods to their favorite hunting spot, they fell into a swamp.

15   Places that were / had been safe in other years suddenly became dangerous.

16   My poor aunt still thinks that they will come back someday, along with the little brown dog that was lost with them, walking in though / through that window just as they used to do / doing .

17   That is why the window is kept open every day until sunrise / sunset .

18   Her husband had his white waterproof coat over his arm, and Ronnie, her youngest brother, was singing 'Bertie, why do you bound?' as he always did to cease / tease her, because she said it got on her nerves.

19   Sometimes on still, quite / quiet evenings like this, I almost get a creepy feeling that they will all walk in through that window—

20   Men always do that sort of thing, aren't / don't they?

21   He made a partially successful effort to change the subject to a less upset / upsetting topic.

22   Her eyes were constantly moving fast / past him to the open window and the lawn beyond.

23   "My doctors ordered me to rest and to avoid both excitement and / or physical exercise," said Framton, who mistakenly believed that strangers were interested in his illnesses, as well as its / their causes and cures.

24   "No?" asked Mrs. Sappleton, barely holding back / down a yawn at the last moment.

25   But they look as if they are / were in the mud up to their eyes!

26   The girl was seeing / staring out through the open window with horror in her eyes.

27   Suddenly feel / feeling fear in his stomach, Framton turned around in his seat and looked in the same direction.

28   He almost / barely noticed the driveway and the front gate as he ran away from the house.

29   A man riding his bike along the road had to ride into a bush to avoid crashing / to crash into him.

30   Our clothes got a bit muddy, but they're mostly dry / wet now.

31   He talked only about his illnesses and dashed off without saying goodbye or apologize / apologizing when you arrived.

32   He was once hunted into a cemetery somewhere along the banks of the Ganges by a pack / peck of wild dogs and had to spend the night in a newly dug grave by / with the creatures barking furiously just above him.

33   Coming up with elaborate / elegant tales on short notice was her speciality.

교과서 **본문 익히기** ② 틀린 부분 고치기

정답 및 해설 p. 42

♣ 다음 밑줄 친 부분이 옳으면 ○표 하고, 틀리면 바르게 고쳐 쓰시오.

01 Framton Nuttel tried to say something that would flatter the niece without <u>make it seems</u> like he was focusing on her rather than her aunt, who had yet to come down.

02 He doubted whether these formal visits to the homes of total strangers <u>would do much to help cure</u> his nervousness.

03 "I know <u>how will it be</u>," his sister had said when he was preparing to move to this rural area.

04 You will hide yourself down there and <u>not speaking</u> to anyone.

05 I will tell all the people <u>I know there</u> that you're coming.

06 Some of them, as far as I can remember, <u>was quite nice</u>.

07 Framton wondered whether Mrs. Sappleton, the woman he was now visiting, <u>belong</u> in the "nice" category.

08 "Hardly <u>no one</u>," said Framton.

09 My sister stayed here four years ago, and she gave me the names of some of the people she <u>wants me meet</u>.

10 He was wondering whether Mrs. Sappleton <u>married or widowed</u>.

11 <u>Undefinable something</u> about the room suggested that a man lived there.

12 Somehow, tragedies seemed out of place in <u>a such calm</u> and peaceful countryside.

13 "You may wonder why we have left that window wide open on an October afternoon," said the niece, <u>pointing to</u> a French window that opened onto a lawn.

14 But does that window have anything <u>to do the tragedy</u>?

15 <u>While they crossing</u> the woods to their favorite hunting spot, they fell into a swamp.

16 Places that <u>has been</u> safe in other years suddenly became dangerous.

17 Their bodies <u>never found</u>.

18 My poor aunt still thinks that they will come back someday, along with the little brown dog that was lost with them, walking in through that window just as they <u>used to doing</u>.

19 That is <u>because</u> the window is kept open every day until sunset.

20 She stopped <u>to speak</u> suddenly and shook a little.

21 Framton was relieved when the aunt rushed into the room and apologized <u>for late</u>.

22 "I hope you <u>mind</u> the open window," said Mrs. Sappleton.

23 My husband and brothers will soon <u>are back</u> from hunting, and they always come in this way.

24 To Framton, it was dreadful <u>to listening</u> her.

25 It was an unfortunate coincidence that <u>he had visited</u> her on such a tragic anniversary.

26 "My doctors ordered me <u>rest and avoid</u> both excitement and physical exercise," said Framton.

27 "However, they are not so much in agreement on what exactly <u>should be my diet</u>," he continued.

28 "No?" asked Mrs. Sappleton, barely <u>held back</u> a yawn at the last moment.

29 Then she suddenly smiled and sat up straight—but it was not <u>because</u> what Framton was saying.

30 Framton trembled slightly and turned towards the niece with a look <u>what</u> expressed sympathy for her aunt's condition.

31 Suddenly feeling fear in his stomach, Framton <u>turns around</u> in his seat and looked in the same direction.

32 A man <u>rode his bike</u> along the road had to ride into a bush to avoid crashing into him.

33 "Here <u>are we</u>, my dear," said the man with the white coat, coming in through the open window.

34 Who was that <u>which</u> just ran out of the room as we arrived?

35 "An unusual <u>man naming</u> Mr. Nuttel," said Mrs. Sappleton.

36 That would be enough to make anyone <u>to lose</u> their nerve.

교과서 본문 익히기 ❸ 빈칸 완성하기

♣ 다음 빈칸에 알맞은 말을 쓰시오.

"My aunt will be down soon, Mr. Nuttel," said the very **(1)** _____ _____ _____ _____.

"이모가 곧 내려오실 거예요, Nuttel 씨," 매우 자신감 넘치는 열다섯 살의 소녀가 말했다.

"In the meanwhile, you **(2)** _____ _____ _____ _____ _____."

"그동안 저를 참고 견디셔야겠네요."

Framton Nuttel tried to say something that would flatter the niece **(3)** _____ _____ _____

_____ like he was focusing on her rather than her aunt, who had yet to come down.

Framton Nuttel은 이모보다 조카에게 집중하는 것처럼 보이지 않으면서, 조카를 추켜세울만한 뭔가를 말하려고 노력했고, 이모는 아직 내려오지 않았다.

He **(4)** _____ _____ these formal visits to the homes of total strangers would do much to help cure his

nervousness.

그는 완전히 낯선 사람의 집에 공식적으로 방문하는 것이 그의 신경과민증을 치료하는 데 큰 도움이 될지 확신하지 못했다.

"I know how it will be," his sister had said when he was preparing **(5)** _____ _____ _____ this

rural area.

"나는 어떻게 될지 알아," 그가 이 시골 지역으로 이사할 준비를 하고 있었을 때 그의 누나가 말했다.

"You **(6)** _____ _____ _____ down there and not speak to anyone.

"넌 거기서 몸을 숨기고 아무에게도 말하지 않을 거야.

Then your nervousness **(7)** _____ _____ _____ than ever.

그러면 네 신경과민증은 그 어느 때보다 더 심해지겠지.

I will tell **(8)** _____ _____ _____ I know there that you're coming.

그곳에서 내가 아는 모든 사람들에게 네가 간다고 말할 거야.

Some of them, **(9)** _____ _____ _____ _____ _____ _____, were quite nice."

내가 기억하는 한 그들 중 몇몇은 꽤 친절했거든."

Framton **(10)** _____ _____ Mrs. Sappleton, the woman he was now visiting, belonged in the "nice"

category.

Framton은 그가 지금 방문하고 있는 Sappleton 부인이 '친절한' 범주에 속하는지 궁금했다.

"Do you know many of the people around here?" asked the niece when she decided that they had **(11)** _____

_____ for long enough.

"이 주변의 사람들을 많이 아세요?" 조카가 그들이 충분히 오랫동안 침묵하고 있었다고 판단했을 때 물었다.

"**(12)** _____ _____," said Framton. "My sister stayed here four years ago, and she gave me the names

of some of the people she **(13)** _____ _____ _____ _____."

"거의 몰라," Framton이 말했다. "누나가 4년 전에 여기 살았는데, 내가 만났으면 하는 몇몇 사람들의 이름을 알려주긴 했어."

He **(14)** _____ _____ _____ _____ in a tone of distinct regret.

그는 뚜렷한 후회가 묻어나는 어조로 마지막 말을 했다.

"Then you **(15)** _____ _____ _____ about my aunt?" asked the confident young lady.

"그러면 제 이모에 대해서 사실상 아무것도 모르시는 거네요?" 자신감 넘치는 소녀가 물었다.

"Only her (16) _____ _____ _____," admitted Framton.

"오직 이름과 주소만 알지," Framton이 인정했다.

He was wondering whether Mrs. Sappleton was (17) _____ _____ _____.

그는 Sappleton 부인이 기혼인지 또는 과부인지 궁금해하고 있었다.

(18) _____ _____ about the room suggested that a man lived there.

그 방에서 표현할 수 없는 무언가가 거기에 남자가 산다는 것을 암시했다.

"A great tragedy happened just three years ago," said the girl. "(19) _____ _____ _____ your sister left."

"불과 3년 전에 엄청난 비극이 일어났어요," 소녀가 말했다. "아저씨의 누나가 떠난 후였어요."

"A tragedy?" asked Framton.

"비극?" Framton이 물었다.

Somehow, tragedies seemed (20) _____ _____ _____ in such a calm and peaceful countryside.

왠지 이 고요하고 평화로운 시골에 비극은 어울리지 않는 것 같았다.

"You may wonder why we have left that window (21) _____ _____ on an October afternoon," said the niece, (22) _____ a French window that opened onto a lawn.

"저희가 10월의 오후에 왜 저 유리문을 활짝 열어놓았는지 궁금하실지도 모르겠네요." 조카가 잔디밭 쪽으로 열린 유리문을 가리키며 말했다.

"Well, (23) _____ _____ _____ _____ for this time of the year," said Framton.

"글쎄, 이 시기치고 꽤 따뜻하긴 하구나," Framton이 말했다.

"But does that window (24) _____ _____ _____ _____ _____ the tragedy?"

"하지만 저 유리문이 그 비극과 관련이 있니?"

"Three years ago today, her husband and her two younger brothers (25) _____ _____ _____ a hunting trip through that window. They never came back.

"3년 전 오늘, 이모의 남편과 두 남동생이 저 유리문을 통해 사냥 여행을 떠났어요. 그들은 다시 돌아오지 못했어요.

(26) _____ _____ the woods to their favorite hunting spot, they fell into a swamp.

숲을 가로질러 가장 좋아하는 사냥터로 가던 중, 그들은 늪에 빠졌어요.

It had been very (27) _____ _____ _____ that summer, you know.

아시다시피 그해 여름은 매우 습하고 진창이었어요.

Places that had been safe in other years (28) _____ _____ _____.

다른 해에는 안전했던 장소가 갑자기 위험해졌어요.

Their bodies (29) _____ _____ _____. That was the worst part of this story."

그들의 시신은 결국 발견되지 않았어요. 그게 이 이야기의 최악인 부분이죠."

Here the girl's voice (30) _____ _____ _____ and began to tremble.

여기서 소녀의 목소리는 자신감 넘치는 어조를 잃고 떨리기 시작했다.

"My poor aunt still thinks that they will come back someday, along with the little brown dog (31) _____ _____ _____ with them, walking in through that window just as they used to do.

"우리 불쌍한 이모는 여전히 그들이 언젠가 그들과 같이 사라진 작은 갈색 강아지와 함께 예전에 그랬던 것처럼 저 유리문을 통해 걸어 들어오며 돌아올 것이라고 생각하세요.

(32) _____ _____ _____ the window is kept open every day until sunset.

그게 매일 해 질 녘까지 유리문이 열려 있는 이유예요.

My aunt often told me (33) _____ _____ _____ .

이모는 자주 제게 그들이 어떻게 떠났는지 말해주셨어요.

Her husband had his white waterproof coat over his arm, and Ronnie, her youngest brother, was singing 'Bertie, why do you bound?' (34) _____ _____ _____ _____ to tease her, because she said it

(35) _____ _____ _____ _____ .

그녀의 남편은 그의 흰색 방수 코트를 팔에 걸치고 있었고, 그녀의 막내 남동생 Ronnie는 그녀를 놀리기 위해 늘 하던 대로 'Bertie, why do you bound?'를 부르고 있었는데, 그건 그 노래가 신경에 거슬린다고 그녀가 말했기 때문이죠.

Sometimes on still, quiet evenings like this, I almost get a creepy feeling that they will all walk in (36) _____ _____ _____—"

가끔 이렇게 고요하고 조용한 저녁이면, 저는 그들이 모두 저 유리문으로 걸어 들어올 것만 같은 으스스한 느낌이 들어요—"

(37) _____ _____ _____ suddenly and shook a little.

그녀는 갑자기 말을 멈추고 살짝 떨었다.

Framton was relieved when the aunt rushed into the room and apologized (38) _____ _____ _____ .

이모가 방으로 급하게 달려와 늦은 것에 대해 사과했을 때 Framton은 안도했다.

"I hope Vera has been (39) _____ _____ ," she said.

"Vera가 당신을 즐겁게 해주고 있었길 바라요," 그녀가 말했다.

"(40) _____ _____ _____ very interesting," said Framton.

"그녀는 매우 재미있었어요," Framton이 말했다.

"I hope (41) _____ _____ _____ the open window," said Mrs. Sappleton.

"열린 유리문은 신경 쓰지 마시길 바라요," Sappleton 부인이 말했다.

"My husband and brothers (42) _____ _____ _____ _____ from hunting, and they always come in this way.

"제 남편과 동생들이 곧 사냥에서 돌아오는데, 그들은 항상 여기를 통해 들어와요.

They've been out (43) _____ _____ _____ today, so they'll make a mess of my poor carpets.

오늘 종일 숲에 있었으니, 그들은 제 불쌍한 카펫을 엉망으로 만들 거예요.

Men always do that sort of thing, (44) _____ _____ ?"

남자들은 항상 그런 짓을 하잖아요, 그렇죠?"

She talked cheerfully about hunting and the (45) _____ _____ _____ in the area.

그녀는 사냥과 그 지역에 새가 부족하다는 것에 대해 쾌활하게 이야기했다.

To Framton, it was dreadful (46) _____ _____ _____ _____ .

Framton에게 그녀의 이야기를 듣는 것은 끔찍한 일이었다.

He made a (47) _____ _____ _____ to change the subject to a less upsetting topic.

그는 주제를 덜 속상한 주제로 바꾸려는, 부분적으로 성공적인 노력을 했다.

He (48)_____ _____ _____ Mrs. Sappleton was giving him only a small part of her attention.

그는 Sappleton 부인이 자신에게 아주 작은 관심만을 기울이고 있다는 것을 알고 있었다.

Her eyes were (49)_____ _____ past him to the open window and the lawn beyond.

그녀의 시선은 거듭해서 그를 지나 열려있는 유리문과 그 너머에 있는 잔디밭을 향해 움직이고 있었다.

It was an unfortunate coincidence (50)_____ _____ _____ _____ her on such a tragic anniversary.

그가 그런 비극적인 기일에 그녀를 방문했다는 것은 불행한 우연의 일치였다.

"My doctors ordered me to rest and to avoid (51)_____ _____ _____ _____ _____," said Framton, who mistakenly believed that strangers were interested in his illnesses, as well as their causes and cures.

"제 의사들은 제가 휴식을 취하고 흥분과 운동을 자제할 것을 지시했어요,"라고 Framton이 말했는데, 그는 낯선 사람들이 자신의 병에 더하여 그 원인과 치료법에 대해서도 관심 있어 한다고 잘못 생각했다.

"However, they are not so much in agreement on (52)_____ _____ _____ _____ _____ _____ _____," he continued.

"하지만, 제 식단이 정확히 어떻게 되어야 하는지에 대해서는 의견이 별로 잘 맞진 않았어요," 그는 말을 이어갔다.

"No?" asked Mrs. Sappleton, (53)_____ _____ _____ a yawn at the last moment.

"그렇지 않다고요?" Sappleton 부인이 마지막 순간에 하품을 간신히 참으며 물었다.

Then she suddenly smiled and sat up straight—but it was (54)_____ _____ _____ what Framton was saying.

그리고 그녀는 갑자기 웃으며 허리를 펴고 앉았다—그러나 그것은 Framton이 이야기하던 것 때문은 아니었다.

"(55)_____ _____ _____ at last!" she cried in delight. "Just in time for tea.

"마침내 그들이 왔어요!" 그녀가 기쁘게 외쳤다. "차 마실 시간에 딱 맞춰 왔네요.

But they look (56)_____ _____ _____ in the mud up to their eyes!"

그렇지만 마치 눈까지 진흙 속에 빠진 것처럼 보여요!"

Framton trembled slightly and turned towards the niece with a look (57)_____ _____ _____ for her aunt's condition.

Framton은 살짝 떨고, 이모의 상태에 대해 동정을 표하는 표정으로 조카를 향해 고개를 돌렸다.

The girl was (58)_____ _____ through the open window with horror in her eyes.

소녀는 공포에 질린 눈으로 유리문 밖을 바라보고 있었다.

Suddenly (59)_____ _____ _____ _____ _____, Framton turned around in his seat and looked in the same direction.

갑자기 두려움을 느끼면서, Framton은 앉은 채로 돌아서 같은 방향을 바라보았다.

In the evening darkness, three figures were walking across the lawn (60)_____ _____ _____.

저녁 어둠 속에서, 세 사람의 형체가 잔디밭을 지나 유리문을 향해 걸어오고 있었다.

They all carried guns (61)_____ _____ _____, and one of them had a white coat over his shoulders.

그들은 모두 겨드랑이에 총을 끼고 있었고, 그중 한 사람은 어깨에 흰 코트를 걸치고 있었다.

A tired brown dog (62) _____ _____ _____ _____.

지친 갈색 강아지가 그들의 발치에서 걸었다.

They silently neared the house, and then a young voice (63) _____ _____ _____ in the dark, "Bertie, why do you bound?"

그들은 조용히 집으로 가까이 다가왔고, 어둠 속에서 젊은 목소리가 'Bertie, why do you bound?'라고 노래 부르기 시작했다.

Framton (64) _____ _____ for his umbrella and hat.

Framton은 그의 우산과 모자를 거칠게 잡아챘다.

He barely noticed the driveway and the front gate (65) _____ _____ _____ _____
_____ the house.

그는 집에서 달아나면서 진입로와 대문도 거의 의식하지 못했다.

A man riding his bike along the road had to ride into a bush to (66) _____ _____ into him.

길에서 자전거를 타고 가던 한 남자는 그와 부딪히는 것을 피하기 위해 덤불 속으로 자전거를 몰아야 했다.

"Here we are, my dear," said the man (67) _____ _____ _____ _____, coming in through the open window.

"우리 왔소, 여보." 흰 코트를 입은 남자가 열린 유리문으로 들어오며 말했다.

"Our clothes (68) _____ _____ _____ _____, but they're mostly dry now.

"우리 옷에 진흙이 조금 묻긴 했는데, 이제 거의 말랐소.

Who was (69) _____ _____ _____ _____ out of the room as we arrived?"

우리가 도착했을 때 방에서 뛰어나간 저 사람은 누구였소?"

"An (70) _____ _____ _____ Mr. Nuttel," said Mrs. Sappleton.

"Nuttel 씨라는 특이한 남자예요." Sappleton 부인이 말했다.

"He talked only about his illnesses and dashed off (71) _____ _____ _____ or apologizing when you arrived. It was like he had seen a ghost."

"그는 자기 병에 대해서만 이야기하다가, 당신이 도착했을 때 작별 인사나 사과도 없이 급히 떠났어요. 마치 유령을 보기라도 한 것처럼요."

"I think it was the dog," said the niece calmly. "He told me (72) _____ _____ _____ _____ dogs.

"제가 생각했을 땐 개 때문인 것 같아요." 조카가 차분하게 말했다. "그가 개를 무서워한다고 제게 말했거든요.

He was once hunted into a cemetery somewhere along the banks of the Ganges (73) _____ _____
_____ _____ _____ _____ and had to spend the night in a newly dug grave with the creatures barking furiously just above him.

한번은 들개 떼에게 쫓겨 갠지스강둑 따라 어딘가에 있는 묘지로 들어가서, 바로 위에서 맹렬하게 짖는 개들과 함께 새로 파놓은 무덤 속에서 밤을 지새워야 했다고 해요.

That would be enough (74) _____ _____ _____ _____ their nerve."

누구라도 겁먹게 하기 충분한 상황이죠."

(75) _____ _____ _____ elaborate tales on short notice was her speciality.

순식간에 정교한 이야기를 지어내는 것은 그 소녀의 특기였다.

01 밑줄 친 부분 중, 문맥상 낱말의 쓰임이 적절하지 <u>않은</u> 것은?

"Do you know many of the people around here?" asked the niece when she decided that they had stayed ①silent for long enough.

"②Hardly anyone," said Framton. "My sister stayed here four years ago, and she gave me the names of some of the people she wants me to meet." He made the last ③statement in a tone of distinct regret.

"Then you know practically nothing about my aunt?" asked the confident young lady.

"Only her name and address," ④admitted Framton. He was wondering whether Mrs. Sappleton was married or widowed. Something ⑤definable about the room suggested that a man lived there.

02 밑줄 친 부분 중, 문맥상 낱말의 쓰임이 적절하지 <u>않은</u> 것은?

Three years ago today, her husband and her two younger brothers went off on a hunting trip ①through that window. They never came back. While crossing the woods to their favorite hunting spot, they fell into a swamp. It had been very wet and muddy that summer, you know. Places that had been safe in other years suddenly became ②dangerous. Their bodies were never found. That was the worst part of this story."

Here the girl's voice lost its ③confident tone and began to tremble. "My poor aunt still thinks that they will come back someday, along with the little brown dog that was ④found with them, walking in through that window just as they used to do. That is why the window is kept open every day until ⑤sunset.

03 (A), (B), (C)의 각 네모 안에서 문맥에 맞는 낱말로 가장 적절한 것은?

My aunt often told me how they left. Her husband had his white waterproof coat over his arm, and Ronnie, her youngest brother, was singing 'Bertie, why do you bound?' as he always did to (A) cease / tease her, because she said it got on her nerves. Sometimes on still, quiet evenings like this, I almost get a (B) creeping / creepy feeling that they will all walk in through that window—" She stopped speaking suddenly and shook a little. Framton was (C) relieved / revived when the aunt rushed into the room and apologized for being late.

	(A)	(B)	(C)
①	cease	creeping	relieved
②	cease	creeping	revived
③	cease	creepy	relieved
④	tease	creepy	revived
⑤	tease	creepy	relieved

04 밑줄 친 부분 중, 문맥상 낱말의 쓰임이 적절하지 <u>않은</u> 것은?

"I hope Vera has been amusing you," she said.

"She has been very interesting," said Framton.

"I hope you don't ①mind the open window," said Mrs. Sappleton. "My husband and brothers will soon be back from hunting, and they always come in this way. They've been out in the forest today, so they'll make a ②mess of my poor carpets. Men always do that sort of thing, don't they?"

She talked ③cheerfully about hunting and the lack of birds in the area. To Framton, it was ④dreadful to listen to her. He made a partially successful effort to change the subject to a ⑤more upsetting topic. He was conscious that Mrs. Sappleton was giving him only a small part of her attention.

05 밑줄 친 부분 중, 문맥상 낱말의 쓰임이 적절하지 <u>않은</u> 것은?

"My doctors ordered me to rest and to ①<u>avoid</u> both excitement and physical exercise," said Framton, who ②<u>mistakenly</u> believed that strangers were interested in his illnesses, as well as their causes and cures. "However, they are not so much in ③<u>agreement</u> on what exactly my diet should be," he continued.

"No?" asked Mrs. Sappleton, ④<u>barely</u> holding back a yawn at the last moment. Then she suddenly smiled and sat up straight—but it was not because of what Framton was saying.

"Here they are at last!" she cried in ⑤<u>despair</u>. "Just in time for tea. But they look as if they were in the mud up to their eyes!"

06 (A), (B), (C)의 각 네모 안에서 문맥에 맞는 낱말로 가장 적절한 것은?

"Here we are, my dear," said the man with the white coat, coming in through the open window. "Our clothes got a bit muddy, but they're mostly (A) dry / wet now. Who was that who just ran out of the room as we arrived?"

"An (B) usual / unusual man named Mr. Nuttel," said Mrs. Sappleton. "He talked only about his illnesses and dashed off without saying goodbye or apologizing when you arrived."

"I think it was the dog," said the niece calmly. "He told me he was scared of dogs. He was once hunted into a cemetery by a pack of wild dogs and had to spend the night in a newly dug grave with the creatures barking (C) calmly / furiously just above him. That would be enough to make anyone lose their nerve."

	(A)		(B)		(C)
①	dry	···	usual	···	calmly
②	wet	···	usual	···	calmly
③	dry	···	usual	···	furiously
④	wet	···	unusual	···	furiously
⑤	dry	···	unusual	···	furiously

07 (A), (B), (C)의 각 네모 안에서 어법에 맞는 표현으로 가장 적절한 것은?

"Then you know practically nothing about my aunt?" asked the confident young lady.

"Only her name and address," admitted Framton. He was wondering (A) whether / whom Mrs. Sappleton was married or widowed. Something undefinable about the room suggested that a man lived there.

"A great tragedy happened just three years ago," said the girl. "It was after your sister left."

"A tragedy?" asked Framton. Somehow, tragedies seemed out of place in (B) so / such a calm and peaceful countryside.

"You may wonder (C) if / why we have left that window wide open on an October afternoon," said the niece, pointing to a French window that opened onto a lawn.

	(A)		(B)		(C)
①	whether	···	so	···	if
②	whom	···	so	···	if
③	whether	···	so	···	why
④	whom	···	such	···	why
⑤	whether	···	such	···	why

08 다음 글의 밑줄 친 부분 중, 어법상 틀린 것은?

My aunt often told me ①<u>how they left</u>. Her husband had his white waterproof coat over his arm, and Ronnie, her youngest brother, was singing 'Bertie, why do you bound?' as he ②<u>always was</u> to tease her, because she said it got on her nerves. Sometimes on still, quiet evenings like this, I almost get a creepy ③<u>feeling that</u> they will all walk in through that window—"

She ④<u>stopped speaking</u> suddenly and shook a little. Framton was relieved when the aunt rushed into the room and apologized for ⑤<u>being late</u>.

09 (A), (B), (C)의 각 네모 안에서 어법에 맞는 표현으로 가장 적절한 것은?

"I hope Vera has been (A) amusing / amused you," she said.

"She has been very interesting," said Framton.

"I hope you don't mind the open window," said Mrs. Sappleton. "My husband and brothers will soon be back from hunting, and they always come in this way. They've been out in the forest today, so they'll make a mess of my poor carpets. Men always do that sort of thing, (B) aren't / don't they?"

She talked cheerfully about hunting and the lack of birds in the area. To Framton, it was dreadful (C) listening / to listen to her. He made a partially successful effort to change the subject to a less upsetting topic.

	(A)		(B)		(C)
①	amusing	···	aren't	···	listening
②	amused	···	aren't	···	listening
③	amusing	···	aren't	···	to listen
④	amused	···	don't	···	to listen
⑤	amusing	···	don't	···	to listen

10 다음 글의 밑줄 친 부분 중, 어법상 틀린 것은?

"My doctors ordered me to rest and ①avoiding both excitement and physical exercise," said Framton, who mistakenly believed that strangers were interested in his illnesses, as well as their causes and cures. "However, they are not so much in agreement on what exactly my diet ②should be," he continued.

"No?" asked Mrs. Sappleton, barely ③holding back a yawn at the last moment. Then she suddenly smiled and sat up straight—but it was not because of ④what Framton was saying.

"Here they are at last!" she cried in delight. "Just in time for tea. But they look as if ⑤they were in the mud up to their eyes!"

11 다음 글의 밑줄 친 부분 중, 어법상 틀린 것은?

Framton trembled slightly and turned towards the niece with a look ①that expressed sympathy for her aunt's condition. The girl was staring out through the open window with horror in her eyes. Suddenly ②felt fear in his stomach, Framton turned around in his seat and looked in the same direction.

In the evening darkness, three figures ③were walking across the lawn towards the window. They all carried guns under their arms, and one of them had a white coat over ④his shoulders. A tired brown dog walked at their feet. They silently neared the house, and then a young voice began ⑤to sing in the dark, "Bertie, why do you bound?"

12 (A), (B), (C)의 각 네모 안에서 어법에 맞는 표현으로 가장 적절한 것은?

"Who was that (A) which / who just ran out of the room as we arrived?"

"An unusual man named Mr. Nuttel," said Mrs. Sappleton. "He talked only about his illnesses and dashed off without saying goodbye or (B) apologizing / apologized when you arrived. It was like he had seen a ghost."

"I think it was the dog," said the niece calmly. "He told me he was scared of dogs. He was once hunted into a cemetery somewhere along the banks of the Ganges by a pack of wild dogs and had to spend the night in a newly dug grave with the creatures (C) barking / barked furiously just above him. That would be enough to make anyone lose their nerve."

	(A)		(B)		(C)
①	which	···	apologizing	···	barking
②	which	···	apologized	···	barking
③	who	···	apologizing	···	barking
④	who	···	apologized	···	barked
⑤	who	···	apologizing	···	barked

내신 1 등급
실전 공략

[01~02] 다음 글을 읽고, 물음에 답하시오.

"My aunt will be down soon, Mr. Nuttel," said the very confident 15-year-old girl. "In the meanwhile, you must ①put up with me."

Framton Nuttel tried to say something that would flatter the niece without making it seem like he was focusing on her ②rather than her aunt, who had yet to come down. He doubted whether these formal visits to the homes of total strangers would ③do much to help cure his nervousness.

"I know how it will be," his sister had said when he was preparing to move to this rural area. "You will hide yourself down there and not speak to anyone. Then your nervousness will be ④worse than ever. I will tell all the people I know there that you're coming. Some of them, ⑤as far as I can remember, were quite nice."

01 윗글을 읽고 유추할 수 있는 내용이 <u>아닌</u> 것은?

① Framton과 소녀는 처음 보는 사이이다.
② 소녀는 이모를 대신해서 Framton을 맞이하고 있다.
③ Framton은 신경과민증을 앓고 있다.
④ Framton의 누나는 그의 이주를 반기지 않았다.
⑤ Framton은 소녀의 이모를 만나면 자신의 병에 도움이 될 거라 기대한다.

02 윗글의 밑줄 친 부분을 우리말로 바르게 옮기지 <u>않은</u> 것은?

① put up with: ~을 참고 견디다
② rather than: ~보다
③ do much: 오래 일하다
④ worse than ever: 한층 심하게
⑤ as far as: ~하는 한

[03~04] 다음 글을 읽고, 물음에 답하시오.

Framton wondered _____ Mrs. Sappleton, the woman he was now visiting, belonged in the "nice" category.

(A) "Only her name and address," admitted Framton. He was wondering _____ Mrs. Sappleton was married or widowed.
(B) "Do you know many of the people around here?" asked the niece when she decided that they had stayed silent for long enough.
(C) "Then you know practically nothing about my aunt?" asked the confident young lady.
(D) "Hardly anyone," said Framton. "My sister stayed here four years ago, and she gave me the names of some of the people she wants me to meet."

03 주어진 문장 다음에 이어질 글의 순서로 가장 적절한 것은?

① (A) – (C) – (D) – (B)
② (B) – (A) – (D) – (C)
③ (B) – (D) – (C) – (A)
④ (C) – (A) – (D) – (B)
⑤ (D) – (A) – (C) – (B)

04 윗글의 빈칸에 공통으로 알맞은 말을 주어진 철자로 시작하여 쓰시오.

→ w_____

[05~07] 다음 글을 읽고, 물음에 답하시오.

"ⓐ<u>A great tragedy</u> happened just three years ago," said the girl. "It was after your sister left."

"A tragedy?" asked Framton. Somehow, tragedies seemed out of place in such a calm and peaceful countryside.

"You may wonder why we have left that window wide open on an October afternoon," said the niece, pointing to a French window that opened onto a lawn.

"Well, it is quite warm for this time of the year," said Framton. "But does that window have anything to do with the tragedy?"

"Three years ago today, her husband and her two younger brothers went off on a hunting trip through that window. They never came back. While crossing the woods to their favorite hunting spot, they fell into a swamp. It had been very wet and muddy that summer, you know. Places that had been safe in other years suddenly became _____. Their bodies were never found. ⓑ<u>That</u> was the worst part of this story."

05 윗글의 밑줄 친 ⓐ A great tragedy에 관해 답할 수 있는 질문이 **아닌** 것은?

① When did it happen?
② Who were the victims of it?
③ How is it related to the open window?
④ What did the girl's aunt do to forget it?
⑤ What is the worst part of it?

06 윗글의 빈칸에 알맞은 말을 주어진 조건에 맞게 쓰시오.

> **조건**
> • 글에 쓰인 단어의 반대말로 쓸 것
> • 철자 d로 시작할 것

→ _____

07 윗글의 밑줄 친 ⓑ that이 가리키는 내용을 글에서 찾아 쓰시오.

→ _____

[08~09] 다음 글을 읽고, 물음에 답하시오.

Here the girl's voice lost its confident tone and began to tremble. "My poor aunt still thinks that they will come back someday, along with the little brown dog that was lost with them, walking in through that window just as they used to ___(A)___. That is why the window is kept open every day until sunset. My aunt often told me how they left. Her husband had his white waterproof coat over his arm, and Ronnie, her youngest brother, was singing 'Bertie, why do you bound?' as he always ___(B)___ to tease her, because she said it got on her nerves. Sometimes on still, quiet evenings like this, I almost get a creepy feeling that they will all walk in through that window—" <u>She stopped speaking suddenly and shook a little.</u> Framton was relieved when the aunt rushed into the room and apologized for being late.

08 윗글의 빈칸 (A), (B)에 들어갈 말이 바르게 짝지어진 것은?

	(A)		(B)
①	be	…	was
②	do	…	did
③	did	…	be
④	do	…	do
⑤	be	…	did

09 윗글의 밑줄 친 문장이 의미하는 바로 가장 적절한 것은?

① The girl felt scared that the missing men would come back.
② Framton was not listening to the girl.
③ The girl's aunt did not like the girl talking about their secret.
④ The girl did not remember the whole story.
⑤ The missing men were approaching the window.

"I hope Vera has been amusing you," she said.

"She has been very interesting," said Framton.

"I hope you don't mind the open window," said Mrs. Sappleton. "My husband and brothers will soon be back from hunting, and they always come in this way. They've been out in the forest today, so they'll make a mess of my poor carpets. Men always do that sort of thing, _____(A)_____ "

She talked cheerfully about hunting and the lack of birds in the area. To Framton, it was dreadful to listen to her. He made a partially successful effort to _____(B)_____ . He was conscious that Mrs. Sappleton was giving him only a small part of her attention. Her eyes were constantly moving past him to the open window and the lawn beyond. It was an unfortunate coincidence that he had visited her on such a tragic anniversary.

10 윗글의 빈칸 (A)에 알맞은 부가의문문을 쓰시오.

→ _____

11 윗글의 빈칸 (B)에 들어갈 말로 가장 적절한 것은?

① comfort her sorrow

② complain about Vera

③ let her talk about the details of the tragedy

④ change the subject to a less upsetting topic

⑤ get to know who her husband and brothers were

"My doctors ordered me to rest and to avoid both excitement and physical exercise," said Framton, who mistakenly believed that strangers were interested in his illnesses, as well as ⓐtheir causes and cures. "However, ⓑthey are not so much in agreement on what exactly my diet should be," he continued.

"No?" asked Mrs. Sappleton, barely holding back a yawn at the last moment. Then she suddenly smiled and sat up straight—but ⓒ그것은 Framton이 말하는 것 때문이 아니었다.

"Here they are at last!" she cried in delight. "Just in time for tea. But they look as if they were in the mud up to their eyes!"

12 윗글의 밑줄 친 ⓐ, ⓑ가 가리키는 것을 글에서 찾아 쓰시오.

ⓐ their → _____

ⓑ they → _____

13 윗글의 밑줄 친 ⓒ의 우리말과 일치하도록 보기 에 주어진 표현을 활용하여 문장을 완성하시오.

> 보기   because of, what, say

→ Then she suddenly smiled and sat up straight—but
_____ .

[14~15] 다음 글을 읽고, 물음에 답하시오.

Framton trembled slightly and turned towards the niece with a look (A) that / what expressed sympathy for her aunt's condition. The girl was staring out through the open window with horror in her eyes. Suddenly (B) feeling / felt fear in his stomach, Framton turned around in his seat and looked in the same direction.

In the evening darkness, three figures were walking across the lawn towards the window. They all carried guns under their arms, and one of them (C) had / having a white coat over his shoulders. A tired brown dog walked at their feet. They silently neared the house, and then a young voice began to sing in the dark, "Bertie, why do you bound?"

14 윗글에서 Framton이 느꼈을 심경으로 가장 적절한 것은?

① terrified
② relieved
③ satisfied
④ excited
⑤ furious

15 (A), (B), (C)의 각 네모 안에서 어법에 맞는 표현으로 가장 적절한 것은?

	(A)		(B)		(C)
①	that	…	feeling	…	had
②	that	…	felt	…	had
③	that	…	feeling	…	having
④	what	…	felt	…	having
⑤	what	…	feeling	…	having

[16~17] 다음 글을 읽고, 물음에 답하시오.

"Here we are, my dear," said ①the man with the white coat, coming in through the open window. "Our clothes got a bit muddy, but they're mostly dry now. Who was ②that who just ran out of the room as we arrived?"

"An unusual man named Mr. Nuttel," said Mrs. Sappleton. "③He talked only about his illnesses and dashed off without saying goodbye or apologizing when you arrived. It was like ④he had seen a ghost."

"I think it was the dog," said the niece calmly. "⑤He told me he was scared of dogs. He was once hunted into a cemetery somewhere along the banks of the Ganges by a pack of wild dogs and had to spend the night in a newly dug grave with the creatures barking furiously just above him. That would be enough to make anyone lose their nerve."

Coming up with elaborate tales on short notice was her speciality.

16 윗글의 밑줄 친 부분 중, 가리키는 대상이 나머지와 다른 것은?

①   ②   ③   ④   ⑤

17 윗글의 내용과 일치하지 않는 것은?

① Sappleton 부인의 남편은 유리문으로 돌아왔다.
② Sappleton 부인의 남편은 진흙이 묻고 젖은 옷을 입고 있었다.
③ Nuttel이란 이름의 남자는 인사도 없이 방에서 뛰어나갔다.
④ 소녀에 따르면 Nuttel 씨는 개를 무서워한다.
⑤ 소녀는 이야기를 지어내는 능력이 있었다.

내신 1 등급
수능형 고난도

[01~02] 다음 글을 읽고, 물음에 답하시오.

"My aunt will be down soon, Mr. Nuttel," said the very ①confident 15-year-old girl. "In the meanwhile, you must put up with me."

Framton Nuttel tried to say something that would flatter the niece without making it seem like he was focusing on her ②rather than her aunt, who had yet to come down. He doubted whether these formal visits to the homes of total strangers would do much to _____.

"I know how it will be," his sister had said when he was preparing to move to this ③urban area. "You will hide yourself down there and not speak to anyone. Then your nervousness will be ④worse than ever. I will tell all the people I know there that you're coming. Some of them, as far as I can remember, were ⑤quite nice."

01 윗글의 빈칸에 들어갈 말로 가장 적절한 것은?

① help cure his nervousness
② get along well with his neighbors
③ make a good impression on the girl
④ relieve his sister's worries
⑤ change his personality

02 밑줄 친 부분 중, 문맥상 낱말의 쓰임이 적절하지 <u>않은</u> 것은?

①   ②   ③   ④   ⑤

[03~04] 다음 글을 읽고, 물음에 답하시오.

"Then you know practically nothing about my aunt?" asked the confident young lady.

"Only her name and address," admitted Framton. He was wondering whether Mrs. Sappleton was married or widowed.

(A) "You may wonder why we have left that window wide open on an October afternoon," said the niece, pointing to a French window that opened onto a lawn.

(B) "A great tragedy happened just three years ago," said the girl. "It was after your sister left."

(C) "A tragedy?" asked Framton. Somehow, tragedies seemed out of place in such a calm and peaceful countryside.

(D) "Well, it is quite warm for this time of the year," said Framton. "But does that window have anything to do with the tragedy?"

03 주어진 문장 다음에 이어질 글의 순서로 가장 적절한 것은?

① (A) – (B) – (D) – (C)
② (A) – (D) – (B) – (C)
③ (B) – (C) – (A) – (D)
④ (B) – (D) – (A) – (C)
⑤ (D) – (A) – (C) – (B)

04 윗글을 읽고, 유추할 수 있는 내용이 <u>아닌</u> 것은?

① 소녀는 Sappleton 부인의 조카이다.
② 남자는 Sappleton 부인에 관해 아는 것이 거의 없다.
③ 소녀가 말하는 비극은 10월에 일어났다.
④ 남자의 누나는 이 마을을 2년 전에 떠났다.
⑤ 지금은 10월치고 날씨가 따뜻한 편이다.

[05~06] 다음 글을 읽고, 물음에 답하시오.

Here the girl's voice lost its confident tone and began to tremble. "My poor aunt still thinks that they will come back someday, along with the little brown dog that was lost with them, walking in through that window just as they used to do. That is _____(A)_____ the window is kept open every day until sunset. My aunt often told me _____(B)_____ they left. Her husband had his white waterproof coat over his arm, and Ronnie, her youngest brother, was singing 'Bertie, why do you bound?' as he always did to tease her, because she said it got on her nerves. Sometimes on still, quiet evenings like this, I almost get a creepy feeling that they will all walk in through that window—" She stopped speaking suddenly and shook a little. Framton was relieved when the aunt rushed into the room and apologized for being late.

05 윗글의 분위기로 가장 적절한 것은?

① cheerful and festive
② calm and peaceful
③ sad and gloomy
④ scary and horrible
⑤ urgent and desperate

06 윗글의 빈칸 (A), (B)에 들어갈 말이 바르게 짝지어진 것은?

	(A)		(B)
①	why	…	that
②	because	…	how
③	how	…	when
④	why	…	how
⑤	because	…	when

[07~08] 다음 글을 읽고, 물음에 답하시오.

"I hope Vera has been amusing you," she said.

"She has been very interesting," said Framton.

"I hope ①you don't mind the open window," said Mrs. Sappleton. "My husband and brothers will soon be back from hunting, and they always come in this way. They've been out in the forest today, so they'll make a mess of my poor carpets. Men always do that sort of thing, ②don't they?"

She talked cheerfully about hunting and the lack of birds in the area. To Framton, ③that was dreadful to listen to her. He made a partially successful effort to change the subject to a ④less upsetting topic. He was conscious that Mrs. Sappleton _____. Her eyes were constantly moving past him to the open window and the lawn beyond. It was an unfortunate coincidence that he ⑤had visited her on such a tragic anniversary.

07 윗글의 빈칸에 들어갈 말로 가장 적절한 것은?

① was worried about Vera
② was much interested in him
③ was eager to close the open window
④ already knew why he visited her house
⑤ was giving him only a small part of her attention

08 윗글의 밑줄 친 부분 중, 어법상 틀린 것은?

① ② ③ ④ ⑤

"Here they are at last!" she cried in delight. "Just in time for tea. But they look as if they (A) are / were in the mud up to their eyes!"

Framton trembled slightly and turned towards the niece with a look that expressed sympathy for her aunt's condition. The girl was staring out through the open window with horror in her eyes. Suddenly (B) feeling / felt fear in his stomach, Framton turned around in his seat and looked in the same direction.

In the evening darkness, three figures were walking across the lawn towards the window. They all carried guns under their arms, and one of them had a white coat over his shoulders. A tired brown dog walked at their feet. They silently neared the house, and then a young voice began to sing in the dark, "Bertie, why do you bound?"

Framton grabbed wildly for his umbrella and hat. He barely noticed the driveway and the front gate as he ran away from the house. A man riding his bike along the road had to ride into a bush to avoid (C) crashing / to crash into him.

09 윗글의 밑줄 친 three figures에 관해 글의 내용과 일치하지 않는 것은?

① 여자는 그들이 돌아오기를 기다리고 있었다.
② 그들은 몸에 진흙을 묻히고 있었다.
③ 여자의 조카가 남자보다 먼저 그들을 발견했다.
④ 그들은 총을 들고 다 함께 노래를 부르며 걸어왔다.
⑤ Framton은 그들을 보고 두려움을 느꼈다.

10 (A), (B), (C)의 각 네모 안에서 어법에 맞는 표현으로 가장 적절한 것은?

	(A)	(B)	(C)
①	are	feeling	crashing
②	are	felt	crashing
③	were	feeling	crashing
④	were	felt	to crash
⑤	were	feeling	to crash

"Here we are, my dear," said the man with the white coat, coming in through the open window. "Our clothes got a bit muddy, but ① they're (A) most / mostly dry now. Who was that who just ran out of the room as we arrived?"

"An unusual man named Mr. Nuttel," said Mrs. Sappleton. "② He talked only about his illnesses and dashed off (B) with / without saying goodbye or apologizing when ③ you arrived. It was like he had seen a ghost."

"I think it was the dog," said the niece calmly. "He told ④ me he was scared of dogs. He was once hunted into a cemetery somewhere along the banks of the Ganges by a pack of wild dogs and had to spend the night in a newly dug grave with the creatures barking furiously just above ⑤ him. That would be enough to make anyone (C) lose / take their nerve."

11 윗글의 밑줄 친 부분 중 가리키는 대상이 바르지 <u>않은</u> 것은?

① they: our clothes
② He: Mr. Nuttel
③ you: the man with the white coat
④ me: Mrs. Sappleton
⑤ him: Mr. Nuttel

12 (A), (B), (C)의 각 네모 안에서 문맥에 맞는 낱말로 가장 적절한 것은?

	(A)	(B)	(C)
①	most	with	lose
②	most	with	take
③	mostly	with	lose
④	mostly	without	take
⑤	mostly	without	lose

[01~02] 다음 글을 읽고, 물음에 답하시오.

"A tragedy?" asked Framton. Somehow, tragedies seemed out of place in such a calm and peaceful countryside.

"You may wonder ＿＿＿＿＿＿＿＿ on an October afternoon," said the niece, pointing to a French window that opened onto a lawn.

"Well, it is quite warm for this time of the year," said Framton. "But does that window have anything to do with the tragedy?"

"Three years ago today, her husband and her two younger brothers went off on a hunting trip through that window. They never came back. While crossing the woods to their favorite hunting spot, they fell into a swamp. It had been very wet and muddy that summer, you know. 다른 해에는 안전했던 장소들이 갑자기 위험해졌어요. Their bodies were never found. That was the worst part of this story."

01 윗글의 빈칸에 들어갈 말을 [보기]에 주어진 표현을 바르게 배열하여 완성하시오.

[보기]
we / open / have left / why / that window / wide

→ You may wonder ＿＿＿＿＿＿＿＿＿＿＿
＿＿＿＿＿＿＿＿＿＿ on an October afternoon.

02 윗글의 밑줄 친 우리말과 일치하도록 주어진 [조건]에 맞게 문장을 완성하시오.

[조건]
• 관계대명사 that을 사용할 것
• 동사의 시제에 주의할 것
• 사용할 표현: other years, suddenly, become

→ Places ＿＿＿＿＿＿＿＿＿＿＿＿＿＿
＿＿＿＿＿＿＿＿＿＿＿＿＿＿＿＿ .

[03~04] 다음 글을 읽고, 물음에 답하시오.

Here the girl's voice lost its confident tone and began to tremble. "My poor aunt still thinks that they will come back someday, along with the little brown dog that was lost with them, ⓐwalk in through that window just as they used to do. That is (1) 유리문이 열려져 있는 이유 every day until sunset. My aunt often told me (2) 그들이 어떻게 떠났는지. Her husband had his white waterproof coat over his arm, and Ronnie, her youngest brother, was singing 'Bertie, why do you bound?' as he always ⓑdo to tease her, because she said it got on her nerves. Sometimes on still, quiet evenings like this, I almost get a creepy feeling that they will all walk in through that window—"

She stopped ⓒspeak suddenly and shook a little. Framton was relieved when the aunt rushed into the room and apologized for being late.

03 윗글의 밑줄 친 ⓐ, ⓑ, ⓒ를 알맞은 형태로 바꿔 쓰시오.

ⓐ walk → ＿＿＿＿＿＿＿＿＿＿＿＿

ⓑ do → ＿＿＿＿＿＿＿＿＿＿＿＿

ⓒ speak → ＿＿＿＿＿＿＿＿＿＿＿＿

04 윗글의 밑줄 친 우리말과 일치하도록 [보기]에 주어진 표현을 활용하여 문장을 완성하시오.

[보기]
how, why, they, the window, open, left, is kept

(1) → That is ＿＿＿＿＿＿＿＿＿＿＿＿＿
every day until sunset.

(2) → My aunt often told me ＿＿＿＿＿＿＿＿＿ .

[05~06] 다음 글을 읽고, 물음에 답하시오.

"I hope Vera has been amusing you," she said.

"She has been very interesting," said Framton.

"I hope you don't mind the open window," said Mrs. Sappleton. "My husband and brothers will soon be back from hunting, and they always come in this way. They've been out in the forest today, so they'll make a mess of my poor carpets. Men always ⓐ do that sort of thing, don't they?"

She talked cheerfully about hunting and the lack of birds in the area. To Framton, it was dreadful to listen to her. He made a partially successful effort to change the subject to a less upsetting topic. He was conscious that Mrs. Sappleton was giving him only a small part of her attention. Her eyes were constantly moving past him to the open window and the lawn beyond. ⓑ 그가 그런 비극적인 기일에 그녀를 방문했다는 것은 불행한 우연의 일치였다.

05 윗글의 밑줄 친 ⓐ가 구체적으로 가리키는 내용을 글에서 찾아 쓰시오.

→ _____

06 윗글의 밑줄 친 ⓑ의 우리말과 일치하도록 주어진 조건에 맞게 문장을 완성하시오.

조건
• 가주어 It으로 문장을 시작할 것
• 동사의 시제에 주의할 것
• 사용할 표현: unfortunate coincidence

→ _____
_____ on such a tragic anniversary.

[07~09] 다음 글을 읽고, 물음에 답하시오.

"Here we are, my dear," said the man with the white coat, coming in through the open window. "Our clothes got a bit muddy, but they're mostly dry now. ⓐ 우리가 도착했을 때 방에서 뛰어나간 저 사람은 누구였소?"

"An unusual man ⓑ name Mr. Nuttel," said Mrs. Sappleton. "He talked only about his illnesses and dashed off without saying goodbye or apologizing when you arrived. It was like he had seen a ghost."

"I think it was the dog," said the niece calmly. "He told me he ⓒ scare of dogs. He was once hunted into a cemetery somewhere along the banks of the Ganges by a pack of wild dogs and had to spend the night in a newly dug grave _____. That would be enough to make anyone lose their nerve."

07 윗글의 밑줄 친 ⓐ의 우리말과 일치하도록 주어진 조건에 맞게 문장을 완성하시오.

조건
• who를 두 번 사용할 것
• 사용할 표현: that, run out of

→ _____
as we arrived?

08 윗글의 밑줄 친 ⓑ, ⓒ를 알맞은 형태로 바꿔 쓰시오. (필요시 단어를 추가할 것)

ⓑ name → _____

ⓒ scare → _____

09 윗글의 빈칸에 들어갈 말을 보기에 주어진 표현을 바르게 배열하여 쓰시오.

보기
the creatures / furiously / with / him / just above / barking

→ _____

최종 점검 기말고사

[01~02] 다음 글을 읽고, 물음에 답하시오.

When we talk about "creativity," you might think of a painter, an author, or a movie director. In other words, you might think of people ①who actually make artistic "creations." What are the differences between "creation" and "creativity"? "Creation" is the act of bringing something into existence. It ②is mainly focused on the outcome of one's efforts to produce something. It can often be the result of someone's artistic expression or thinking. The word "creativity" means the ability ③to generate something new or original. It includes not only using one's imagination for artistic purposes, ④but also come up with fresh ideas or solutions to problems. It emphasizes the quality of ⑤being innovative and original regardless of the field. We should remember this broader definition of creativity.

01 윗글의 제목으로 가장 적절한 것은?

① Defining Creativity: More Than Just Making Things
② Why Artists Are the Only Creative People
③ Understanding Artistic Expression
④ Creativity and the Art World
⑤ The Meaning of Creation

02 윗글의 밑줄 친 부분 중, 어법상 틀린 것은?

①   ②   ③   ④   ⑤

[03~04] 다음 글을 읽고, 물음에 답하시오.

Look at these two paintings. Believe it or not, they both ①depict the same person, Holy Roman Emperor Rudolf II. The one on the left might look familiar, as it is a ②standard style of portrait that you would see in a gallery or an art book. However, the one on the right, called *Vertumnus*, is very ③unconventional. Created by a 16th-century Italian painter named Giuseppe Arcimboldo, the painting shows striking creativity and originality. Fruits, flowers, and vegetables are arranged like the pieces of a puzzle to create a human head. A cherry and a mulberry become the dark eyes, while an apple and a peach act as the pink cheeks. This painting is representative of the artist's ④signature style of "composite portraits." He used plants, animals, and other objects to ⑤create many other portraits like this.

03 윗글의 밑줄 친 부분과 바꿔 쓸 표현으로 적절하지 <u>않은</u> 것은?

① describe   ② typical
③ unusual   ④ stereotypical
⑤ produce

04 윗글의 내용과 일치하도록 주어진 질문에 대한 답을 완성하시오.

What did Arcimboldo use to create the pink cheeks in *Vertumnus*?

→ _____

[05~06] 다음 글을 읽고, 물음에 답하시오.

Another good example of Arcimboldo's unique creativity can be found in *The Gardener*, one of his "reversible" paintings. When viewed normally, it is just an ordinary still life of vegetables in a bowl. However, when flipped upside down, it is magically transformed into a smiling face! (①) Experts have studied this painting, along with Arcimboldo's other reversible ones. (②) Their research showed that he first painted them as still life paintings and then turned them upside down and made some adjustments to create faces. (③) X-ray examination revealed that he sometimes changed the positions of some of the fruits and vegetables. (④) Why did he make his paintings reversible? (⑤) Viewers feel as if they are playing a visual game, which brings them a sense of pleasure.

05 글의 흐름으로 보아, 주어진 문장이 들어갈 위치로 가장 적절한 곳은?

It was probably because he wanted to add an interactive element to his work by doing so.

①   ②   ③   ④   ⑤

06 윗글의 밑줄 친 reversible의 영어 뜻풀이로 가장 적절한 것은?

① able to be changed to the opposite position
② acting in close relation with each other
③ introducing or using new methods or ideas
④ relating to things that can be seen
⑤ made of different elements or parts

[07~08] 다음 글을 읽고, 물음에 답하시오.

Another series that highlights Stentzel's astonishing creativity is *Edible Creatures*. For this series, she arranges food items you can find in any kitchen to create cute animals. The stars of the series are *Brad Pet* and *Crunchie*, a pair of puppies made of sliced bread and lettuce respectively. Stentzel says she came up with the concept of *Crunchie* while putting together a salad for her family.

What do you think her secret is? Stentzel says that it is her active observation skills ___(A)___ allow her to make magic out of the ordinary. As a child, she would spend time staring at the patterns in the wood of her bed, trying to find different animal shapes. She admits that even today she stares at things longer than is acceptable in society. This keen observation is ___(B)___ enables her to continuously produce creative and imaginative works of art.

07 윗글의 빈칸 (A), (B)에 들어갈 말이 바르게 짝지어진 것은?

	(A)		(B)
①	which	⋯	that
②	that	⋯	that
③	that	⋯	what
④	if	⋯	which
⑤	who	⋯	what

08 윗글의 내용과 일치하지 않는 것은?

① Stentzel의 <먹을 수 있는 존재들>은 그녀의 창의력이 돋보이는 작품으로 유명하다.
② Brad Pet은 자른 빵으로 만들었다.
③ Stentzel은 빨래를 널다가 <먹을 수 있는 존재들>을 생각해 냈다.
④ Stetzel은 어려서 침대의 나무 무늬를 보며 시간을 보냈다.
⑤ 예리한 관찰력이 Stentzel의 예술적 창의력의 원천이다.

[09~10] 다음 글을 읽고, 물음에 답하시오.

While it is well known that exercise is essential for our physical health, not many people know that it can also boost our creativity. This is because physical activity can enhance our mood and reduce negative emotions, (A) that / which are factors that restrict creativity. Also, exercise increases blood flow to the brain, providing it with the nutrients (B) it needs / they need to function better. When at its best, the brain can generate more creative ideas. Moreover, exercise often leads us to go outside and visit different places. By doing so, we can expose ourselves to new sources of inspiration and (C) alter / to alter the way we think.

09 윗글의 요지로 가장 적절한 것은?

① 창의력을 키우려면 집 밖으로 나가야 한다.
② 두뇌의 활동이 건강해야 창의력을 키울 수 있다.
③ 예술적 영감을 키우기 위해서는 긍정적 사고가 중요하다.
④ 신체 활동은 정신 건강에 중요하다.
⑤ 운동은 창의력 증진에 핵심적인 역할을 한다.

10 (A), (B), (C)의 각 네모 안에서 어법에 맞는 표현으로 가장 적절한 것은?

	(A)		(B)		(C)
①	that	…	it needs	…	alter
②	that	…	they need	…	alter
③	which	…	it needs	…	alter
④	which	…	they need	…	to alter
⑤	which	…	it needs	…	to alter

[11~12] 다음 글을 읽고, 물음에 답하시오.

People with a fixed mindset and people with a growth mindset will react to the same situation differently. For example, when getting a poor grade on a math exam, people with a fixed mindset might feel frustrated and give up on studying math. They might also say, "I am just not good at math. I can't improve my math skills." _____, people with a growth mindset might be motivated to try harder at math. They might say, "I'm sure I can get a much better grade next time if I work harder." What kind of mindset do you have? If you have a fixed mindset, why don't you try to adopt a growth mindset?

11 윗글의 빈칸에 들어갈 말로 가장 적절한 것은?

① As a result
② For example
③ In addition
④ In short
⑤ On the other hand

12 윗글의 내용을 요약할 때 빈칸에 들어갈 말이 바르게 짝지어진 것은?

People with a fixed mindset interpret challenges as signs of their ___(A)___ , leading to discouragement. People with a growth mindset view setbacks as motivation to improve and ___(B)___ more.

	(A)		(B)
①	limitations	…	achieve
②	strengths	…	gain
③	advantages	…	challenge
④	improvements	…	motivate
⑤	failures	…	discourage

[13~14] 다음 글을 읽고, 물음에 답하시오.

Yusra had no idea that her life would soon be turned upside down by the horrors of the Syrian civil war, which had broken out in 2011.

(A) However, even this became dangerous. One fateful day, a bomb fell in the pool where she was training. Although it did not explode, this incident was horrifying enough to be a wake-up call for Yusra and her sister Sara.

(B) If they reached Europe, the rest of the family would follow. The decision was not an easy one, but Yusra knew that it was her only option if she wanted to pursue her dream and live without fear.

(C) They realized that they could no longer stay in their home country, and they made up their minds to flee Syria and go to Germany to avoid the war.

(D) Over the next few years, normal activities like going to school became risky. Through all of this chaos, she clung to her dream and kept swimming.

13 주어진 문장 다음에 이어질 글의 순서로 가장 적절한 것은?

① (A) – (B) – (D) – (C)
② (B) – (D) – (A) – (C)
③ (C) – (B) – (D) – (A)
④ (C) – (D) – (B) – (A)
⑤ (D) – (A) – (C) – (B)

14 윗글의 밑줄 친 this chaos가 가리키는 것을 글에서 찾아 쓰시오. (네 단어)

→ _____

[15~16] 다음 글을 읽고, 물음에 답하시오.

In August, 2015, the sisters began their dangerous journey by making their way to their first destination, Türkiye. There, along with 18 other people, including children and babies, they boarded a tiny boat designed for seven passengers. They were heading across the sea towards Greece when disaster struck. The boat's engine failed in the middle of the open sea, and the weather rapidly grew worse. The heavy boat began to sink, and the panicked, desperate passengers had no choice but to throw their possessions into the sea. Yusra는 사람들의 소중한 소지품들이 물결 아래로 사라지는 것을 보며 비통함을 느꼈다. However, she had no time to reflect. She had to take action immediately in order to save herself and the other passengers. She jumped into the water along with Sara and two others, and the four of them guided the drifting boat. They swam for three and a half hours until they arrived safely with all the other passengers on the shore of a Greek island.

15 윗글을 읽고 답할 수 있는 질문이 <u>아닌</u> 것은?

① Where was the boat heading for?
② How many passengers were on the boat?
③ How did the weather change when the boat's engine stopped?
④ What did the passengers do to signal for rescue?
⑤ How many people guided the boat to the shore?

16 윗글의 밑줄 친 우리말과 일치하도록 보기에 주어진 표현을 활용하여 문장을 완성하시오.

보기
feel, heartbroken, watch, treasured, disappear

→ Yusra _____

_____ under the waves.

[17~18] 다음 글을 읽고, 물음에 답하시오.

> She decided to take up training again, and she started looking for a coach in Berlin who could help her reach her full potential. She eventually met Sven Spannekrebs at a swimming club near the refugee center and asked, "Can you be my coach?" When he saw her swim, he immediately recognized her _____(A)_____ talent and agreed to do so. Sven helped Yusra stay focused and persistent in her efforts to pursue excellence.
>
> Yusra soon received a chance to make her dream a reality when she was invited to join the first ever refugee team at the 2016 Summer Olympic Games in Rio de Janeiro. Although it seemed like a great opportunity, Yusra was _____(B)_____. If she joined the refugee team, she thought, people might view her with pity instead of seeing her as a serious athlete. She almost turned down the invitation, but she decided to accept it after she realized that she could inspire hope in millions of other refugees facing similar challenges.

17 윗글의 밑줄 친 부분을 간접화법으로 바르게 바꿔 쓴 것은?

① asked if he could be her coach
② asked that he can be her coach
③ asked if you could be her coach
④ asked that you could be my coach
⑤ asked if he can be my coach

18 윗글의 빈칸 (A), (B)에 알맞은 말을 다음 영어 뜻풀이를 참고하여 주어진 철자로 시작하여 쓰시오.

> (A) much better than averange
> (B) slow to act or speak due to being unsure or embarrassed

(A) → o_____

(B) → h_____

[19~20] 다음 글을 읽고, 물음에 답하시오.

> "My aunt will be down soon, Mr. Nuttel," said the very confident 15-year-old girl. "In the meanwhile, you must put up with ⓐme."
>
> Framton Nuttel tried to say something _____(A)_____ would flatter the niece without making it seem like he was focusing on her rather than her aunt, _____(B)_____ had yet to come down. He doubted whether these formal visits to the homes of total strangers would do much to help cure his nervousness.
>
> "I know how it will be," his sister had said when he was preparing to move to this rural area. "You will hide yourself down there and not speak to anyone. Then your nervousness will be worse than ever. ⓑI will tell all the people I know there that you're coming. Some of them, as far as I can remember, were quite nice."

19 윗글의 밑줄 친 ⓐ, ⓑ가 가리키는 대상을 글에서 찾아 쓰시오.

ⓐ me → _____

ⓑ I → _____

20 윗글의 빈칸 (A), (B)에 들어갈 말이 바르게 짝지어진 것은?

	(A)		(B)
①	that	…	that
②	which	…	who
③	which	…	that
④	that	…	who
⑤	who	…	which

"I hope Vera has been amusing you," she said.

"She has been very interesting," said Framton.

"I hope you don't mind the open window," said Mrs. Sappleton. "My husband and brothers will soon be back from hunting, and they always come in this way. They've been out in the forest today, so they'll make a mess of my poor carpets. Men always do that sort of thing, _____."

She talked cheerfully about hunting and the lack of birds in the area. To Framton, it was dreadful to listen to her. He made a partially successful effort to change the subject to a less upsetting topic. He was conscious that Mrs. Sappleton was giving him only a small part of her attention. Her eyes were constantly moving past him to the open window and the lawn beyond. It was an unfortunate coincidence that he had visited her on such a tragic anniversary.

21 윗글의 빈칸에 들어갈 말로 가장 적절한 것은?

① wasn't he?   ② aren't they?

③ do they?   ④ doesn't he?

⑤ don't they?

22 윗글의 밑줄 친 문장을 통해 유추할 수 있는 내용으로 가장 적절한 것은?

① Sappleton 부인은 Framton의 방문이 반갑지 않다.

② Sappleton 부인은 Vera가 손님을 잘 맞이했을지 안절부절 못하고 있다.

③ Sappleton 부인은 집이 엉망이 될까봐 염려하고 있다.

④ Sappleton 부인은 남편과 동생들이 돌아오기를 고대하고 있다.

⑤ Sappleton 부인은 자신의 비극에 관해 Framton이 알게 될까봐 두려워한다.

"My doctors ordered me to rest and to avoid both excitement and physical exercise," said Framton, who mistakenly believed that strangers were interested in his illnesses, as well as their causes and cures. "However, they are not so much in agreement on what exactly my diet should be," he continued.

"No?" asked Mrs. Sappleton, barely holding back a yawn at the last moment. Then she suddenly smiled and sat up straight—but it was not because of what Framton was saying.

"Here they are at last!" she cried in delight. "Just in time for tea. But 그들은 마치 눈까지 진흙 속에 빠진 것처럼 보여요!"

Framton trembled slightly and turned towards the niece _____ a look that expressed sympathy for her aunt's condition. The girl was staring out through the open window _____ horror in her eyes. Suddenly feeling fear in his stomach, Framton turned around in his seat and looked in the same direction.

23 윗글의 밑줄 친 우리말과 일치하도록 주어진 조건 에 맞게 문장을 완성하시오.

> **조건**
> • as if를 사용할 것
> • 사용할 표현: look, in the mud

→ But _____ up to their eyes!

24 윗글의 빈칸에 공통으로 들어갈 말로 가장 적절한 것은?

① by   ② for   ③ in

④ of   ⑤ with

25 윗글의 내용과 일치하지 않는 것은?

① Framton은 지병을 가지고 있다.

② Framton은 사람들이 자신의 병에 관심이 있다고 생각했다.

③ Sappleton 부인은 Framton의 말을 흥미롭게 들었다.

④ Sappleton 부인은 기다리던 가족들이 돌아와 기뻤다.

⑤ Sappleton 부인의 조카는 유리문 밖을 보고 두려움을 느꼈다.

빠른 독해를 위한
바른 선택

빠바 시리즈
400
만부 돌파!

빠른독해 바른독해

이상엽 박세광 권은숙 류혜원
NE능률 영어교육연구소
신유승 이지형 손원희

구문독해

NE_능률

교재구성
**미리
보기**

시리즈 구성

기초세우기

구문독해

유형독해

수능실전

1 최신 수능 경향 반영

최신 수능 경향을 반영한 독해 지문과
수능 기출 문장 중심으로 구성된 구문 훈련

2 실전 대비 기능 강화

실제 사용에 기반한 사례별 구문 학습과 최신 수능 경향을 반영한
수능 독해 Mini Test로 유형별 수능 대비 훈련

3 서술형 주관식 문제

내신과 수능의 출제 경향을 반영한 서술형 및 주관식 문제 수록

BOOK LIST 고등

도/서/목/록

어휘 · 문법 · 구문

능률 VOCA

대한민국 어휘서의 표준

초등 기본 | 초등 필수
중등 기본 | 중등 필수 | 중등 고난도 | 중등 숙어
고등 기본 | 수능 필수 | 수능 고난도
어원편 중등 | 어원편 고등

•

GRAMMAR ZONE

대한민국 영문법 교재의 표준

중등 기본 | 중등 필수 |
고등 기본 | 고등 필수 | Complete

•

필히 통하는 시리즈

시험에 필히 통하는 고등 영문법과 서술형

필히 통하는 고등 영문법 | 기본편 | 실력편
필히 통하는 고등 서술형 | 기본편 | 실전편

•

문마고

문제로 마스터하는 고등 영문법

•

천문장

구문이 독해로 연결되는 해석 공식

입문 | 기본 | 완성

NE능률

정답 및 해설

고등 기출문제집
English I

오선영

교과서 **어휘 익히기** ·············· p. 7

01 지도	26 explorer
02 전념, 몰두	27 breeding
03 장비	28 insufficient
04 이용할 수 있는	29 attempt
05 계획하다	30 transform
06 강조하다	31 economics
07 직업	32 define
08 엄청난	33 reptile
09 한계, 경계	34 pursue
10 헌신	35 rewarding
11 격려하다	36 perception
12 불운, 불행	37 diagnose
13 보존, 보호	38 portable
14 유명한, 중요한	39 extensive
15 호기심을 불러일으키다	40 companion
16 기회	41 encounter
17 힘든	42 when it comes to
18 모으다	43 discourage
19 열렬한, 열정적인	44 persistence
20 지장을 주다	45 dedicate
21 저명한, 유명한	46 physical therapy
22 수반하다, 포함하다	47 compelling
23 동물학자	48 inspire
24 낙관주의	49 specialize
25 ~에 몰두하다	50 regardless of

교과서 **핵심 문법** ·············· pp. 8~11

POINT 1 to부정사를 목적격 보어로 취하는 동사

Q 1 to pick 2 to reduce 3 prepare
Check-Up
01 ③, ⑤
02 (1) follows → follow
   (2) taking → take
   (3) entered → to enter
   (4) participate → to participate
03 (1) encouraged me to exercise
   (2) expected the students to think
   (3) help us (to) carry

04 (1) advise you to be
   (2) expect this project to continue
   (3) ask you to stay

Q 1. 수지는 휴가 동안 자신의 우편물을 받아 달라고 이웃에게 부탁했다.
2. 의사는 환자에게 카페인 섭취를 줄이라고 조언했다.
3. 그는 여동생이 취업 면접을 준비하는 것을 도와주었다.

Check-Up

01 want, expect, encourage, ask는 목적격 보어로 to부정사를 취한다. help는 목적격 보어로 동사원형과 to부정사를 모두 쓸 수 있다.
   ① eat → to eat
   ② finish → to finish
   ④ help → to help
   ① 그녀는 자녀들이 건강한 음식을 먹기를 원한다.
   ② 그들은 우리가 오늘 밤까지 그 일을 끝내기를 기대한다.
   ③ 그는 친구에게 새로운 것을 시도해 보라고 독려했다.
   ④ 나는 친구에게 내 숙제를 도와달라고 부탁했다.
   ⑤ Mike는 내가 어려운 수학 문제를 푸는 것을 도와주었다.

02 want, tell, allow, encourage는 목적격 보어로 to부정사를 취하는 동사들이다.
   (1) 그녀는 내가 그녀의 지시를 주의 깊게 따르기를 원한다.
   (2) 의사는 나에게 약을 규칙적으로 복용하라고 말했다.
   (3) 직원들은 우리가 제한 구역에 들어가는 것을 허락해 주었다.
   (4) 선생님은 우리가 대회에 참가하도록 권장했다.

03 (1) encourage는 목적격 보어로 to부정사를 취하므로 「encourage +목적어+to부정사」 형태로 쓴다.
   (2) expect는 목적격 보어로 to부정사를 취하므로 「expect+목적어+to부정사」 형태로 쓴다.
   (3) help는 목적격 보어로 to부정사와 동사원형을 모두 쓸 수 있으므로 「help+목적어+(to+)동사원형」 형태로 쓴다.

04
건물 입주민들은 모두 주목해 주세요. 주차장 구역에 건설 공사가 예정되어 있음을 알고 계시기를 권합니다. 이 프로젝트는 약 나흘 동안 계속될 것으로 예상합니다. 이 기간에 **East Building** 근처에 있는 주차 공간을 사용하실 수 없을 것입니다. 안전상의 이유로 공사 구역에서 멀리 떨어져 있기를 부탁드립니다. 여러분의 협조에 대단히 감사드립니다. 이로 인해 발생할 수 있는 불편에 대해 사과드립니다.
관리팀

(1) 「advise+목적어+to부정사」 구문으로 advise you to be가 알맞다.
(2) 「expect+목적어+to부정사」 구문으로 expect this project to continue가 알맞다.
(3) 「ask+목적어+to부정사」 구문으로 ask you to stay가 알맞다.

POINT 2 so ~ that ... 구문

Q 1 so 2 clearly 3 could 4 easy

Check-Up

01 (1) Lewis는 너무 빨리 달려서 경주를 쉽게 이겼다.
 (2) 폭풍이 너무 심해서 항공편이 취소되었다.
 (3) 나는 기말시험에서 좋은 성적을 얻기 위해 열심히 공부했다.
 (4) Hailey는 새 노트북을 사기 위해 돈을 모았다.

02 (1) The music was so loud that we couldn't hear each other.
 (2) The suitcase was so heavy that he couldn't lift it alone.
 (3) The traffic was so heavy that we were late for the meeting.
 (4) He was so tired that he fell asleep as soon as he sat on the sofa.

03 (1) so realistic that I felt like I was actually driving
 (2) so entertaining that we decided to go there again

Q 1. Tom은 너무 화가 나서 밤새 잠을 자지 못했다.
 2. Jenny는 너무 분명하게 말해서 모두가 그녀의 메시지를 이해했다.
 3. 관광객들은 일출을 보기 위해 일찍 떠났다.
 4. 시험이 너무 쉬워서 나는 높은 점수를 받았다.

Check-Up

01 so ~ that ...은 '너무 ~해서 …하다'라고 해석하고, so that ~은 '~하기 위하여, ~하도록'이라고 해석한다.

02 '너무 ~해서 …하다'라는 의미의 「so+형용사/부사+that …」 구문으로 쓴다.
 (1) 음악 소리가 너무 커서 우리는 서로의 말을 들을 수 없었다.
 (2) 여행 가방이 너무 무거워서 그는 그것을 혼자 들 수 없었다.
 (3) 교통이 너무 혼잡해서 우리는 회의에 늦었다.
 (4) 그는 너무 피곤해서 소파에 앉자마자 잠이 들었다.

03
> 나는 오늘 언니와 함께 VR 게임 카페에 갔다. 나는 그런 종류의 카페에 가는 것이 처음이었다. 그곳엔 정말 많은 종류의 게임이 있었다. 하나를 고르는 데 시간이 조금 걸렸다. 마침내, 우리는 특수한 장비를 착용하고 경주 게임을 했다. 게임이 너무 현실적이어서 내가 진짜로 자동차를 운전하고 있는 것처럼 느껴졌다! VR 게임 카페가 너무 재미있어서 우리는 다음 주에 또 그곳에 가기로 했다. 다음번에 우리는 가상 스포츠 게임을 할 것이다. 난 항상 테니스 치는 법을 배우고 싶었기 때문에, VR 테니스를 해 볼 것이다!

'너무 ~해서 …하다'라는 의미의 so ~ that ... 구문이다. so와 that 사이에는 형용사나 부사가 오고 that 뒤에는 「주어+동사」의 절이 오며, 결과를 나타낸다.

교과서 본문 익히기 ❶ 옳은 어법·어휘 고르기 ····· pp. 19~21

01 decisions	02 Mapping
03 others	04 useful
05 start	06 shaping

07 documenting	08 becoming
09 swimming	10 to explore
11 insufficient	12 to create
13 which	14 released
15 promoted	16 himself
17 to push	18 Because of
19 what	20 that
21 who	22 herself
23 Although	24 took care of
25 from	26 so
27 that	28 female
29 incorporating	30 myself
31 where	32 passions
33 who	34 to work
35 despite	36 enthusiastic
37 deficiency	38 to discourage
39 as	40 with
41 so	42 start
43 that	44 challenges
45 If	46 shared
47 optimism	48 searching
49 to take	

교과서 본문 익히기 ❷ 틀린 부분 고치기 ·········· pp. 22~24

01 Choosing	02 Mapping
03 others	04 ○
05 (to) start	06 ○
07 shaping	08 ○
09 exploring	10 becoming
11 ○	12 to explore
13 ○	14 Instead of
15 which	16 released
17 promoted	18 challenge
19 to push	20 Because of
21 what	22 ○
23 have heard	24 that
25 During	26 Although
27 ○	28 ○
29 so	30 knowledge
31 ○	32 impressed
33 female	34 allowed for
35 myself	36 deeply
37 ○	38 who
39 ○	40 despite
41 ○	42 disrupted
43 to discourage	44 ○
45 economics	46 ○

47 start   48 that
49 a lot of   50 ○
51 encounter   52 shared
53 ○   54 searching for
55 to take

교과서 **본문 익히기** ❸ 빈칸 완성하기 ·············· pp. 25~29

(1) the biggest life decisions
(2) Mapping out the right career path
(3) struggle to define them
(4) can be useful
(5) by providing them with guidance
(6) the qualities they admire most
(7) when it comes to shaping
(8) a French ocean explorer
(9) dedicated his life to exploring
(10) dreamed of becoming
(11) part of his physical therapy
(12) became intrigued by
(13) the diving equipment available
(14) create his own equipment
(15) succeeded in developing
(16) shared his underwater experiences
(17) the need for marine conservation
(18) drove him to constantly challenge himself
(19) inspired me to push
(20) try different things
(21) what suits me best
(22) ask me about my role model
(23) may not have heard of
(24) who specialized in reptiles
(25) devotion to a particular field
(26) immersed herself in
(27) her father hated reptiles
(28) took care of
(29) prevented her from attending
(30) so strong that
(31) accumulated extensive knowledge
(32) in order to share
(33) so impressed that he hired
(34) the first female curator
(35) contributed to
(36) allowed for better care
(37) want to dedicate myself to
(38) where my true interests lie
(39) lead to a rewarding career
(40) who loves animation

(41) the first Korean animator
(42) Beyond the fact that
(43) despite the difficulties he faced
(44) enthusiastic about drawing
(45) was diagnosed with
(46) allow this misfortune to discourage
(47) viewed his condition as
(48) graduated with a degree in economics
(49) related to art
(50) sent his portfolio to
(51) gave him an opportunity
(52) It was his hard work and talent
(53) credit for his persistence
(54) never give up
(55) encounter difficulties
(56) emphasize the importance of
(57) regardless of their field
(58) If you haven't found
(59) Try to find
(60) encourage you to take

내신 1등급 어휘 공략   pp. 30~31

01 ① **02** ② **03** ③ **04** ① **05** ⑤ **06** ⑤ **07** ④ **08** ③

01 ① 대부분의 사람들에게 올바른 진로를 찾는 것은 쉽지 않은 일이므로 easy 대신 difficult나 demanding 등이 적절하다.

02 (A) 불가능을 현실로 만든 원동력은 '열정'이므로 passion이 적절하다.
(B) push the boundaries는 '한계를 뛰어넘다'라는 관용 표현으로 push가 적절하다.
(C) 자신에게 잘 맞는 것을 찾을 때까지 '탐구'를 계속 하겠다는 흐름이므로 exploring이 적절하다.
오답 (A) indifference: 무관심
(B) pull: 당기다
(C) ignoring: 무시하기

03 ③ 그 당시에는 사용할 수 있는 잠수 장비가 불충분해서 Cousteau가 직접 'Aqua-Lung'이라는 장비를 개발했으므로 insufficient(불충분한)가 적절하다.

04 ① infamous(악명 높은)는 부정적 뉘앙스를 지닌 단어로, Joan Procter가 국제적으로 '저명한(notable)' 동물학자라는 사실과 모순된다.

05 (A) George Boulenger가 Procter에게 '감명을 받아' 그녀를 조수로 고용했다는 흐름이므로 impressed가 적절하다.
(B) 문맥상 '~에 헌신하다'라는 의미의 dedicate oneself to ~ 구문이 적절하다.

(C) 자신의 열정이 보람 있는 경력으로 이어질 수 있는 것은 '운이 좋은' 상황이므로 fortunate가 적절하다.

오답 (A) depressed: 우울한
(B) indicate: 나타내다
(C) unfortunate: 불운한

06 ⑤ 김상진은 색약 진단을 누구에게나 일어날 수 있는 '사소한' 문제로 여기고 좌절하지 않았다는 흐름이므로 minor가 적절하다.

07 ④ 끈기와 적극적인 태도로 높게 평가받은 것이므로 resistance (저항)가 아니라 persistence(끈기)가 적절하다.

08 (A) 십 대들이 자신의 진로 목표를 '향해' 나아가도록 이끌어준다는 의미이므로, toward가 적절하다.
(B) 역할 모델의 긍정적 특성인 persistence, commitment와 어울리는 단어는 '낙관주의'이므로 optimism이 적절하다.
(C) 진로 탐색의 첫걸음을 '격려하는' 행동이 흐름상 자연스러우므로 encourage가 적절하다.

오답 (A) forward: 앞으로, 전방에
(B) pessimism: 비관주의
(C) discourage: 낙담시키다

내신 1등급 어법 공략

01 ③ **02** ② **03** ⑤ **04** ⑤ **05** ④ **06** ③ **07** ③ **08** ①

01 ③ 「help+목적어+(to+)동사원형」 구문으로 starting이 아니라 (to) start가 적절하다.

오답 ① 「one of+the+최상급+복수 명사」
② some teenagers와 호응을 이루는 others
④ '가장'이라는 뜻으로 동사 admire를 수식하는 부사
⑤ when it comes to 뒤에 쓰인 동명사

02 (A) enable은 목적격 보어로 to부정사를 취하므로 to make가 적절하다.
(B) '~하는 것'이라는 의미의 선행사를 포함하는 관계대명사 what이 적절하다.
(C) '~하기를 계속하다'라는 의미의 「keep v-ing」 구문으로 exploring이 적절하다.

03 ⑤ 다큐멘터리 영화는 만들어진 후 '개봉되는' 것이므로 과거분사 released가 적절하다.

오답 ①, ② 전치사의 목적어로 쓰인 동명사이다.
③ 보어 역할을 하는 과거분사이다.
④ 용도를 나타내는 동명사이다.

04 ⑤ such 뒤에는 명사가 온다. 이 문장은 「so+형용사[부사]+that ~」 구문으로 so가 적절하다.

오답 ① zoologist를 수식하는 주격 관계대명사이다.
② '~동안'이라는 의미의 전치사이다.
③ '비록 ~이지만'이라는 의미의 접속사이다.
④ 'A로 하여금 ~하지 못하게 하다'라는 의미의 「prevent A from v-ing」 구문이다.

05 (A) George Boulenger가 감명을 받은 상태를 나타내므로 impressed가 적절하다.
(B) '자신을 ~에 헌신하다'라는 의미의 「dedicate oneself to+ (동)명사」 구문으로 myself가 적절하다.
(C) 「one of+복수 명사」로 passions가 적절하다.

06 ③ 뒤에 studying art in college로 동명사구가 오므로 동격을 나타낼 때 접속사 that이 아니라 전치사 of가 적절하다.

오답 ① 선행사가 사람이면서 단수인 주격 관계대명사와 단수동사이다.
② '~에도 불구하고'라는 의미의 전치사이다.
④ '~동안'이라는 의미의 전치사이다.
⑤ '목적어가 ~하는 것을 허락하다'라는 의미의 「allow+목적어+to 부정사」 구문이다.

07 (A) 예술과 '관련된' 직업을 찾았다는 의미이므로, 명사 job을 수식하는 형용사 역할로 related가 적절하다.
(B) 「It was ~ that ....」 강조구문으로 that이 적절하다.
(C) 조건을 나타내는 부사절(if절)에서는 현재시제를 사용하므로 encounter가 적절하다.

08 ① 독자들에 의해 '공유된' 이야기라는 의미이므로 과거분사 shared 가 적절하다.

오답 ② 주어가 복수 명사(Role models)인 문장의 동사 inspire
③ haven't p.p.: 현재완료 부정문
④ someone을 수식하는 주격 관계대명사
⑤ '목적어가 ~하는 것을 격려하다'라는 의미의 「encourage+목적어+to부정사」 구문

내신 1등급 실전 1회

01 ③ **02** ⑤ **03** Choosing a career is one of the biggest life decisions young people face. **04** ③ **05** ② **06** ④ **07** physical therapy **08** ④ **09** passion, ability **10** ② → to put **11** ④ **12** was so strong that it kept her moving forward **13** ③ **14** ①, ⑤ **15** ④ **16** ⑤ **17** I encounter difficulties, I will simply find another way to pursue them **18** persistence

01 과학 공부와 음악 사이에서 고민하고 있음을 표현하는 주어진 문장은 기타 연주를 하며 시간을 보내는 것을 더 좋아한다고 말하는 문장 뒤인 ③의 위치에 오는 것이 적절하며, 이어서 고민을 구체적으로 설명하는 흐름에도 자연스럽게 연결된다.

02 ⑤ 김 선생님은 하나를 선택하라고 조언하는 것이 아니라 직업에서 가장 중요하게 여기는 것을 알아보라고 조언하고 있다.

03 주어 역할을 하는 동명사가 필요하므로 Choosing으로 수정하고, 「one of+the+최상급+복수 명사」 구문이 사용된 문장이므로 복수 명사 decisions로 바꾼다.

04 ③ help는 목적격 보어로 동사원형이나 to부정사를 취하므로 (to) start가 적절하다.

오답 ① 주어 역할을 하는 동명사

② '몇몇은 ~이고, 다른 몇몇은 …이다'라는 의미의 「some ~ others …」 구문
④ '~을 더 잘 이해하게 되다'라는 의미의 get a better idea of
⑤ when it comes to ~ 구문에서 전치사의 목적어 역할을 하는 동명사

05 마지막 문장에서 직업 목표 설정에 있어서 롤모델이 미칠 수 있는 영향에 대해 더 잘 이해할 수 있게 해주는 학생들의 이야기가 이어질 것이라고 했으므로, ②가 가장 적절하다.

06 Cousteau의 탐험 정신과 새로운 도전을 강조하는 문맥상 ④ '인생에서 다양한 것들에 도전하는 것'이 빈칸에 적절하다.
오답 ① 내 원래 계획을 고수하는 것
② 바다에서 수영하는 법을 배우는 것
③ 내 경력에서 도전을 피하는 것
⑤ 오로지 학업 성취에만 집중하는 것

07 '관절이나 근육 등 신체 부위에 발생하는 문제에 대한 의학적 치료'는 physical therapy(물리 치료)에 대한 설명이다.

08 (A) exploring과 병렬 연결되므로 documenting이 적절하다.
(B) 앞에 콤마(,)가 있는 계속적 용법의 관계대명사이므로 which가 적절하다.
(C) '개봉된' 영화이므로 과거분사 released가 적절하다.

09 직업을 선택할 때 열정과 능력 중 무엇이 더 중요한가?

10 '목적어가 ~하도록 동기를 부여하다'라는 뜻의 「motivate+목적어+to부정사」 구문이다.

11 ④ 여기서 재귀대명사 herself는 재귀 용법으로 쓰인 재귀대명사로 생략할 수 없다.

12 '너무 ~해서 …하다'라는 의미의 so ~ that … 구문으로 so와 that 사이에는 형용사가 오고 that 뒤에는 「주어+동사」의 절이 온다.

13 ③ 필자는 Joan Procter의 사례에서 영감을 받아 자신의 열정을 추구하려는 결의를 나타내므로 determined(결의에 찬)가 적절하다.
오답 ① envious: 부러워하는
② pleased: 기쁜
④ satisfied: 만족한
⑤ depressed: 우울한

14 밑줄 친 to think와 ②, ③, ④는 목적을 나타내는 부사적 용법의 to부정사이다.
① 그들은 매주 주말마다 동물 보호소에서 자원봉사를 하기로 결정했다. (목적어 역할을 하는 명사적 용법)
⑤ 도시 지역에서 고대 유물을 발견한 것은 놀라운 일이었다. (진주어 역할을 하는 명사적 용법)
오답 ② 과학자들은 바이러스의 확산을 막기 위해 백신을 개발했다.
③ Lisa는 자신의 대중 연설 능력을 향상시키기 위해 토론 동아리에 가입했다.
④ Tony는 프로 운동선수가 되기 위해 최선을 다했다.

15 디즈니 최초의 한국 애니메이터를 소개하며, 그가 색약 진단으로 미대에 진학하지 못했지만 자신의 문제를 심각하게 받아들이지 않고 꿈을 이루었다는 내용이므로, ④가 가장 적절한 주제이다.

16 (A) pursue는 '추구하다'라는 의미로 '어려움에도 불구하고'와 자연스럽게 연결된다. 전치사 뒤이므로 동명사 pursuing이 적절하다.
(B) 색약 진단으로 미대 진학 계획이 중단된 상황을 설명하므로 '지장을 주다'라는 동사의 과거분사형 disrupted가 적절하다.
(C) 불운이 김상진을 '좌절시키지' 못하게 했다는 흐름이 자연스러우므로 discourage가 적절하다.

17 조건절이 '만약 내가 어려움에 부딪힌다면'이므로 I encounter difficulties를 쓰고, 주절로 I will simply find another way to pursue them을 쓴다. to pursue them은 앞에 있는 way를 수식하는 형용사적 용법의 to부정사이다.

18 '어려움이 있어도 누군가가 무언가를 계속해서 하게 해주는 자질'은 persistence(끈기)이다.

내신 1등급 실전 2회

pp. 38~41

01 ④ **02** ③ **03** ④ **04** ③ **05** ⑤ **06** ③ **07** Cousteau's curiosity drove him to constantly challenge himself in new areas **08** ③ **09** ③ **10** health problems prevented her from attending university **11** ③ **12** (A) impressed (B) incorporating (C) am **13** ④ **14** ③, ⑤ **15** ① **16** 동물 보호소에서 정기적으로 자원봉사를 한 것

01 대화에서 남학생은 자신의 진로에 대해 고민하고 있다. 이 맥락에서 남학생이 할 수 있는 말로 가장 적절한 것은 ④ '나도 내 꿈의 직업이 무엇인지 알 수 있으면 좋겠어.'이다.
오답 ① 나는 너무 바빠서 내 미래를 생각할 수 없다.
② 나는 먼저 세계 여행을 하고 싶다.
③ 부모님이 나를 위해 직업을 선택해주셨다.
⑤ 나는 이미 꿈의 직업을 결정했다.

02 ③ 대화 초반에 남학생은 자신의 진로에 대해 답답함과 '좌절한(frustrated)' 심경이었지만 여학생이 '진로 성격 테스트'라는 구체적인 해결책을 제시하고, 그 방법과 예시를 설명해주자 적극적이고 '열정적인(enthusiastic)' 심경으로 변화했다.
오답 ① 신이 난, 들뜬 → 안도한
② 혼란스러운 → 좌절한
④ 실망한 → 희망에 찬
⑤ 걱정하는 → 당황한

03 청소년의 진로 선택 과정에서 롤모델의 영향력을 강조하는 글로, 구체적 사례를 통해 독자에게 롤모델의 중요성을 전달하려는 의도를 보여준다. 따라서 ④가 글의 목적으로 적절하다.

04 career(직업)에 대한 알맞은 설명은 ③ '한 사람이 오랫동안 하는 직업이나 직종'이다.
오답 ① 무언가를 하는 이유: purpose(목적)
② 무엇을 하거나 어떻게 해야 하는지에 대한 도움이나 조언: guidance(지도)
④ 누군가 또는 무언가의 특징이나 특성: quality(자질)
⑤ 어떤 것이 사람이나 상황에 미치는 강력한 영향이나 효과: impact(영향)

정답 및 해설 **5**

05 ⑤ 사고 극복 → 기술 혁신 → 사회적 영향의 흐름을 포괄하는 주제로 적절하다.

06 ③ become intrigued by는 '~에 의해 매료되다'라는 의미이다.

07 주어 Cousteau's curiosity, 동사 drove, 목적어 him을 쓰고, 목적격 보어인 to constantly challenge himself와 부사구 in new areas를 쓴다.

08 ③ 동격의 전치사 of 뒤에는 명사(구)가 와야 하는데 절이 왔으므로 동격절을 이끄는 접속사 that이 적절하다.
　오답 ① 선행사가 someone인 주격 관계대명사 who
　② the first Korean animator를 수식하는 형용사적 용법의 to부정사
　④ 전치사(about) 뒤에 쓰인 동명사 drawing
　⑤ allow의 목적격 보어로 쓰인 to부정사

09 ③ Joan Procter의 아버지는 파충류를 싫어했다고(her father hated reptiles) 했으므로 일치하지 않는 내용이다.

10 'A가 ~하는 것을 막다, A가 ~하지 못하게 하다'라는 의미의 「prevent A from v-ing」 구문에 맞게 문장을 완성한다.

11 ③ '흥미롭게도, London Zoo에는 세계에서 가장 오래된 파충류관 중 하나가 남아 있어 매년 수천 명의 방문객을 끌어들인다.'는 London Zoo의 파충류관에 대한 부수적인 정보로, Procter의 구체적인 경력이나 필자의 진로 고민과 직접적인 관련이 없다.

12 (A) Boulenger가 Procter의 능력에 '감명 받은' 상태를 나타내므로 impressed가 적절하다.
　(B) 전치사(by) 뒤에는 동명사가 와야 하므로 incorporating이 적절하다.
　(C) 조건을 나타내는 if절에서는 미래를 나타내더라도 현재시제를 쓰므로 am이 적절하다.

13 ④ 「It is[was] ~ that」 강조 구문에 쓰인 that으로 '~한 것은 바로 …이다[이었다]'라고 해석한다. 이 문장은 주어(his hard work and talent)를 It was와 that 사이에 넣어 강조하고 있다.

14 김상진이 일했던 한국의 애니메이션 스튜디오가 어디인지와 그가 디즈니에서 어떤 애니메이션 작품에 참여했는지는 글을 통해 알 수 없으므로 ③과 ⑤가 정답이다.
　오답 ① 경제학
　② 색을 다루지 않으면서 미술과 관련된 직업
　④ 37세

15 수의사가 되기 위한 미래 목표, 동물 보호소에서의 자원봉사 경험, 수의학 관련 공부 계획, 그리고 수의사가 된 후의 꿈과 포부에 대해 서술하고 있으므로 ① '수의사가 되고 싶은 나의 꿈'이 제목으로 가장 적절하다.
　오답 ② 동물 보호소에서 자원봉사 하는 것의 중요성
　③ 집에서 반려동물을 돌보는 방법
　④ 의학 공부의 어려움
　⑤ 시골 지역을 여행한 나의 경험

16 this experience는 앞 문장 I regularly volunteered at an animal shelter.(나는 동물 보호소에서 정기적으로 자원봉사를 했다.)를 통해 알 수 있다.

내신 1등급 실전 3회 　　　　pp. 42~45

01 ② **02** ④ **03** ③ **04** when it comes to shaping career goals **05** 청소년들에게 지도와 성공하는 데 필요한 목적의식을 제공하여 그들이 진로 계획을 시작하도록 도와준다. **06** ⑤ **07** ② **08** notable **09** ④ **10** ③ → I want to dedicate myself to a field that I have a passion for. **11** ③ **12** ③ **13** ② **14** It was his hard work and talent that eventually led him to a position at Disney at the age of 37. **15** ③ **16** ③ **17** ⑤

01 ・a safe career path: 안정적인 '직업' 경로
　・what you value most in a career: 네가 '직업'에서 중요하게 여기는 것

02 '직업과 성격 유형이 일치할 때 행복과 생산성이 높아진다'는 존 홀랜드의 이론에 관한 내용으로 matches(일치하다)가 빈칸에 가장 적절하다.

03 ③의 them이 가리키는 말은 young people이다.

04 '~하는 데 있어서, ~에 관한 한'이라는 의미의 when it comes to ~ 구문을 사용하되 to가 전치사이므로 동명사 shaping을 쓰고 career goals로 마무리한다.

05 This is where role models can be useful. 뒤의 문장, They help young people start to plan their careers by providing them with guidance and the sense of purpose they need to succeed.에서 롤모델이 청소년의 진로 계획에 어떻게 도움이 되는지 알 수 있다.

06 ⑤ 영화는 '개봉되는' 것이므로 releasing이 아니라 released가 적절하다.

07 ⓐ, ⓒ, ⓓ는 계속적 용법의 관계대명사, ⓑ는 의문형용사, ⓔ는 의문대명사이다.
　ⓐ 그는 그림을 한 점 구매했는데, 그것은 1920년에 제작된 것이다.
　ⓒ 내 친구가 내게 책을 한 권 주었는데, 그 책은 매우 흥미로웠다.
　ⓓ 나는 오래된 박물관을 방문했는데, 그것은 19세기에 설립되었다.
　오답 ⓑ 나는 교통체증을 피하기 위해 어느 길로 가야 할지 모르겠다.
　ⓔ 건강과 성공 중 어느 것이 더 중요하다고 생각하시나요?

08 '매우 중요하고 유명한'은 notable(저명한, 유명한)에 대한 설명이다.

09 (A) 명사절을 이끄는 접속사 that이 적절하다.
　(B) 뒤에 「주어+동사」의 절이 왔으므로 접속사 Although가 적절하다.
　(C) '너무 ~해서 …하다'라는 의미의 so ~ that ... 구문으로 so가 적절하다.

10 주어와 목적어가 동일할 경우 재귀대명사를 쓴다. 따라서 me 대신 myself를 써야 하며, dedicate oneself to 구문으로 표현해야 한다. 이는 '특정 분야에 전념한다'라는 의미의 관용 표현이다.

11 ③ Procter는 George Boulenger와 편지를 주고받으며 의견을 나누었다고 했으므로 일치하지 않는 내용이다.

12 ③ his dream과 studying art in college가 동격을 이루므로 알맞은 전치사는 of이다.
오답 ① work for: '~에서 근무하다, 일하다'라는 뜻으로 뒤에 기관이나 회사가 나온다.
② be enthusiastic about: '~에 대해 열정적이다'라는 의미로 about은 적절하다.
④ during high school: 특정 기간을 나타내므로 '~동안'이라는 의미의 during은 적절하다.
⑤ view A as B: 'A를 B로 간주하다[여기다]'라는 의미의 관용 표현으로 적절하다.

13 ② discourage(좌절시키다)는 '누군가를 어떤 일에 대해 덜 희망적이거나, 자신감이 없거나, 긍정적이지 않게 만들다'를 의미한다.
오답 ① 무언가를 하거나 이루기 위해, 흔히 오랜 기간 동안 노력하다: pursue(추구하다)
③ 어떤 일이 평소처럼 또는 예상대로 계속되는 것을 막다: disrupt(지장을 주다)
④ 질병이나 문제의 원인을 밝혀내다: diagnose(진단하다)
⑤ 오랜 기간에 걸쳐 무언가를 모으거나 얻다: accumulate(모으다)

14 「It is[was] ~ that」 강조 구문에서는 강조하고 싶은 부분을 It is[was]와 that 사이에 넣는다.

15 ③ 37세에 디즈니에 입사했다는 언급은 있지만 포트폴리오를 보낸 직후 디즈니에 바로 채용되었다는 언급은 없다.
오답 ① 김상진은 대학에서 경제학을 전공했다.
② 김상진은 색을 사용하지 않아도 되는 예술 관련 직업에서 일하고 싶어 했다.
④ 어떤 애니메이터들은 색을 사용하지 않고 연필로만 작업한다.
⑤ 필자는 김상진의 끈기를 존경한다.

16 ③ Organizers는 체계적 업무를 선호하며, 은행원이나 비서가 대표 직업이다.
오답 ①은 creators, ②는 thinkers, ④는 helpers, ⑤는 persuaders에 대한 설명이다.

17 ⑤ Persuaders(설득자)에는 sales manager(영업 관리자), school principal(학교 교장), lawyer(변호사) 등이 속한다. accountant(회계사), bank clerk(은행원)는 Organizers(조직자)에 속하는 직업이므로 연결이 바르지 않다.
오답 ① 행동주의자 - 정비공, 기술자
② 사고자 - 컴퓨터 프로그래머, 과학자
③ 창조자 - 책 편집자, 그래픽 디자이너, 배우
④ 조력자 - 간호사, 사회복지사

내신 1등급 수능형 고난도
pp. 46~49

01 ②   02 ③   03 ②   04 ④   05 ①   06 ④   07 ②   08 ③   09 ③
10 ②   11 ⑤   12 ④   13 ④   14 ④   15 ②   16 ①

---

01 ② 다섯 개의 독립적인 단계(five separate stages) 중 첫 번째 단계(The first stage)에 대해 말하고 있으므로 ②의 위치가 가장 적절하다.

02 ③ 방송 내용은 진로 발달의 5단계 이론을 체계적으로 설명하는 데 초점을 맞추고 있다. 진행자는 '탐색(exploration) 단계'의 특징과 활동을 구체적으로 언급하며, 다양한 경험의 중요성을 강조하고 있다.

03 진로 선택의 중요성 강조 – 진로 결정의 어려움과 롤모델의 필요성 언급(A) – 롤모델의 구체적 역할과 청소년 독자들에게 롤모델에 대해 물었다고 소개(C) – 학생들의 이야기를 읽으면 롤모델이 진로 목표 형성에 얼마나 큰 영향을 미치는지 알 수 있다고 결론(B)

04 빈칸에는 롤모델이 제공하는 구체적 지원 요소가 필요하므로, ④ '지침과 목적 제공'이 가장 적절하다.
오답 ① 경제적 위험 회피
② 시장 동향 비교
③ 사회적 영향 분석
⑤ 학업 성취 강조

05 ① mental therapy는 '정신적 치료'를 의미하는데 문맥상 '물리 치료'의 일환으로서의 수영이므로 physical이 적절하다.

06 ④ After a long series of failed attempts로 보아 오랜 기간 동안 실패를 거듭한 끝에 자신만의 휴대용 호흡 기계를 개발했음을 알 수 있다.

07 (A) 아버지는 파충류를 싫어했지만, 그녀는 파충류를 애완동물로 키웠다는 대조적 상황이므로 Although(~에도 불구하고)가 적절하다.
(B) 건강 문제로 대학 진학에 실패했으나 동물학에 대한 열정은 지속되었다는 의미적 전환을 나타내므로 However(그러나)가 적절하다.
오답 ① ~때문에 – 그러므로
③ 만약 ~라면 – 한편
④ 비록 ~이지만 – 그 결과
⑤ 그러나 – 그럼에도 불구하고

08 (A) may have p.p.: ~했을지도 모른다(과거 사실에 대한 추측)
(B) '~에 몰두하다'라는 뜻의 immerse oneself in 구문으로 herself가 적절하다.
(C) 「prevent+목적어+from+v-ing」 구문으로 동명사 attending이 적절하다.

09 ③ A few years later는 시간적 흐름을 이어주는 역할을 하며 대영 박물관 조수직 이후 런던 동물원 큐레이터로의 경력 변화를 자연스럽게 연결한다. 또한 뒤에 나오는 There가 가리키는 런던 동물원에서의 파충류관 설계 기여와도 자연스럽게 이어진다.

10 ② 문맥상 VR 게임을 하려면 특수 장비(the special gear)를 착용해야 하므로, took off(벗었다)가 아니라 put on(착용했다)이 적절하다.

11 ⑤ They가 가리키는 Holland Codes는 '사용되는' 것으로 「be p.p.」 형태의 수동태가 되어야 하므로 used가 적절하다.

12 Dr. Holland에 따르면, 당신의 <u>성격</u> 유형이 무엇인지 파악하는 것이 중요하다. 왜냐하면 그것(성격 유형)에 맞는 직업을 찾는 것이 직장에서 더 행복하고 <u>생산적으로</u> 만들어 주기 때문이다.

　오답 ① 능력 – 성공적인
　② 흥미 – 효율적인
　③ 기술 – 조직적인, 체계적인
　⑤ 미래 – 만족한

13 ④ 김상진은 한국의 애니메이션 스튜디오에서 경력을 쌓은 후 37세에 디즈니에 입사했으므로 일치하지 않는 내용이다.

14 ④ '관련된' 직업이라는 의미로 과거분사 related가 적절하다.

15 경제학을 전공했지만 예술과 관련된 직업을 찾기 위해 끈기 있게 노력했고, 포트폴리오를 여러 곳에 보낸 끝에 기회를 얻어 결국 디즈니에 입사하게 되는 과정에서 강조되는 것은 ② '그의 노력과 재능'이다.

　오답 ① 그의 운과 시기
　③ 업계에서의 그의 인맥
　④ 그의 가족의 재정적 지원
　⑤ 그의 경제학 학위

16 김상진은 색각 이상을 <u>극복하고</u> 애니메이션에 대한 열정을 계속 <u>추구</u>했다. 그 결과, 그는 월트 디즈니 애니메이션 스튜디오의 첫 한국인 애니메이터가 되었으며, 그의 끈기는 다른 이들에게 영감을 주었다.

내신 1등급 서술형

pp. 50~52

01 (1) Choosing a career is one of the biggest life decisions young people face.
　(2) They help young people start to plan their careers by providing them with guidance and the sense of purpose they need to succeed.

02 what

03 (1) dedicate　(2) intrigue　(3) equipment　(4) portable

04 ① exploring: 여기서 to는 전치사이므로 뒤에는 동명사가 와야 한다.
　⑤ promoted: 앞의 동사 transformed와 병렬 구조를 이루므로 과거형 promoted가 되어야 한다.

05 (1) 미래에 어떤 직업을 가질 것인지 모르겠다는 것
　(2) 직업 선택에서 중요한 요소가 무엇인지 스스로에게 물어보기

06 I wish I could find

07 (p)refer

08 필자는 Procter처럼 자신이 열정을 가지고 있는 분야에 전념하고 싶어 한다.

09 He was so impressed that he hired her as his assistant at the British Museum.

10 I will take my time to think deeply about where my true interests lie.

11 고등학교 시절 색약 진단을 받으면서 대학에서 미술을 공부하고자 했던 그의 꿈에 지장이 가게 된 것

12 ⓐ for　ⓑ of　ⓒ with　ⓓ as

13 enthusiastic

14 ⓐ devotion[devoting]　ⓑ exploration

15 (1) whom → who[that]　(2) such → so

---

01 (1) 「one of+the+최상급+복수 명사」 구문으로 decision을 decisions로 고쳐야 한다.
　(2) by는 전치사로 뒤에는 동명사(v-ing)가 와야 하므로, provided를 providing으로 고쳐야 한다.

02 앞에 선행사가 없이 '~한 것'을 나타내는 명사절을 만드는 관계대명사 what이 공통으로 들어갈 말로 적절하다.

03 (1) 전념하다, 바치다: 시간이나 에너지 등을 어떤 일에 모두 쓰다
　(2) 호기심을 불러일으키다: 누군가가 어떤 것에 매우 관심을 갖게 하다
　(3) 장비: 특정 목적을 위해 필요한 도구 세트
　(4) 휴대용의: 쉽게 옮기거나 들고 다닐 수 있는

05 (1) A의 고민은 My biggest concern these days is that I don't know what I want to be in the future.에 나타나 있다.
　(2) B의 조언은 What about starting by asking yourself what factor is the most important to you when choosing a career?에 나타나 있다.

06 '~라면 좋을 텐데'라는 의미의 'I wish+가정법 과거' 구문이다. 과거형 조동사 could를 쓰는 것에 주의한다.

07 두 문장 모두 '~하기를 선호하다'라는 의미가 필요하며, 주어진 철자 p로 시작하는 동사는 prefer이다.

08 필자가 본받고 싶어 하는 점은 Like her, I want to dedicate myself to a field that I have a passion for.에 나타나 있다.

09 「so+형용사(impressed)+that ~」의 형태로 나타낸다.

10 I will take my time을 쓰고 목적을 나타내는 to think deeply about을 쓴 뒤, 간접의문문(의문사+주어+동사)의 어순에 따라 where my true interests lie를 쓴다.

11 this misfortune은 However로 시작하는 문장에 서술된 내용을 가리킨다.

12 ⓐ work for: ~에서 근무하다
　ⓑ 앞의 명사 the dream과 동격을 나타내는 전치사 of
　ⓒ '~으로 진단받다'라는 의미로 be diagnosed with
　ⓓ view A as B: A를 B로 여기다

13 '누군가 또는 무언가에 대해 관심이나 흥분을 느끼거나 드러내는'은 enthusiastic(열렬한, 열정적인)에 대한 설명이다.

14 두 군데 모두 명사형이 필요하다 ⓐ에는 devote의 명사형 devotion이나 동명사형 devoting을 쓸 수 있고, ⓑ에는 explore의 명사형은 exploration을 쓸 수 있다.

15 (1) 선행사가 사람이고 주격이므로 관계대명사는 who 또는 that이 적절하다. whom은 목적격 관계대명사이다.
　(2) '너무 ~해서 …하다'라는 의미의 so ~ that ... 구문이다.

Lesson 02 | The Power of Good Habits

교과서 **어휘 익히기** ·· p. 55

01 반응, 응답	**26** angle
02 타당성	**27** argument
03 광고	**28** instinct
04 계속해서	**29** investigate
05 활용[이용]하다	**30** reasonable
06 특징, 특성	**31** purchase
07 믿을 만한	**32** audience
08 생각해 내다	**33** alert
09 신경 과학	**34** option
10 엄청난, 거대한	**35** confront
11 처음에	**36** reinforce
12 효율적으로	**37** reliant
13 만들어 내다	**38** intelligence
14 믿을 수 있는	**39** automatic
15 계산	**40** conclusion
16 추리, 추론	**41** frequently
17 자극하다	**42** reveal
18 부정확하게	**43** rely on
19 필수적인	**44** unfamiliar
20 대단히 중요한	**45** capability
21 지름길, 손쉬운 방법	**46** fundamental
22 굉장한, 강렬한	**47** resist
23 대단히 흥미로운	**48** countless
24 의도적인	**49** reflect
25 갑자기 생각나다	**50** be responsible for

교과서 **핵심 문법** ································ pp. 56~59

POINT 1 단순 조건문 (if 조건문)

Q 1 rains 2 studies 3 will miss 4 were 5 would

Check-Up

01 ④

02 (1) gets (2) will feel (3) could start

03 (1) have, will watch
  (2) is, will borrow
  (3) read, will make
  (4) spoke, could work

04 ③ → will need to be

Q 1. 내일 비가 오면, 우리는 집에서 영화를 볼 것이다.
  2. 그녀가 열심히 공부하면, 반에서 가장 높은 점수를 받을 것이다.
  3. 관광객들이 서두르지 않으면, 그들은 기차를 놓칠 것이다.
  4. 내가 새라면, 산과 바다 위를 날아다닐 텐데.
  5. 내가 진실을 안다면, 너에게 즉시 말해줄 텐데.

Check-Up

01 ④ 「if+주어+동사의 과거형, 주어+조동사의 과거형(would/could/might)+동사원형」 형태의 가정법 과거 문장으로 will take가 아니라 would take가 알맞다.
① 날씨가 춥다면, 우리는 실내에서 보드게임을 할 것이다.
② 일찍 일어나면 조용한 아침을 즐길 수 있을 것이다.
③ 네가 더 열심히 연습하면, 너의 실력이 향상될 것이다.
④ 내가 너라면, 나는 다른 접근 방식을 취할 텐데.
⑤ 그가 나에게 다시 전화하지 않으면, 나는 그에게 다시 메시지를 보낼 것이다.

02 (1) 단순 조건문에서 if절은 현재시제를 사용하므로 gets가 알맞다.
(2) 단순 조건문에서 주절은 「will+동사원형」의 형태로 쓴다.
(3) 가정법 과거에서 주절은 「would/could/might+동사원형」의 형태로 쓴다.
(1) 날씨가 더 더워지면, 나는 에어컨을 켤 것이다.
(2) 이 약을 먹으면, 당신은 기분이 훨씬 더 나아질 것이다.
(3) John에게 시간이 더 있다면, 그는 새로운 취미를 시작할 수 있을 텐데.

03 (1)~(3) 단순 조건문으로 「if+주어+동사의 현재형, 주어+will+동사원형」의 형태로 쓴다.
(4) 가정법 과거 문장으로 「if+주어+동사의 과거형, 주어+조동사의 과거형(would/could/might)+동사원형」의 형태로 쓴다.

04
> 좋은 아침입니다, 여러분! 오늘의 일기 예보에 오신 걸 환영합니다. 여러분이 밖에서 어떠한 활동을 할 계획이 있다면, 그 계획을 취소해야 할 겁니다. 하루 종일 비가 아주 많이 올 것으로 예상됩니다. 여러분이 운전을 한다면, 도로가 젖어있을 것이기 때문에 각별히 조심해야 할 겁니다. 또한, 오전 9시경에 폭우로 인해 차가 밀릴 것으로 예상됩니다. 여러분이 더 일찍 출발한다면, 교통 체증을 피할 수 있을 겁니다.

③이 포함된 문장은 단순 조건문으로 「if+주어+동사의 현재형, 주어+will+동사원형」의 형태로 써야 한다. 따라서 will need to be가 적절하다.

POINT 2 동격을 나타내는 전치사 of

Q 1 reducing plastic waste by 50 percent
  2 finding a cure for the disease
  3 global warming is accelerating

Check-Up

01 (1) 우주를 탐험하고자 하는 그의 꿈은 어린 시절에 시작되었다.
  (2) 매일 책을 읽는 습관은 지식을 넓히는 데 도움이 된다.
  (3) Danny는 유명한 음악가가 되는 꿈을 가지고 있다.
  (4) 수지는 전 세계를 여행한다는 생각에 신이 났다[흥분했다].

02 (1) Her dream of becoming a singer

(2) the idea of meeting his favorite artist

(3) The process of starting a new business

(4) The hope of winning the championship

03 (1) danger of becoming extinct

(2) our goal of conserving endangered species

(3) the dream of protecting all living things on earth

Q 1. 그들은 올해 플라스틱 폐기물을 50% 줄이겠다는 목표를 세웠다.

2. 그 질병의 치료법을 발견할 가능성이 환자들에게 희망을 준다.

3. 지구 온난화가 가속화되고 있다는 사실이 많은 과학자들을 걱정시킨다.

Check-Up ☃

01 「명사 + of + 동명사(구)」의 형태에서 of는 '~이라고 하는, ~인, ~의' 등으로 해석한다.

02 '~이라고 하는, ~인, ~의'라는 의미의 동격을 나타내는 전치사 of를 사용하여 「명사 + of + 동명사(구)」의 형태로 쓴다.

03

> 환경오염으로 인해 많은 식물과 동물 종이 멸종될 위기에 놓여 있습니다. 환경 단체로서, 저희는 자연의 다양성을 복원하기 위한 많은 계획을 개발해 왔습니다. 이 계획을 실행하기 위해서 여러분의 도움이 필요합니다. 기부하고 우리의 아름다운 행성을 보호합시다! 여러분의 도움은 저희가 멸종 위기에 처한 종을 보존하는 목표를 성취하는 데 꼭 필요합니다. 지구상의 모든 생명체를 보호하는 꿈을 달성하기 위해 저희와 함께 해주세요!

「danger/goal/dream of + 동명사(구)」의 형태로 쓴다. 전치사 of의 앞뒤에 있는 명사(구)가 서로 동격임을 나타낸다.

교과서 **본문 익히기 ❶** 옳은 어법·어휘 고르기 ⋯⋯ pp. 67~69

01 it is	02 to work
03 becoming	04 asking
05 to purchase	06 that
07 what	08 would
09 will realize	10 that
11 without	12 like
13 coming	14 with
15 regularly	16 for
17 encounter	18 make
19 its	20 a few
21 on	22 for
23 as	24 it
25 to be	26 to save
27 that	28 less
29 make	30 accepting
31 harmful	32 deeply
33 instead of	34 generating

35 if	36 unfamiliar
37 to dive	38 as
39 something new	40 Learning
41 any	42 vitally
43 so	44 and
45 of	46 her

교과서 **본문 익히기 ❷** 틀린 부분 고치기 ⋯⋯ pp. 70~72

01 how important it is	02 ○
03 to becoming	04 ○
05 to purchase	06 ○
07 what	08 ○
09 pause	10 that 또는 삭제
11 ○	12 is based on, ○
13 ○	14 because, ○
15 ○, ○	16 regularly encounter
17 ○	18 encounter
19 need to focus	20 ○, its
21 ○, to check	22 ○
23 That is why	24 as dependable as
25 ○, ○	26 ○
27 Having, that require	28 ○
29 becomes	30 the more likely
31 Those who	32 ○, have never been proven
33 ○	34 these
35 thinking	36 instead of
37 generating	38 ○
39 ○	40 to dive
41 as	42 something new
43 ○, more efficiently	44 any
45 that	46 so that
47 in order to use	48 ○
49 her	

교과서 **본문 익히기 ❸** 빈칸 완성하기 ⋯⋯ pp. 73~77

(1) Welcome to

(2) how important it is

(3) to work out your mind

(4) we can become better thinkers

(5) Thank you for having

(6) what is the secret to

(7) by asking the audience

(8) Suppose

(9) to purchase

(10) The total price is

(11) Raise

(12) that came to mind

(13) popped into my head

(14) the error in your calculation

(15) make the total price

(16) It seems like

(17) realize your mistake

(18) reveals the fundamental way

(19) have two different systems

(20) is based on instinct

(21) without our conscious control

(22) large words on advertisements

(23) process enormous amounts of information

(24) came up with

(25) we regularly encounter

(26) is responsible for

(27) the validity of an argument

(28) conscious mental activities

(29) requires time and effort

(30) taking a few seconds to reflect

(31) tend to rely heavily on

(32) That is why it's common

(33) not as dependable as

(34) it is impossible to make

(35) quite reasonable and effective

(36) allows us to save energy

(37) becomes a habit

(38) requires intense concentration

(39) the less

(40) the more likely

(41) make errors and bad decisions

(42) develop a habit of accepting

(43) can be harmful

(44) these lazy brain habits

(45) practice thinking deeply

(46) reconsider your initial thoughts

(47) Keep generating more ideas

(48) supports your original conclusion

(49) If not

(50) make use of

(51) motivate us to investigate

(52) from multiple angles

(53) serve as a foundation for

(54) in order to stimulate your brain

(55) allow information to flow through

(56) final words for our audience

(57) creatures of habit

(58) vitally important

(59) remain alert so that

(60) how to think deeply

(61) relying too much on

(62) reinforce your mental capabilities

(63) give her a big hand

01 ④   02 ③   03 ⑤   04 ④   05 ③   06 ①   07 ③

01 ④ System 1은 본능적이고 빠르게 작동하는 시스템이므로 slowly(느리게) 대신 quickly(빠르게)가 적절하다.

02 (A) 몸을 '운동시키다'라는 뜻으로, 건강을 위해 신체를 단련하는 것의 중요성을 강조하고 있으므로 exercise가 적절하다.
(B) 뇌 훈련은 '정신'과 관련이 있으므로 mind가 적절하다.
(C) 진행자가 Yoon 박사에게 함께 해주셔서 감사하다고 말하는 상황이므로 joining이 적절하다.

03 (A) System 2를 적용하는 데는 시간과 노력이 필요하다는 의미로, requires(필요로 하다)가 적절하다.
(B) System 1의 첫 응답을 검토하기 위해 System 2를 사용한다는 의미로, initial(초기의)이 적절하다.
(C) System 1에 의존하는 경향이 강해 잘못된 답을 먼저 내는 것이 흔하다는 의미로, common(흔한)이 적절하다.
오답 (A) acquire: 획득하다
(B) final: 최종의
(C) uncommon: 흔하지 않은

04 (A) 모든 결정 하나하나를 의식적으로 내리는 것은 불가능하므로 impossible이 적절하다.
(B) 게으른 뇌가 에너지를 절약하도록 허락한다는 의미이므로 allows가 적절하다.
(C) System 1에 지나치게 의존하게 되면, 고도의 집중력이 필요한 문제에 직면했을 때 System 2를 제대로 적용하지 못한다고 말하는 흐름이 자연스러우므로 intense가 적절하다.
오답 (A) possible: 가능한
(B) prevent: 방해하다
(C) extensive: 광범위한

05 ③ 깊이 사고하는 방법을 배우는 데 시간을 투자해야 한다는 흐름이므로 invest가 적절하다.

06 ① '처음 생각을 곧바로 거부하는 대신 다시 생각하라'는 모순된 조언으로, 문맥상 어색하므로 rejecting(거부하기)이 아니라 accepting (받아들이기)이 적절하다.

07 ③ 보상은 원하는 활동을 한 후에 좋은 것을 받는 것이므로 give (주다)가 아니라 receive(받다)가 적절하다.

01 ③	02 ②	03 ④	04 ④	05 ③	06 ②	07 ⑤

01 (A) the secret to ~는 '~에 대한 비결'이라는 의미로 여기서 to는 전치사로 뒤에 (동)명사가 와야 하므로 becoming이 적절하다.
(B) 문맥상 목적을 나타내는 부사적 용법의 to부정사가 알맞으므로 to purchase가 적절하다.
(C) 명령문이므로 동사원형 Raise가 적절하다.

02 ② 「if+주어+동사의 과거형, 주어+조동사의 과거형+동사원형」 형태의 가정법 과거 문장으로, will이 아니라 조동사의 과거형 would가 적절하다.

03 (A) 앞의 동사 compare, check와 함께 병렬 구조를 이루므로 encounter가 적절하다.
(B) seconds는 셀 수 있는 복수 명사이므로 a few가 적절하다.
(C) That이 가리키는 것이 사람들이 처음에 문제에 틀리게 대답하는 이유를 설명하므로 why가 적절하다.
오답 (B) a little+셀 수 없는 명사
(C) how는 방법을 나타내는 관계부사

04 ④ '~할수록 …하다'라는 의미의 「the+비교급 ~, the+비교급 …」 구문으로 little의 비교급 less가 적절하다.

05 ③ -thing으로 끝나는 부정대명사는 형용사가 뒤에서 수식하므로 something new가 적절하다.
오답 ① keep v-ing: 계속 ~하다
② '~인지'라는 의미로 명사절을 이끄는 접속사
④ 주어 역할을 하는 동명사
⑤ allow의 목적격 보어 역할을 하는 to부정사

06 (A) 의문문에서는 any를 사용한다.
(B) '~하기 위하여'라는 의미의 so that 구문이다.
(C) 문맥상 '사고하는 방법'이라는 의미의 how to think가 적절하다.
오답 (A) some은 긍정문과 권유를 나타내는 의문문에 사용한다.
(C) what to think: 무엇을 생각할지

07 ⑤ allow는 목적격 보어로 to부정사를 취하므로 eating이 아니라 to eat이 적절하다.
오답 ① 주어 역할을 하는 동명사
② a signal을 수식하는 주격 관계대명사
③ an alarm clock을 후치 수식하는 현재분사
④ 선행사가 the part로 장소를 나타내는 관계부사

01 ⑤	02 ③	03 ③	04 ④	05 ②	06 (1) 1.05 (2) 0.05	07 ③

08 ②   **09** ⑤   **10** ③   **11** ②   **12** the less, the more likely   **13** ②
14 (s)timulate   **15** ④   **16** ①   **17** eat healthier, sugary   **18** the trap of making careless decisions

01 큰 목표도 작은 시작에서부터 이루어진다는 내용의 대화와 가장 잘 어울리는 것은 ⑤ '천 리 길도 한 걸음부터 시작된다.'이다.
오답 ① 백문이 불여일견이다.
② 연습이 완벽을 만든다.
③ 쇠가 뜨거울 때 쳐라.
④ 말보다 행동이 더 영향력이 크다.

02 ③ 여학생의 말 I'll start with making that playlist.를 통해 대화 후 여학생이 할 일은 '신나는 노래로 플레이리스트 만들기'임을 알 수 있다.

03 나쁜 습관을 인식하고, 이를 좋은 습관으로 바꾸는 구체적인 방법에 대해 설명하고 있으므로 ③이 주제로 가장 적절하다.

04 ④ 문맥상 나쁜 습관을 좋은 습관으로 '대체하다'라는 의미가 필요하므로 replace가 가장 적절하다.

05 ② 대화에서 언급된 대안은 listen to music(음악 듣기), read a book(책 읽기), take a walk(산책하기), chat with your family(가족과 가벼운 대화하기)이다. '일기 쓰기'는 언급되지 않았다.

06 펜의 가격을 묻는 문제로 공책(notebook)이 펜(pen)보다 $1 더 비싸고, 두 개의 총합이 $1.10이다. 펜의 가격을 x라고 가정하면, 공책의 가격은 x+$1가 된다. 두 물건의 합은 $1.10이므로, 식은 다음과 같다.
$$x+(x+1)=1.10$$
$$2x+1=1.10$$
$$2x=0.10$$
$$x=0.05$$
따라서 공책은 $1.05이고, 펜은 $0.05이다.

07 ③ sentences는 명사이므로 부사 simply가 아니라 형용사 simple이 알맞다. simply는 '간단히, 단순히'라는 뜻의 부사로, 명사 sentences를 수식할 수 없다.

08 ② it works without our conscious control(의식적인 통제 없이 작동한다)로 보아 일치하지 않는 내용이다.

09 mental shortcuts는 사람들이 빠르고 효율적으로 결정을 내리기 위해 사용하는 무의식적 사고 과정 또는 인지 전략을 의미한다. 이러한 과정은 깊은 분석이나 논리적 추론 없이, 자동적이고 즉각적으로 이루어지므로 ⑤ unconscious processes(무의식적 과정)에 가장 가깝다.
오답 ① 정확한 계산 ② 신중한 분석
③ 상세한 계획 ④ 논리적 추론

10 System 1은 빠르고 자동적인 사고에 사용되고, System 2는 신중한 사고에 사용되므로 ③은 일치하지 않는 내용이다.

11 (A) 우리는 알아차리지 못한 채 매일 약 35,000번의 '결정'을 내리므로 decisions가 적절하다.
(B) 우리의 집중과 '주의'를 필요로 하는 중요한 일들이므로 attention이 적절하다.
(C) 어떠한 사실이 한 번도 증명되지 않았음에도 불구하고 그것을 사실로 받아들이는 '습관'을 키울 수도 있다는 것이므로 habit이 적절하다.

12 '~할수록 …하다'라는 의미의 「the+비교급 ~, the+비교급 …」 구문을 사용한다. little의 비교급은 less이고, likely의 비교급은 more likely이다.

13 ② 깊이 있는 사고, 호기심과 새로운 것을 배우는 것은 게으른 뇌 습관을 극복하는 것을 돕는다.
　오답 ① 뇌는 효율성을 위해 항상 System 1에 의존해야 한다.
③ 처음 떠오른 생각을 받아들이는 것이 결정을 내리는 가장 좋은 방법이다.
④ 새로운 것을 배우는 것은 쉽지 않지만 필요하다.
⑤ System 2로 사고하는 것은 더 많은 에너지를 필요로 한다.

14 '특히 정신이나 신체에서 더 많은 활동을 만들어 내다'는 stimulate(자극하다)에 대한 설명이다.

15 habit stacking의 목적은 기존에 이미 형성된 습관에 새로운 습관을 덧붙여, 새로운 습관을 효과적으로 정착시키는 데 있으므로 ④ '새로운 습관을 효과적으로 형성하기 위해'가 가장 적절하다.
　오답 ① 나쁜 습관을 깨기 위해
② 새로운 습관을 시작하는 것을 피하기 위해
③ 현재의 일상을 고수하기 위해
⑤ 당신의 일상 루틴을 더 복잡하게 만들기 위해

16 (A) 문맥상 '~라고 불리는'의 의미로 과거분사 called가 적절하다.
(B) 앞에 선행사가 없으므로 선행사를 포함하는 관계대명사 what이 적절하다.
(C) 진주어 역할을 하는 to부정사 to turn이 적절하다.

17 지우는 설탕이 많이 든 간식 대신 견과류 같은 더 건강한 간식을 먹을 계획이다.

18 「명사+of+동명사(구)」 형태로 문장을 완성한다.

내신 1등급 실전 2회　　　　pp. 86~89

01 ③　**02** ②　**03** (A) constantly eating sugary snacks (B) eating healthier snacks like nuts　**04** ③　**05** (1) careless (2) remarkable　**06** ③　**07** ⑤　**08** how we can become better thinkers　**09** ③　**10** ①　**11** ④　**12** ②　**13** ③　**14** ①　**15** ③　**16** ④　**17** ③　**18** ③

01 독서 습관을 새로 만들기 위해 구체적으로 어떻게 계획하고 실천할지에 대한 내용의 대화이므로 ③이 주제로 가장 적절하다.

02 구체적인 계획이 있는지 묻는 B의 질문에 대한 A의 대답(하루에 10분 동안 읽는 것으로 시작해서 점차 시간을 늘릴 것)이 자연스럽게 이어지므로, ②의 위치가 가장 적절하다.

03 (A) The habit I plan to replace is constantly eating sugary snacks.로 보아 this habit은 constantly eating sugary snacks를 가리킨다.
(B) To replace this habit, I plan to eat healthier snacks like nuts instead.로 보아 this change는 eating healthier snacks like nuts를 가리킨다.

04 지우는 나쁜 습관을 더 건강한 습관으로 바꾸고 싶어 하므로 ③이 일치하는 내용이다.
　오답 ① 지우는 설탕이 든 간식을 더 많이 먹을 계획이다.
② 지우는 자신의 현재 습관이 건강에 좋다고 생각한다.
④ 지우는 자신의 습관을 바꾸는 법을 모른다.
⑤ 지우는 간식 먹는 것을 완전히 그만둘 것이다.

05 (1) '부주의한'이라는 의미의 형용사가 필요하므로 careless가 알맞다.
(2) 명사 achievement를 수식하는 형용사가 필요하므로 remarkable이 알맞다.

06 ③ the secret to ~에서 to는 전치사로 뒤에는 동명사가 와야 하므로 becoming이 적절하다. to부정사가 아니라는 점에 주의한다.

07 밑줄 친 to purchase와 ①~④는 부사적 용법의 to부정사이고, ⑤는 진주어 역할을 하는 명사적 용법의 to부정사이다.

08 간접의문문(의문사+주어+동사)의 어순에 따라 쓴다.

09 환경오염으로 인해 많은 동식물 종이 멸종 위기에 처해 있으며, 이를 보존하기 위한 계획과 후원의 필요성을 강조하고 있으므로 ③이 목적으로 가장 적절하다.

10 빈칸에는 모두 동격을 나타내는 전치사 of가 들어가는 것이 적절하다. 각각 빈칸 앞에 있는 danger, goal, dream과 빈칸 뒤에 있는 명사구가 동격을 이룬다.

11 (A) 주절이 미래시제라도 조건절에서는 현재시제를 사용하므로 becomes가 알맞다.
(B) 「the+비교급 ~, the+비교급 …」 구문으로 little의 비교급 less가 알맞다.
(C) '입증되다'라는 의미의 수동태가 되어야 하므로 been proven이 알맞다.

12 a lazy brain은 System 1에 지나치게 의존하여 깊이 생각하지 않고, 쉽게 결정을 내리는 뇌를 의미하므로 ② '노력이 필요한 사고를 피하는 뇌'가 적절하다.
　오답 ① 항상 활동적인 뇌
③ 결코 실수하지 않는 뇌
④ 오직 System 2만 사용하는 뇌
⑤ 모든 것을 질문하는 뇌

13 이어지는 문장에서 '계속해서 더 많은 아이디어를 내고, 결정을 내리기 전에 신중히 비교하라'고 언급하고 있으므로 ③ '처음 떠오른 생각을 다시 생각해보라'는 의미가 빈칸에 적절하다.
　오답 ① 즉각적인 결정을 내리다
② 다른 사람들의 아이디어에 대해 불평하다
④ 다른 사람들의 관점을 이해하다
⑤ 가능한 한 많은 창의적인 아이디어를 생각해 내다

14 keep proving more ideas는 '더 많은 아이디어를 증명하라'는 뜻인데, 문맥상 '더 많은 아이디어를 계속 생각해 내라'는 의미가 되어야 하므로 generating이 적절하다.

15 well-balanced thinking habits(균형 잡힌 사고 습관)의 중요성을 강조하고, 이를 기르도록 권장하는 데 있으므로 ③이 적절하다.

16 ④ '~하도록'이라는 의미의 so that이 빈칸에 알맞다.

오답 ① ~이기 때문에 ② 만약 ~하지 않는다면
③ ~와 같은 ⑤ 비록 ~일지라도

17 ③ 조건을 나타내는 if절에는 미래시제 대신 현재시제를 써야 하므로 will drive 대신 drive를 쓴다.

18 ⓑ 조건절에서는 미래시제 대신 현재시제를 써야 하므로 You will feel much better if you take this medicine.이 되어야 한다.
ⓓ 동격을 나타내는 of가 필요하므로 Tourists should be aware of the danger of getting lost in the forest.가 되어야 한다.
ⓐ 날씨가 좋으면 우리는 캠핑을 갈 수 있을 것이다.
ⓑ 네가 이 약을 먹으면 훨씬 더 기분이 좋아질 것이다.
ⓒ Katie는 매일 밤 너무 늦게까지 깨어 있는 자신의 습관을 걱정하고 있다.
ⓓ 관광객들은 숲에서 길을 잃는 위험에 대해 주의해야 한다.
ⓔ 식당이 열려 있으면, 우리는 거기서 저녁을 먹을 것이다.

내신 1등급 실전 3회

pp. 90~93

01 ⑤ **02** how important it is for us to exercise our bodies **03** ⑤ **04** ② **05** replacements **06** ⑤ **07** ① **08** They are the trigger, the action, and the reward. **09** ② **10** ③ **11** ⑤ **12** ⑤ **13** ③ **14** 그것을 덜 사용할수록 게으르게 생각하는 사람이 될 가능성이 더 커진다 **15** ⑤ **16** ③: such → so ⑤: from → of **17** 뇌에서 정보가 더 효율적으로 흐르게 해주는 새로운 길을 만들어준다. **18** ③

01 주어진 문장은 자기 보상(self-rewarding)에 대한 언급이 나오는 문장 I'll reward myself.(나는 나 자신에게 보상을 줄 것이다.) 뒤에 오는 것이 가장 자연스럽다.

02 간접의문문(의문사+주어+동사)의 어순에 따라 how important it is를 쓴 뒤, 의미상의 주어(for+목적격)와 to부정사를 쓴다.

03 ⑤ '나쁜 습관을 좋은 습관으로 바꾸는 방법을 제안하기 위해'가 목적으로 가장 적절하다.

오답 ① 스마트폰 사용의 이점을 설명하기 위해
② 음악을 듣는 방법을 소개하기 위해
③ 가족과 더 많은 시간을 보내는 방법을 설명하기 위해
④ 운동의 중요성을 강조하기 위해

04 (A) 예시를 들고 있으므로 For example(예를 들어)이 적절하다.
(B) 나쁜 습관을 없애는 것은 어렵지만 좋은 습관으로 바꾸는 방법이 있다는 대조적인 내용을 연결하고 있으므로 However(그러나, 하지만)가 적절하다.
(C) '만약 휴대폰을 너무 자주 보고 싶지 않다면'이라는 조건을 나타내므로 If(만약 ~라면)가 적절하다.

오답 ① 게다가 – 그러므로 – 만약 ~하지 않는다면
③ 그 결과 – 또한 – ~할 때
④ 그렇지 않으면 – 예를 들어 – 왜냐하면, ~때문에
⑤ 게다가 – 한편 – 비록 ~일지라도

05 형용사 positive 뒤이므로 replace의 명사형 replacement가 와야 한다. 또한, 여러 가지 긍정적인 대체 습관들을 의미하므로 복수형 replacements가 적절하다.

06 ⑤ 조건을 나타내는 if절에서는 미래시제를 쓰지 않고, 현재시제를 사용하므로 associates가 알맞다. 주어가 your brain으로 3인칭 단수이므로 동사도 3인칭 단수 현재형이 되어야 한다는 것에 주의한다.

07 빈칸 뒤에 나오는 내용이 앞에 언급된 something good의 구체적인 예시에 해당하므로 ① For example(예를 들어)이 가장 적절하다.

오답 ② 결론적으로 ③ 그러나, 하지만
④ 게다가, 또한 ⑤ 반면에, 다른 한편으로

08 Q: 습관의 세 가지 단계는 무엇인가?
A: 그것들은 방아쇠, 행동, 그리고 보상이다.

09 주어진 문장의 They는 Our brains를 의미하고 이 문장이 System 1과 System 2를 처음 소개하고 있으므로 System 1에 대한 설명이 나오는 문장 바로 앞인 ②의 위치가 알맞다.

10 ③ 문맥상 '셀 수 없이 많은(countless)' 일상 상황이 자연스럽다.

오답 ① 부주의한 ② 무해한 ③ 쓸모 없는 ⑤ 의미없는

11 ⑤ '두 개 또는 그 이상의 것들 사이의 유사점과 차이점을 살펴보다'가 compare(비교하다)의 영어 뜻풀이에 해당한다.

오답 ① 어떤 것에 대해 깊이 생각하다: reflect(곰곰이 생각하다)
② 어떤 상황을 실제인 것처럼 생각하다: suppose(가정하다)
③ 알려지지 않은 것을 드러내다: reveal(드러내 보이다, 밝히다)
④ 어떤 상황에서 아이디어나 방법을 사용하다: apply(적용하다)

12 ⑤는 System 1에 관한 설명이다.

13 '게으른 뇌 습관'의 위험성과 그로 인한 문제점에 대해 중점적으로 설명하고 있으므로 ③이 주제로 가장 적절하다.

14 「the+비교급 ~, the+비교급 …」 구문으로 '~할수록 더 …하다'라는 뜻으로 해석한다.

15 윗글에 따르면, System 1에 지나치게 의존하는 것은 위험할 수 있는데, 그 이유는 필요할 때 시스템 2를 사용하는 것을 방해하기 때문이다.

오답 ① 그것은 항상 에너지를 절약한다
② 그것은 우리가 더 나은 결정을 하도록 도와준다
③ 그것은 절대로 실수하지 않는다
④ 그것은 우리를 더 똑똑하게 만든다

16 ③ '~하기 위하여'라는 의미의 목적을 나타낼 때는 so that이 알맞다.
⑤ 「a habit of+동명사」 구문으로 동격을 나타내는 전치사는 from이 아니라 of이다.

17 these new activities will create new paths that allow information to flow through your brain more efficiently에서 답을 알 수 있다.

18 ③ '오로지 직관에만 의존하는 것'은 오히려 게으른 두뇌 습관의 예시이며, 극복 방법으로 언급되지 않았다.

내신 1등급 수능형 고난도

pp. 94~97

01 ③	02 ②	03 ②	04 ③	05 ③	06 ④	07 ①	08 ③
09 ④	10 ③	11 ①	12 ⑤	13 ③	14 ④	15 ②	16 ④	17 ②

01 ③ '새로운 습관을 기르는 비결'에 대한 대화이다.
오답 ① 언어 능력을 향상시키는 방법
② 책을 읽는 것의 이점
④ 실현 가능한 목표를 설정하는 방법
⑤ 여가 시간을 현명하게 보내는 요령

02 ② early는 뒤에 than이 있으므로 비교급 earlier가 알맞다.

03 나쁜 습관을 좋은 습관으로 바꾸는 것의 중요성과 방법에 대한 대화이므로 ② '나쁜 습관을 바꾸는 방법'이 제목으로 가장 적절하다.
오답 ① 규칙적으로 운동하는 방법들
③ 책을 더 많이 읽는 요령
④ 가족 대화의 중요성
⑤ 휴대폰을 사용하는 시간을 줄이는 방법

04 빈칸 뒤에 휴대폰을 보는 대신 할 수 있는 일들이 나열되어 있으므로 빈칸에는 ③ '더 나은 무언가를 하다'가 적절하다.
오답 ① 도서관에 가다
② 나쁜 습관을 없애다
④ 의사소통할 다른 방법을 찾다
⑤ 해야 할 일의 목록을 만들다

05 System 2가 담당하는 역할과 특징에 대해 설명하고 있으므로 ③이 가장 적절하다.
오답 ① System 1과 System 2의 유사점
② 일상적인 과업에 미치는 System 2의 영향
④ 의사결정에 미치는 System 1의 영향
⑤ 인지 처리에서 System 2의 필요성

06 ④ '제품의 가격과 특징을 비교하다'가 문맥상 자연스러우므로 compare(비교하다)가 적절하다.
오답 ① 무시하다 ② 잊다 ③ 구입하다 ⑤ 생성하다

07 (B)의 앞에서는 System 2의 장점을 말하고, 뒤에서는 단점을 말하므로 대조를 나타내는 However가 적절하다.
(C)의 앞에서는 System 2에 대해 설명하다가, 뒤에서는 System 1의 경향을 말하므로 역시 대조를 나타내는 However가 적절하다.
오답 ② 그러므로, 따라서 ③ 마침내
④ 게다가, 더욱이 ⑤ 그 결과

08 게으른 뇌는 에너지를 아낄 수 있게 해준다고 긍정적인 면을 설명한 후, '그러나(However)', 이것이 습관이 되면 위험하다로 전환하는 것이 자연스러우므로 ③의 위치가 가장 적절하다.

09 System 1에 지나치게 의존하면 오히려 실수와 잘못된 결정을 하게 되고, System 2를 덜 사용하면 게으른 사고를 하게 된다고 했으므로, ④는 내용과 일치하지 않는다.

10 습관이 형성되기 위해 필요한 방아쇠, 행동, 보상이라는 세 가지 단계에 대해 설명하고 있으므로 제목으로는 ③ '습관의 세 단계 이해하기'가 적절하다.
오답 ① 운동 후에 자신에게 보상하는 방법
② 일상생활에서 알람시계의 중요성
④ 나쁜 습관이 고치기 어려운 이유
⑤ 하루 동안 시간을 절약하는 요령

11 (A) 사역동사 make의 목적격 보어이므로 동사원형 stick이 알맞다.
(B) 앞의 명사 an alarm clock을 후치 수식하는 현재분사 telling이 알맞다.
(C) 조건을 나타내는 if절에서는 미래시제 대신 현재시제를 사용해야 하므로 associates가 알맞다.

12 lazy brain habits는 System 1에 지나치게 의존해 자동적이고 노력 없는 사고에 머무르는 습관을 의미하므로 ⑤ '자동적이고 수월한 사고에 지나치게 의존하는 것'이 적절하다.
오답 ① 정기적으로 새로운 기술을 배우는 것
② 호기심을 이용해 탐구하는 것
③ 깊이 있는 사고를 장려하는 습관들
④ 항상 자신의 결론을 의심하는 것

13 ③ 동사 motivate의 목적격 보어로 쓰이고 있으므로 investigating이 아니라 to investigate가 적절하다.

14 박사에 따르면, 호기심은 우리가 탐구하고 더 깊이 생각하도록 동기를 부여하기 때문에 중요하다.
오답 ① 우리가 시스템 1에 더 많이 의존하게 만든다
② 우리가 결정을 내리지 못하게 한다
③ 우리가 새로운 경험을 피하도록 격려한다
⑤ 우리가 증거 없이 어떤 것을 사실로 받아들이게 만든다

15 (A) 방과 후에 달리기를 '습관(habit)'으로 만들 계획이라고 하는 것이 자연스럽다.
(B) '작은(small)' 것부터 시작해야 습관이 잘 만들어진다고 하는 것이 자연스럽다.
(C) 달리기 시간을 조금씩 '늘리면(increase)' 달리기가 습관이 된다고 하는 것이 자연스럽다.

16 소녀의 말 it's not easy for me로 보아 ④ '소녀는 달리기를 습관으로 만드는 것이 쉽다고 생각한다.'는 일치하지 않는 내용이다.
오답 ① 민호는 매일 30분씩 달린다.
② 소녀는 달리기 플레이리스트를 만들 계획이다.
③ 민호는 세 곡이 나오는 동안 달리면서 시작하라고 제안한다.
⑤ 소녀는 그 습관이 자신을 건강하고 튼튼하게 해주길 바란다.

17 ② '많은 사람들은 여가 시간에 책을 읽거나 음악 듣는 것을 즐긴다.'는 생각 습관에 관한 전체 글의 흐름과 어울리지 않는다.

01 (1) 설탕이 든 간식을 끊임없이 먹는 것
(2) 견과류와 같은 더 건강한 간식을 먹는 것

02 habits

03 harmful

04 나쁜 습관을 없애는 것

05 음악 듣기, 책 읽기, 산책하기, 가족과 가벼운 대화하기

06 habits, replace, positive[good]

07 ⓐ reasonable ⓑ reliant ⓒ concentration

08 (1) 자주 실수를 하고 잘못된 결정을 내린다.
(2) 증명되지 않은 것을 사실로 받아들이는 습관을 키울 수 있다.

09 하루에 10분 동안 읽는 것으로 시작해서 서서히 시간을 늘리는 습관

10 (1) pay attention (2) rely on (3) come up with

11 (1) 처음 생각을 곧바로 받아들이는 대신 다시 생각하기
(2) 타고난 호기심을 이용하기
(3) 뇌를 자극하고 더 똑똑해지기 위해 새로운 무언가를 배우기

12 (A) generating (B) to dive (C) Learning

13 of

14 invest time into learning how to think deeply

15 (1) will take → takes (2) won't → don't

---

01 나쁜 습관은 constantly eating sugary snacks이고, 습관을 바꾸기 위한 계획은 eating healthier snacks like nuts이다.

02 ones는 앞에 나온 habits를 대신하는 말이다.

03 설탕이 든 간식을 끊임없이 먹는 습관은 건강에 해롭기 때문에 harmless(해롭지 않은)를 harmful(해로운)로 고쳐야 한다.

04 여기서 this는 앞 문장에서 언급한 getting rid of such habits (그러한 습관을 없애는 것)를 가리키며 such habits는 bad habits를 말한다.

05 You could listen to music, read a book, take a walk, or chat with your family.를 통해 음악 듣기, 책 읽기, 산책하기, 가족과 가벼운 대화하기임을 알 수 있다.

06 나쁜 습관들을 없애는 가장 좋은 방법은 먼저 그것들을 인식하고, 그것들이 언제 그리고 얼마나 자주 일어나는지 이해하는 것이다. 그 다음에는 그런 나쁜 습관들을 긍정적인[좋은] 습관으로 대체하는 것이다.

07 ⓐ 부사 quite의 수식을 받으며 보어 역할을 하므로 형용사형 reasonable이 적절하다.
ⓑ 부사 too의 수식을 받으므로 형용사형 reliant가 적절하다.
ⓒ 형용사 intense의 수식을 받는 명사형 concentration이 적절하다.

08 (1) frequently make errors and bad decisions로 보아 자주 실수를 하고 잘못된 결정을 내리는 것이다.
(2) develop a habit of accepting things to be true even though they have never been proven으로 보아 증명되지 않은 것을 사실로 받아들이는 습관을 키울 수 있다는 것이다.

09 I'll start by reading for ten minutes a day and gradually increase the amount of time.에서 this habit이 의미하는 바는 '하루에 10분 동안 읽는 것으로 시작해서 서서히 시간을 늘리는 습관'이라는 것을 알 수 있다.

10 (1) 집중하다, 주의를 기울이다: pay attention
(2) ~에 의존하다: rely on
(3) 생각해 내다, (아이디어 등을) 내놓다: come up with

11 reconsider your initial thoughts instead of accepting them right away, make use of your natural curiosity, learn something new in order to stimulate your brain and become more intelligent에 세 가지 방법이 나타나 있다.

12 (A) 아이디어를 '만들어 내는' 것이므로 generate가 필요하고, '계속해서 ~하다'라는 의미의 「keep v-ing」 구문으로 generating이 알맞다.
(B) 주제에 '파고드는' 것이므로 dive가 적절하고, 「encourage+목적어+to부정사」 구문으로 to dive가 알맞다.
(C) 새로운 것을 '배우는' 것이므로 learn이 적절하고, 문장에서 주어 역할을 하므로 동명사 Learning이 알맞다.

13 두 문장 모두 동격을 나타내는 전치사 of가 필요하다.

14 '~하는 데 시간을 투자하다'라는 의미의 invest time into를 쓴 뒤, 목적어 역할을 하는 명사구 '깊이 생각하는 방법을 배우는 것'에 해당하는 learning how to think deeply를 쓴다.

15 조건의 부사절에서는 미래시제 대신 현재시제를 쓴다.
(1) 그녀가 이른 기차를 탄다면, 그녀는 정오 전에 목적지에 도착할 것이다.
(2) 서두르지 않으면, 너는 수업에 늦을 것이다.

교과서 **어휘 익히기** ······················· p. 103

01 예산, 비용	26 resident
02 위치하다, 있다	27 removal
03 손실	28 experience
04 젊은	29 assistance
05 많은	30 recently
06 입주해서 사는	31 unusual
07 필요로 하다	32 neighbor
08 활기찬	33 social
09 아주 흥미로운	34 perspective
10 ~의 대가로	35 elderly
11 알리다, 알아내다	36 reduction
12 ~과 함께	37 go through
13 감사하는, 고마워하는	38 knowledge
14 위로, 위안	39 spot
15 상기시키다, 생각나게 하다	40 acquire
16 큰 슬픔, 비통	41 rush around
17 소중한, 귀중한	42 accommodation
18 적당한, 감당할 수 있는	43 unique
19 현재	44 counseling
20 거의	45 in return for
21 ~할 작정이다, 의도하다	46 meaningful
22 확실히, 분명히	47 transformative
23 괜찮은, 제대로 된	48 supportive
24 세대 간의	49 educational
25 ~와 시간을 보내다	50 proposal

교과서 **핵심 문법** ······················· pp. 104~107

POINT 1 분사의 후치수식

Q 1 fallen 2 crying 3 covered 4 wearing
Check-Up ♥
01 (1) shining (2) decorated (3) hidden
02 (1) building → built
   (2) worn → wearing
   (3) broken window → window broken
03 (1) the special dishes recommended by the chef
   (2) The people injured in the traffic accident
   (3) a video introducing a man
04 (1) written (2) named

Q 1. 떨어진 나뭇잎들이 길 전체를 덮었다.
  2. 우는 아기가 가족 모두를 잠 못 들게 했다.
  3. 공원에서 눈으로 덮인 나무들은 멋져 보인다.
  4. 노란 드레스를 입고 있는 여성이 우리의 새로운 수학 선생님이다.

Check-Up ♥
01 (1) '반짝이는' 별들로 능동·진행이므로 현재분사 shining이 알맞다.
   (2) 신선한 과일로 '장식된' 케이크로 수동·완료이므로 과거분사 decorated가 알맞다.
   (3) 동굴에 '숨겨진' 보물로 수동·완료이므로 과거분사 hidden이 알맞다.
   (1) 밤하늘에서 밝게 빛나는 별들을 보아라.
   (2) 이 빵집은 신선한 과일로 장식된 케이크로 유명하다.
   (3) 동굴에 숨겨진 보물은 모험가들에 의해 발견되었다.

02 (1) 집은 건축가에 의해 지어진 것이므로(수동) 과거분사 built가 알맞다.
   (2) 선수들이 옷을 입고 있는 것이므로(능동) 현재분사 wearing이 알맞다.
   (3) 창문이 낯선 사람에 의해 깨진 것이므로(수동) 과거분사 broken은 알맞다. 그러나 분사에 수식어구(by a stranger)가 있는 경우는 명사 뒤에서 수식하므로 window broken이 알맞다.
   (1) 그 음악가는 유명한 건축가가 지은 집에서 살았다.
   (2) 빨간 유니폼을 입은 선수들이 우승했다.
   (3) 낯선 사람에 의해 깨진 창문은 빠르게 수리되었다.

03 분사에 목적어나 수식어(구) 등이 있을 때는 명사를 뒤에서 수식한다. 명사와 분사의 관계가 능동·진행일 때는 현재분사를 쓰고, 수동·완료일 때는 과거분사를 쓴다.

04
> *Dumplin'*은 Julie Murphy가 쓴 영감을 주는 이야기이다. 그것은 Willowdean Dickson이라는 10대 소녀에 대한 이야기이다. Willowdean은 과체중이지만, 그녀는 자신을 자랑스러워한다. 그녀는 미인 대회에 출전하기로 결심하고, 그 과정에서 그녀는 자신이 믿는 것을 지지하는 방법을 배운다. 이 책은 당신에게 계속 영감을 주고, 자아 수용에 대한 중요한 교훈을 가르쳐줄 것이다. 나는 재미있고 감동적인 이야기를 읽는 것을 즐기는 모든 사람들에게 이 책을 추천한다.

(1) 흥미로운 이야기가 작가에 의해 '쓰여진' 것이므로 과거분사 written이 알맞다.
(2) Willowdean Dickson이라는 이름으로 '불리는' 10대 소녀이므로 과거분사 named가 알맞다.

POINT 2 의문사＋to부정사

Q 1 when to launch 2 how to write 3 what to say
Check-Up ♥
01 (1) where to go (2) what to do
   (3) who to follow (4) how to make

02 (1) when to return the library books

(2) how to operate the new machine

(3) where to find reliable information

(4) where to buy tickets

03 (1) what to do

(2) how to recover

(3) where to get

Q 1. 우리는 제품을 언제 출시해야 할지 결정할 것이다.

2. Jessica는 노래 가사를 쓰는 방법을 배우고 있다.

3. 면접에서 내가 무엇을 말해야 할지 알려줄 수 있나요?

Check-Up ☝

01 '(의문사) ~할지'는 「의문사+to부정사」 형태의 명사구로 쓸 수 있다.

02 '(의문사) ~할지'에 해당하므로 「의문사+to부정사」 형태의 명사구로 쓸 수 있다.

03

담당자님께,

저는 최근에 당신의 매장에서 컴퓨터를 구매했고, 그것이 품질에 실망했습니다. 그것은 너무 큰 소음을 내고 화면이 계속 꺼지기 때문에 무엇을 해야 할지 모르겠습니다. 또한, 제 데이터 중 일부가 분실되었는데, 그것을 어떻게 복구해야 할지도 모르겠습니다. 어디에서 그것을 고칠 수 있는지 알려주세요.

'(의문사) ~할지'에 해당하므로 「의문사+to부정사」 형태의 명사구로 쓸 수 있다.

(1) 무엇을 해야 할지: what to do

(2) 어떻게 복구해야 할지: how to recover

(3) 어디에서 그것을 고칠 수 있는지: where to get (it fixed)

교과서 **본문 익히기** ❶ 옳은 어법·어휘 고르기 ···pp. 115~117

01 located	02 who
03 something unusual	04 amount
05 loss	06 left
07 to offer	08 so
09 for	10 As
11 than	12 how
13 shopping	14 feel
15 that	16 advice
17 gathered	18 realizing
19 of	20 rushing
21 used to	22 much
23 meaningful	24 least
25 possible	26 a lot
27 when	28 was
29 create	30 before, in
31 held	32 how

33 compared	34 that
35 Speaking	36 what
37 what	38 which
39 nice	40 better
41 nothing	42 having, forget
43 be offered	44 lives
45 while	46 are, harmony

교과서 **본문 익히기** ❷ 틀린 부분 고치기 ········ pp. 118~120

01 located	02 ○
03 something unusual	04 ○
05 amount	06 ○
07 to fill the gap	08 ○
09 so	10 ○
11 at least	12 than that
13 ○	14 go shopping
15 a part of	16 ○
17 much experience	18 little but important
19 ○	20 ○
21 used to	22 much
23 for	24 ○, possible
25 a lot	26 ○
27 laugh	28 more
29 invited	30 ○
31 compared	32 have become
33 Speaking	34 what
35 ○	36 during, ○
37 feels nice, for others	38 better
39 ○	40 helps, enjoy
41 ○, be offered	
42 how people of different ages can help	
43 ○	44 ○, bringing

교과서 **본문 익히기** ❸ 빈칸 완성하기 ········ pp. 121~125

(1) located in

(2) houses more than

(3) Along with

(4) offers something unusual

(5) elderly residents share

(6) reduced the amount of money

(7) led to the loss

(8) seek an affordable solution

(9) had numerous empty rooms available

(10) were struggling to afford

(11) about this intriguing place

(12) I've been living

(13) in exchange for free accommodations

(14) In reality

(15) how to use social media

(16) have meals together

(17) feel like a care home

(18) consider it a community

(19) tell my neighbors

(20) useful advice to share

(21) With so much experience

(22) little but important things

(23) having a casual chat

(24) from rushing around

(25) used to feel sorry for

(26) see all the things

(27) much more than

(28) meaningful friendships

(29) intend to stay at

(30) really grateful for

(31) have learned so much

(32) when we were first informed

(33) once they moved in

(34) make us laugh and create

(35) a decent place to live

(36) held a pajama party

(37) taught us how to play

(38) hear loud music from

(39) compared to

(40) have become part of our community

(41) Speaking of

(42) went through a difficult time

(43) listened to what she said

(44) which made me feel

(45) capable of doing things

(46) have bad knees

(47) get any better

(48) There is nothing much

(49) helps me forget

(50) hoping to be offered

(51) share their lives with one another

(52) gain a more youthful perspective

(53) bringing the young and old together

01 ② **02** ④ **03** ④ **04** ③ **05** ⑤ **06** ⑤ **07** ② **08** ④

01 ② 문맥상 Humanitas가 제공하는 '젊은 이웃'은 평범하지 않고 독특한 것이므로 unusual(특이한)이 적절하다.

02 (A) 서비스들이 사라지면서 남은 공백을 메우기 위한 solution(해결책)이 자연스럽다.
(B) 노인 거주자들과 함께 시간을 보내는 것의 대가이므로 free(무료의)가 자연스럽다.
(C) 앞문장의 내용은 지역의 대학생들에게 제안(proposal)하는 것이다.
오답 (A) problem: 문제
(B) expensive: 비싼
(C) refusal: 거부, 거절

03 ④ Humanitas에서는 학생들에게 '무료(free)' 거처를 제공하는 대신 일정 시간 노인들과 시간을 보내도록 하고 있으므로 expensive(비싼)는 적절하지 않다.

04 (A) 과거에는 노인들이 할 수 없는 것만 보고 '안타깝게(sorry)' 여겼지만, 지금은 할 수 있는 것들을 본다는 흐름이다.
(B) 적어도 1년 더 머물 계획이라는 의도를 강조하므로 intend(~할 작정이다)가 적절하다.
(C) Humanitas에서의 경험이 인생을 변화시켰으므로, transformative(변화를 가져다주는)가 적절하다.

05 ⑤ 노인 이웃들과 커피를 마시며 나누는 대화를 긍정적이고 편안한 휴식의 시간으로 묘사하고 있으므로 serious(진지한) 대신 casual(가벼운, 편안한)이 적절하다.

06 ⑤ 이어지는 문장에서 '사소한 문제'라고 했으므로 '고요한' 소리가 아닌 '큰(loud)' 소리였을 것이다.

07 ② 화자는 슬픔에 빠진 학생을 위로했으며, 학생은 이를 '불편함(discomfort)'이 아니라 '위안(comfort)'으로 받아들였다고 하는 것이 자연스럽다.

08 (A) 다른 연령대의 젊은 학생들과 노인들이 서로 도움을 주고받는다는 의미이므로 different(다른)가 적절하다.
(B) 노인들이 젊은 사람들로부터 얻을 수 있는 것은 experience(경험)가 아니라 삶에 대한 더 젊은 perspective(관점)라고 할 수 있다.
(C) 문맥상 젊은 세대와 노년 세대를 함께 생활하게 하는 방식을 뜻하므로 intergenerational(세대 간의)이 적절하다.
오답 (A) similar: 비슷한
(B) experience: 경험
(C) international: 국제적인

01 ②   **02** ③   **03** ⑤   **04** ①   **05** ①   **06** ②   **07** ⑤   **08** ②

01 (A) '~에 위치한'이라는 의미의 과거분사 located가 적절하다.
(B) 선행사가 residents로 사람이므로 주격 관계대명사 who가 적절하다.
(C) -thing으로 끝나는 대명사는 형용사가 뒤에서 수식한다.

02 (A) '남겨진'이라는 의미의 과거분사 left가 적절하다.
(B) '~의 대가로'라는 의미의 「in return for+동명사(v-ing)」 구문으로 동명사 spending이 적절하다.
(C) '~하기 어려워하다'라는 의미의 「struggle+to부정사」 구문으로 to afford가 적절하다.

03 (A) 현재완료(have+p.p.) 시제 문장으로, enjoyed가 적절하다.
(B) 비교급 more를 수식할 수 있는 것은 a lot이다. very는 비교급을 수식할 수 없다.
(C) '~하는 방법'은 「how+to부정사」이다.

04 ② 경험은 '모아지는' 것으로 수동의 의미이므로 과거분사 gathered가 적절하다.
오답 ① 앞의 명사 advice를 수식하는 형용사적 용법의 to부정사
③ 전치사(without) 뒤에 쓰인 동명사
④ 동격을 나타내는 전치사 of 뒤에 쓰인 동명사
⑤ 앞의 명사 way를 수식하는 형용사적 용법의 to부정사

05 ① be used to는 '~에 익숙하다'라는 뜻으로, 뒤에는 명사나 동명사(v-ing)가 와야 한다. 여기서는 '(과거에) ~하곤 했다'라는 의미의 used to가 적절하다.
오답 ② a free place를 수식하는 형용사적 용법의 to부정사
③ at least: 적어도
④ 동명사 주어
⑤ a lot+비교급(more)

06 ② 사역동사 make는 목적격 보어로 동사원형을 취하므로 laugh가 적절하다.
오답 ① 현재완료 진행형
③ a lot(비교급 강조)+비교급
④ 「의문사+to부정사」 형태의 명사구
⑤ compared to: ~과 비교하여

07 ⑤ 동명사구(having young, vibrant people around) 주어는 단수 취급하므로 helps가 적절하다.
오답 ① Speaking of: ~에 대해 말하자면
② 선행사를 포함하는 관계대명사 what
③ 계속적 용법의 관계대명사 which
④ 「feel+형용사(보어)」 구문

08 (A) 학생들이 한 자리를 '제공받기'를 희망한다는 수동의 의미이므로 to be offered가 적절하다.
(B) 문맥상 '더 젊은' 관점이라는 의미이므로 more youthful이 적절하다. 최상급 앞에는 the가 있어야 하므로 적절하지 않다.
(C) 주어 care homes가 복수이므로 동사는 are가 적절하다.

01 ②   **02** ③   **03** 요양 시설의 노인 거주자들이 대학생들과 그들의 생활 공간을 공유하는 것   **04** ⓐ left ⓑ spending ⓒ to afford   **05** ⑤   **06** ③   **07** the elderly   **08** ⑤   **09** ①   **10** Willowdean is overweight, but she is proud of who she is.   **11** ①   **12** how to use social media   **13** 젊은이들을 이웃으로 두는 것   **14** ①, ③   **15** (A) Speaking of my young neighbor, she has been here for more than two years now. (B) But having young, vibrant people around helps me forget about the pain and enjoy my life!   **16** ②   **17** ⑤   **18** ④

01 ② Let's pick up some trash before we head to the subway station.으로 보아 두 사람은 경기 후 남겨진 쓰레기를 함께 주울 것이다.

02 ③ Humanitas는 노인 거주자들이 대학생들과 생활 공간을 공유하는 요양 시설로, 대학생들은 젊은 '이웃들(neighbors)'이라고 하는 것이 자연스럽다.
오답 ① 감독들 ② 종업원들 ④ 교사들 ⑤ 환자들

03 this unique "intergenerational living" project는 세대가 다른 (노인과 대학생) 구성원이 한 공간에서 함께 생활하며 서로 교류하는 프로그램을 의미한다.

04 ⓐ '남겨진'의 의미로, gap을 수식하는 과거분사 left가 알맞다.
ⓑ 전치사(for) 뒤이므로 동명사 spending이 알맞다.
ⓒ 「struggle to+동사원형」 구문으로 to afford가 알맞다.

05 ⑤ 대학생들은 노인들과 시간을 보내는 것의 대가로 무료 거처를 제공받았을 뿐, 급여를 받지는 않았다.

06 I used to feel sorry for the elderly를 통해 필자가 처음에 어르신들에 대해 느꼈을 심경으로 적절한 것은 ③ '안타까움(sorry)'이다.

07 여기서 they는 앞에 나온 the elderly(어르신들)를 의미한다.

08 ⑤ at least는 '적어도, 최소한'이라는 의미로 at least one more year는 '적어도 1년은 더'라는 의미이다.

09 ① Dumplin'은 Julie Murphy에 의해 '쓰여진' 이야기이므로 과거분사 written이 적절하다.

10 전치사 of의 목적어 역할을 하는 간접의문문이므로 「의문사+주어+동사」의 어순인 who she is가 알맞다.

11 (A) 현재완료와 함께 사용된 '~동안'이라는 의미의 for가 적절하다. during도 '~동안'이라는 뜻이지만 특정한 사건이나 기간 앞에 사용한다.
(B) '~하도록 요구받다'라는 의미의 수동태이므로 required가 적절하다.
(C) 앞에 나온 sometimes와 호응을 이루는 other times가 적절하다. another 뒤에는 복수 명사가 올 수 없다.

12 '~하는 방법'은 「how+to부정사」 형태의 명사구로 표현한다.

13 it은 바로 앞 문장 we would have young people as neighbors, 즉 '젊은이들을 이웃으로 두는 것'을 의미한다.

14 ⓑ와 ①, ③은 선행사를 포함하는 관계대명사 what이고 ②, ④, ⑤는 의문사 what이다.
① 그는 회의 중에 무슨 일이 있었는지 설명했다.
② 이 단어가 무슨 뜻인지 설명해 줄 수 있나요?
③ 그들이 발견한 것이 모두를 놀라게 했다.
④ 나는 그녀의 생일에 무엇을 요리할지 결정할 수 없다.
⑤ 새로운 언어를 빠르게 배우는 가장 좋은 방법이 무엇이라고 생각하나요?

15 (A) speaking of는 '~에 대해 말하자면'이라는 의미의 관용 표현이다.
(B) 동명사구(having young, vibrant people around) 주어는 단수 취급하므로 helps가 적절하다.

16 grief(큰 슬픔, 비통)는 ② '누군가를 잃어서 생기는 깊은 슬픔'이다.
[오답] ① 특정 주제에 대한 관점: perspective(관점, 시각)
③ 격려와 지지를 받는 느낌: comfort(위로, 위안)
④ 개인적, 사회적, 또는 심리적 문제에 대한 조언과 지원: counseling(상담, 조언)
⑤ 도움이나 지원을 주는 행위, 또는 주어진 도움: assistance(도움, 지원)

17 영화관에서 휴대전화를 사용하는 사람 때문에 불편했던 것을 얘기하고 있으므로, ⑤ '공공장소에서 에티켓을 지키는 것'이 빈칸에 적절하다.
[오답] ① 영화 보는 동안 간식을 즐기는 것
② 영화 감상 경험을 준비하는 것
③ 엔딩 크레딧 전에 극장을 떠나는 것
④ 동행 없이 영화를 보는 것

18 ④ 누군가가 반전을 스포일러 했는지 묻는 남학생의 질문에 Susan이 No.라고 답했으므로, 일치하지 않는 내용이다.

---

01 ⑤ **02** (A) Humanitas is a yellow brick house located in the city of Deventer, the Netherlands. (B) Along with its supportive environment, Humanitas offers something unusual: young neighbors. **03** ② **04** ④ **05** ③ **06** the value of having a casual chat **07** Living here has changed my life in ways I never thought possible **08** ① **09** ⓐ laugh ⓑ to live ⓒ compared **10** ④ **11** comfort **12** 화자의 젊은 이웃이 아버지를 여의고 나서 겪었던 슬픔의 시간 **13** (A) what to do (B) how to recover **14** ③ **15** she noticed a message written on the cup **16** 친절을 받는 사람들 **17** ①, ④

01 ⑤ 사회, 교육, 그리고 상담 서비스를 포함한 여러 가지 필수적인 노인 프로그램의 손실로 이어지기 위해서는 growth(성장)가 아니라 reduction(삭감)이 적절하다.

02 (A) house와 locate가 수동·완료의 관계이므로 과거분사를 써야 한다. located 이하는 a yellow brick house를 뒤에서 수식하는 과거분사구이다.
(B) something처럼 –thing으로 끝나는 대명사는 형용사가 뒤에서 수식하므로, something unusual(특별한 무언가)이 올바른 표현이다.

03 (A) 서비스들이 '사라지면서' 남은 공백이므로 removal(제거)이 적절하다.
(B) 건물에 '사용 가능한' 빈 방이 많았기 때문에 지역 대학생들에게 무료 거처를 제공하는 것이므로 available(이용 가능한)이 적절하다.
(C) 많은 학생들이 그 지역의 비싼 집세를 감당하기 위해 '애쓰고 있다'는 것이 자연스러우므로 struggling(애쓰고 있는)이 적절하다.
[오답] (A) approval: 승인
(B) unavailable: 이용 불가능한
(C) be planning to: ~할 계획이다

04 affordable(적당한, 감당할 수 있는)에 해당하는 영어 뜻풀이는 ④ '가격이 너무 비싸지 않은; 가격 면에서 합리적인'이다.
[오답] ① 도움과 격려를 제공하는: supportive(지원하는)
② 감사함을 느끼거나 표현하는: grateful(감사하는, 고마워하는)
③ 에너지와 생기가 넘치는: vibrant(활기찬)
⑤ 중요성이나 가치를 지닌: meaningful(의미 있는)

05 주어진 문장은 '하지만 실제로 우린 그것보다 훨씬 더 많은 시간을 함께 보내요.'라는 뜻으로 입주 학생이 무료 거처에 대한 대가로 한 달에 최소 30시간을 노인 이웃들과 함께 보내야 한다는 내용 뒤인 ③의 위치에 오는 것이 자연스럽다.

06 '~의 가치'를 의미하는 the value of를 쓰고 '가볍게 대화하다'라는 의미의 have a casual chat을 쓰되 전치사 of 뒤이므로 동명사형 having을 쓴다.

07 '여기에서 사는 것'이라는 의미로 문장의 주어 역할을 하는 동명사구 Living here와 '변화시켰다'라는 의미의 현재완료 has changed와 목적어 my life를 쓴다. '~한 방식으로'라는 의미의 in ways를 쓰고 '제가 가능하다고 생각하지 못했던'이라는 의미의 관계사절 I never thought possible로 마무리한다.

08 ① 필자의 말, When I have a problem, they always have useful advice to share.로 보아 일치하는 내용이다.
[오답] ② 필자는 Humanitas에 최소 1년 더 머물 계획이라고 했다.
③ 필자는 아직 배울 것이 많다고 했다.
④ 필자는 예전에는 안타까워했지만 지금은 그렇지 않다고 했다.
⑤ 필자는 세대 차이 극복에 한계가 있다고 말하지 않았다.

09 ⓐ 사역동사 make는 목적격 보어로 동사원형을 취하므로 laugh가 알맞다.
ⓑ place 뒤에는 '~할 장소'를 의미하는 형용사적 용법의 to부정사 to live가 알맞다.
ⓒ '~과 비교하여'라는 의미의 compared to 구문이므로 compared가 알맞다.

10 ④ 처음 젊은이들이 이웃으로 온다고 했을 때 모두 다 좋아한 것은 아니었지만 곧 분위기가 밝아지고 재미있어졌으므로 일치하는 내용이다.

오답 ① Helena Smit는 현재 93세이고, Humanitas에서 15년 동안 살았다고 했지, 93세에 입주했다고는 하지 않았다.
② Humanitas에서 15년 동안 거주할 수 있다는 내용은 없고, 단지 Helena가 15년 동안 거주해 왔다고 했다.
③ 처음 젊은이들이 이웃으로 온다고 했을 때 모두가 좋아하지는 않았다고 했다.
⑤ Helena는 학생들이 들려주는 큰 음악 소리가 가끔 들리지만 괜찮다고 했으며, 가장 싫어한다고 하지 않았다.

11 '격려와 지지를 받는 느낌'은 comfort(위로, 위안)의 설명이다.

12 문맥상 that difficult time은 젊은 이웃이 아버지를 잃고 힘들었던 시기를 가리킨다.

13 '~해야 할지'는 「의문사+to부정사」 형태의 명사구로 표현할 수 있다.
(A) '무엇을 해야 할지'는 what to do이다.
(B) '어떻게 복구해야 할지'는 how to recover이다.

14 Amy가 카페에서 받은 작은 메시지가 하루를 바꿨고, 친절을 베푸는 사람들은 그 영향력을 과소평가하지만, 받는 사람은 크게 느낀다는 내용이므로 ③ '우연한 친절 행위의 힘'이 주제로 적절하다.
오답 ① 감사를 표현하는 적절한 방법
② 감동적인 메시지를 쓰는 데 유용한 조언들
④ 한 잔의 커피가 주는 놀라운 효과
⑤ 친절한 서비스가 어떻게 손님을 행복하게 하는지

15 주어와 동사 she noticed와 목적어 a message를 쓴다. message를 수식하는 과거분사구 written on the cup으로 마무리한다.

16 recipient는 '수령인, 수취인, 받는 사람'이라는 뜻이다. 여기서는 문맥상 '친절을 받는 사람들'을 의미한다.

17 특별한 옷을 입거나 특별한 음식을 먹을 필요가 없다고 했으므로, ① '특별한 음식 먹기'와 ④ '특별한 옷 입기'는 친절한 행동의 예가 아니다.
오답 ② 지역 자선 단체에서 자원봉사하기
③ 누군가에 대해 좋은 말 하기
⑤ 누군가의 커피 값 내주기

내신 1등급 실전 3회 pp. 138~141

01 budget 02 ① 03 ⑤ 04 ① 05 (B)-(A)-(C)-(D) 06 ②
07 ④ 08 ③ 09 ② 10 ⑤ 11 ③ 12 ④ 13 (1) 지하철 칸에 들어가기 전에 승객이 나오는 것을 기다리기 (2) 특정 사람들을 위한 우대석에 앉지 말기 14 ④ → They taught us how to play some new games / They taught us how we could play some new games 15 ⑤ 16 ③ 17 ④

01 '어떤 목적을 위해 사용 가능하거나 배정된 금액'은 budget(예산, 비용)이다.

02 ① a yellow brick house는 문장의 보어이고, located는 문장의 동사가 아니라 앞에 있는 a yellow brick house를 후치 수식하는 과거분사이다.

03 빈 방이 많다는 점과 학생들이 높은 임대료 때문에 어려움을 겪는 점을 고려할 때, 무료 '숙소(accommodations)'가 가장 적절하다.
오답 ① 식사 ② 조언 ③ 책 ④ 돈

04 Humanitas의 빈 방을 대학생들에게 무료로 제공하는 대신, 학생들이 노인들과 시간을 보내도록 하여 노인과 대학생 모두에게 도움이 되는 상생 프로그램을 소개하고 있으므로 ①이 주제로 적절하다.

05 (B) 경기가 재미있었지만 쓰레기가 남아 있어 실망이라고 한다. - (A) 그 말에 공감하며 아쉬움을 표현한다. - (C) 쓰레기를 같이 치우자고 제안한다. - (D) 제안에 긍정으로 답한다.

06 ② at least는 '최소한, 적어도'라는 뜻으로 '한 달에 최소한 30시간'이라는 의미이다.

07 윗글의 as와 ⓒ, ⓔ의 as는 '~로서'라는 의미의 전치사이다.
오답 ⓐ: 접속사(~함에 따라)
ⓑ: 접속사(~할 때)
ⓓ: 접속사(~이기 때문에)
ⓐ 기술이 발전함에 따라 우리의 삶은 더 쉬워진다.
ⓑ 내가 방에 들어서자 모두가 나를 돌아보았다.
ⓒ Lucas는 팀 주장으로 선출되었다.
ⓓ 날씨가 나빴기 때문에 비행기가 지연되었다.
ⓔ Davis 선생님은 많은 젊은 학생들의 멘토 역할을 했다.

08 빈칸의 앞뒤로 상반되는 두 세대(노인과 젊은이)가 각각 얻는 이점을 설명하고 있으므로, ③ while(반면에)이 적절하다.

09 I want to thank you for helping me make new friends this year.로 보아 혜린이 태민에게 친구를 사귀도록 도와준 것에 대해 감사를 표현하기 위해 쓴 것임을 알 수 있으므로 ② '친구의 도움에 감사하기 위해'가 편지를 쓴 목적으로 알맞다.
오답 ① 새로운 활동을 제안하기 위해
③ 친구를 파티에 초대하기 위해
④ 내성적인 것에 대해 사과하기 위해
⑤ 친구 사귀는 것에 대한 조언을 구하기 위해

10 (A) '평생 동안 쌓은 많은 경험과 함께'라는 의미가 문맥상 자연스러우므로 With가 적절하다.
(B) 커피 한 잔을 하며 가볍게 대화하는 것의 '가치'를 노인들로부터 배웠다는 것이 문맥상 자연스러우므로 value가 적절하다.
(C) 노인들이 하지 못하는 것에만 집중해서 그들에게 '안타까움'을 느꼈다고 하는 것이 자연스러우므로 sorry가 적절하다.

11 ③ 「used to+동사원형」은 '(과거에) ~하곤 했다'라는 의미의 관용표현이다. '~하는 데 익숙하다'는 「be used to v-ing」 구문으로 표현한다.

12 ④ '특정 사람들을 위한(reserved for certain people)' 좌석은 '우대석, 노약자석(priority seats)'이다.
오답 ① 복도 ② 구석 ③ 창가 ⑤ 앞

13 (1) wait for passengers to exit before entering the train car의 내용이다.

22

(2) don't sit in priority seats reserved for certain people의 내용이다.

14 「teach+간접목적어+직접목적어」 구문이 되어야 한다. 직접목적어 자리에 「how+to부정사」 형태의 명사구가 오거나 「how+주어+ 조동사+동사원형」 형태의 명사절이 와야 한다.

15 ⑤ I sometimes hear loud music from my young next-door neighbor's apartment, but that is okay.로 보아 개의치 않았다는 것을 알 수 있다.

16 'I'는 이웃을 위로하고, 남을 도울 수 있음에 기뻐하는 성격으로 ③ generous(관대한)가 적절하다.
　[오답] ① 부끄러워하는 ② 이기적인 ④ 활기찬 ⑤ 비인격적인, 인간미 없는

17 (A) speaking of는 '~에 대해 말하자면'이라는 의미의 관용 표현이다.
　(B) 앞 절 전체를 선행사로 하는 계속적 용법의 관계대명사 which가 적절하다.
　(C) 동명사구(having young, vibrant people around) 주어는 단수 취급하므로 helps가 적절하다.

내신 **1등급 수능형 고난도**
pp. 142~145

| 01 ② | 02 ⑤ | 03 ③ | 04 ② | 05 ① | 06 ⑤ | 07 ② | 08 ① |
| 09 ⑤ | 10 ② | 11 ④ | 12 ② | 13 ① | 14 ④ | 15 ⑤ | 16 ③ | 17 ④ |

01 (A) 건물이나 장소가 어디에 '위치해 있다'는 의미로는 located가 적절하다.
　(B) 선행사가 사람일 때 관계대명사는 who가 적절하다.
　(C) money는 셀 수 없는 명사이므로 amount가 적절하다.

02 ⑤ 네덜란드 전역의 모든 요양원에서 시행되고 있다는 내용은 언급되지 않았으며, Humanitas라는 특정 요양원에 대한 사례이므로 일치하지 않는 내용이다.

03 ③ 마지막 문장, Now, let's hear more about this intriguing place from two of the residents.를 통해 '주거민의 의견, 경험, 소회'가 이어질 것임을 예고하고 있다.

04 많은 학생들이 그 지역의 비싼 집세를 감당하기 어려워하고 있었고, 그래서 그 제안은 진정한 윈윈(win-win) 상황이 되었다. 그 결과, 노인들과 학생들 모두가 이 방식에서 혜택을 얻었다.
　[오답] ① 대조적으로 ③ 그럼에도 불구하고
　④ 예를 들어 ⑤ 다른 한편으로, 반면에

05 ① Jacob이 2년 넘게 살고 있는 것이므로 현재완료 진행형 have been living이 적절하다.

06 ⑤ teach them things, such as how to use social media로 보아 Jacob은 노인들에게 소셜 미디어 사용법을 가르치고 있으므로, 일치하지 않는다.

07 문맥상 평생에 걸쳐 '모아진' 경험이라는 의미가 자연스러우므로 gathered가 가장 적절하다.
　[오답] ① 낭비된 ③ 무시된 ④ 나누어진 ⑤ 공유된

08 ① '(과거에) ~하곤 했다'라는 의미의 「used to+동사원형」 구문으로 feeling이 아니라 feel이 적절하다.

09 (C) 공동체로서 Humanitas에서의 생활과 배움 → (A) 공동체 생활을 통해 변화된 자신의 시각과 깊어진 관계 → (B) 앞으로의 계획과 감사의 마음

10 주어진 문장의 it이 가리키는 내용이 '젊은이들을 이웃으로 두는 것 (have young people as neighbors)'이므로 ②의 위치가 가장 적절하다.

11 (A) 뒤에 오는 비교급 more를 수식하는 부사가 필요하므로 a lot이 적절하다. a lot of는 뒤에 명사가 온다.
　(B) '~하는 방법'이라는 의미의 명사구 how to play가 적절하다.
　(C) '~하는 것'이라는 의미의 선행사를 포함하는 관계대명사 what이 적절하다.

12 아버지를 잃은 후 힘든 시간을 겪었다고 했으므로, ② '슬픔(grief)'이 가장 적절하다.
　[오답] ① 경이, 놀라움 ③ 안도, 안심
　④ 흥분, 신남, 기대감 ⑤ 실망, 낙담

13 (A) 어려운 시기에 '위로'가 되었다고 하는 것이 자연스러우므로 comfort가 적절하다.
　(B) 다른 사람들을 위해 무언가 '할 수 있다'는 것을 의미하므로 capable이 적절하다.
　(C) 젊고 '활기찬' 사람들로 인해 통증을 잊고 삶을 즐길 수 있었다는 의미이므로 vibrant가 적절하다.
　[오답] (A) conflict: 분쟁, 갈등 (B) careful: 신중한
　(C) violent: 폭력적인

14 I truly appreciate what you did for me 등에서 편지 내내 감사의 마음이 반복적으로 표현되고 있으므로 ④ grateful(감사하는, 고마워하는)이 가장 적절하다.
　[오답] ① 걱정하는, 염려하는
　② 짜증나는, 화가 난
　③ 무관심한, 개의치 않는
　⑤ 실망한, 낙담한

15 편지의 전체적인 메시지는 친구의 도움으로 태민이 내성적인 성격을 극복하고 새로운 환경에 잘 적응할 수 있었다는 점이므로 ⑤ '친구의 친절은 누군가가 수줍음을 극복하는 데 도움이 될 수 있다.'가 요지로 적절하다.
　[오답] ① 조용한 것이 외향적인 것보다 더 낫다.
　② 새로운 친구를 사귀는 것은 항상 쉽다.
　③ 방과 후에 활동을 하는 것이 중요하다.
　④ 학교에서 도움을 요청하는 것은 중요하다.

16 윗글은 '작은 친절의 행위가 생각보다 훨씬 큰 힘을 가지고 있으며, 우리는 그 영향력을 과소평가하는 경향이 있다'는 실험 결과와 메시지를 전달하고 있으므로 ③ '친절의 힘: 당신이 생각한 것보다 더 강하다'가 제목으로 적절하다.

오답 ① 친절한 행동은 사람들을 하나로 모으는 열쇠이다
② 우리가 종종 다른 사람에게 친절을 베푸는 것을 망설이는 이유
④ 한 잔의 핫초콜릿이 우리에게 친절에 대해 가르쳐 줄 수 있는 것
⑤ 친절한 행동이 우리의 뇌에 미치는 영향

17 ④ 실제 연구 결과가 핫초콜릿을 받은 사람이 준 사람이 기대한 것보다 높게 평가했다는 것이 자연스러우므로 lower가 아니라 higher가 적절하다.

내신 1등급 서술형

pp. 146~148

01 It is a care center that houses more than 160 elderly residents who require assistance.
02 (1) ⓐ, ⓓ (2) ⓑ, ⓒ
03 (1) go through (2) in exchange for
(3) hang out with (4) rush around
04 (1) With so much experience gathered over a lifetime
(2) the value of having a casual chat over a cup of coffee
05 to take a break from rushing around all the time
06 처음에는 노인들이 할 수 없는 일에만 집중하여 그들을 안타깝게 여겼으나, 지금은 그들이 할 수 있는 많은 것들을 보게 되었고, 그들의 다양한 능력을 인정하게 되었다.
07 residents
08 (A) for (B) as (C) about (D) in
09 (1) They make us laugh and create a joyful mood.
(2) They taught us how to play some new games
10 (1) grief (2) comfort (3) vibrant
11 ③ to feel → feel: 사역동사 make는 목적격 보어로 동사원형을 취한다.
⑤ help → helps: 동명사구가 주어인 경우 단수 취급하므로 동사도 3인칭 단수 현재형을 써야 한다.
12 작은 친절이 연쇄적으로 좋은 결과를 가져오는 것
13 (1) 지역 자선단체에서 자원봉사하기
(2) 누군가에게 좋은 말 해주기
(3) 누군가에게 커피 한 잔 사주기

---

01 선행사가 a care center로 단수이므로 단수 동사 houses가 적절하고, 선행사가 residents로 사람이므로 관계대명사 who가 적절하다.

02 ⓐ 우리는 그들의 지혜와 인생 경험으로부터 배울 수 있다.
ⓑ 다른 의사 소통 방식을 가진다는 것은 때때로 오해를 불러일으킬 수 있다.
ⓒ 생활방식과 가치관의 차이를 감당하기 어려울 수 있다.
ⓓ 우리는 그들과 함께 사는 동안 정서적인 지지를 받을 수 있다.

03 (1) ~을 겪다: go through
(2) ~의 대가로: in exchange for
(3) ~와 시간을 보내다: hang out with
(4) 분주히 돌아다니다: rush around

04 (1) 「with+명사+과거분사」 형태로 쓴다.
(2) 「명사+of+동명사」 형태로 쓴다.

05 명사를 수식하는 to부정사구 to take a break를 쓰고 from rushing around all the time으로 완성한다.

07 문맥상 '거주자'라는 의미의 resident가 필요한데 복수형으로 써야 하므로 residents가 적절하다.

08 (A) for: ~동안 (B) as: ~로서 (C) about: ~에 관하여
(D) in one's 20s: 20대에

09 (1) 「make+목적어+동사원형」 구문으로 laugh가 적절하다.
(2) 「의문사+to부정사」 형태의 명사구로 how to play가 적절하다.

10 (1) 큰 슬픔, 비통: 누군가를 잃은 데서 오는 깊은 슬픔
(2) 위로, 위안: 격려와 위로의 느낌
(3) 활기찬: 에너지와 생기가 넘치는

12 a chain reaction은 한 사람의 작은 친절이 또 다른 친절을 낳고, 그 친절이 다시 다른 사람에게 이어지면서 계속해서 좋은 행동이 확산되는 현상을 의미한다.

13 How about volunteering at a local charity? We can also say nice things about someone or pay for someone's cup of coffee.에서 Pay It Forward Day에 사람들이 할 수 있는 일이 언급되어 있다.

01 ②　**02** ③　**03** (1) useful　(2) exploration　(3) removal
(4) harmless　(5) resident　(6) valuable　(7) proposal　(8)
participant　**04** (1) possess　(2) draw　(3) seek　(4) generate
05 ④　**06** ⑤　**07** ④　**08** ②　**09** ③　**10** ②　**11** ⑤　**12** ①　**13** It was
his hard work and talent that eventually led him to a position
at Disney at the age of 37.　**14** ⓐ Having　ⓑ becomes　ⓒ
less　ⓓ accepting　**15** ④　**16** ④　**17** (1) ⓑ: play → to play / ask
는 목적격 보어로 to부정사를 취한다. (2) ⓔ: will leave → leave /
조건의 if절에서는 미래의 일이라도 현재시제를 사용한다.　**18** ③　**19** ③
20 ⑤　**21** ③　**22** ③　**23** ②　**24** ④　**25** ⑤

---

01 투어를 시작하기 전 방문객에게 미술관에서 지켜야 할 규칙을 안내
하고 있으므로 ② '방문객에게 미술관의 규칙을 상기시키기 위해'가
목적으로 적절하다.
　오답 ① 미술관의 역사를 설명하기 위해
　③ 방문객에게 일시적인 폐쇄를 알리기 위해
　④ 새로운 전시회 개막을 홍보하기 위해
　⑤ 전시 중인 작품들에 대한 정보를 제공하기 위해

02 ③ to prevent damage(손상을 막기 위해)라는 목적에 가장 부합
하는 행동은 '작품을 만지지 않는 것'이다.
　오답 ① 소지품을 가방에 넣고 다니지 않기
　② 친구와 대화하지 않기
　④ 다른 사람들에게 무례하게 말하지 않기
　⑤ 더 안전한 장소로 작품 옮기기

03 (1) use(사용)의 형용사형은 useful(유용한, 쓸모 있는)이다.
　(2) explore(탐험하다, 탐구하다)의 명사형은 exploration(탐험,
탐구)이다.
　(3) remove(제거하다, 없애다)의 명사형은 removal(제거, 철거)이
다.
　(4) harmful(해로운)의 반의어는 harmless(해롭지 않은, 무해한)
이다.
　(5) reside(거주하다)의 사람을 나타내는 명사형은 resident(거주
자, 주민)이다.
　(6) value(가치)의 형용사형은 valuable(가치 있는, 소중한)이다.
　(7) propose(제안하다)의 명사형은 proposal(제안)이다.
　(8) participate(참가하다, 참여하다)의 사람을 나타내는 명사형은
participant(참가자, 참여자)이다.

04 (1) 광범위한 '지식(knowledge)'을 가지고 있다는 의미로
possess가 알맞다.
　(2) '주의(attention)'를 끈다는 의미로 draw가 알맞다.
　(3) 제조업자가 문제의 '해결책(solution)'을 계속 찾았다는 의미로
seek가 알맞다.
　(4) '전기(electricity)'를 만들어 낸다는 의미로 generate가
알맞다.

05 habit stacking이라는 방법을 통해 좋은 습관을 쉽게 형성하는
법을 안내하고 있으므로 ④가 주제로 적절하다.

06 ⑤ 문맥상 그것이 얼마나 쉬운지 보라는 의미의 see how easy it
is가 되어야 한다. difficult는 앞뒤 내용과 모순되어 문맥상 적절하
지 않다.

07 ④ succeed는 「succeed in v-ing」 형태로 써야 하므로,
succeeded in developing이 적절하다.

08 ② As a young man, he dreamed of becoming a pilot, but
then he broke both of his arms in a terrible car accident.
를 통해 두 팔이 모두 부러졌고 조종사의 꿈을 포기했다는 것을
알 수 있으므로 일치하지 않는 내용이다.

09 ③ alert(경계하는)의 영어 뜻풀이는 watchful and ready to
act(주의 깊게 지켜보고 즉시 행동할 준비가 된)이다. without
much thought(깊이 생각하지 않고)는 careless(부주의한)의
영어 뜻풀이이다.
　오답 ① 타당성: 옳거나 건전함의 성질
　② 진단하다: 질병이나 문제의 원인을 확인하다
　④ 기회: 무언가를 하거나 성취할 수 있게 만드는 상황
　⑤ 계산: 수학을 사용하여 답을 찾는 과정

10 ② reliable(믿을 만한)의 영어 뜻풀이는 able to be trusted(신뢰
할 수 있는, 믿을 수 있는)이다. appropriate or rational(알맞거나
논리적인)은 reasonable(합리적인, 타당한)의 영어 뜻풀이이다.
　오답 ① 조사하다: 어떤 것을 더 깊이 살펴보다
　③ 큰 슬픔, 비통: 누군가를 잃어서 생기는 극심한 슬픔
　④ 거주자, 주민: 어떤 곳에 영구적으로 또는 오랫동안 사는 사람
　⑤ 끈기: 어렵더라도 어떤 일을 계속할 수 있게 해주는 성질

11 김상진이 색각 이상이라는 어려움에도 불구하고 예술에 대한 열정과
끈기로 꿈을 포기하지 않고, 결국 디즈니 최초의 한국인 애니메이터
가 된 과정을 다루고 있으므로 ⑤가 제목으로 적절하다.

12 (A) 그림 그리는 것에 열정적이었다는 앞 문장과 대조적인 색약 진단
으로 인해 꿈에 지장이 간 내용이 나오므로 However(그러나)가
적절하다.
　(B) 색약 진단을 불행이라고 여기는 대신 사소한 문제로 여겼다고
하는 것이 자연스러우므로 Instead(대신에)가 적절하다.
　(C) 경제학을 전공했지만, 색을 쓰지 않는 미술 관련 직업을 찾았다
는 점에서 Although(비록 ~이지만)가 적절하다.
　오답 ② 그럼에도 불구하고 – 한편 – ~ 때문에
　③ 그러므로 – 예를 들어 – ~이기 때문에
　④ 게다가 – 그러므로 – ~ 후에
　⑤ 그렇지 않으면 – 마찬가지로 – ~하지 않는다면

13 주어 his hard work and talent를 It was와 that 사이에 넣고
나머지를 that 이하에 쓴다.

14 ⓐ 동명사 주어가 필요하므로 Having이 적절하다.
　ⓑ 조건절(if)에서는 미래시제 대신 현재시제를 써야 하므로
becomes가 적절하다.
　ⓒ 「the+비교급 ~, the+비교급 …」 구문으로 little의 비교급 less
가 적절하다.

ⓓ 동격을 나타내는 전치사 of 뒤에는 동명사가 오므로 accepting 이 적절하다.

15 (A) 하루에 35,000번의 결정을 모두 의식적으로 내리는 것은 불가능하므로 impossible이 적절하다.
(B) 두뇌가 가끔 게으른 것은 에너지 절약 측면에서 효과적이므로 effective가 적절하다.
(C) 게으른 두뇌 습관을 기르는 것은 해로울 수 있으므로 harmful이 적절하다.

16 (C) 수의사가 되고 싶은 동기와 계기 – (A) 대학 진학 및 수의학 공부에 대한 앞으로의 계획 – (B) 수의사가 된 이후의 미래 계획

17 (1) 「ask+목적어+to부정사」 구문으로 to부정사가 적절하다.
(2) 「if+주어+현재동사, 주어+will/shall/can/may+동사원형」 구문으로 현재시제가 적절하다.

18 ③은 '학생들의 시간 관리 어려움'에 대한 내용으로, Jacob의 Humanitas 생활이나 노인 이웃과의 활동과는 직접적인 연관이 없다.

19 문맥상 they는 Jacob이 함께 생활하며 교류하는 이웃들을 가리킨다. Jacob은 이웃들과 시간을 보내며 그들로부터 인생 경험과 지혜를 배우고 있다고 언급하고 있다.

20 ⑤ 마지막 문장에서 at first는 System 1에 의해 즉각적으로 답하는 것을 의미한다. 하지만 System 1은 실수가 잦으므로, 사람들은 처음에 '정확하게(correctly)'가 아니라 '부정확하게(incorrectly)' 답하는 것이 일반적이라고 하는 것이 자연스럽다.

21 이 글은 System 2의 역할과 특징, 그리고 System 1과의 차이점을 설명하며 정보를 제공하는 데 초점을 두고 있으므로 ③ '정보를 제공하고 설명하는'이 어조로 적절하다.
[오답] ① 창의적이고 상상력이 풍부한
② 비판적이고 논리적인
④ 희망적이고 긍정적인
⑤ 묘사적이고 서술적인

22 Helena Smit는 학생들과의 교류 덕분에 Humanitas의 생활이 훨씬 더 즐겁고 활기차졌다고 했으므로 ③ '더 활기찬'이 가장 적절하다.
[오답] ① 더 외로운 ② 더 지루한 ④ 더 불편한 ⑤ 더 위험한

23 not everyone was happy about it으로 보아 처음에 학생들이 이사 온다는 소식에 모든 노인들이 기뻐한 것은 아니라고 했다. 오히려 처음에는 일부가 불만이었으나, 학생들이 실제로 이사 온 후 분위기가 바뀌었다고 설명하고 있으므로 ②는 일치하지 않는 내용이다.

24 pay it forward(선행을 돌려주는 것의 힘)라는 개념과 그것이 사회에 긍정적인 파급 효과를 가져 온다는 내용의 글이므로 ④ '선행 나누기의 힘'이 가장 적절하다.
[오답] ① 새로운 친구를 사귀는 안내서
② 호의를 직접 보답하는 방법
③ 영화 속 친절의 역사
⑤ 친절은 왜 비밀로 해야 하는가

25 (A) 「help+목적어+동사원형」 구문으로 move가 적절하다.
(B) Trevor라는 '이름의' 소년이라는 의미로 과거분사 named가 적절하다.
(C) suggest의 목적어로 doing과 asking이 병렬 연결되는 구조이므로 asking이 적절하다.

Spark Your Creativity

교과서 **어휘 익히기** .... p. 157

01 묘사하다	26 potential	
02 독창성	27 innovative	
03 빤히 쳐다보다	28 extraordinary	
04 즉시	29 portrait	
05 색다른	30 illusion	
06 재치 있는, 익살맞은	31 exclusive	
07 강조하다, 돋보이다	32 laundry	
08 특징적인	33 arrange	
09 가정(용)의	34 adjustment	
10 확인하다	35 element	
11 ~을 보다	36 belief	
12 (말한 순서대로) 각각	37 edible	
13 드러내다	38 visual	
14 일반적인, 보통의	39 upside down	
15 뒤집을 수 있는	40 interactive	
16 조정하다	41 observation	
17 발상	42 admit	
18 눈에 띄는	43 keen	
19 만들다	44 acceptable	
20 창작물	45 belong to	
21 특출난	46 examination	
22 휙 뒤집다, 젖히다	47 composite	
23 대표, 전형	48 surrealism	
24 운동복 상의	49 give a glance	
25 웃기는, 재미나는	50 approach	

교과서 **핵심 문법** .... pp. 158~161

POINT 1 부사절의 「주어+be동사」 생략

Q 1 reading 2 Though 3 asked

Check-Up
01 (1) unless given permission
(2) While young
(3) Although exhausted
(4) once used
02 (1) While I was walking
(2) If they were given a chance
(3) Though we were uncertain
(4) Since she was feeling tired
03 (A) seated (B) when (C) scheduled

Q 1. 추리 소설을 읽으면서, 나는 범인의 다음 움직임을 예측하려고 했다.
2. 실망했음에도 불구하고, Kevin은 마지막 경기까지 최선을 다했다.
3. 그녀의 행방에 대해 질문을 받았을 때, 그녀의 부모님은 침묵을 지켰다.

Check-Up
01 부사절의 주어가 주절의 주어와 일치하고 be동사로 되어 있으면 「주어+be동사」를 생략하고, 「접속사+분사/형용사」로 간결하게 표현할 수 있다.
(1) 허락을 받지 않으면 자리를 이동할 수 없다.
(2) 젊었을 때, 삼촌은 혼자 세계를 여행했다.
(3) 지쳤지만 선수들은 축구 시합을 위해 열심히 연습했다.
(4) 한번 사용되면 바늘은 폐기되어야 한다.

02 「접속사+분사/형용사」는 부사절의 주어가 주절의 주어와 일치하고 동사가 be동사일 때 주어와 동사를 생략하여 간략하게 나타내는 표현이다. 원래의 부사절은 「접속사+주어+be동사+분사/형용사」로 나타낸다.
(1) 거리를 걸어 내려가며 나는 엄마의 차를 봤다.
(2) 기회가 주어진다면 그들은 전국을 여행할 것이다.
(3) 미래에 관해 확신이 없었지만 우리는 낙관적이려고 노력했다.
(4) 피곤했기 때문에 그녀는 모임에 참석하지 않기로 했다.

03 승객 여러분, 탑승을 환영합니다. 다음 안내 방송에 주의를 기울여 주시기 바랍니다. 첫째, 자리에 앉아 계실 때에는 반드시 안전벨트를 착용해 주십시오. 둘째, 여러분의 안전을 위해서 승무원의 요청이 있을 때 협조해 주시길 바랍니다. 우리 비행기는 예정된 대로 2시간 후에 시카고에 도착할 것입니다. 즐거운 비행 되십시오!

(A) while you are seated를 줄인 표현이므로 seated가 적절하다.
(B) '~할 때'라는 의미이므로 접속사 when이 적절하다.
(C) 부사절 as it is scheduled에서 「주어+be동사」가 생략된 형태이므로 과거분사가 적절하다.

POINT 2 대동사 do를 이용한 표현

Q 1 Doing 2 do 3 so

Check-Up
01 (1) try on the clothes (at the store)
(2) Booking the hotel in advance
(3) built some birdhouses (in the forest)
(4) applied for a passport
02 (1) I didn't do so
(2) Unless you do so
(3) requested me to do so
(4) By doing so
03 (A) Resting your forehead on the floor and relaxing your entire body
(B) maintain your balance

Q 1. 안전 수칙을 명심해라. 그렇게 하면 비상시에 도움이 될 것이다.
2. 우리는 TV로 야구 경기를 보고 싶었지만, 그렇게 할 수 없었다.
3. 진실을 말하라는 요청을 받았을 때, 그는 주저하지 않고 그렇게 했다.

01 do so는 앞에 쓰인 일반동사와 동사의 목적어나 보어의 반복을 피하기 위해 사용한다. 시제, 태, 용법에 따라 **do so, doing so, did so, done so** 등 다양한 형태를 취한다.

(1) 가게에서 옷을 입어보고 싶다면 편하게 그리 해도 된다.

(2) 미리 호텔을 예약하는 게 어때? 그렇게 하는 것이 시간과 돈을 아껴줄 것이다.

(3) 우리는 숲에 새집을 지으려 계획했고, 지난 일요일에 그렇게 했다.

(4) 아직 하지 않았다면 여권을 신청해야 한다.

02 일반동사와 동사의 목적어 또는 보어의 반복을 피하기 위해 **do so**를 써서 나타낸다.

03
> 초보자를 위한 기본 요가
> 〈1〉아기 자세
> • 무릎을 꿇고 앉아서 시작한다. 그런 다음 상체를 낮추며 부드럽게 앞으로 숙인다.
> • 이마를 바닥에 대고 몸 전체에 힘을 뺀다. 그렇게 하는 것은 당신이 가지고 있을 수도 있는 허리 통증을 완화해 줄 것이다.
> 〈2〉나무 자세
> • 양발을 모으고 곧게 선다. 무게 중심을 오른쪽 다리로 옮기고 천천히 왼쪽 발을 바닥에서 들어 올린다.
> • 균형을 유지한다. 서 있는 발을 바닥으로 단단히 누르면 그렇게 하는 데에 도움이 될 것이다.

do so는 앞에 쓰인 일반동사와 동사의 목적어나 보어를 대신하는 표현이다.

교과서 **본문 익히기** ❶ 옳은 어법·어휘 고르기 ···pp. 169~171

01 what	02 quality, or
03 that, those	04 however
05 takes	06 creativity
07 hidden	08 not
09 familiar	10 called
11 Created, striking	12 are arranged
13 while	14 representative
15 objects	16 Another
17 bowl	18 down
19 with	20 still, made
21 because, doing	22 which
23 is	24 imaginative
25 who	26 Take
27 hanging	28 by
29 to look	30 been called
31 best	32 while
33 adding, into	34 crossing
35 nothing	36 creativity
37 find	38 puppies
39 putting	40 What
41 that	42 staring
43 at	44 what
45 exclusive	46 that
47 Whether	48 so
49 glance	50 might

교과서 **본문 익히기** ❷ 틀린 부분 고치기 ·········pp. 172~174

01 either born with or without	02 that we can be divided
03 far from	04 to be creative
05 ○	06 by looking
07 hidden	08 both depict
09 ○	10 Created by
11 other objects	12 paintings
13 When viewed	14 transformed into
15 ones	16 made
17 doing so	18 ○
19 works is	20 ○
21 who came after	22 ○
23 you to look, what	24 has been called
25 best known for	26 while
27 By simply adding	28 crossing
29 nothing more than	30 that highlights
31 ○	32 made of sliced
33 while (she was) putting	34 her secret is
35 her to make	36 trying
37 ○	38 to continuously produce
39 that belongs	40 (that) we choose
41 ○	42 something extraordinary
43 give them	44 that sparks

교과서 **본문 익히기** ❸ 빈칸 완성하기 ···········pp. 175~179

(1) instantly pops into your mind

(2) that only artists and writers possess

(3) accept the idea that

(4) those who are not

(5) This common belief

(6) the ability to be creative

(7) just takes a little effort

(8) spark their creativity

(9) hidden within these common objects

(10) Look at

(11) Believe it or not

(12) as it is a standard style

(13) is very unconventional

(14) striking creativity and originality

(15) like the pieces of a puzzle

(16) act as the pink cheeks

(17) the artist's signature style

(18) to create many other portraits

(19) Another good example

(20) When viewed normally

(21) when flipped upside down

(22) have studied this painting

(23) made some adjustments to create faces

(24) sometimes changed the positions

(25) Why did he make

(26) because he wanted to add

(27) as if they are playing

(28) is a careful study

(29) such as a bowl of vegetables

(30) His innovative approach to

(31) Take a look at

(32) standing in a field

(33) hanging on a clothesline

(34) witty and amusing creation

(35) Using everyday items

(36) force you to look twice

(37) has been called

(38) best known for

(39) while she was hanging her laundry

(40) By simply adding

(41) she was able to transform

(42) standing on some hills

(43) crossing the desert

(44) nothing more than

(45) Another series that highlights

(46) you can find in any kitchen

(47) a pair of puppies made of

(48) she came up with the concept

(49) do you think

(50) it is

(51) that allow her to make

(52) would spend time staring at

(53) longer than is acceptable

(54) what enables her to continuously produce

(55) exceptional skill that belongs

(56) anytime we choose to

(57) Whether we realize it or not

(58) By doing so

(59) has never been seen before

(60) but don't just give them

(61) discover something that sparks

내신 1등급 어휘 공략   pp. 180~181

01 ②　02 ②　03 ④　04 ①　05 ③　06 ④　07 ②　08 ④

01 ② 앞 문장의 흐름에 따라 많은 사람들은 우리가 창의적인 사람과 그렇지 않은 사람으로 나뉜다는 생각을 '받아들인다'고 해야 자연스러우므로, ② doubt가 아닌 accept가 쓰여야 한다.

02 왼쪽의 그림은 일반적이지만(standard) 오른쪽의 그림은 ② '색다르다'가 문맥상 자연스러우므로 unconventional이 알맞다.

03 ④ 정물화: still life painting
오답 ① normally: 정상적으로　② transform: 변형하다
③ reversible: 뒤집을 수 있는　⑤ adjustment: 수정, 보정

04 (A) interactive: 상호작용하는　(B) typical: 전형적인, 일상의
(C) approach: 접근법
오답 (A) international: 국제적인　(B) unique: 독창적인
(C) aspect: 측면

05 (A) confirm: 확인하다　(B) inspiration: 영감
(C) transform: 바꾸다
오답 (A) conform: 따르다　(B) interest: 관심
(C) transfer: 옮기다

06 (A) '놀라운'이라는 의미의 astonishing이 적절하다.
(B) '쌍'이라는 의미의 pair가 적절하다.
(C) '각각'이라는 의미의 respectively가 적절하다.
오답 (A) amused: 즐거운　(B) fair: 공정한; 장터
(C) respectfully: 공손하게

07 (A) active: 능동적인, 적극적인　(B) admit: 인정하다
(C) produce: 만들어 내다
오답 (A) passive: 수동적인　(B) permit: 허용하다
(C) consume: 소비하다

08 ④ 문맥상 '빠르게' 힐끗 보지 말고 주의 깊게 보라는 내용이므로 thorough(빈틈 없는, 철저한) 대신 quick을 써야 한다.
오답 ① belong: 속하다　② constantly: 지속적으로
③ extraordinary: 비범한, 특이한　⑤ spark: 촉발시키다

내신 1등급 어법 공략   pp. 182~183

01 ③　02 ②　03 ①　04 ⑤　05 ④　06 ②　07 ④　08 ②

01 ③ the idea와 동격의 명사절을 이끄는 접속사 that이 필요하다.

02 ② '~라고 불리는'이라는 수동의 의미이므로 과거분사 형태(called)가 적절하다.

03 ① other reversible paintings를 대신하므로 one이 아닌 복수 형태 ones를 써야 한다.
오답 ② 목적어로 쓰이는 명사절을 이끄는 접속사이다.
③ make의 목적격 보어로 쓰인 형용사이다.

④ 앞에 쓰인 동사구 making his paintings reversible을 대신한다.
⑤ 앞의 절을 선행사로 하는 계속적 용법의 관계대명사이다.

04 (A) a horse와 능동의 관계이므로 현재분사가 적절하다.
(B) force+목적어+to-v: (목적어)가 ~하게 (강요)하다
(C) 그녀의 독특한 스타일이 '불려온' 것이므로 현재완료 수동태가 적절하다.

05 (A) 앞에 Another가 수식하고 있으므로 series는 단수로 쓰였고, 이를 수식하는 관계사절의 동사도 단수 형태가 적절하다.
(B) '만들어진'이라는 의미의 과거분사 형태가 알맞다.
(C) while she was putting에서 주어와 be동사를 생략한 형태이다.

06 ② it is ~ that 강조 구문으로 her active observation skills를 강조하고 있다. which가 아닌 that을 써야 한다.

07 ④ 선행사 something과 관계사절의 동사 see는 수동의 관계이므로, 현재완료 수동태 has never been seen으로 나타내야 한다.

08 (A) 앞에 나온 exercise를 대신하므로 it이 적절하다.
(B) 앞에 쓰인 negative emotions를 선행사로 하는 계속적 용법의 관계대명사이므로 which가 적절하다.
(C) go와 함께 병렬 연결되어 lead A to-v의 구문으로 쓰이고 있으므로 동사원형이 자연스럽다.

내신 1등급 실전 1회
pp. 184~187

01 ② **02** ③ **03** Everyone has the ability to be creative. **04** ①
05 ② **06** (1) depict (2) originality **07** upside down **08** ①
09 ③ **10** it is her active observation skills that allow her to make magic out of the ordinary **11** ⑤ **12** ① **13** ⑤ **14** (1) 책을 사고, 팔고, 교환하는 학교 행사를 준비한다. (2) 필요 없는 책을 모아 지역 도서관에 기증한다. **15** (1) Exercise (2) blood **16** ②

01 남학생의 일일 창의적 도전 활동에 여학생이 공감하며, 어떻게 하는지 활동에 대한 조언을 얻고 있으므로, 대화의 주제로는 ② '일일 창의력 도전에 대한 충고'가 가장 적절하다.
오답 ① 그림 그리기 실력을 키우는 방법
③ 매일 간단한 과업을 하는 것의 이점
④ 복잡한 일을 단순하게 만드는 방법
⑤ 전화기로 사진을 찍는 팁

02 여학생이 자신도 창의력을 증진시키는 활동을 하고 싶다고 말하며 조언을 구하면, 남학생이 주어진 문장과 같이 답을 하고, 주어진 문장의 구체적인 이유를 설명하는 내용이 이어지는 것이 자연스럽다.

03 창의적인 능력은 원래 타고나는 것이라는 일반적인 믿음은 '진실'과 동떨어진 것으로, 진실은 바로 뒤에 언급된 문장, 즉 모든 사람은 창의력을 발휘할 수 있는 능력을 지니고 있다는 것이다.

04 • into your mind: 당신의 마음에
• turn A into B: A를 B로 바꾸다

05 ② 오른쪽의 그림은 Arcimboldo에 의해 제작된 〈Vertumnus〉라는 작품이지만, 왼쪽의 그림을 누가 그렸는지는 언급되지 않았다.

06 (1) 그림에서 누군가 또는 무언가를 그리다: depict(묘사하다)
(2) 특이하게 새롭고 다른 성질: originality(독창성)

07 거꾸로: upside down

08 doing so는 앞에 나온 일반동사 표현의 반복을 피하기 위해 사용하는 것으로, 바로 앞 문장의 make his paintings reversible(그림을 뒤집을 수 있도록 만드는 것)을 가리킨다.

09 ③ Brad Pet을 완성하는 데에 얼마나 걸렸는지는 알 수 없다.
오답 ① 〈먹을 수 있는 존재들〉을 만드는 데에 무엇이 쓰였는가? → 빵, 양상추 등 식재료
② Crunchie의 아이디어를 떠올렸을 때 그녀는 무엇을 하고 있었는가? → 샐러드를 만들고 있었다.
④ 아이였을 때 그녀는 적극적인 관찰 기술을 어떻게 보여 주었는가? → 침대의 나무 무늬를 보며 시간을 보냈다.
⑤ 그녀가 상상력이 풍부한 예술작품을 만들 수 있도록 한 것은 무엇인가? → 예리한 관찰력

10 문장의 주어, 목적어, 또는 부사구를 it is ~ that 구문을 사용하여 강조할 수 있다. It is와 that 사이에 강조하고자 하는 표현을 넣어 나타낸다.

11 창의력은 한정된 집단의 특출난 기술이 아니다.
(C) 그것(=창의력)은 우리 일상의 일부로서 우리가 인식하지 못하더라도 발휘하며 살고 있다.
(A) 그렇게 하여 평범한 것들을 새로운 것으로 변화시키고 있다.
(B) 주위를 주의 깊게 살펴보는 것이 중요하다.

12 창의력은 특별한 사람들의 전유물이 아니며, 주위를 유심히 관찰함으로써 키울 수 있는 능력이라는 것이 글의 요지이다.

13 (A) 전치사 by의 목적어로 쓰이는 동명사가 적절하다.
(B) 선행사가 의미상 관계사절의 부사구 역할을 하므로(at the school event) 관계부사 where가 적절하다.
(C) collecting과 함께 suggest의 목적어 역할을 하므로 동명사가 적절하다.

14 학년말에 버려지는 책 쓰레기를 줄이는 방법으로 두 가지를 제안하고 있다.

15 운동은 신체에 도움이 되고 또한 당신을 보다 창의적으로 만들어 줄 수 있다. 그것은 기분을 좋게 만들고 혈류를 증가시켜 두뇌가 더 잘 작동하도록 도와주며, 당신을 새로운 아이디어에 노출시킨다.

16 운동이 신체 건강뿐 아니라 창의력을 키우는 데에도 도움이 된다는 내용의 글이다. 운동이 창의력을 키우는 데 도움이 되는 이유는 우리의 기분을 좋게 만들고 ② '창의력을 제약하는 요소인' 부정적인 감정을 줄여주기 때문이다.
오답 ① 창의력을 증진할 수 있는
③ 보다 강력한 관계의 주요 원인인
④ 늘어난 스트레스로 예방할 수 있는
⑤ 정신 건강을 위해 피해야 하는

01 (1) treadmill (2) creativity **02** next time you're faced with a task that requires creativity, I suggest **03** ④ **04** ⓐ (C), (E) ⓑ (B) **05** ④ **06** ④ **07** ① **08** ② **09** ③ **10** puppies **11** Keen observation **12** ③ **13** ⑤ **14** ① **15** ⓐ Creation ⓑ Creativity **16** ⑤ **17** collecting unwanted books and donating them to our local library

01 연구에 따르면 트레드밀에서 걷는 것이 앉아 있는 것과 비교했을 때 창의적 사고를 두 배 많이 생산했다. 그러므로 걷기는 창의력을 효과적으로 신장한다.

02 next time이 접속사처럼 절과 절을 연결할 수 있다. 동사 suggest 뒤에는 명사절이 이어진다.

03 창의력은 타고나는 것이라고 생각하는 사람이 많지만, 실제로 창의력은 누구든 조금만 노력을 기울이면 키울 수 있다는 것이 글의 주요 내용이다.

04 ⓐ 선행사를 수식하는 형용사절을 이끄는 관계대명사이다.
ⓑ 앞에 쓰인 the idea와 동격의 명사절을 이끄는 접속사이다.
오답 (A) It is[was] ~ that 형태의 강조구문이다.
(D) It seems that ~: ~인 것 같다

05 단락의 첫문장이 Another good example of Arcimboldo's unique creativity ...로 시작하고 있으므로, 이 단락의 앞에서는 Arcimboldo의 다른 작품에 관해 다루었을 것이다.

06 주어진 문장이 이유를 묻고 있으므로, 뒤에는 그 이유를 설명하는 문장이 이어지는 것이 자연스럽다. ④ 뒤의 It was probably because ....가 이유를 설명하고 있으므로 주어진 문장은 ④에 들어가야 한다.

07 'this picture'는 들판에 선 말, 또는 빨랫줄에 걸린 옷가지처럼 보이며, '집 안의 초현실주의' 작가인 Stentzel이 검정색 운동복을 사용하여 만들었다.

08 때, 조건, 양보 등의 부사절에서 주어가 주절의 주어와 같을 때에는 「주어+be동사」를 생략할 수 있다.

09 nothing more than: ~에 불과한 (= only)
오답 ① better than: ~보다 나은
② at least: 적어도
④ no sooner than: ~하자마자
⑤ not so much as: ~조차 아닌

10 이어지는 내용에서 이 시리즈의 주인공이 자른 빵과 양상추로 만든 한 쌍의 강아지라고 했으므로 puppies가 알맞은 답이다.

11 Stentzel이 창의적이고 상상력이 풍부한 예술작품을 만들 수 있도록 하는 것은 무엇인가? → 예리한 관찰력

12 바로 뒤에 이어지는 문장에서 Look carefully라고 했으므로 ③ '단지 힐끗 보기만 하지 (마라)'가 가장 자연스럽다.
오답 ① 일상생활을 특별하게 만들지 (마라)

② 끊임없이 자신의 창의력을 사용하지 (마라)
④ 비범한 무언가를 만들려고 노력하지 (마라)
⑤ 자신을 창의적인 사람이라고 생각하지 (마라)

13 (A) 뒤에 or not이 이어지고 양보의 부사절을 이끄는 접속사는 whether이다.
(B) 일반동사를 대신하는 동사는 do이다.
(C) 선행사 something이 단수이므로 관계사절의 동사도 단수 형태가 적절하다.

14 창작과 창의력의 차이를 예술에 국한하지 않고 설명하는 글이므로, 제목으로는 ① '창작 대 창의력: 예술 너머'가 가장 적절하다.
오답 ② 창작의 광범위한 이해
③ 신선한 아이디어를 떠올리는 방법
④ 예술의 목적은 무엇인가?
⑤ 다양한 분야의 창작

15 ⓐ It은 앞문장에 나온 창작(creation)을 가리키고, ⓑ It은 앞문장의 창의력(creativity)을 가리킨다.

16 필자는 학년말에 버려지는 책이 쓰레기가 되는 것을 안타깝게 여기며, 책을 사고팔거나 교환하는 행사를 개최하거나 도서관에 기증하자고 제안한다. ⑤ '후배들에게 책을 물려주자'는 의견은 필자의 생각과 일치하지 않는다.
오답 ① Josh: 학기가 끝날 때 우리는 너무 많은 책을 버린다.
② Theo: 버려진 책은 많은 쓰레기를 만든다.
③ Caryn: 다 쓴 책을 도서관에 기증하자.
④ 민지: 우리는 벼룩 시장을 열어 중고책을 거래할 수 있다.

17 doing so는 앞에 나온 일반동사와 그 목적어, 보어, 또는 부사구를 대신하는 표현으로, 이 글에서는 바로 앞에 쓰인 suggest 이하의 명사구를 대신한다.

01 ⑤ **02** ④ **03** ② **04** ① **05** ② **06** belief **07** ④ **08** Fruits, flowers, and vegetables are arranged like the pieces of a puzzle to create a human head. **09** ⑤ **10** ⓑ viewed ⓒ flipped **11** ④ **12** colorful clothespins, a dish towel, a black sweatshirt, dark grey pants **13** ④ **14** (1) realize (2) carefully **15** something that has never been seen before **16** ① **17** 학년말에 버려지는 책들이 많은 양의 쓰레기를 만들어 내는 것

01 ⑤ 그림 그리기는 남학생이 하고 있는 활동이고, 여학생에게는 전화기로 사진을 찍어 보라고 제안했다.

02 남학생은 여학생에게 창의적 도전 활동으로 단순한 것을 권하는데, 그 이유는 복잡한 것은 ④ '매일 도전을 완수할 수 없기' 때문일 것이다.
오답 ① 쉽게 창의력을 키울 수 있다
② 사진을 잘 찍지 못한다
③ 매일 같은 일을 하는 데 싫증날 것이다
⑤ 무언가를 창조하는 기술을 키울 수 있을 것이다

03 (A) experiment: 실험 (B) Participants: 참가자들
(C) enhance: 신장하다
오답 (A) experience: 경험 (B) Participation: 참가
(C) enable: 가능하게 하다

04 창의적인 아이디어가 앉아 있을 때보다는 걸을 때 두 배 가까이 떠오른다는 연구 결과를 설명하고 있으므로, 필자가 제안하고자 하는 내용은 창의력이 필요한 과업에 직면했을 때 ① '걸으라'는 것이다.
오답 ② 나의 영상을 볼 것을
③ 온라인 콘텐츠를 만들어 볼 것을
④ 가능한 한 많은 아이디어를 생성할 것을
⑤ 일상의 물건들을 다양한 방법으로 사용할 것을 (제안한다)

05 주어진 문장은, 창의력은 특별한 사람들만이 지닌 것이라는 일반적인 생각에 이어지는 문장으로, ② 뒤의 This common belief가 지칭하는 내용이 바로 주어진 문장이다.

06 belief(믿음, 신념): 무엇이 존재하거나 사실이라고 확신하는 느낌

07 체리, 오디, 사과, 복숭아가 얼굴의 눈과 볼을 구성한다. ④ '자두'에 대한 언급은 없다.

08 과일, 꽃, 채소가 '배열되는' 것이므로 동사는 수동태로 나타내고, 목적을 나타내는 표현은 to부정사를 사용한다.

09 ⑤ 엑스레이 검사를 통해, 화가가 정물화를 그린 후 약간의 수정을 했다는(made some adjustments) 것을 알아냈다.

10 둘 다 접속사 뒤에 주어와 be동사가 생략된 형태이다. 주어와 동사가 수동의 관계이므로 과거분사 형태가 적절하다.

11 앞에 쓰인 paintings를 대신하는 대명사이므로 ④ ones가 알맞다.

12 알록달록한 빨래집게, 행주, 검정색 운동복 상의, 짙은 회색 바지를 이용해 만들었다.

13 (A) 예술작품이 '창작되는' 것이므로 과거분사가 적절하다.
(B) '당신이 방금 본 것'이라는 의미로 선행사를 포함하는 관계대명사 what이 적절하다.
(C) '횡단하는'이라는 의미의 현재분사구가 a zebra를 수식한다.

14 비록 인식하지 못하더라도 우리는 끊임없이 창의력을 발휘하고 있다. 그러므로 우리는 주위를 주의 깊게 살펴 보고 우리의 창의력을 자극하는 것을 찾아야 한다.

15 that이 이끄는 관계대명사절이 something을 수식하고, 동사는 현재완료 수동태(have been p.p.)가 적절하다.

16 학년말에 책이 버려지는 문제를 지적하며 자신의 의견을 제안하고 있으므로 글의 어조로는 ① '설득적인'이 알맞다.
오답 ② 재미있는
③ 희망적인
④ 비판적인
⑤ 공감하는

17 this problem의 구체적인 내용이 앞문장에 언급되어 있다.

내신 1등급 수능형 고난도

pp. 196~199

01 ⑤	02 ⑤	03 ⑤	04 ②	05 ④	06 ①	07 ③	08 ④
09 ①	10 ⑤	11 ②	12 ②	13 ②	14 ④	15 ④	16 ②

01 연구에 따르면 걷는 것이 앉아 있는 것과 비교했을 때 창의적 사고를 두 배 많이 생산했다고 했으므로, 글의 요지로는 ⑤ '걷기가 창의력과 새로운 아이디어를 고안하는 능력을 획기적으로 신장시킨다.'가 가장 적절하다.
오답 ① 콘텐츠 크리에이터에게 가장 중요한 자질은 아이디어를 생산하는 것이다.
② 많이 걷는 사람들은 걷지 않는 사람들보다 더 건강한 삶을 산다.
③ 아이디어를 떠올리는 가장 좋은 방법은 숙고하는 것이다.
④ 연구에 따르면 실외 활동이 정신 건강에 좋다.

02 ⑤ 문맥상 '창의력을 요구하는 과업을 마주할 때'라는 의미이므로 requires가 들어가야 한다. restrict는 '제한하다'라는 뜻이다.

03 창의력은 모든 사람들이 지닌 타고난 능력이다. 의식적인 노력을 기울임으로써 누구든 창의적 잠재력을 발휘할 수 있고 평범한 것들을 예술적인 것으로 변형시킬 수 있다.

04 빈칸 바로 뒤에 이어지는 내용으로 보아 ② '우리는 두 부류로 나뉠 수 있다'가 자연스럽다.
오답 ① 화가와 작가들만이 창의력이 있다
③ 모든 사람은 창의적이 될 잠재력이 있다
④ 숨겨진 창의력을 찾는 데에는 시간이 걸린다
⑤ 주의깊은 관찰은 창의력을 기르는 데 도움이 된다

05 ④ 체리, 오디, 사과, 복숭아가 얼굴의 눈과 볼을 구성하고 있는 것이지, 그림 속 인물이 과일을 먹고 있는 것은 아니다.
오답 ① 이것은 신성 로마 제국 황제 루돌프 2세의 초상화이다.
② 이것은 보는 사람들에게 색다르게 보인다.
③ 이것은 Giuseppe Arcimboldo가 그렸다.
⑤ 이것은 화가의 '합성 초상화' 화풍을 대표한다.

06 ① 주어가 they이므로 동사는 3인칭 단수형으로 쓰면 안 된다.

07 Arcimboldo의 뒤집을 수 있는 그림들을 분석한 결과와, 화가가 그런 기법을 사용한 이유를 추론한 내용을 설명하는 글로서, ③ '연구는 그의 그림을 본 사람들이 혼란스러움을 느꼈다고 주장한다'는 글의 흐름과 관련이 적다.

08 ④ Arcimboldo의 뒤집을 수 있는 그림: 정물화에서 초상화까지
오답 ① 이탈리아 화가 Arcimboldo의 생애
② 16세기 이탈리아의 정물화
③ 명작들의 과학적 분석
⑤ 정교한 과일과 채소를 그리기 위한 예술적 기법

09 앞문장에서 〈빨랫줄 동물들〉이라고 시리즈의 이름이 소개되었으므로 빈칸에는 ① '빨래를 널다가'가 가장 자연스럽다.
오답 ② 부엌 식탁에서
③ 동물원을 방문했을 때
④ 동물들을 유심히 관찰함으로써
⑤ '집 안의 초현실주의'를 창조하기 위해

10 (A) illusion: 환각, 착각 (B) transform: 변형하다 (C) desert: 사막
오답 (A) allusion: 암시 (B) trasfer: 옮기다 (C) dessert: 후식

11 두 번째 단락의 첫 문장인 질문에 대한 답이 주어진 문장이므로 ②의 위치에 들어가는 것이 가장 자연스럽다. 이어지는 문장들은 주어진 문장을 부연 설명한다.

12 ② Crunchie는 양상추로 만들어졌다. 자른 빵으로 만들어진 것은 Brad Pet이다.
오답 ① Stentzel의 잘 알려진 작품 가운데 하나는 〈먹을 수 있는 존재들〉이다.
③ Stentzel은 〈먹을 수 있는 존재들〉에 대한 영감을 부엌에서 얻었다.
④ 어린 Stentzel은 주위의 사물을 관찰하며 시간을 보냈다.
⑤ Stentzel은 자신의 창의력이 관찰 기술에서 비롯되었다고 믿는다.

13 창작과 창의력의 차이는 무엇인가?
(B) 창작은 한 사람의 노력의 결과물이다.
(A) 창의력은 새로운 것을 만들어내는 능력이다.
(D) 그것은 예술뿐 아니라 문제에 대한 참신한 해결책도 포함한다.
(C) 창의력의 넓은 의미를 이해해야 한다.

14 빈칸 앞 문장의 내용을 빈칸 뒤의 문장이 부연 설명하고 있으므로, 빈칸에는 '다시 말해'라는 의미의 ④ In other words가 적절하다.
오답 ① 예를 들어 ② 그 결과 ③ 반면에 ⑤ 게다가

15 운동이 신체적 건강뿐만 아니라 창의력 증진에도 도움이 된다는 내용이므로 가장 적절한 제목은 ④ '운동이 어떻게 창의력을 신장하는가'이다.
오답 ① 밖으로 나가 예술의 영감을 얻어라
② 신체 활동의 중요성
③ 언제 두뇌가 가장 잘 작동하는가?
⑤ 운동과 정신 건강

16 (A) enhance와 함께 조동사 can 뒤에 쓰이는 말이므로 동사원형이 적절하다.
(B) 연속동작을 나타내는 분사구문으로 현재분사 형태가 적절하다.
(C) 전치사 뒤에 동명사가 와야 하므로 doing이 적절하다.

내신 1등급 서술형
pp. 200~202

01 some special talent you are either born with or without / some special talent either you are born with or without
02 ⓐ takes ⓑ hidden
03 a cherry, a mulberry, an apple, a peach
04 Created by a 16th-century Italian painter named
05 He first painted them as still life paintings and then turned them upside down and made some adjustments to create faces.
06 he wanted to add an interactive element to his work (by doing so)
07 (1) sliced (2) star
08 while putting together a salad for her family

09 what enables her to continuously produce creative and imaginative works of art
10 ⓐ Whether we realize it or not
ⓑ By doing so
11 extraordinary
12 ⓐ exercise ⓑ the brain
13 (1) 기분을 향상시키고 부정적인 감정을 줄일 수 있다.
(2) 뇌로 가는 혈류를 증가시켜 뇌가 더 잘 기능하게 한다[하는 영양분을 공급한다].
(3) 우리가 여러 장소를 찾아가 새로운 영감의 원천에 노출되게 한다.

01 either A or B: A 또는 B 중 하나

02 ⓐ 주어가 동명사(Finding)이므로 동사는 단수 형태가 적절하다.
ⓑ 앞에 쓰인 명사 the beauty를 수식하며 수동의 관계이므로 과거분사 형태가 알맞다.

03 체리와 오디가 짙은 눈을, 사과와 복숭아가 뺨을 구성하였다.

04 앞에 Being이 생략된 분사구문으로 '창작되어'라는 의미의 과거분사 Created로 문장을 시작한다. name은 동사로 '이름 붙이다'라는 뜻이므로 과거분사로 쓰여 painter와 수동의 관계로 뒤에서 수식한다.

05 '뒤집을 수 있는 그림'의 제작 기법은, 먼저 정물화로 그림을 그리고 나서 거꾸로 뒤집어 얼굴을 만들기 위해 약간의 수정을 한 것이다.

06 Arcimboldo가 뒤집을 수 있는 그림을 창작한 이유는 무엇인가? Why did he make his paintings reversible?이라는 질문 뒤에 이어지는 문장에 답이 언급되어 있다.

07 Stentzel은 Brad Pet을 자른 빵으로 만들었는데, 그것은 그녀의 〈먹을 수 있는 존재들〉 시리즈의 스타이다.

08 때, 조건, 양보 등의 부사절에서 주어가 주절의 주어와 일치할 경우, 「주어+be동사」를 생략할 수 있다.

09 • 관계대명사 what은 '~하는 것'이라는 의미로 선행사를 포함한다.
• enable A to-v: A가 ~할 수 있게 하다

10 ⓐ whether ~ or not: ~하든 하지 않든
ⓑ By doing so: 그렇게 함으로써

11 끊임없이 창의력을 발휘함으로써 평범한 것을 '비범한' 무언가로 바꿀 수 있다. ordinary의 반의어는 extraordinary이다.

12 ⓐ 앞에 쓰인 exercise를 가리킨다.
ⓑ 운동이 뇌로 가는 혈류를 증가시켜 그것(=뇌)에 필요한 영양분을 제공한다.

13 Also, Moreover로 연결되는 내용에 주의하여 운동의 세 가지 역할을 정리한다.

교과서 **어휘 익히기** ·· p. 205

01 역경	26 refugee
02 대표하다	27 chaos
03 위험한	28 border
04 ~과 함께	29 hesitant
05 달아나다, 도망치다	30 journey
06 정착하다	31 treasure
07 무서운	32 make up one's mind
08 겁에 질려 어쩔 줄 모르다	33 overwhelming
09 소지품, 재산	34 persistent
10 실현되다	35 pity
11 지도, 가르침	36 explode
12 비통해 하는	37 former
13 폭탄	38 undergo
14 (배, 기차 등에) 타다	39 turn down
15 어려움, 고난	40 drift
16 성명, 진술	41 fateful
17 소지품, 재산	42 excellence
18 발생하다	43 sink
19 굳게 결심한	44 break out
20 ~에 매달리다	45 exhausted
21 사건	46 athlete
22 언급하다	47 compete
23 뛰어난	48 international
24 전문적인	49 desperate
25 성과를 내다	50 destination

교과서 **핵심 문법** ·· pp. 206~209

POINT 1 help+목적어+동사원형

Q 1 follow 2 to improve 3 help

Check-Up

01 (1) can help you (to) relieve stress
   (2) will help students (to) cultivate reading habits
   (3) helps us (to) think logically
   (4) helped him (to) feel less lonely

02 (1) The scientists helped the baby elelphant (to) survive in the forest.
   (2) The director of the movie wanted to help people (to) understand the environmental crisis.

(3) Michel helped me (to) learn French during my stay in Paris.
(4) Self-confidence will make you face challenges in your life. / Self-confidence will help you to face challenges in your life.

03 ④

Q 1. Briton 부인은 딸이 자신의 꿈을 쫓도록 도왔다.
2. 코치는 선수들이 기량을 향상하도록 도왔다.
3. 규칙적인 운동은 사람들이 건강을 유지하도록 도울 수 있다.

Check-Up

01 help는 「help+목적어+목적격 보어」 형식으로 '(목적어)가 ~하는 것을 돕다'라는 의미를 가진다. 목적격 보어 자리에는 동사원형이나 to부정사가 올 수 있다.

02 (1), (2), (3) help는 준사역동사로 목적격 보어 자리에 동사원형이나 to부정사가 와야 한다.
(4) 사역동사 make는 목적격 보어로 동사원형을 쓰고, 준사역동사 help는 동사원형이나 to부정사를 쓸 수 있으므로, 동사를 help로 고치거나 목적격 보어를 동사원형으로 고쳐야 한다.
(1) 과학자들은 새끼 코끼리가 숲에서 생존할 수 있도록 도왔다.
(2) 그 영화의 감독은 사람들이 환경 위기를 이해하도록 돕고자 했다.
(3) Michel은 내가 파리에 머무는 동안 프랑스어 배우는 것을 도와줬다.
(4) 자신감은 당신이 삶에서 도전에 맞설 수 있도록 할 것이다.

03

> 여러분의 옷에서 더러운 얼룩을 제거하려고 노력하는 것에 지쳤나요? Power Clean을 사용해 보세요! 이 새로운 제품은 여러분의 옷이 원래의 밝기와 색깔을 되찾을 수 있도록 도울 것입니다. Power Clean을 쓴다면, 여러분의 옷은 항상 새것처럼 좋아 보일 수 있습니다! 또한, Power Clean은 옷에서 더 오랫동안 상쾌하고 깨끗한 냄새가 나도록 돕는 특별한 성분이 들어있습니다. 저희 제품을 사용해 보고 그 차이를 직접 확인하세요!

Power Clean의 효과를 광고하는 글로, ④ 땀의 배출을 도와준다는 설명하지 않았다.

POINT 2 의문문의 화법 전환

Q 1 where 2 that 3 if 4 had

Check-Up

01 (1) if[whether] I wanted to play soccer
   (2) what time she went to school
   (3) who had broken her cup
   (4) if[whether] they had finished the project

02 (1) asked if[whether] she worked at this restaurant
   (2) asked if[whether] I was[we were] ready for the math test
   (3) asked if[whether] I had ever been to Paris
   (4) asked why the singer had canceled her concert

03 (1) asked if[whether] I had left something behind

(2) asked if[whether] he had seen it

Q 1. Joan은 내가 어디에서 꽃을 샀는지 물었다.

2. 그들은 그가 그들의 형이라고 말했다.

3. 교사는 우리가 그 프로젝트에 질문이 있는지 물었다.

4. 그는 내가 해리포터 시리즈를 읽었는지 물었다.

Check-Up 🍎

01 의문문을 간접화법으로 나타낼 때에는 의문사나 접속사 if[whether]를 사용하며, 평서문의 어순으로 나타낸다. (3), (4)는 물어볼 때(asked)보다 앞서는 시제이므로 대과거인 had p.p. 형태로 쓴다.

02 직접화법을 간접화법으로 바꿀 때 의문문에 의문사가 있으면 의문사를 접속사처럼 사용하여 절을 연결하고, 의문사가 없을 때에는 접속사 if나 whether를 사용하여 연결한다. 의문문은 평서문의 어순으로 바꾸고, 동사의 시제와 인칭대명사의 사용도 알맞게 바꿔야 한다.

(1) 나는 그녀가 이 식당에서 일하는지 물었다.

(2) 교사는 내가[우리가] 수학 시험 준비가 되었는지 물었다.

(3) 그녀는 내가 파리에 가 본 적이 있는지 물었다.

(4) 우리는 그 가수가 왜 공연을 취소했는지 물었다.

03

> 가게 매니저님께,
>
> 저는 당신의 직원 중 한 명이 제공한 뛰어난 서비스에 깊은 감사를 표하고 싶습니다. 지난주에 저는 딸을 위한 스카프를 사러 당신의 가게에 들렀고, 거기에 제 휴대폰을 두고 왔습니다. 놀랍게도, 제가 가게에 돌아가자마자 그는 저를 기억하고 제가 두고 간 것이 있는지 물었습니다. 저는 그에게 제 휴대폰을 잊어버렸다고 말했고, 그가 그것을 보았는지 물어봤습니다. 그는 친절하게 다른 직원들에게 제 휴대폰에 관해 물었고, 저는 그들 중 한 명에게서 그것을 돌려받았습니다. 제가 휴대폰을 잃어버렸다면 실망했을 텐데, 그의 친절한 행동 덕분에 즐거운 하루를 보낼 수 있었어요.

접속사 if나 whether를 써서 의문문을 연결한다. 의문문의 동사가 과거이므로, 간접화법에서 동사의 시제는 대과거로 바꾸고, 인칭대명사는 (1)은 I로, (2)는 he로 바꾼다.

교과서 본문 익히기 ❶ 옳은 어법·어휘 고르기 ⋯pp. 217~219

01 centered	**02** how
03 that	**04** which
05 true	**06** upside, out
07 risky	**08** clung
09 where	**10** enough
11 made, to avoid	**12** would
13 if	**14** destination
15 designed	**16** when
17 desperate, throw	**18** disappear
19 the other	**20** for
21 from, on	**22** were
23 settled	**24** Despite

25 home	**26** to take, reach
27 he could	**28** recognized
29 persistent	**30** pay
31 reality, refugee	**32** hesitant
33 instead of	**34** down, inspire
35 both	**36** determined
37 came	**38** without
39 have, even if	**40** it's

교과서 본문 익히기 ❷ 틀린 부분 고치기 ⋯⋯⋯pp. 220~222

01 ○	**02** how to swim
03 that	**04** which led
05 seemed like	**06** idea that
07 clung to	**08** where
09 horrifying enough	**10** they made up
11 reached, would follow	**12** ○
13 by making	**14** designed
15 grew worse	**16** had no choice but to throw
17 disappear[disappearing]	**18** herself
19 until they arrived	**20** had to cross every border
21 No matter how	**22** made it to Germany
23 underwent	**24** to feel at home
25 who	**26** if he could be
27 ○	**28** stay focused
29 day and night	**30** ○
31 Although it seemed	**32** instead of seeing
33 other refugees facing	**34** and
35 ○	**36** ○
37 did not matter	**38** ○, have
39 impossible	

교과서 본문 익히기 ❸ 빈칸 완성하기 ⋯⋯⋯⋯pp. 223~227

(1) centered around swimming

(2) how to swim from

(3) When she was nine years old

(4) It was clear that

(5) which led her to dream about

(6) the chance to represent

(7) might someday come true

(8) had no idea that

(9) had broken out in 2011

(10) Over the next few years

(11) kept swimming

(12) However, even this

(13) where she was training
(14) horrifying enough to be
(15) made up their minds
(16) to avoid the war
(17) If they reached Europe
(18) her only option
(19) live without fear
(20) began their dangerous journey
(21) including children and babies
(22) across the sea towards
(23) the weather rapidly grew worse
(24) had no choice but to throw
(25) felt heartbroken
(26) no time to reflect
(27) in order to save herself
(28) guided the drifting boat
(29) for three and a half hours
(30) had to travel through
(31) even though they caught rides
(32) No matter how exhausted
(33) they finally made it to
(34) Despite all the hardships
(35) to feel at home
(36) decided to take up training
(37) if he could be her coach
(38) he immediately recognized
(39) stay focused and persistent
(40) day and night
(41) to make her dream a reality
(42) Although it seemed like
(43) might view her with pity
(44) turned down the invitation
(45) facing similar challenges
(46) the 100-meter butterfly
(47) When she stepped onto
(48) 41st out of 45 competitors
(49) proud to have made
(50) did not matter
(51) strong for their goals
(52) even if I fail
(53) it's hard to arrive
(54) everyone can do it

01 ④ 02 ② 03 ⑤ 04 ④ 05 ④ 06 ⑤ 07 ① 08 ④

01 ④ 올림픽에서 '경쟁하다'라는 의미의 competing이 들어가야 자연
   스럽다. complete는 '완료하다, 끝마치다'라는 의미이다.

36

02 ② 발발하다: break out
   오답 ① upside down: 거꾸로
   ③ cling to: ~에 매달리다
   ④ wake-up call: 정신을 차리게 하는 신호
   ⑤ make up one's mind: 결심하다

03 (A) '목적지'라는 의미의 destination이 알맞다.
   (B) '~을 향하여'라는 의미의 전치사 towards가 적절하다.
   (C) '소지품'이라는 의미의 명사 possessions가 알맞다.
   오답 (A) destiny: 운명
   (B) forwards: 앞으로
   (C) possess: 소유하다

04 (A) disappear: 사라지다
   (B) reflect: 깊이 생각하다
   (C) drifting: 표류하는
   오답 (A) appear: 나타나다
   (B) refer: 참고하다, 조회하다
   (C) drafting: 선발하는

05 (A) crowded: 복잡한 (B) exhausted: 지친 (C) adversity: 역경
   오답 (A) clouded: 흐린, 멍한 (B) excited: 흥분한
   (C) adversary: 상대방

06 ⑤ 문맥상 '그의 가르침에 따라'라는 의미가 적절하므로
   instructions를 써야 한다. construction은 '건설, 구성'이라는 뜻
   의 단어이다.

07 (A) hesitant: 망설이는 (B) pity: 동정, 연민 (C) hope: 희망
   오답 (A) persistent: 끈질긴 (B) respect: 존경 (C) horror: 공포

08 ④ 점수판의 기록은 '중요하지' 않다는 의미이므로 work가 아닌
   matter(중요하다, 문제가 되다)를 써야 자연스럽다.

01 ③ 02 ④ 03 ② 04 ③ 05 ③ 06 ⑤ 07 ③ 08 ⑤

01 ③ people이 '남겨지는' 것이므로 수동태 were left가 알맞은 표현
   이다.
   오답 ① enough+명사+to-v: ~하기에 충분한 (명사)
   ② help의 목적격 보어로 쓰인 동사원형
   ④ by v-ing: ~함으로써
   ⑤ so that: ~할 수 있도록

02 ④ 선행사가 앞의 절인 계속적 용법의 관계대명사이므로 that이 아
   닌 which가 적절하다.
   오답 ① a young girl을 뒤에서 수식하는 현재분사구이다.
   ② how to-v: ~하는 방법
   ③ It이 가주어이고, that이 이끄는 절이 진주어이다.
   ⑤ seem like: ~처럼 보이다

03 (A) keep 뒤에는 동명사를 목적어로 쓴다.

(B) 선행사와 관계사절이 의미상 she was training in the pool
이므로 장소의 관계부사가 적절하다.
(C) 주절의 시제가 과거이므로 reached로 나타낸다.

04 (A) '만들어진'이라는 수동의 의미를 가진 과거분사가 적절하다.
(B) have no choice but to-v: ~할 수밖에 없다
(C) watched가 지각동사이므로 목적격 보어로 동사원형을 써야
한다.

05 (A) 선행사가 a coach이므로 사람을 수식하는 주격 관계대명사
who가 적절하다.
(B) 간접의문문을 이끄는 접속사 if가 적절하다.
(C) 능동의 분사구문으로 현재분사를 쓴다.

06 ⑤ 수식 받는 명사 other refugees와 능동의 관계이므로 현재분사
facing이 알맞은 형태이다.
오답 ① a chance를 수식하는 형용사적 용법의 to부정사이다.
② 부사절과 주절이 대조를 이루므로 양보의 접속사 Although가 사
용되었다.
③ might: 추측을 나타내는 조동사
④ decide는 to부정사를 목적어로 취하는 동사이다.

07 ③ want의 목적격 보어 역할을 하므로 to부정사 형태인 to stay
strong으로 써야 한다.
오답 ① 주절의 시제보다 앞선 행위를 나타내는 완료부정사이다.
② 의문문을 간접화법으로 전환한 것이다.
④ 양보의 부사절을 이끄는 접속사이다.
⑤ 진주어 역할을 하는 to부정사이다.

08 (A) 주어가 one이므로 동사도 단수 형태이다.
(B) get used to v-ing: ~하는 데 익숙해지다
(C) 직접목적어 역할을 하는 명사절을 이끄는 접속사 that이 적절
하다.

내신 1등급 실전 1회   pp. 232~235

01 ④   **02** ④   **03** ④   **04** ③   **05** enjoyed watching Olympic
swimming events with her father, which led her to dream
about competing   **06** ②   **07** ⑤   **08** ②   **09** ⑤   **10** ④   **11** ③
12 ④   **13** ②   **14** helped Yusra (to) stay focused and persistent
in her efforts to pursue excellence   **15** (1) medal   (2) dreams
16 to arrive at your dreams   **17** ②   **18** sharing knowledge in
disaster situations

01 ④ 여학생은 프랑스 여행 시 번역 앱을 사용하여 큰 어려움 없이 사
람들과 의사소통할 수 있었다.

02 ④는 that 이하의 내용을 대신하는 가주어이고, 나머지는 모두 여학
생이 사용한 번역 애플리케이션을 가리킨다.

03 어린 나이에 수영에 재능을 보여 올림픽 출전의 꿈을 꾸고, 그것이
실현될 것처럼 보였다 했으므로, 글의 분위기로는 ④ '희망적이고 낙
관적인'이 적절하다.

오답 ① 활기차고 축제와 같은
② 우울하고 슬픈
③ 긴장되고 필사적인
⑤ 비판적이고 냉소적인

04 ③ 몇 살에 그녀가 수영을 시작했는가? → 어려서 시작했다고 했지만
몇 살에 시작했는지는 알 수 없다.
오답 ① 그녀의 고국은 어디인가? → 시리아
② 그녀 아버지의 직업은 무엇이었나? → 수영선수
④ 그녀는 누구와 함께 올림픽 수영 경기 보는 걸 즐겼는가? → 그녀
의 아버지
⑤ 어려서 그녀의 꿈은 무엇이었나? → 올림픽에 출전하는 것

05 (1) enjoy는 to부정사가 아닌 동명사를 목적어로 취한다.
(2) 앞의 절을 선행사로 하는 계속적 용법의 관계대명사는 which이다.

06 내전으로 혼란스러운 와중에도 수영을 계속했지만 그것마저 위험해
졌다. 그 구체적인 이유가 주어진 문장의 폭탄이 수영장에 떨어진 사
건이었고, (B) 뒤의 it이 주어진 문장의 폭탄을 가리킨다.

07 ⑤ make up one's mind: 결심하다

08 ② → Yusra, 언니 Sara, 그리고 어린아이와 아기를 포함한 다른
18명의 승객이 배에 타고 있었다.

09 사람들의 소중한 소지품이 사라지는 걸 볼 때는 ⑤ '비통한' 감정이었
을 것이다.
오답 ① 흥분한 ② 실망한 ③ 긴장한 ④ 혐오감을 느낀

10 ④ 조치를 취하다: take action

11 ③ make it to: ~에 이르다, 도착하다 (= reach)
오답 ① from time to time: 때때로
② no matter how: 아무리 ~하더라도
④ Despite: ~에도 불구하고

12 힘겹게 걸어서 국경을 넘어 베를린의 난민 센터에 정착한 고난스러
운 상황이므로, 수영은 그녀에게 ④ '이국땅에서 편안함을 느끼기 위
해' 할 수 있는 유일한 일이었을 것이다.
오답 ① 올림픽 수영 경기에 참가하기 위해
② 가능한 한 빨리 고국에 돌아가기 위해
③ 그 나라에 머물기 위해
⑤ 베를린에 있는 다른 시리아인들을 돕기 위해

13 ② 간접화법으로 의문문을 전환할 때 의문사가 없는 의문문을 이끄
는 접속사는 if나 whether이다.
오답 ① help+목적어+동사원형
③ 지각동사 saw의 목적어와 목적격 보어(동사원형)
④ 이유를 나타내는 분사구문
⑤ 그녀가 초대받는 것이므로 수동태

14 ・help+목적어+(to+)동사원형: (목적어)가 ~하도록 돕다
・~하려는 노력: effort to-v

15 Yusra가 비록 올림픽에서 메달을 따지는 못했지만, 그녀는 최선을
다했고 그녀가 꿈에 도달할 거라는 것을 알았기 때문에 스스로를 자
랑스러워 했다.

16 it은 가주어로, 뒤에 나오는 **to arrive at your dreams**가 진주어이다. '꿈에 도달하는 것'이 어려운 일이지만, 불가능한 것은 아니라고 말했다.

17 (A) 빈칸 뒤에서 피해 복구를 위한 원조의 구체적 사례를 열거하고 있으므로 빈칸에는 **For example**이 적절하다.
(B) 국제적 원조를 빈칸 뒤에서 부연 설명하고 있으므로 '더구나'라는 의미의 **Furthermore**가 적절하다.
오답 ① In other words: 다시 말해, Therefore: 그러므로
③ To make matters worse: 설상가상으로
④ Meanwhile: 반면, 한편, On the other hand: 반면
⑤ In short: 요컨대

18 doing so는 앞에 나온 일반동사와 그 목적어, 보어, 부사구 등을 대신하는 표현이다. 주어진 문장에서 doing so는 앞에서 언급된 '재난 상황에서 지식을 공유하는 것'을 가리킨다.

내신 1등급 실전 2회
pp. 236~239

01 ④ **02** ② **03** ② **04** ⑤ **05** ① **06** ⑤ **07** ⓐ a bomb ⓑ to flee Syria and go to Germany / fleeing Syria and going to Germany **08** ② **09** No matter how exhausted they were, they kept moving. **10** ③ **11** asked if[whether] he could be her coach **12** ③ **13** turn down **14** ③ **15** it's hard to arrive at your dreams, but it's not impossible **16** ② **17** ⓔ speaking

01 고정형 사고방식과 성장형 사고방식을 비교하며, 성장형 사고방식이 보다 성공적인 삶에 도움이 된다고 주장하는 내용이다.

02 고정형 사고방식을 가진 사람들에 관해 설명한 뒤 성장형 사고방식을 가진 사람들을 소개하고 있으므로 앞의 내용과 대조되는 관계이다. 대조를 나타내는 연결어 ② '반면에'가 가장 적절하다.
오답 ① 예를 들어
③ 다시 말해
④ 요컨대
⑤ 그런 경우

03 (B) 뒤에 쓰인 they가 가리키는 것이 주어진 문장의 over 100 countries and organizations이다. 주어진 문장을 시작으로 국제 사회의 도움이 상세히 진술되고 있다.

04 ⑤ 문맥상 전 세계 시민들이 성금과 물품을 '받은' 것이 아니라 '기부했다(donated)'라고 해야 자연스럽다.

05 ① '전 세계의 구호 노력이 없었다면' 상황은 더 심각했을 것이다.
오답 ② 자연재해가 증가하면서
③ 재해 예방 시스템이 없었다면
④ 국제 원조의 도움 덕분에
⑤ 의료 지원이 없었다면

06 ⑤ 시리아를 떠나 독일로 가서 꿈을 추구하고 안전하게 살기로 결정했다.

오답 ① → 2011년 내전이 발발했다.
② → 내전이 일어났지만 한동안 학교에 가고 수영을 했다.
③ → 폭탄이 떨어졌지만 폭발하지는 않았다.
④ → Yusra와 언니가 먼저 유럽에 도착하면 다른 가족이 뒤따르기로 계획했다.

07 ⓐ it은 수영장에 떨어진 폭탄을 가리킨다.
ⓑ it은 시리아를 떠나 독일에 가는 것을 가리킨다.

08 ② 주로 걸어서 국경을 이동했지만, 때때로 작은 차나 붐비는 버스를 타기도 했다.

09 • '아무리 ~할지라도'라는 양보의 표현은 No matter how로 나타낸다.
• keep(~을 계속하다)은 목적어로 동명사를 취한다.

10 ③ pursue excellence: 탁월함을 추구하다

11 의문사가 없는 의문문이 포함된 문장을 간접화법으로 바꿀 때에는 ask if[whether]로 연결한다. 과거시제이므로 조동사 could로 나타내고 인칭대명사도 문맥에 맞게 변형한다.

12 (A) '~할 기회'라는 의미로 chance를 수식하는 형용사적 용법의 to부정사가 적절하다.
(B) 양보의 의미를 나타내는 접속사 Although가 적절하다.
(C) realized의 목적어로 쓰이는 명사절을 이끄는 접속사 that이 적절하다.

13 • accept: 받아들이다, 수용하다
• turn down: 거절하다

14 바로 앞문장에서 '비록 메달 없이 올림픽을 떠났지만 그녀는 자부심을 느꼈다'고 했으므로, ③ '점수판에 있는 기록'은 중요하지 않았다.
오답 ① 참가자의 수
② 기자들과의 인터뷰
④ 올림픽 경기에서 경쟁
⑤ 경기에 그녀가 쏟은 모든 것

15 가주어 it으로 시작하고 뒤에 진주어가 되는 to부정사구를 넣어 절을 완성한다.

16 사람들 앞에서 연설하는 것에 대한 두려움을 가지고 있었으나, 발표 동아리에 들어가 연습을 거듭한 끝에 성공적으로 발표를 한 경험을 얻었으므로, 심경 변화로는 ② '좌절한 → 자부심을 느끼는'이 가장 적절하다.
오답 ① 흥분한 → 실망한
③ 걱정하는 → 분노한
④ 걱정하는 → 안도한
⑤ 기대하는 → 긴장한

17 ⓔ get used to v-ing: ~하는 데에 익숙해지다, making과 함께 전치사 to의 목적어 역할을 하는 동명사 형태가 적절하다.

01 ④   **02** ④   **03** ①   **04** ⓐ growing   ⓑ to represent   **05** ④   **06** possessions   **07** ⑤   **08** ④   **09** (A) who (B) if   **10** he saw her swim, he immediately recognized her outstanding talent and agreed to do so   **11** ②   **12** ②   **13** ①   **14** was so nervous that I made a lot of mistakes   **15** ④   **16** disaster survivors

01 주어진 문장은 자신이 앱을 사용하여 어려움 없이 사람들과 의사소통했던 경험을 말하는 것이므로, 작년에 프랑스에서 그 앱을 사용했었다는 말 뒤에 이어지는 것이 자연스럽다.

02 ④ 대화 마지막에서 I'm going to download it.이라고 말하고 있다.

03 어려서부터 수영을 배워 아홉 살 때 이미 나이 많은 선수들을 앞서기 시작했으므로, ① '그녀가 특별한 재능을 가진 것'이 분명했다.
[오답] ② 시리아 사람들은 수영을 좋아했다
③ 그녀의 아버지는 올림픽 메달리스트였다
④ 그녀는 올림픽 경기에서 이길 것이었다
⑤ 그녀는 수영 경기 보는 걸 좋아했다

04 ⓐ a young girl을 수식하며 능동의 관계이므로 현재분사 형태가 자연스럽다.
ⓑ '대표할 기회'라는 의미로 a chance를 수식하는 형용사적 용법의 to부정사가 적절하다.

05 (C) 그리스로 향하던 보트가 바다 가운데에서 멈춰섰다.
(A) 배가 가라앉으며 승객들이 소지품을 바다로 던졌다.
(D) Yusra 자매와 몇몇 승객이 바다로 뛰어내려 보트를 끌었다.
(B) 3시간 반 동안 배를 끌어 해변에 안전히 도착했다.

06 어떤 사람이 소유하거나, 가지고 있거나, 통제하는 것들: possessions (소지품)

07 ⑤ Yusra가 베를린의 어느 곳에서 수영을 시작했는지는 언급되지 않았다.
[오답] ① 얼마나 많은 나라를 건넜는가? → 4개국을 거쳐 독일에 도착했다.
② 어디에 도착해 정착했는가? → 독일에 도착해 베를린의 난민 센터에 정착했다.
③ 난민 센터에 도착하기까지 얼마나 걸렸는가? → 25일
④ 스스로를 위안하기 위해 무엇을 했는가? → 수영

08 (A) '때때로 차를 타기도 했다'와 '국경을 걸어서 넘었다'는 대조의 관계이므로 양보의 접속사 even though가 적절하다.
(B) 역경에도 '불구하고' 수영을 향한 열정이 사그라들지 않은 것이므로, 전치사 Despite가 적절하다.

09 (A) a coach를 수식하는 주격 관계대명사 who가 적절하다.
(B) 간접화법에서 의문사가 없는 의문문을 이끄는 접속사 if가 적절하다.

10 (1) saw는 지각동사이므로 목적격 보어 자리에 to부정사가 아닌 동사원형(또는 분사)을 써야 한다.
(2) 주어 he에 대해 동사가 recognized와 agreed이므로 과거시제가 바르다.

11 ② the first ever refugee team이라고 했으므로 최초의 난민 올림픽 선수단이었다.
[오답] ① → 난민 선수단에 초청받았다.
③ → 처음에는 망설였다.
④ → 동정을 받을까 Yusra가 걱정했지만 실제 동정을 받았는지는 언급되어 있지 않다.
⑤ → 수많은 사람들에게 희망을 주기 위해 수락했다.

12 it은 난민 올림픽 선수단에 합류하라는 초대(the invitation)를 가리킨다.

13 마지막 문장(끈질긴 노력으로 어려움을 극복할 수 있다)이 필자의 주장을 나타내므로, 알맞은 격언은 ① '훈련이 완벽을 만든다.'이다.
[오답] ② 제때의 바늘 한 번이 아홉 바늘을 던다.
③ 구르는 돌은 이끼가 끼지 않는다.
④ 웅변은 은이나 침묵은 금이다.
⑤ 로마에서는 로마법을 따르라.

14 • so ~ that: 너무 ~해서 …하다
• make a mistake: 실수를 저지르다

15 ④ 국제적 원조가 발전소, 대중교통, 병원 같은 핵심 시설의 재건에 도움이 된다.

16 them은 바로 앞 문장의 재난 생존자를 지칭한다.

01 ②   **02** ③   **03** ②   **04** ③   **05** ②   **06** ④   **07** ④   **08** ②   **09** ⑤   **10** ④   **11** ③   **12** ②   **13** ①   **14** ③   **15** ④   **16** ④

01 (A) 예를 들어 고정형 사고방식을 가진 사람은 수학 시험을 망치면 포기한다.
(D) 그들은 수학 실력을 향상할 수 없다고 말한다.
(B) 반면 성장형 사고방식을 가진 사람은 더 노력한다.
(E) 그들은 노력하면 더 잘할 수 있다고 말한다.
(C) 고정형 사고방식을 가지고 있다면 성장형 사고방식을 받아들이는 게 좋다.

02 두 가지의 사고방식 가운데 고정형 사고방식보다 개방형 사고방식을 채택하는 것이 좋다고 ③ '독려하는' 글이다.
[오답] ① 회의적인 ② 재미있는 ④ 불만스러운 ⑤ 감사하는

03 튀르키예와 시리아에서 일어난 지진에 국제적 구호의 손길이 미쳤던 사례를 소개하며 자연재해에 국제적 도움의 중요성을 말하는 글이다. ② '재난에 맞선 국제적 연대'가 가장 적절한 제목이다.
[오답] ① 전세계의 점증하는 자연재해
③ 지진 예보의 중요성
④ 기아로 고통받는 사람들을 위한 국제적 구호
⑤ 2023년 튀르키예-시리아 지진의 영향

04 100여 개의 나라와 기구들이 '대응한' 것이므로 수동태가 아닌 능동 태(quickly responded)가 적절하다.

05 내전으로 일상이 파괴되어 안전한 곳으로 도피를 계획하는 이야기이 므로 글의 분위기는 ② 긴급하고 절박하다.
오답 ① 차분하고 평화로운
③ 재미있고 흥미로운
④ 무관심하고 초연한
⑤ 활기차고 축제와 같은

06 빈칸이 포함된 절 뒤에 and로 이어지는 내용이 '시리아를 떠나기로 결심했다'는 것이므로, ④ '더 이상 조국에 머물 수 없다'는 것을 깨달 았을 것이다.
오답 ① 내전이 곧 발발할 것이다
② 그들이 유럽에 있는 나라들을 방문해야 한다
③ 그들이 새 수영장을 찾아야 한다
⑤ 올림픽에 출전할 거란 그들의 꿈은 결코 실현될 수 없다

07 ④ 보트가 가라앉기 시작하자 승객들은 자신의 소지품을 바다로 던 질 수밖에 없었다.
오답 ① Yusra는 2015년 봄에 여정을 시작했다. → 여름(8월)에 시작했다.
② 배에는 18명의 승객이 있었다. → Yusra 자매와 다른 18명이므 로 20명의 승객이 있었다.
③ 보트는 튀르키예로 향했다. → 그리스로 향했다.
⑤ Yusra와 네 명의 다른 승객이 배를 해안으로 끌었다. → 그녀를 포함하여 네 명이 끌었다.

08 (A) disaster와 능동의 관계이므로 과거시제 struck이 적절하다.
(B) watched가 지각동사이므로 목적격 보어로 동사원형이 적절 하다.
(C) '그녀 자신'이므로 재귀대명사가 적절하다.

09 여러 나라의 국경을 걸어서 건너 마침내 독일에 도착하고, 수영을 계 속 하려는 노력을 진술하는 글이므로, 주제로는 ⑤ '피난 여정과 수영 을 향한 지속적 열정'이 가장 적절하다.
오답 ① 시리아와 유럽의 지리
② 유럽 국가들의 난민 정책
③ 수영이 육체적 건강에 미치는 혜택
④ 시리아와 독일의 문화적 차이

10 (A) border: 국경
(B) settle: 정착하다
(C) undergo: 겪다
오답 (A) board: 판
(B) battle: 싸우다
(C) understand: 이해하다

11 올림픽에 난민 선수단으로 출전할 기회를 얻었지만 사람들이 동정을 하며 진지한 선수로 보지 않을 것을 우려해 출전을 망설이다 결국 수 용했다는 내용이다. ③ '그녀의 올림픽 꿈이 마침내 실현되었다.'는 글의 흐름상 어색한 내용이다.

12 사람들이 연민을 느끼고 자신을 ② '진지한 선수'로 생각하지 않을까 염려했다.

오답 ① 청소년 수영선수
③ 시리아 난민
④ 올림픽 메달리스트
⑤ 반전 활동가

13 클럽 참여, 연습, 그리고 꾸준한 노력을 통해 대중 앞에서 연설하는 두려움을 극복한 것은 성공적인 연설과 끈기의 중요한 교훈을 얻게 해주었다.

14 빈칸 앞에서는 연설의 두려움을 없애기 위한 노력을 진술하고, 빈칸 뒤에서 그 성과를 언급하고 있으므로, 빈칸에는 ③ '그 결과'가 가장 적절하다.
오답 ① 요컨대 ② 다시 말해 ④ 예를 들어 ⑤ 반면에

15 주어진 문장의 them은 ④ 앞의 disaster survivors를 가리킨다.

16 ④ 국제기구 설립과 관련된 내용은 글에서 언급되지 않았다.

내신 1등급 서술형 pp. 248~250

01 I am just not good at math. I can't improve my math skills.

02 I'm sure I can get a much better grade next time if I work harder. / I'm sure I can get a much better grade if I work harder next time.

03 Yusra had no idea that her life would soon be turned upside down, which had broken out

04 to flee Syria and go to Germany to avoid the war

05 panicked, desperate, heartbroken

06 (1) eighteen[18] (2) sink (3) guided

07 (1) ⓓ to throw
(2) ⓔ disappear[disappearing]

08 (1) She crossed Macedonia, Serbia, Hungary, and Austria.
(2) It took 25 days.

09 No matter how exhausted they were, they kept moving.

10 (A) outstanding
(B) persistent

11 난민 선수단에 합류하면 사람들이 자신을 진지한 선수로 여기지 않고 연민을 가지고 바라볼 거라 생각해서

12 (1) About 6,800 natural disasters occur
(2) Food, shelter, and medical support

13 These efforts help global communities (to) respond better to future disasters.

---

01 고정형 사고방식을 가진 사람은 수학 시험을 망치면 자신이 수학을 못하고 향상할 수 없다고 생각한다.

02 · get a much better grade: 훨씬 더 좋은 성적을 얻다
· work harder: 더 열심히 하다

03 (1) have no idea 뒤에 접속사 that이 이끄는 절을 연결하여 '~할 거라고 생각하지 못했다'라는 표현을 나타낸다.

(2) 시리아 내전을 설명하는 계속적 용법의 관계대명사 which를 사용하고, 전쟁이 발발한 것이 더 이전의 일이므로 대과거(had p.p.)로 나타낸다.

04 the decision이 가리키는 내용은 they made up their minds의 목적어로 쓰인 to부정사구이다.

05 배가 가라앉으며 승객들은 겁에 질리고(panicked) 필사적이 되었고(desperate), 사람들이 소중한 소지품을 바다에 버리는 모습을 보며 Yusra는 비통함을(heartbroken) 느꼈다.

06 Yusra와 언니가 다른 18명의 승객과 함께 탄 작은 보트는 바다 한가운데에서 가라앉기 시작했다. 자매는 바다로 뛰어들어 해변까지 보트를 끌었다.

07 ⓓ have no choice but to-v: ~하지 않을 수 없다
ⓔ watched는 지각동사이므로 목적격 보어로 동사원형이나 분사를 써야 한다.

08 (1) 독일에 도착하기 위해 Yusra는 어떤 나라들을 지났는가?
→ 마케도니아, 세르비아, 헝가리, 오스트리아를 지났다.
(2) Yusra가 독일에 도착하기까지 얼마나 걸렸는가?
→ 25일이 걸렸다.

09 • No matter how: 아무리 ~하더라도
• keep v-ing: 계속 ~하다

10 (A) 평균보다 월등히 나은: outstanding(뛰어난)
(B) 어렵더라도 무언가를 계속하고자 결심한: persistent(끈질긴)

11 이어지는 문장에서 그녀가 망설인 이유가 설명되어 있다.

12 (1) 매년 지구상에 얼마나 많은 자연재해가 발생하는가?
→ 약 6,800건의 자연재해가 전세계에서 매년 발생한다.
(2) 재난 생존자에게 무엇이 가장 시급히 필요한가?
→ 식량, 대피소, 그리고 의료 지원이 가장 시급히 필요하다.

13 「help+목적어+(to+)동사원형」의 구문을 사용하여 문장을 완성한다.

Special Lesson ❷ │ The Open Window

교과서 **어휘 익히기** ⋯⋯⋯⋯⋯⋯⋯⋯ p. 253

01 늪	**26** rural
02 운이 없는	**27** lawn
03 동정	**28** tremble
04 추켜세우다, 아첨하다	**29** yawn
05 묘지	**30** waterproof
06 놀리다	**31** as far as
07 간신히	**32** doubt
08 기념일	**33** grab
09 잘못하여	**34** meanwhile
10 누르다, 참다	**35** niece
11 맹렬하게	**36** distinct
12 신경과민(증)	**37** tragedy
13 사과하다	**38** bound
14 충돌하다	**39** mess
15 사실상	**40** run away
16 전문 (분야), 특기	**41** coincidence
17 낫게 하다	**42** figure
18 으스스한, 오싹한	**43** bush
19 의식하다	**44** grave
20 신경에 거슬리게 하다	**45** elaborate
21 끔찍한	**46** bark
22 과부가 된	**47** confident
23 신경 쓰다, 싫어하다	**48** regret
24 표현하기 힘든	**49** illness
25 ~을 참고 견디다	**50** muddy

교과서 **본문 익히기** ❶ 옳은 어법·어휘 고르기 ⋯ pp. 261~262

01 confident	**02** up
03 who	**04** do
05 it will	**06** speak
07 that	**08** whether
09 silent	**10** distinct
11 married	**12** why
13 anything	**14** crossing
15 had been	**16** through, do
17 sunset	**18** tease
19 quiet	**20** don't
21 upsetting	**22** past
23 and, their	**24** back
25 were	**26** staring

27 feeling

29 crashing

31 apologizing

33 elaborate

28 barely

30 dry

32 pack, with

교과서 **본문 익히기** ❷ 틀린 부분 고치기 ·········· pp. 263~264

01 making it seem

03 how it will be

05 ○

07 belonged

09 wants me to meet

11 Something undefinable

13 ○

15 While (they were) crossing

17 were never found

19 why

21 for being late

23 be back

25 ○

27 my diet should be

29 because of

31 turned around

33 we are

35 man named

02 ○

04 not speak

06 were quite nice

08 anyone

10 was married or widowed

12 such a calm

14 to do with the tragedy

16 had been

18 used to do

20 speaking

22 don't mind

24 to listen to

26 to rest and (to) avoid

28 holding back

30 that

32 riding his bike

34 who

36 lose

교과서 **본문 익히기** ❸ 빈칸 완성하기 ·········· pp. 265~269

(1) confident 15-year old girl

(2) must put up with me

(3) without making it seem

(4) doubted whether

(5) to move to

(6) will hide yourself

(7) will be worse

(8) all the people

(9) as far as I can remember

(10) wondered whether

(11) stayed silent

(12) Hardly anyone

(13) wants me to meet

(14) made the last statement

(15) know practically nothing

(16) name and address

(17) married or widowed

(18) Something undefinable

(19) It was after

(20) out of place

(21) wide open

(22) pointing to

(23) it is quite warm

(24) have anything to do with

(25) went off on

(26) While crossing

(27) wet and muddy

(28) suddenly became dangerous

(29) were never found

(30) lost its confident tone

(31) that was lost

(32) That is why

(33) how they left

(34) as he always did

(35) got on her nerves

(36) through that window

(37) She stopped speaking

(38) for being late

(39) amusing you

(40) She has been

(41) you don't mind

(42) will soon be back

(43) in the forest

(44) don't they

(45) lack of birds

(46) to listen to her

(47) partially successful effort

(48) was conscious that

(49) constantly moving

(50) that he had visited

(51) both excitement and physical exercise

(52) what exactly my diet should be

(53) barely holding back

(54) not because of

(55) Here they are

(56) as if they were

(57) that expressed sympathy

(58) staring out

(59) feeling fear in his stomach

(60) towards the window

(61) under their arms

(62) walked at their feet

(63) began to sing

(64) grabbed wildly

(65) as he ran away from

(66) avoid crashing

(67) with the white coat

(68) got a bit muddy

(69) that who just ran
(70) unusual man named
(71) without saying goodbye
(72) he was scared of
(73) by a pack of wild dogs
(74) to make anyone lose
(75) Coming up with

내신 1등급 어휘·어법 공략
pp. 270~272

01 ⑤	02 ④	03 ⑤	04 ⑤	05 ⑤	06 ⑤	07 ⑤	08 ②
09 ⑤	10 ①	11 ②	12 ③				

01 방에서 ⑤ '표현할 수 없는(undefinable)' 무언가가 거기에 남자가 산다는 것을 암시했다고 말해야 자연스럽다. definable은 '한정할 수 있는, 정의할 수 있는'이라는 의미이다.

02 ④ 그들과 함께 '사라진' 개를 의미하므로 found가 아닌 lost가 자연스럽다.

03 (A) tease: 놀리다 (B) creepy: 으스스한
(C) relieved: 안도한
오답 (A) cease: 멈추다
(B) creeping: 서서히 진행되는
(C) revived: 활기를 되찾은

04 Sappleton 부인의 이야기를 듣는 것이 끔찍해서 이야기의 주제를 '덜 속상한' 주제로 바꾸려 한 것이므로 ⑤ more upsetting이 아닌 less upsetting이 적절한 표현이다.

05 '마침내 그들이 돌아왔다!'라고 기쁘게 외쳤으므로 ⑤ despair(절망)가 아닌 delight(기쁨)를 써야 한다.

06 (A) 옷에 흙이 묻었지만 지금은 거의 '말랐다(dry)'가 적절하다.
(B) 자기 병 얘기만 하다가 인사도 없이 떠났으므로 '특이한 (unusual)'사람이다.
(C) 들개떼가 '맹렬하게 (furiously)' 짖었을 것이다.

07 (A) '~인지 아닌지'라는 의미의 접속사 whether가 적절하다.
(B) such a(n)+형용사+명사: 그토록 ~한 (명사)
(C) '왜 그녀가 문을 열어두는지'라는 의미의 이유를 나타내므로 why가 적절하다.

08 ② 일반동사 sang(노래했다)을 대신하는 대동사이므로 was가 아닌 did를 써야 한다.
오답 ① told의 직접목적어인 간접의문문으로, 평서문의 어순이다.
③ feeling과 동격의 명사절을 이끄는 접속사 that이다.
④ stop의 목적어로 동명사를 쓴다.
⑤ 전치사 for의 목적어 역할을 하는 동명사구이다.

09 (A) '즐겁게 하다'라는 능동의 동사로 쓰이고 있으므로 현재분사가 적절하다.

(B) 일반동사(do)가 쓰인 문장의 부가의문문이므로 don't가 알맞다.
(C) it이 가주어이고, to부정사구가 진주어인 구조이다.

10 ① to rest와 함께 ordered의 목적격 보어로 쓰이는 표현이므로 to avoid가 알맞은 형태이다.

11 ② 분사구문에서 분사가 주어 Framton과 능동의 관계이므로 felt가 아닌 feeling이 적절하다.

12 (A) who라고 that(저 사람)을 묻고 있으므로 that은 사람을 가리킨다. 사람을 선행사로 하는 관계사는 who가 적절하다.
(B) saying과 함께 전치사 without의 목적어로 쓰이므로 동명사가 적절하다.
(C) the creatures와 능동의 관계이므로 현재분사가 적절하다.

내신 1등급 실전 공략
pp. 273~276

01 ⑤	02 ③	03 ③	04 (w)hether	05 ④	06 dangerous

07 Their bodies were never found. **08** ② **09** ① **10** don't they? **11** ④ **12** ⓐ his illnesses ⓑ my doctors **13** it was not because of what Framton was saying **14** ① **15** ① **16** ① **17** ②

01 ⑤ Framton은 이웃을 방문하는 것이 자신의 병 치료에 도움이 될지 의심스러웠다. (He doubted whether these formal visits ... would do much to help cure his nervousness.)

02 ③ do much: 큰 기여를 하다, 보탬이 되다

03 (B) 소녀가 '이 주변에 아는 사람이 많은지' 묻는다.
(D) 남자가 '거의 없고, 누나가 몇몇을 알려주었다'고 답한다.
(C) '그러면 이모에 대해 모르는 거죠?'라고 소녀가 묻는다.
(A) 남자가 '이름과 주소만 안다'고 답한다.

04 wonder의 목적어가 되는 명사절을 이끌며 '~인지'라는 뜻을 가지므로 whether가 적절하다.

05 ④ '비극을 잊기 위해 소녀의 이모가 무엇을 했는지'는 언급되지 않았다.
오답 ① 비극이 언제 발생했는가? → 3년 전 오늘
② 비극의 희생자는 누구였는가? → 이모의 남편과 두 남동생
③ 비극은 열린 유리문과 어떻게 관련되어 있는가? → 이모의 남편과 두 남동생이 유리문을 통해 떠났고, 이모는 그들이 유리문으로 다시 돌아올 거라 믿고 있다.
⑤ 비극의 최악인 부분은 무엇인가? → 시신을 발견하지 못한 것

06 safe(안전한)의 반대말은 dangerous(위험한)이다.

07 That이 가리키는 것은 바로 앞의 문장, '그들의 시신이 발견되지 않은 것'이다.

08 (A) used to 뒤에는 동사원형을 써야 하고 일반동사 walk를 대신하므로 do가 적절하다.
(B) 일반동사 sang을 대신하는 대동사이므로 did가 적절하다.

09 소녀가 '갑자기 말을 멈추고 살짝 떤' 것은 무서운 이야기의 극적 효과를 높이기 위한 동작으로, ① 실종된 사람들이 돌아올까봐 두렵다는 뜻이다.

오답 ② Framton은 소녀의 말을 듣고 있지 않았다.
③ 소녀의 이모는 소녀가 자신들의 비밀을 말하는 걸 좋아하지 않았다.
④ 소녀는 전체 이야기를 기억하지 못했다.
⑤ 실종된 남자들이 유리문으로 다가오고 있었다.

10 앞에 쓰인 동사가 일반동사(do)의 긍정문이므로 don't를 쓰고, 주어 Men을 받는 인칭대명사 they를 쓴다.

11 바로 앞 문장에서 '그녀의 이야기를 듣고 있는 것은 끔찍한 일이었다.'라고 했으므로, 빈칸에는 ④ '주제를 덜 속상한 것으로 바꾸려는' 노력을 했다는 말이 자연스럽다.

오답 ① 그녀의 슬픔을 위로하려는
② Vera에 관해 불평하는
③ 그녀가 비극에 관해 상세하게 말하도록 하는
⑤ 그녀의 남편과 동생들이 누구였는지를 알게 되는

12 ⓐ는 그의 질병을 가리키고, ⓑ는 그의 이사들을 가리킨다.

13 because of 뒤에 what이 이끄는 명사절을 쓴다.

14 Suddenly feeling fear in his stomach라는 표현으로 보아, Framton이 느꼈을 심경은 ① '겁이 난'일 것이다.

오답 ② 안도한 ③ 만족한 ④ 흥분한 ⑤ 분노한

15 (A) a look을 수식하는 주격 관계대명사 that이 알맞다.
(B) 동시동작을 나타내는 분사구문으로서, 주어와 능동의 관계이므로 현재분사가 적절하다.
(C) 접속사 and로 연결되는 완전한 절이므로 과거시제의 동사 had가 적절하다.

16 ①은 흰 코트를 가지고 유리문으로 들어온 남자이고, 나머지는 모두 Mr. Nuttel을 가리킨다.

17 ② 진흙이 묻어 있었지만 거의 말라 있었다. (Our clothes got a bit muddy, but they're mostly dry now.)

내신 1등급 수능형 고난도
pp. 277~279

01 ①	02 ③	03 ③	04 ④	05 ④	06 ④	07 ⑤	08 ③	09 ④
10 ③	11 ④	12 ⑤						

01 뒤에 이어지는 내용이, 누나가 몸을 숨기고 아무하고도 말하지 않으면 남자의 신경과민증이 더 심해질 거라 걱정하며 친절한 이웃을 몇 명 소개하겠다고 얘기했으므로, 남자가 방문한 목적은 누나의 조언에 따라 ① 신경과민증을 치료하는 데 도움이 되기 위한 것이었다.

오답 ② 그의 이웃들과 잘 지내다
③ 소녀에게 좋은 인상을 주다
④ 누나의 걱정을 덜어주다
⑤ 그의 성격을 바꾸다

02 ③ 이어지는 문장에서 '너는 거기서 몸을 숨기고 아무에게도 말하지 않을 거야.'라고 말하는 것으로 보아, 남자가 이사하려는 곳은 '도시' 지역이 아닌 '시골' 지역이다. '시골의'라는 뜻의 rural을 써야 자연스럽다.

03 (B) 3년 전에 엄청난 비극이 있었어요.
(C) 비극이라고?
(A) 10월 오후에 저 유리문을 열어두는 이유가 궁금하시겠죠.
(D) 유리문이 비극과 관련이 있니?

04 ④ 비극은 남자의 누나가 마을을 떠난 후인 3년 전에 일어났으므로, 남자의 누나는 그 전에 떠났다.

05 실종된 가족들이 돌아올 거라 믿고 유리문을 열어두는 이모에 관해 소녀가 이야기하며, 이런 저녁에는 그들이 올 것 같은 오싹한 기분이 든다고 말하고 있으므로, 글의 분위기는 ④ 공포스럽고 무섭다.

오답 ① 활기차고 축제 같은
② 차분하고 평화로운
③ 슬프고 울적한
⑤ 긴박하고 절박한

06 (A) That(앞의 내용)이 창문을 열어두는 이유이므로 why가 적절하다.
(B) 이어지는 내용이 이모의 남편과 동생이 떠날 때 어땠는지를 설명하고 있으므로 how가 적절하다.

07 다음 문장에서 '그녀의 시선이 열린 유리문과 그 너머를 향해 움직였다'고 했으므로, Sappleton 부인이 ⑤ '자신에게 작은 관심만을 기울이고 있다'는 것을 알고 있었을 것이다.

오답 ① Vera에 관해 걱정했다
② 그에게 많은 관심이 있었다
③ 유리문을 닫고 싶었다
④ 그가 왜 그녀의 집을 방문했는지 이미 알았다

08 ③ 문장의 주어는 to부정사구인 to listen to her이므로, 가주어 it을 문장 앞에 사용하고 진주어는 문장의 뒤로 보낸다.

오답 ① 앞에 접속사 that이 생략된 명사절이다.
② 일반동사의 긍정문에 대한 부가의문문이다.
④ '덜 ~한'이라는 열등비교를 나타내는 표현이다.
⑤ 그가 방문한 것이 더 앞서는 시제의 일이므로 대과거 형태로 나타낸다.

09 ④ 그들은 총을 들고 있었고, 그들 중 젊은 사람이 노래를 부르기 시작했다.

10 (A) as if 뒤에 가정법을 써서 '마치 ~인 것처럼'이라는 의미를 나타낸다.
(B) 주어와 능동의 관계이므로 현재분사가 적절하다.
(C) avoid는 동명사를 목적어로 취한다.

11 ④ me는 the niece를 가리킨다.

12 (A) mostly dry: 대부분 마른
(B) without saying goodbye: 작별 인사 없이
(C) lose one's nerve: 겁먹다

01 why we have left that window wide open

02 that had been safe in other years suddenly became dangerous

03 ⓐ walking ⓑ did ⓒ speaking

04 (1) why the window is kept open
   (2) how they left

05 make a mess of my poor carpets

06 It was an unfortunate coincidence that he had visited her

07 Who was that who just ran out of the room

08 ⓑ named ⓒ was scared

09 with the creatures barking furiously just above him

01 간접의문문이므로 평서문의 어순(we have left)으로 나타낸다.

02 '다른 해에는 안전했던'을 관계대명사절로 표현한다. 이때 장소가 '위험해진' 것보다 '안전했던' 것이 먼저 일어난 일이므로 대과거 형태(had p.p.)로 표현한다.

03 ⓐ '~하면서'라는 의미의 동시동작을 나타내는 현재분사 형태가 적절하다.
ⓑ 전체 시제가 과거이므로 do의 과거형을 쓴다.
ⓒ stopped의 목적어로 동명사를 써야 한다.

04 (1) '~한 이유'는 why로 시작하고, (2) '어떻게 ~(했는지)'는 how로 시작하며, 둘 다 동사의 보어/목적어로 쓰이므로 평서문의 어순(주어+동사)으로 표현한다.

05 바로 앞 문장의 내용(내 불쌍한 카펫을 엉망으로 만든다)이다.

06 가주어 It과 진주어인 that이 이끄는 명사절로 문장을 구성한다. '그가 그녀를 방문한' 것은 대과거(had p.p.)로 나타낸다.

07 의문사 who로 문장을 시작하고, 관계대명사 who가 이끄는 형용사절을 사용하여 지시대명사 that을 수식한다.

08 ⓑ '~라는 이름을 가진'이라는 의미의 과거분사가 적절하다.
ⓒ 주어가 He이므로 동사와 수동의 관계이고, 시제가 과거이므로 과거형 수동태로 나타낸다.

09 with+명사+v-ing: (명사)가 ~한 채로

---

01 ①   02 ④   03 ④   04 He used an apple and a peach (to create the pink cheeks in the painting).   05 ⑤   06 ①   07 ③   08 ③   09 ⑤   10 ③   11 ⑤   12 ①   13 ⑤   14 the Syrian civil war   15 ④   16 felt heartbroken as she watched people's treasured belongings disappear   17 ①   18 (A) (o)utstanding (B) (h)esitant   19 ⓐ the very confident 15-year-old girl ⓑ his sister   20 ④   21 ⑤   22 ④   23 they look as if they were in the mud   24 ⑤   25 ③

01 창작과 창의력을 비교하며, 창의력은 예술가들의 창작의 결과물에 국한되지 않는, 새롭고 독창적인 것을 만들어내는 능력을 의미한다고 강조하는 글이다. 제목으로는 ① '창의력의 정의: 무엇을 만드는 것 이상'이 가장 적절하다.
오답 ② 예술가들만이 창의적인 사람인 이유
③ 예술적 표현의 이해
④ 창의력과 예술계
⑤ 창작의 의미

02 ④ not only A but also B 구문으로, A와 B 자리에는 어법상 동등한 형태의 표현이 쓰여야 한다. using과 같은 동명사 형태인 coming이 알맞은 형태이다.
오답 ① people을 수식하는 관계대명사와 동사이다.
② 주어 It(= Creation)와 focus가 수동의 관계이므로 수동태가 적절하다.
③ ability를 수식하는 형용사적 용법의 to부정사이다.
⑤ 전치사 of의 목적어로 쓰인 동명사구이다.

03 ④ signature는 '특징적인'이라는 뜻이고, stereotypical은 '틀에 박힌, 진부한'이라는 뜻이다.
오답 ① depict: 묘사하다 / describe: 묘사하다
② standard: 일반적인, 보통의 / typical: 전형적인
③ unconventional: 색다른 / unusual: 특이한
⑤ create: 창조하다 / produce: 만들다

04 Arcimboldo는 〈Vertumnus〉에서 분홍빛 뺨을 만들기 위해 무엇을 사용했는가?
→ 그는 (그림에서 분홍빛 뺨을 만들기 위해) 사과와 복숭아를 사용했다.

05 주어진 문장은 이유를 설명하는 문장이다. 그가 그림을 뒤집을 수 있도록 만든 이유를 묻는 문장인 Why did he make his paintings reversible? 뒤에 들어가는 것이 가장 자연스럽다.

06 ① reversible(뒤집을 수 있는): 반대 방향으로 바꿀 수 있는
오답 ② 서로 밀접한 관계로 작용하는: interactive(상호작용을 하는)
③ 새로운 방식이나 생각을 제안하거나 사용하는: innovative(혁신적인)
④ 보이는 것들과 관계된: visual(시각의)
⑤ 서로 다른 요소나 부분으로 만들어진: composite(합성의)

07 (A) It ~ that 강조구문으로, her active observation skills를 강조한다.

(B) 선행사가 포함된 관계대명사 what이 이끄는 절로, is의 보어 역할을 한다.

08 〈먹을 수 있는 존재들〉은 샐러드를 만들다가 떠올린 작품이다

09 신체 활동이 기분을 향상시키고 뇌로 가는 혈류를 증가시키며, 밖으로 나가 영감을 얻을 수 있게 해 창의력을 증진시킨다.

10 (A) 계속적 용법의 관계대명사이므로 which가 적절하다. that은 계속적 용법으로 쓰지 않는다.
(B) '뇌가 필요로 하는'이라는 의미이므로 단수 형태인 it needs가 적절하다.
(C) 조동사 can에 연결되는 동사이므로 동사원형이 적절하다

11 고정형 사고방식과 성장형 사고방식을 가진 사람들을 비교하는 글이다. 빈칸 앞에서는 고정형 사고방식을 가진 사람이 수학 시험을 망쳤을 때의 사례를 설명하고, 뒤에서는 성장형 사고방식을 가진 사람의 사례를 설명하고 있으므로, 빈칸에는 대조를 나타내는 연결어, ⑤ '반면에'가 가장 적절하다.
오답 ① 그 결과 ② 예를 들어 ③ 게다가 ④ 요컨대

12 고정형 사고방식을 가진 사람은 도전을 자신의 한계로 인식하여 용기를 잃게 된다. 성장형 사고방식을 가진 사람은 차질을 성장하고 더 성취하는 동기로 인식한다

13 (D) (전쟁이 발발한) 이후 몇 년간 평범한 활동이 위험해졌지만, 그녀는 수영을 계속 했다.
(A) 그녀의 수영장에 폭탄이 떨어졌고, 이것은 그녀와 언니에게 정신이 들게 했다.
(C) 그들은 시리아를 떠나 독일로 가기로 결심했다.
(B) 그들이 유럽에 도착하면 다른 가족들이 뒤따르기로 했고, 이것이 그들의 유일한 선택임을 알았다.

14 '혼란'이 가리키는 것은 2011년 발발한 시리아 내전이다.

15 ④ '승객들이 구조신호를 보내기 위해 무엇을 했는가?'는 글에 나와 있지 않다.
오답 ① 보트는 어디로 향하고 있었는가? → 그리스
② 배에는 몇 명의 사람이 있었는가? → 20명 (자매와 다른 18명의 승객)
③ 보트의 엔진이 꺼졌을 때 날씨는 어떻게 변했는가? → 급격히 나빠졌다.
⑤ 몇 명의 사람들이 배를 해안으로 끌었는가? → 4명

16 문장의 시제는 과거시제이고, felt 뒤에 감정을 나타내는 형용사를 쓴다. 그리고 watch는 지각동사로 목적격 보어 자리에 동사원형 또는 분사를 써야 한다.

17 의문사가 없는 의문문을 간접화법으로 바꿀 때 접속사로 if를 사용한다. you는 Sven을 가리키고, my는 Yusra를 가리키므로 각각 he, her로 바꾼다.

18 (A) 평균보다 훨씬 잘하는: outstanding(뛰어난)
(B) 불확실하거나 당황스러워서 행하거나 말하는 데 늦은: hesitant(망설이는)

19 ⓐ '나'는 Framton을 맞이하고 있는 15세 소녀를 가리키고, ⓑ '나'는 Framton의 누나를 가리킨다.

20 (A) something을 수식하는 관계대명사가 필요하다. -thing으로 끝나는 부정대명사가 선행사일 때는 관계대명사로 보통 that을 사용한다.
(B) her aunt를 부가적으로 설명하는 계속적 용법의 관계대명사이다. 사람을 선행사로 하므로 who가 적절하다.

21 부가의문문의 주어는 Men의 인칭대명사인 they가 적절하고, 동사는 앞에 쓰인 동사가 현재시제 긍정문의 일반동사(do)이므로 don't가 적절하다.

22 열린 유리문에 대해 설명하며 사냥을 나간 남편과 남동생들에 관해 즐겁게 얘기하는 것으로 보아 ④ 남편과 동생이 돌아오기를 기다리느라, Framton의 말을 건성으로 듣는 것이다.

23 as if+가정법 과거: 마치 ~인 것처럼

24 · with a look that: ~한 표정으로
· with horror in her eyes: 공포에 질린 눈으로

25 ③ Sappleton 부인이 마지막 순간 하품을 간신히 참으며 물었다는 것으로 보아, 그녀는 Framton의 말에 별 흥미를 느끼지 못했다.

· MEMO ·

독해

Reading TUTOR 리딩튜터

체계적인 초·중·고등 독해 프로그램

Starter 1 | 2 | 3
Junior 1 | 2 | 3 | 4
Challenger 1 | 2 | 3

READING EXPERT

중고등 대상 7단계 원서 독해 교재

Level 1 | Level 2 | Level 3 | Level 4 | Level 5 |
Advanced 1 | Advanced 2

기강 잡고

기본을 강하게 잡아주는 고등영어

독해 잡는 필수 문법 | 기초 잡는 유형 독해

빠른 독해를 위한 바른 선택

기초세우기 | 구문독해 | 유형독해 | 수능실전

The 상승

독해 기본기에서 수능 실전 대비까지

직독직해편 | 문법독해편 | 구문편 |
수능유형편 | 어법·어휘+유형편

수능

맞수

맞춤형 수능영어 단기특강 시리즈

구문독해 기본편 | 실전편
수능유형 기본편 | 실전편
수능문법어법 기본편 | 실전편
수능듣기 기본편 | 실전편
빈칸추론

PICK 수능유형

핵심만 콕 찍어주는 수능유형 필독서

독해 기본 | 독해 실력 | 듣기

수능1UP

수능 영어 1등급 올려주는 상위권 수능 독해서

빈순삽함 유형편 | 간접연계 소재편

얇빠 얇고 빠른 미니 모의고사 10+2회

수능 핵심유형들만 모아 얇게! 회당 10문항으로 빠르게!

입문 | 기본 | 실전

수능만만

만만한 수능영어 모의고사

기본 영어듣기 20회 | 기본 영어듣기 35회+5회 |
기본 영어독해 10+1회 | 기본 문법·어법·어휘 150제 |
영어듣기 20회 | 영어듣기 35회 |
영어독해 20회 | 어법·어휘 228제

지은이

오 선 영	現 서울대학교 영어교육과 교수	전 형 주	現 용산고등학교 교사	조 은 비	現 자양고등학교 교사
김 주 혜	現 서울국제고등학교 교사	신 유 승	現 ㈜NE능률 교과서개발연구소	김 은 정	前 ㈜NE능률 교과서개발연구소

고등 기출문제집

내신백신
English Ⅰ 오선영

펴 낸 날	2025년 6월 25일 (초판 1쇄)
	2026년 2월 15일 (제3쇄)
펴 낸 이	이정진
펴 낸 곳	(주)NE능률
개 발 책 임	김지현
영 문 교 열	Curtis Thompson, Alison Li, Courtenay Parker
디자인책임	오영숙
디 자 인	안훈정, 오솔길
제 작 책 임	한성일
등 록 번 호	제1-68호
I S B N	979-11-253-5015-6

대 표 전 화	02 2014 7114
홈 페 이 지	www.neungyule.com
주 소	서울시 마포구 월드컵북로 396(상암동) 누리꿈스퀘어 비즈니스타워 10층